# Managing the service economy
## Prospects and problems

Essays commissioned for the inaugural conference of the Fishman–Davidson Center for the Study of the Service Sector, Wharton School, University of Pennsylvania

Edited by ROBERT P. INMAN
*The Wharton School, University of Pennsylvania*

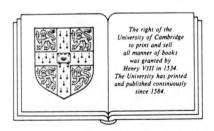

The right of the
University of Cambridge
to print and sell
all manner of books
was granted by
Henry VIII in 1534.
The University has printed
and published continuously
since 1584.

CAMBRIDGE UNIVERSITY PRESS

Cambridge
New York   New Rochelle
Melbourne   Sydney

Published by the Press Syndicate of the University of Cambridge
The Pitt Building, Trumpington Street, Cambridge CB2 1RP
32 East 57th Street, New York, NY 10022, USA
10 Stamford Road, Oakleigh, Melbourne 3166, Australia

First published 1985
First paperback edition 1988

Printed in the United States of America

*Library of Congress Cataloging in Publication Data*

Main entry under title:

Managing the service economy.

Papers from the ARA/Wharton Conference on the Future of
the Service Economy held Nov. 19–20, 1982, at the Wharton
School, University of Pennsylvania, sponsored by the
Fishman–Davidson Center for the Study of the Service
Sector.
Bibliography: p.
Includes index.
1. Service industries – Congresses.   2. Service indus-
tries – Government policy – Congresses.   I. Inman, Robert P.
II. Fishman–Davidson Center for the Study of the Service
Sector.   III. ARA/Wharton Conference on the Future of the
Service Economy (1982: University of Pennsylvania)
HD9980.5.M35   1985     338.4'6        84-29318

ISBN 0-521-30647-7 hard covers
ISBN 0-521-37858-3 paperback

# Contents

                    iii

# Foreword

The ARA/Wharton Conference on the Future of the Service Economy was the first event sponsored by the Fishman–Davidson Center for the Study of the Service Sector, established in 1982 through a generous endowment from ARA Services, Inc. It is an honor for me, as the first director of the Fishman–Davidson Center, to introduce this conference volume devoted to research on the service sector of the economy. Indeed, this work represents a first and impressive effort in pursuit of the Center's mission: bringing to bear the highest quality scholarship and research on the unique problems of the service sector.

Although two-thirds of our domestic economic activity involves the service sector, our understanding of that sector is primitive. Concerns are raised that the rise of the service sector will be accompanied by a fall in productivity, that tangible goods are somehow more real, more valued than intangible services, that services cannot sustain the economic growth that our goods sector provided for so many years. While it is easy to recognize the superficiality of these concerns, nonetheless the research community at large has not yet responded to the need for understanding and insight regarding the nature and direction of the service sector. It is our intent that the Center will respond to that need by encouraging, supporting, and disseminating research in the fields of economics, finance, marketing, management, and accounting, which speaks to this gap in our knowledge.

The research presented by the participants in the ARA/Wharton Conference on the Future of the Service Economy and published in this volume is an initial step on a long and exciting journey. I wish to thank the participants for their pioneering effort, and to thank my colleague Robert Inman for his valuable contribution as conference organizer and as editor of the conference proceedings.

*April 5, 1984*  GERALD R. FAULHABER
Director, Fishman–Davidson Center
for the Study of the Service Sector
Wharton School
University of Pennsylvania
Philadelphia, PA 19104

# Contributors

DR. WILLIAM J. BAUMOL currently holds dual appointments as a Professor of Economics at New York University and at Princeton University. His published books include *Economic Dynamics* (third edition, 1970), *Welfare Economics and the Theory of State* (second edition, 1965), *Performing Arts: The Economic Dilemma* (1966), *Economics, Environmental Policy, and the Quality of Life* (1979) and most recently, *Contestable Markets and the Theory of Industry Structure* (1982). He is past President of the American Economic Association, a Fellow of the Economic Society, and an elected member of the American Philosophical Society.

DR. JERE R. BEHRMAN, the William R. Kenan Professor of Economics at the University of Pennsylvania, is a leading expert on developing economies. He is Director for the Center for Analysis of Developing Economies and Associate Director of the Lauder Institute for Management and International Studies at Penn and past Chairman of the Economics Department. He has written fourteen books and over a hundred research articles that have appeared in the major economics and specialized development journals. He is an editor of the *Journal of Development Economics* and a Fellow of the Econometric Society.

DR. FISHER BLACK is a Professor of Finance, Sloan School of Management, M.I.T., and a Research Associate of the National Bureau of Economic Research. He is a nationally recognized expert in financial theory. His research has been published in the *Journal of Finance, Journal of Political Economy, Financial Analysts Journal,* and the *Journal of Financial Economics,* for which he also serves as an editor. Dr. Black is currently on leave to Goldman–Sacks as Vice-President, Trading and Arbitrage.

DR. ALAN K. CAMPBELL is Vice-Chairman of the Board and Executive Vice-President for Management and Public Affairs, ARA, Inc., and also is Adjunct Professor of Public Management, the Wharton School. Most recently, Dr. Campbell was the Director of the Office of Personnel Management, the central personnel agency for the U.S. government, a position that he was named to by President Carter in January 1979. Prior to that he served as Chairman of the Civil Service Commission. Dr. Campbell received his

Ph.D. from Harvard and was, before entering government, Dean of the Lyndon B. Johnson School of Public Affairs at the University of Texas; Dean of the Maxwell School of Citizenship and Public Affairs at Syracuse University; and Professor and Chairman of the Political Science Department of Hofstra University. He also lectured and served on the faculty of Harvard and Columbia Universities.

DR. MARK J. FLANNERY is an Associate Professor of Finance, University of North Carolina. His research focuses on issues in bank management, financial regulation, and macroeconomic policy. His published articles have appeared in the *American Economic Review, Quarterly Journal of Economics, Journal of Finance,* and the *Journal of Banking Finance.*

DR. IRWIN FRIEND is the Edward J. Hopkinson Professor of Finance and Economics, Wharton School, University of Pennsylvania and Director of the Rodney L. White Center for Financial Research. His published research on financial theory and financial market performance has appeared in the major economic and financial journals. He is past President of the American Finance Association, a Fellow of the Econometric Society, and a Fellow of the American Statistical Association.

DR. VICTOR R. FUCHS is Professor of Economics at Stanford University (Economics Department and the Medical School) and a Research Associate of the National Bureau of Economic Research, where he directs its program of research in health economics. Dr. Fuchs is a member of the Institute of Medicine of the National Academy of Sciences and a Fellow of the American Academy of Arts and Sciences. He is the author of six books, including *How We Live* (Harvard University Press, 1983) and *The Service Economy* (1968) and editor of *Production and Productivity in the Service Industry* (1969).

DR. EDWARD M. GRAMLICH is a Professor of Economics and Public Policy, University of Michigan. Dr. Gramlich received his Ph.D. in economics from Yale. His published research on government performance has appeared in the major economics and policy journals. He is author of *Benefit Cost Analysis of Government Programs* (1981) and *Educational Performance Contracting: An Evaluation of an Experiment* (1975). He serves as an editor for the *National Tax Journal, The Journal of Policy Analysis and Management,* and the *Journal of Economic Literature.*

DR. JEFFREY E. HARRIS is presently an Associate Professor of Economics at M.I.T., and a Clinical Associate, Medical Services, Massachusetts General Hospital. Dr. Harris received his Ph.D. in economics and his M.D. from the University of Pennsylvania. His research interests include medical economics, regulation policy, and environmental policy. His published work has appeared in the *American Economic Review* and the *Bell Journal of Economics*, and he has recently completed a study entitled *Diesel Emissions and Lung Cancer* for the National Academy of Sciences.

DR. BENGT HOLMSTROM is currently Professor of Economics and Organization at Yale University, having received his Ph.D. from Stanford University's Graduate School of Business in 1978. Dr. Holmstrom has taught at Northwestern, the University of Chicago, and the Swedish School of Economics and Business Administration. His published research on insurance markets, finance, accounting, and market economics has appeared in the leading economics and business journals. He is the U.S. Editor for the *Review of Economic Studies,* an Associate Editor for the *Journal of Economic Theory* and *Econometrica* and a Fellow of the Econometric Society.

DR. CHARLES R. HULTEN is currently a Senior Research Associate of the Urban Institute, Washington, D.C. Prior to joining the Urban Institute, Dr. Hulten taught at Johns Hopkins University. His research work on productivity analysis and on public finance has been published in *Econometrica,* the *American Economic Review,* the *Review of Economic Studies, Journal of Econometrics,* the *National Tax Journal,* and *The Wharton Magazine.* He is the author of "Japanese Productivity Slowdown" and the chapter on "Tax Policy" for the recent book, *The Reagan Experiment.*

DR. ROBERT P. INMAN is currently a Professor of Finance, Economics, and Public Management and Director of the Public Enterprise Research Program, University of Pennsylvania. Dr. Inman is a Research Associate of the National Bureau of Economic Research. His published papers have appeared in the *American Economic Review, Journal of Urban Economics, Journal of Public Economics, National Tax Journal, Journal of Regional Science, Public Choice, Journal of Finance,* and the *Harvard Law Review.* He is the Editor (with M. S. Feldstein) of the *Economics of Public Services* and an Associate Editor of the journal *Public Finance Quarterly.*

DR. JOHN W. KENDRICK is a Professor of Economics at George Washington University and an Adjunct Scholar at the American Enterprise Institute. He has been Chief Economist of the U.S. Department of Commerce and Vice-President for Economic Research of the Conference Board. He has published extensively on matters of productivity and growth policy in the leading economics journals. His most recent book is *Improving Company Productivity: Handbook with Case Studies* (1984).

DR. IRVING B. KRAVIS is a University Professor of Economics at the University of Pennsylvania and a Research Associate of the National Bureau of Economic Research. His published research on trade theory and policy has appeared in the major economics journals. He was the Director of the

U.N. International Comparison Project during its first three phases and is a coauthor of three volumes reporting on the international comparison of prices and income, published by Johns Hopkins University Press.

DR. IRVING LEVESON is presently Senior Vice-President and Director of Research of Hudson Strategy Group. He served as Director of Economic Studies of Hudson Institute from 1974 to 1984. Previously, he spent four years with the National Bureau of Economic Research and a year with Rand Corporation. From 1969 to 1974 he directed research and planning departments in the New York City Department of City Planning and the New York City Health Services Administration. Among Dr. Leveson's writings are Hudson publications, *The Modern Service Sector* (1980) and *The Future of the Financial Services Industry* (1982).

DR. DUNCAN P. MANN is an Assistant Professor of Economics at Rutgers University. He received his Ph.D. in Economics from the University of Pennsylvania. His research interests include market outcomes and incentives under asymmetric information.

DR. JANET L. NORWOOD is the Commissioner of Labor Statistics, appointed in May 1979, after serving as Acting Commissioner. She received her Ph.D. in Economics from Tufts University. Her research has included studies of price indices and women in the labor force.

DR. HUGH T. PATRICK is the R. D. Calkins Professor of International Business, Graduate School of Business, Columbia University. He previously taught at the University of Michigan and Yale University, where he was Professor of Economics for some years. He is a specialist on the Japanese economy and on Asia–Pacific economic development, on which he has published extensively.

DR. ANDREW W. POSTLEWAITE is Chairman of the Economics Department, University of Pennsylvania, and Professor of Economics, Finance, and Public Management. Before coming to Penn, he taught at the University of Illinois, University of California, and at Princeton. He is an Associate Editor of the *Journal of Economic Theory* and his own published papers have appeared in *Econometrica, Journal of Economic Theory, Review of Economic Studies,* and *Management Science.*

DR. MARK A. SATTERTHWAITE is the Earl Dean Howard Professor of Managerial Economics, Kellogg School of Management, Northwestern University. In addition to his research in health care management and policy, Dr. Satterthwaite has published extensively on the theory of social decision making, regulation policy, and market economies.

DR. GARY SAXONHOUSE is currently Professor of Economics at the University of Michigan and Director of its Committee on Comparative and Historical Research on Market Economies (CCHROME). Dr. Saxonhouse has written widely on the structure and operation of the Japanese economy, on Japan-U.S. trade relations, on technology transfer, and on econometrics. His articles have appeared in the *American Economic Review*, the *Quarterly Journal of Economics*, the *Journal of Political Economy*, the *Review of Economics and Statistics*; and many other journals. During the academic year 1984–5, Dr. Saxonhouse was a Fellow at the Center for Advanced Study in the Behavioral Sciences in Stanford, California.

DR. JOAN E. SPERO is presently Vice-President, International Corporate Affairs, American Express. Prior to joining American Express, she served as the U.S. Ambassador to the United Nations Economic and Social Council. She was also a Professor of International Business, Columbia University Business School. Dr. Spero's recent publications include *Politics of International Economic Relations* (St. Martin's Press), *Failure of Franklin National Bank: The Challenge to the International Banking System* (Columbia University Press), and "Information: The Policy Void," *Foreign Policy*, Fall 1982.

MS. HELENA STALSON is currently Economist and Fellow, Council on Foreign Relations. She has worked extensively in the areas of U.S. foreign trade policy and the service economy. Her published papers have appeared in edited volumes and policy journals on such topics as foreign trade policy, policies toward a new international economic order, and negotiating international service agreements.

DR. ROBERT SUMMERS is a professor of Economics, University of Pennsylvania. Dr. Summers has taught at Yale as well as at Penn. He is coauthor of the recent three-volume study of international comparisons of prices and income for the United Nations, published by Johns Hopkins University Press. His published articles on productivity, income measurement and growth, and statistical methodology have appeared in *Econometrica*, *Economic Journal*, *Review of Income and Wealth*, *Quarterly Journal of Economics*, and the *American Economic Review*.

# Acknowledgments

The essays, comments, and discussions that are reported here were first presented at the ARA/Wharton Conference on the Future of the Service Economy, held at the Wharton School, University of Pennsylvania, on November 19, 20, 1982. The conference was the inaugural event of the Fishman–Davidson Center for the Study of the Service Sector. The Center was established to honor William S. Fishman, the founder with Davre J. Davidson, of ARA Services, Inc. ARA's generous financial support made the conference and the subsequent publication of these papers possible.

Numerous individuals contributed to the success of the conference. In many ways, Alan ("Scotty") Campbell, Executive Vice-President, Management and Public Affairs at ARA, is a coeditor, or at least the godfather, of this volume. The idea for the Center and the conference was his, and in our early conversations he helped define the research agenda of this volume. His strong emphasis on scholarly rigor and quality research set the standard for the papers finally selected for the conference.

No academic conference can be a success without the support of the host university. Dean Donald Carroll of the Wharton School was a most congenial host indeed. Not only did he open the doors of Wharton to all of our activities and provide the administrative support needed to run the conference, but he and Associate Dean John Lubin acted as the early liaison to ARA in planning for the Center and this conference. At Wharton Anne Hearn, Karen Freedman, and (most of all) Barbara Hesselgrave made the conference work. I now know to be true what my "real world" friends keep saying: It's easy to plan, but harder to execute. Happily I had very good people to help me.

As editor, my greatest debt is to the authors and commentators. Everyone responded with quality research under a very short time horizon and for that we should all be thankful. Duncan Mann and Judith Farnbach assisted me with the editor's chores, and Stephanie Hogue ably typed various versions of the manuscript.

ROBERT P. INMAN

# Introduction and overview

ROBERT P. INMAN

In the last three decades we have witnessed a quiet revolution in the composition of economic activity in most major developed economies. The provision of services has replaced the manufacturing of goods as the predominant production activity of advanced economies. For example, in the United States, the share of services in nonfarm employment has risen from nearly 50 percent in 1952 to just under 68 percent in 1981. Services are no less important in the economic affairs of other developed economies.[1] As we watch the daily affairs of workers and consumers in developed economies we would no longer observe nations of factories, but rather societies predominantly involved in the provision and consumption of services – an economy of doctor's visits, of data collection and processing, of psychological and financial consultations, of teaching, of dining, and of traveling. The transition has been quiet – there has been no public announcement of a "service revolution" – but the economic implications of the change are potentially deep and fundamental. This volume is directed to the task of understanding the evolution from a manufacturing to a service economy and to anticipating the problems and the prospects that lie before us in this new economic regime.

The volume begins (Part I) with a careful examination of the growth of the service sector in world economies. An analysis of the recent history of the service sector in the United States by Irving Leveson and in Japan by Gary Saxonhouse is complemented by a cross-national and intertemporal analysis of service sector growth by Robert Summers. The results update previous work on services in the United States and document the importance of services in the other major Western economies, developed and less developed. Given the importance of the service sector in both developed and developing economies, are there economic policy issues central, perhaps even unique, to this sector, which require study? In Part II of the book, three major policy topics are identified and analyzed in detail: John Kendrick examines the trends and prospects for productivity improvement in services; Helena Stalson and Irving Kravís, in separate papers, look at the difficulties associated with international trade in services; and Bengt Holmstrom examines, from the perspective of economic theory, what the likely problems are, and will be, in the provision of services through

1

markets. The conceptual analysis of Part II is complemented by more detailed studies of three major service industries in Part III. Fischer Black speculates on future trends in financial services. Mark Satterthwaite examines the role of competition in the provision of physician's services. Edward Gramlich overviews the differences between market-provided and government-provided services and discusses the problems unique to the provision of services through a political process. The volume concludes in Part IV with commentaries by the two men who initiated and encouraged, by their example, the serious contemporary analysis of the service economy. William Baumol returns to the theme he first explored nearly twenty years ago: productivity policy and the service sector. The paper here extends his early work in important, new directions. Victor Fuchs assumes the role of senior counselor as he comments on these papers and on service sector research in general.

The contemporary analysis of the service economy, which this volume seeks to advance, does not begin without precedent. In the early, truly path-breaking studies of the role of services in economic development, Victor Fuchs (1968) and William Baumol (1967) described the growth of the service economy and began to speculate on the implications of this important trend.[2] Fuchs carefully documented the emerging prominence of services in the U.S. economy and offered, and then tested, three hypotheses for the relative growth of service employment.[3] The first hypothesis argues that services have an income elasticity of demand greater than 1 so that as real income per capita increases, real services per capita grow more than the proportional growth in income. Thus services consume an increasing share of national income and (all else equal) national employment as well. The second hypothesis suggests as economic specialization and automation increase with economic growth, it becomes efficient for services once provided within the firm or household to be contracted out to experts outside the organization. Legal, accounting, and data processing services are examples for firms whereas restaurants, day care, and housekeeping are examples for the household sector. This may mean that the same volume of services is being provided as before, but that these services are now *measured* as a separate market activity. But it is also possible that increased specialization leads to higher service quality and/or lower average costs, which would increase the demand for, and production of, such services. The third hypothesis explains the growing relative importance of services in national employment by the *slower* relative growth of labor productivity in services than in agriculture or in industry. The slower than average growth in worker productivity in services will mean higher than average costs in services. If the demand for services is relatively insensitive to rising prices, then as the economy expands, service's share of total employment will increase. Fuchs reviews the evidence for the period from 1929 to 1965 and concludes that, although each hypothesis is valid and explains a portion of the growth of the service sector, the major explanation for the increasing *relative* importance of services in U.S. employment is the third hypothesis of lagging productivity growth.[4]

William Baumol (1967) has given us a simple two-sector growth model of an economy with differential productivity growth, which makes precise Fuchs's important insight into the relative roles of productivity changes and demand in service sector growth. The Appendix to this Introduction and Overview presents an extended version of Baumol's model, but the model's main conclusions are easily summarized by the following relationship for the rate of growth over time in the relative share of service employment:

$$\dot{l}_s = (\alpha - 1)r_m + \Delta + (r_m - r_s)(1 + \beta) \tag{1}$$

where $l_s$ is the service share of employment ( = service employment/total non-agricultural employment), $\dot{l}_s$ is the rate of growth in this share [ $= (dl_s/dt)/l_s$], $r_m$ and $r_s$ are the rates of growth in labor productivity in the manufacturing ($m$) and service ($s$) sectors, respectively, $\beta$ and $\alpha$ are the price ($\beta < 0$) and income ($\alpha > 0$) elasticities of demand for services, and $\Delta$ is the rate of exogenous change in the demand for services over time. The general equilibrium version of Fuchs's first hypothesis is measured in the first term $(\alpha - 1)r_m$. In the Baumol model, wages grow at the rate of growth in labor productivity in the numeraire good (manufacturing), so wages per worker rise at rate $r_m$. This percentage increase in income stimulates an increase in the demand for service output at the percentage rate of $r_m \alpha$. All output must rise at the rate $r_m$, however. The service *share* therefore rises only if the increase in services is proportionally greater than the overall increase; that is, if $r_m \alpha > r_m$ or if $r_m(\alpha - 1) > 0$. The service share declines if $r_m(\alpha - 1) < 0$. Fuchs's second hypothesis is represented by the term $\Delta$, which measures the exogenous shift in demand for services due to changes in the structure of family life (e.g., increased female labor force participation) or business practice (e.g., contracting for services once performed inside the organization). The third component, $(r_m - r_s)(1 + \beta)$, measures the effects of lagging productivity, Fuchs's third hypothesis. If the growth of labor productivity in manufacturing exceeds the growth in labor productivity in services $(r_m > r_s)$, then producing services will become relatively more expensive over time. This will increase the share of labor allocated to service activities. However, the rising relative price of services will reduce service demand at the rate $\beta$, the price elasticity of demand for services. This fall in demand will reduce services' shares in total employment. The net effect is $(r_m - r_s)(1 + \beta)$, where $\beta < 0$.

Baumol's simple general equilibrium framework tells much the same story about the pattern of U.S. service employment over time as Fuchs's careful, disaggregated accounting. For example, using Fuchs's (1968) estimates of labor productivity growth in industry ($r_m = .022$) and services ($r_s = .011$) and plausible average estimates of the income elasticity ($\alpha = 1.05$) and the price elasticity ($\beta = -.6$) of demand for services yields for $\dot{i}_s$:[5]

$$\dot{i}_s = (1.05 - 1)(.022) + \Delta + (.022 - .011)(1 - .6),$$

or

$$\dot{i}_s = .0011 + \Delta + .0044. \tag{2}$$

Fuchs's estimated annual rate of increase in the service employment share over the period from 1929 to 1965 is .008.[6] As $\dot{i}_s = .008$, $\Delta$ must equal .0025 ($= .008 - .0055$). Of the three possible explanations for the growth in the service shares, the hypothesis of lagging productivity accounts for 55 percent ($= .0044/.008$) of the annual rate of change in the service share. The rising income hypothesis accounts for only 14 percent ($= .0011/.008$) of the annual change. The exogenous demand shift hypothesis accounts for the remaining 31 percent of annual service share growth ($= .0025/.008$).[7] Baumol's general equilibrium analysis and Fuchs's microaccounting analysis converge to the same general conclusion: The growing importance of service employment in the U.S. economy over the period from 1929 to 1965 is due in large part to the lagging performance of labor productivity in the service sector.[8]

Will lagging productivity continue to drive the U.S. economy toward services? Does lagging productivity account for the move to services in other economies? If not, what does? Irving Leveson (for the U.S. economy), Gary Saxonhouse (for Japan), and Robert Summers (for a variety of developed and developing nations) address just these questions using contemporary data. Any empirical analysis of the service economy must begin with a definition of a service transaction. Like beauty, the definition of a service activity is often in the eye of the beholder. The crucial, underlying characteristics of a service transaction, which have been emphasized previously [Fuchs (1968), Stigler (1956), and Marshall (1929)] and which receive central emphasis by all the authors in this volume, are the intangible nature of the service product, the difficulty of storage, and the need for direct, often face-to-face, exchange between consumers and producers. Although there may never be full agreement as to whether a given economic activity is, or is not, a service, we must be clear how we define services in any study at hand. For only with common definitions are comparisons possible. The empirical studies by Leveson, Saxonhouse, and Summers permit such comparisons, though their definitions are not identical. Leveson employs the taxonomy proposed by Fuchs (1968, Chapter 2, Appendix I), and counts wholesale and retail trade, finance (banking, real estate, and insurance), professional, business and personal services, and general government as part of the service sector. Saxonhouse follows the Fuchs–Leveson definition but excludes business services. For his study, Summers uses data from the United Nations International Comparison Project, which is not strictly comparable to the U.S. and Japanese national income accounts data. Summers includes in "services" housing, transportation and communication (both excluded in Leveson and in Saxonhouse), medical care, recreation and education, and government (all included in Leveson and in Saxonhouse), and a category called "other consumption services" (which overlaps with personal services in Leveson and in Saxonhouse). Fortunately, Summers performs most of his empirical work on each service subgroup so comparisons to Leveson and to Saxonhouse are possible.

The Saxonhouse and Summers studies provide international evidence that supports the emphasis in the Baumol–Fuchs hypothesis on lagging productivity as the central cause of the worldwide drift to service economies. Summers's carefully constructed dissection of the demand for services using international, cross-section data yields evidence against the simple hypothesis that increases in income lead to the rising *share* of services in output and therefore in employment. The test of this hypothesis reduces to a test that the income elasticity of demand for services is significantly greater than 1 – for example, that a 10 percent rise in income leads to a greater than 10 percent increase in service consumption. When the income elasticity of demand [$\alpha$ in equation (1)] exceeds 1, services consume an increasing share of income and contribute to the rising share in employment [see equation (1)]. Summers finds, however, that for the category of all services, $\alpha = .98$ for his sample and cannot be judged significantly different from unity. The analysis of the various subgroups of services reveals that housing, medical care, and "other consumption services" do have income elasticities of demand significantly greater than 1, but the subgroups of recreation and education, transportation and communication, and government have income elasticities of 1 or less. Overall, the income elasticity is unity. Summers's cross-national analysis also provides an estimate of the price elasticity of demand for services [$\beta$ in equation (1)]. The elasticity is significantly lower than previous estimates ($\beta = -.06$) and if valid, implies an even more important role than previously thought for the decline in relative productivity as a source of rising service employment. The implications of Summers's results are twofold: (1) services have not been growing as a *share of real income* in world economies, contrary to popular belief; and (2) although services jobs have been growing as a *share of employment* in most economies, the reason for this growing share cannot be the growth in service output share. To explain the increasing relative importance of services in employment, we must look to causes other than simple income growth.

Saxonhouse's analysis of the Japanese service economy finds these other causes in lagging service productivity and in the unique structure of Japan's wholesale and retail trade for the distribution of goods. Both the pre- and post-World War II data show a falling share of services in national income but a rising share of services in total employment. The increasing share in total employment is attributed to the slower growth of labor productivity in services than in manufacturing; a comparison of Japan to other industrialized nations shows Japan's productivity shortfall in services (relative to manufacturing) to be the most pronounced. One possible explanation for the very poor relative performance of service productivity is the unique, and government-protected, position of small retailers and wholesalers in Japan. In 1981, distribution activities employed nearly 25 percent of Japan's active labor force, compared to 20 percent in the United States and only 12 percent in England and West Germany. Further, almost 70 percent of this segment of the labor force work in establishments employing fewer than ten people.

Additional country-specific studies of the service economy such as Saxonhouse has done for Japan are needed to establish firmly the importance of the Baumol–Fuchs hypothesis of lagging productivity as the *central* cause of the historical drift to a world service economy. Yet as we study and learn from the past, we must also speculate as to what the future portends. Leveson, using the recent history of the U.S. service economy, offers a prediction of the future pattern of development for the U.S. service sector. The relatively disadvantageous trends in service labor productivity have been offset to some extent by the recent rise in energy costs and environmental restrictions, which have raised costs in capital-intensive industries and shifted demand back toward services. The changing roles of women in our economy also have stimulated the demand for *market* services, which often replace *nonmarket* services once provided by women within a more traditional household structure. Inflation, too, has stimulated the demand for services as price volatility increases financial uncertainty and, hence, the need for financial and accounting services. Each of these forces has acted as an exogenous, outward "shock" to relative service demand in recent years – that is, $\Delta$ of equation (1) has been positive and important.[9] Will these trends continue, or be replaced by new stimuli to service sector growth? Leveson sees the relative growth in services slowing over the next decade. His arguments can be conveniently summarized in terms of the components of the relative service growth equation (1). Leveson contends that predicting the future importance of services requires us to predict future demand shocks ($\Delta$) and the relative trend in manufacturing and service productivity ($r_m - r_s$).[10] Whereas favorable demand shocks ($\Delta > 0$) have stimulated service growth in the past, the trend may be against services in the future. In the United States, at least, relative cutbacks in government-provided services are envisioned. Any increases in public allocations are likely to be in defense, which encourages goods, not service, production. Also the federal government and private firms are both seeking to limit their medical care expenditures. The factors that had limited the capital-intensive industries in the 1970s (energy costs and environmental regulation) may be easing. The liberation of women from housework is likely to continue, but the early growth spurt to service demand is probably behind us. The surge in the demand for education created by the maturity of the baby boom generation is also over. In effect, Leveson predicts that $\Delta$ will fall to zero, or even become negative. The gap between manufacturing and service productivity ($r_m - r_s$) may also narrow in the future. Two forces are at work here. First, the prospects for increasing the capital-to-labor ratio in services look excellent, particularly in the retailing, wholesaling, and finance subsectors. This point was emphasized by Saxonhouse as well in his review of the Japanese service economy. Second, as government spending is curtailed and service activities are shifted to the private sector, Leveson predicts that the increased competition of the private sector will act to stimulate productivity growth in these service areas. As the productivity of labor in the service sector rises to the level now enjoyed by the manufacturing sector, the need for more and more workers in services will decline. This will slow the relative growth of the service employment in the future.

The overall picture presented in these three papers is one of extraordinary service sector employment growth since World War II, which now seems to have peaked in the major industrialized nations. The net result of this growth process, however, is a world economy predominantly involved in producing and trading services. In Japan more than half the work force is employed in service production, whereas in the United States two-thirds of the labor force is so employed.[11] The share of gross domestic product that is services ranges from 30 percent in less developed countries to just about 50 percent in most industrialized nations.[12] As services assume a central role in our economic lives, it is necessary to understand how services are produced and consumed and, from that understanding, to seek new ways to improve our management of the service sector.

The papers in Part II provide a conceptual framework for examining the major policy issues in running a service economy: enhancing productivity growth (Kendrick), encouraging international service trade (Kravis and Stalson), and promoting efficient domestic service markets (Holmstrom).

The emergence of services as the dominant sector in the economy raises fundamental questions of public policy. In the United States these issues have surfaced in the debate over the efficiency of a national industrial policy to combat the erosion of the U.S. manufacturing sector; the concern for the decline of the manufacturing sector is simply an alternative to the concern over the growth of the service sector. [13] Because the industrial sector has, at least historically, been the leader in labor productivity growth, the decline of this sector may lead to a decline in the growth in labor productivity for the economy as a whole. Real wage incomes, therefore, would grow less rapidly. Due to their intangible nature, services tend to be domestically produced and consumed. Consequently, world trade in goods dominates world trade in services. A declining manufacturing sector may therefore weaken a country's balance of payment position. Finally, national defense requires a strong manufacturing sector that can be mobilized quickly in time of war; a service economy cannot be transformed easily into a military economy. Each of these arguments has been offered as the basis for a national industrial policy that should (1) subsidize promising manufacturing (often high technology) industries through tax breaks and direct grants, and (2) offer government assistance and import protection for declining manufacturing industries so that these industries can adjust to new economic conditions. The economic implications of these subsidies and trade restrictions will be significant. The use of industrial policies to reverse the economic trend to a service economy will create domestic price distortions and inefficiencies and possibly limit world trade via retaliatory trade barriers. The benefits will have to be sizable to justify the use of such "favored-sector" policies. The presumption behind an industrial policy is that those benefits are large for reasons just mentioned: The manufacturing sector is more productive than the service sector, world trade in services is limited, and an all-service economy is militarily weak.

What is the evidence? The Summers, Saxonhouse, and Leveson analyses should dispel the concern that service economies will be militarily weak. It is most unlikely that any economy will become an all-service economy. In all the economies examined here, the division of national income between services and manufacturing has remained virtually constant over the past two decades. In the United States, for example, the manufacturing share of output actually rose slightly from 23.3 percent in 1960 to 23.8 percent in 1980. The papers by Kendrick on productivity and by Kravis and by Stalson on world service trade address the two, more substantive, arguments for an industrial policy. Their results also argue against an explicitly promanufacturing, antiservice industrial policy.

The Kendrick paper reviews the methodological issues in service sector productivity measurement, updates Fuchs's (1968) original analysis of productivity, and speculates about future trends in service productivity with an eye toward the design of policies to improve efficiency in the service sector. The central methodological problem in the study of the performance of service sector productivity is developing adequate measures of service output. In the case of government services, for example, we have historically measured output in units of labor inputs; clearly there can be no increase in labor productivity if output always equals labor inputs! Fortunately, important new theoretical approaches to measuring output in the service economy have been developed and have been shown to be useful in empirical research on service production.[14] The remaining task is to collect a sufficiently rich data base of service output and input measures so that accurate empirical studies of service sector production can be performed. Both industry-wide production function studies and engineering and managerial analyses of individual service firms are needed. It is at the macro, sector-wide level and with existing published, U.S. government data that Kendrick performs his empirical analysis of service productivity. The results are revealing on several points: (1) from 1948 to 1981 the rates of growth in total factor productivity and labor productivity in "goods" production exceeded their equivalent measures in "service" production, but the gap between productivity growth in the two sectors has narrowed in recent years; (2) within the service sector, retail and wholesale trade have had the best records of productivity improvement, records that compare favorably to the "goods" sector, whereas finance and real estate have experienced poor (often negative) productivity trends; and (3) the financial sector has enjoyed a recent increase in its capital-to-labor ratio, an improvement that may mean significant labor productivity gains in that sector in the future. As to the future, Kendrick is optimistic. Anticipated increases in U.S. aggregate investment should increase the capital-to-labor ratio in service industries, and on the basis of past performance, Kendrick predicts a growth in labor productivity in the service sector of 2 percent per year for the next decade. Kendrick's forecast considerably eases concern over the effects of an expanding service sector on the growth in real labor incomes.

The research by Irving Kravis documents, perhaps more carefully than any study to date, the role of services in world trade. When services are defined to include income from investment (as payment for the services of capital), services constituted approximately 25 percent of world transactions in 1980. When investment income is excluded from the service total, services involved about 17 percent of world trade. The developed nations are net exporters of services, whereas the developing economies are net importers. The United States is by far the dominant exporter of services, including or excluding investment income. Further, world trade in services has been growing over the past decade, both absolutely and relative to world gross domestic product (GDP). Whereas nominal GDP grew fourfold over the decade from 1970 to 1980, the nominal value of world trade in services grew by a factor of five. Will world service trade continue to grow? Kravis sees no absolute decline, but he is doubtful that service trade will continue to show its impressive relative gains of the last decade, unless major policy initiatives to lower trade and investment barriers are forthcoming. On this point, he is not optimistic. The bulk of noninvestment service trade involves sales by domestic affiliates or branches in a host country, rather than direct service sales from a firm located in the export nation. Service trade expansion therefore will require increased direct involvement in foreign host countries. Such investments are often discouraged on social or cultural grounds, however. It is not clear that trade negotiations, which Kravis advocates, will successfully overcome these barriers.

In her paper on world trade policy, Stalson details the existing restrictions on international trade in services and suggests possible strategies for their removal or relaxation. Among the existing barriers to noninvestment trade are host country requirements that restrict imports or limit the sales of foreign-owned companies, discriminatory fees, regulations, and licenses, and subsidies to competitive domestic firms. Barriers to investment are limitations on foreign ownership and restrictions on the level of profits or royalties that may be transferred from the host country. International arrangements to control such restrictions are not new, but they are not extensive either. Various international arrangements now regulate telecommunications, banking, aviation, and shipping. But insurance has never been supervised internationally and the General Agreement on Tariffs and Trade (GATT) refers almost exclusively (the exception is motion pictures) to trade in goods. What can be done to lower the barriers to trade in services and to expand service trade still further? Both Stalson and Kravis agree that the likelihood of quick action on a multilateral level is small, but the initiative toward building a broad international consensus on trade in services should be maintained. At the same time, bilateral agreements can be concluded that may help to ease friction, so long as they provide for ultimate access by other countries willing to accept the agreements' terms. An effort to reach agreement on liberalization of service trade at the multilateral 1982 GATT conference was defeated, largely for political reasons. Since the 1982 conference, however, a number of countries have followed the United States in compiling information on their service industries in preparation for future talks in GATT.

Although a sound trade policy towards services must await a more cooperative international political environment, nations can pursue sensible domestic policies toward the service economy on their own. The design of public policies toward service industries is a subtle matter, however. One of the unique, and central, characteristics of services is that the "commodity" being exchanged is intangible, and thus not easily described or measured – for example, a physician's visit or a legal consultation. This fact creates special problems for the market provision of services. In an important survey paper, Bengt Holmstrom helps us understand these problems. The major difficulty, as Holmstrom sees it, is that the quality of service provision is difficult to assess; whereas the producer may know product quality, the buyer often does not. This asymmetry of information between sellers and buyers of services creates problems for their market provision.[15] These problems are of two types: moral hazard and adverse selection. Moral hazard arises when the buyer is unable to observe the level of care or effort taken by the seller.[16] The problem of moral hazard is one of inducing the seller to provide the right level of effort at the lowest cost to ensure efficient service provision. Adverse selection arises when the buyer cannot observe relevant characteristics of the seller or the conditions under which the seller must work. For example, a doctor contracts to do open-heart surgery but the patient does not know whether the doctor is competent or clumsy or whether the hospital has experienced or inexperienced surgical nurses. All the patient knows is that, on the average, 20 percent of all open-heart patients die in the operating room. This risk may be too great and the patient may refuse surgery. Even though there are good doctors and good hospitals where the risk is very low, the "good" surgeons are driven from the market by the "bad" surgeons, and a valuable service is not provided. How serious are the problems of moral hazard and adverse selection, and is government intervention into the service economy needed to correct the resulting misallocations? At this point, we do not have definitive answers to these questions. We do know that buyers and sellers often create clever market solutions to the problems of moral hazard and adverse selection – warranties and contingent contracts, seller reputation, informative advertising, and certification – but we do not know how effective these corrective measures are. Matters are further complicated by the fact that although problems of adverse selection can be minimized through government action, problems of moral hazard are not necessarily improved by government intervention. As Holmstrom emphasizes, government policies are to be preferred when an externality is present. This is the case with adverse selection where "inferior" sellers impose an externality on "superior" sellers by driving them from the market. This externality can be removed through government quality-testing and certification. There is no externality in the case of moral hazard, however, just poor information about seller effort. Unless governments have an advantage in providing such information there is no reason to believe the political process can allocate resources more efficiently than the marketplace. To advocate government intervention into the workings of the service economy therefore requires us to identify the observed market failure as a problem of moral hazard or adverse selection. Such a distinction is difficult to draw, but necessary for a sound domestic policy towards the service economy.

The conceptual papers of Kendrick, Kravis, Stalson, and Holmstrom help to define the policy issues facing a service economy, but decisions regarding the actual structure of service provision can only be made from the perspective of individual service industries. For that, we need careful analyses of a variety of service industries. There is variety. Services are provided by competitive profit maximizing firms, nonprofit organizations, regulated firms, and governments. Often organizations of each form compete against each other in the same service industry – for example, in providing health care, transmitting information, giving legal counsel, or collecting garbage. The analysis of the service economy challenges our analytic capabilities as well as our ability to create new forms of organization and management structures to solve uncovered problems. The three industry studies in Part III – one for a predominantly competitive market (Black on financial services), one for a predominantly nonprofit market (Satterthwaite on health care), and one for government services (Gramlich) – make important, first steps towards improving our understanding of individual service industries.

Fischer Black's provocative essay on the financial service industry of the future is a case study that applies the fundamental principles of policy as enunciated in Holmstrom's essay. After describing an ideal world with perfect information and no costs of financial management or transaction, Black moves to a more realistic world where financial information is imperfect and costly to acquire. In Black's world, costly information explains not only the existence of a financial service industry, but its structure as well. With costly information, investment firms will dominate the holding of securities of nonfinancial firms. An investment firm will generally be better at evaluating the information that affects its holdings as well as evaluating new securities. Individuals will invest in investment firms to avail themselves of this informational advantage. Stockholder control of nonfinancial firms should also improve as a few investment firms will have an incentive (in a way many stockholders do not) to seek out information on firm performance. Economies-of-scale in gathering and processing financial information will dictate that in equilibrium only a few large investment firms will survive. Security firms will be wholesalers of primary securities, doing financial planning for their corporate customers and selling to investment firms. Accounting firms will be an important source of independent information to investment firms. Banking firms will facilitate financial transactions by check, credit card, or electronic message and they will borrow, sell shares, and lend money. Competition will drive bank charges to the marginal cost of processing transactions and administering loans; all positive balance accounts will be paid the competitive rate of interest. Credit rationing and reputation will play an important role in the market for bank loans when information is imperfect. Having predicted the future structure of the financial service industry, Black asks the last question: Will government regulation be required? Black sees little need for security, banking, or takeover regulations in his competitive, but imperfect information, world. Antitrust regulation may be needed to monitor the large investment firms and to keep entry barriers low. Regulations against fraud and investment firm deception are also needed; such regulations play an important role in minimizing the problems of adverse selection. The essential discipline that ensures an adequate performance of the financial service sector remains, however, the competitive market process.

Although Black is confident that a competitive market process will work well for the financial service industry, Satterthwaite is not so optimistic that market competition will lead to desirable outcomes in the market for physicians' services. The market for physicians' services is characterized by three facts: (1) all physicians have some monopoly power in being able to increase fees without losing all of their patients; (2) entry into any regional physicians' market is generally easy, so the physicians' ability to exploit this monopoly power is limited; and (3) consumers have only imperfect information about the quality of each physician's practice. The market is one of monopolistic competition with imperfect consumer information. Satterthwaite analyzes the performance of this market within the context of an economic model explicitly designed to accommodate these three characteristics. The analysis is instructive not only for what it tells us about the market for physicians' services, but also for what it says, generally, about service markets characterized by imperfect consumer information. The analytic results are counter-intuitive on two points. First, physicians' fees are higher in regions with more physicians, all else being equal. Second, an increase in the aggregate supply of physicians to a region will raise, not lower, the equilibrium price of physicians' services. Why? Since physicians are assumed to be profit-maximizing monopolists, they will price their services in the price-elastic portion of their demand curve at that quantity where marginal revenue equals marginal cost. If marginal cost is constant, and if a physician's demand curve becomes less elastic, the profit-maximizing price will rise. Given these basic results, which hold for any monopolistic market, Satterthwaite then asks: When might a physician's demand curve become less price elastic? One answer is when consumers' information regarding the quality of physicians' practices is reduced; with less information about practice quality, consumers are less likely to switch doctors when their current doctors raise their fees. Thus, with poorer information, each physician's demand curve becomes less price sensitive. The last step in Satterthwaite's argument is to assume that consumer information about the quality of any individual physician declines as the number of physicians in the market increases. The more doctors there are, the less we can learn about any individual doctor, other than our own current physician. Thus, as the number of physicians increases in a market, the equilibrium price for physicians' services will rise, and markets with more physicians, ceteris paribus, will have higher market prices for physicians' services. When tested against the performance of physicians' markets in the 100 largest metropolitan areas, the Satterthwaite predictions are confirmed. [17] What are the policy implications of Satterthwaite's analysis? At a minimum the results lead us to be skeptical of any policy that recommends an increase in the number of new physicians, on the grounds that more doctors mean more price competition, and thus lower prices. Rather, more doctors are likely to mean less information about any individual physician, less price competition, and thus higher prices! Satterthwaite's concluding comment is one we should all heed as we begin our analysis of service industries: Old, comfortable models developed for the "goods" sector are not necessarily the right tools for analysis of the substantively different service economy.

Satterthwaite's warning is nowhere more appropriate than when we begin to study the provision of government services. After a brief survey of the growth of government spending on services, Edward Gramlich asks whether the collective provision of services is, or ever can be, economically efficient. The answer rests on the comparative ability of markets or government to provide the socially optimal allocation of services. Governments will have a *presumed* advantage in just those instances where markets are likely to fail, the prominent instances being the case of Samuelson pure public goods, and the case when judgements of equity or fairness are deemed relevant. Education, health care, housing, protection, and legal justice are leading examples. Whereas governments are potentially more efficient, or fairer, than markets in allocating such services, the question remains: Are they in fact? Gramlich reviews a series of analytic models of government performance and the associated evidence and concludes that, in general, governments are imperfect too. Although democratic referendum politics has much to recommend it, it is not a sure mechanism to economic efficiency or equity. Nor is its polar alternative, centralized bureaucratic decision making. Bureaucracies are likely to overprovide services relative to the efficient allocation, whereas referenda may over- or underprovide public services. The imperfections of government have motivated a search in recent years for possibly preferable mixed market and government structures. Gramlich reviews four alternatives: (1) spending and tax limitations that restrict the size of government and force any extra services desired above the limit to be provided by the market; (2) government financed but privately provided services, with providers chosen through competitive bidding; (3) government provided but privately financed services through the use of "user fees" or prices, and (4) the competitive purchase of government inputs and the extensive use of labor incentive contracts to restrict the power of the government bureaucracy. Although our experience to date with each of the four reforms suggests major difficulties – Gramlich attributes the problems to the fundamental difference between public and private services – an important commitment to experimentation in service provision has been established.

What does the future hold for the service economy? Part IV concludes the volume with speculative essays by the two scholars who began the serious study of the service economy nearly twenty years ago, William Baumol and Victor Fuchs. Baumol returns to his original theme of productivity in the service sector. In the essay here, he refines his earlier analysis of service productivity to include three alternative stages of productivity development: progressive, asymptotically stagnant, and stagnant. [Baumol's original article (1967) studied only the stagnant phase.] Not all services pass through each stage. Indeed, Baumol sees "personal services" where direct provider–consumer contact is essential (e.g., the arts, health care, legal services) as inherently stagnant. "Impersonal" services, which involve little direct producer–consumer contact (e.g., telecommunications) are particularly open to technological change and may be permanently progressive. Nor does Baumol's scheme rule out the possibility that personal services may become impersonal services – live performances become television or movie performances – and thus become open to technological change and increased productivity. The progressive stage is the period of significant technological advance and gains in productivity; the telecommunications industry of the last twenty years is his example. Productivity growth may be limited, however, to the extent that the substitution of capital and technology for labor is limited. For example, the computer industry will always need programmers, television and movies will still need actors and directors, and telecommunications will need operators and repair personnel. As we reach the limit of the capital/technology for labor substitution, productivity can grow only as labor becomes smarter, faster, or stronger. At this point, the industry moves into the asymptotically stagnant phase. Finally, as labor productivity gains are exhausted, we reach the stagnant stage of development. This more detailed view of service sector production clarifies two points, which Baumol emphasizes: (1) productivity growth in the service economy will not be zero – indeed, the potential for growth is quite significant; and (2) when we design public policies for productivity growth we must understand at which stage in the development process a service industry stands. Policies must be targeted to be effective. Baumol cites as examples of ineffective or misguided policies, tax limitations on government services, simple rate of return regulation for regulated service industries, protective trade barriers, and inadequate public support for the service called basic research and development. In each case, Baumol contends, the policy failure is due to our lack of understanding of the true productivity potential of the service industry involved.

In his capstone essay, Victor Fuchs defines five broad areas for future research on the management of the service economy. For each topic, Fuchs emphasizes a theme that underlies all the papers in this volume. Services are fundamentally different from goods; the productive analysis of the service economy will require new data, new economic and management models, and the careful industry-by-industry application of each. The first area of new research is to examine the demand for and production of consumer or household services. Fuchs stresses the need here to consider the consumer as both a demander and a producer of services, and he cites medical care services as a typical example. The patient not only buys the physician's services, but also works with the physician in a cooperative, productive relationship to produce improved health. [18] Further, household demographic changes may have a significant effect on service sector growth, and again we will need to consider both supply-side and demand-side forces. For example, increased labor force participation by women increases the demand for market services but also supplies additional labor to the service sector, thereby lowering costs. The joint effect is an expansion of consumer services; the growth of day care and nursery school education is an example. The second area of the service economy that deserves increased study is government services. Fuchs expands Gramlich's analysis by asking why government services have grown so significantly over the last thirty years. Is it for economic reasons of increasing market failure in an increasingly complicated economy, or is it for political reasons? The growth of producer services is the third topic on Fuchs's research agenda. Are new services being provided, or are firms now finding it efficient to hire outsiders to perform many management functions once provided by firm employees? This question returns us to Holmstrom's essay where we began to explore the role of services in writing, monitoring, and enforcing production contracts. As his fourth research area, Fuchs wants us to examine the production of services in greater detail. To be sure, capital, labor, and technology are important to service production, but Fuchs suggests that the timing of service utilization may be important (is demand uniform or sporadic?) as might be the form of organization (profit, nonprofit, government) used to produce services. Further, since service production is often labor intensive, labor-embodied technological change becomes a topic of research importance in a service economy. Finally, and perhaps most importantly, Fuchs wants us to examine what it will mean to live in a postindustrial society. Just as industrial societies differ from agrarian ones, so too may we expect the service society to differ from the industrial society. New social organizations are often required to implement new production processes. Will a service economy demand additional adjustments in how we relate to one another in our economic lives? There are good reasons to think that it will, and Fuchs wants us to think hard about such matters now.[19]

The Wharton/ARA Conference, held in November 1982, provided the occasion for the research papers and commentary collected in this volume. Whereas these papers contribute in their own right to our understanding of the role of the service sector and its consequences in developed economies, they are also a blueprint for future research. Indeed, the agenda indicated implicitly by this collection, and explicitly by Professor Fuchs, is long and rich in prospects. Analyzing so vital and preeminent a sector of our economy as services will require efforts ranging from the collection of new data, to the development of new conceptual tools, to the need for careful industry studies. The essays, commentaries, and discussions in this volume are a first step toward defining, and fulfilling, that agenda.

## Appendix: Introduction and overview

William Baumol (1967) has presented a simple model of the relative growth of two economic activities with differential rates of change in labor productivity. The version of the model presented here is an extension of Baumol's original framework. There are two sectors, manufacturing $(m)$ and services $(s)$, whose production technologies are represented by:

$$Q_m = aL_m e^{r_m t},\tag{A.1}$$

and

$$Q_s = bL_s e^{r_s t},\tag{A.2}$$

where output levels in time $t$ ($t$ subscripts are omitted), $Q_m$ and $Q_s$, depend upon labor inputs, $L_m$ and $L_s$, and the rate of increase in labor productivity, $r_m$ and $r_s$. The total labor force is $L_s + L_m = L$. The demand for the two outputs is described by the budget constraint (equal to the wage per worker, $W$) and the demand for one of the outputs, in this case services:

$$(Q_s/L) = c(p_s/p_m)^\beta W^\alpha e^{\Delta t}\tag{A.3}$$

and

$$p_m(Q_m/L) = W - p_s(Q_s/L). \tag{A.4}$$

Equation (A.3) is the demand for services per worker, which depends upon the relative prices of services to manufacturing ($p_s/p_m$), wage income per worker ($W$), and exogenous shifts in demand at rate $\Delta$ over time. The coefficient $\beta$ is the price elasticity of demand and $\alpha$ is the income elasticity of demand for services. Equation (A.4) defines the demand for manufacturing output as the difference between wage income and expenditures on services. We can allow manufacturing to be the numeraire good, so $p_m \equiv 1$.

Wages in the economy are determined in a competitive labor market by equating the demand for labor to the supply of labor ($L$). Profit-maximizing firms will demand labor until the value of the marginal product of a unit of labor equals the wage. The marginal products of labor in the two sectors are defined by:

$$\partial Q_m/\partial L_m = mp_m = ae^{r_m t}, \tag{A.5}$$

and

$$\partial Q_s/\partial L_s = mp_s = be^{r_s t}. \tag{A.6}$$

Equating the value of the marginal products in manufacturing to the wage gives:

$$W = p_m ae^{r_m t}, \tag{A.7}$$

or since $p_m \equiv 1$,

$$W = ae^{r_m t}. \tag{A.7'}$$

Finally, market prices for manufacturing and services are set in competitive markets where price must equal marginal cost. With only one input, marginal cost is defined by ($W/mp_m$) in manufacturing and ($W/mp_s$) in services. Only relative prices ($p_s/p_m$) are relevant for our analysis, however. They are defined as:

$$(p_s/p_m) = (W/mp_s)/(W/mp_m) = (mp_m/mp_s), \tag{A.8}$$

or using (A.5) and (A.6), as:

$$(p_s/p_m) = (a/b)e^{(r_m - r_s)t}. \tag{A.8'}$$

Note that if the rate of change in labor productivity in manufacturing exceeds that in services ($r_m > r_s$), then the relative price of services rises over time [$\partial(p_s/p_m)/\partial t > 0$].

We can now describe the path of services' share in total employment over time in this simple economy. Services' share of total employment is defined as:

$$\frac{L_s}{L_s + L_m} = \frac{L_s}{L} = l_s. \tag{A.9}$$

From the production function (A.2) for services, we know:

$$L_s = (1/b)Q_s e^{-r_s t}, \tag{A.10}$$

or in per worker units:

$$(L_s/L) = (1/b)(Q_s/L)e^{-r_s t}. \tag{A.10'}$$

In equilibrium, service output per worker $(Q_s/L)$ must equal service demand per worker defined by equation (A.3) for the equilibrium relative prices [equation (A.8′)] and the equilibrium wage [equation (A.7′)]:

$$(Q_s/L) = c\{(a/b)e^{(r_m - r_s)t}\}^{\beta}\{ae^{r_m t}\}^{\alpha}e^{\Delta t} \tag{A.11}$$

or

$$(Q_s/L) = Ae^{\{(r_m - r_s)\beta + r_m \alpha + \Delta\}t}, \tag{A.11'}$$

where $A = (c/b^{\beta})a^{\alpha + \beta}$. Substituting (A.11′) into (A.10′) defines the equilibrium path of services' share of total employment:

$$(L_s/L) = l_s = (A/b)e^{\{(r_m - r_s)\beta + r_m \alpha - r_s + \Delta\}t}. \tag{A.12}$$

The rate of change of this share over time is:

$$\frac{d(L_s/L)/dt}{(L_s/L)} = \dot{l}_s = (r_m - r_s)\beta + (r_m \alpha - r_s) + \Delta. \tag{A.13}$$

If we add $r_m$ and subtract $r_m$ to the right-hand side of expression (A.13) we obtain (A.14), which also appears as equation (1) of the Introduction and Overview:

$$\dot{l}_s = (\alpha - 1)r_m + \Delta + (r_m - r_s)(1 + \beta). \tag{A.14}$$

### Notes

1. See the papers by Irving Leveson, Robert Summers, and Gary Saxonhouse in this volume.
2. Colin Clark (1957), and Petty [1691, as quoted in Clark (1957, p. 492)] before them all, also noted the rising share of services in income over the course of economic growth.
3. For the purpose of his study Fuchs defined services to include wholesale trade, retail trade, finance and insurance, real estate, household and institutions, professional, personal, business and repair services, and general government.
4. Fuchs finds that the share of U.S. services in U.S. output when measured in fixed prices was the same in 1965 as in 1929. That is, the quantities of services

and income grew at roughly the same rate. The implication is that services in the aggregate have a unitary income elasticity of demand. Also see R. Summers in this volume. There is other evidence from demand studies, which supports this result; see Houthakker and Taylor (1966) and Inman (1978b). An income elasticity of demand equal to 1, however, will not explain why services have become relatively *more* important over time. The first hypothesis must therefore be rejected. The second hypothesis – increased specialization – does account for some of the increased relative importance of services since 1945, but it does not provide a complete explanation. Fuchs concludes from a comparison of input–output tables for the years 1947 and 1958 that less than 10% of the total growth in service employment can be attributed to the growth of intermediate demand by the goods-producing industries. The third hypothesis of lagging service productivity is the most important explanation for the growth of U.S. service employment from 1929 to 1965. During this period Fuchs estimates output per worker in agriculture grew at an annual rate of 3.4%, in industry at an annual rate of 2.2%, and in services at a rate of 1.1%. Faster technological change and improved labor quality in the industrial sector accounted for the majority of the productivity differences between industry and services during this period.

Recently Haig (1975) has tested Fuchs's three hypotheses for the relative growth of services in the Australian economy over the period 1960–70. The results suggest greater roles for demand through the growth in income (Fuchs's first hypothesis) and for increased demand for services as intermediate goods (Fuchs's second hypothesis), but lagging service sector productivity (Fuchs's third hypothesis) is also a major determinant of the relative growth of services in Australia.

5. Productivity estimates are from Fuchs (1968, p. 4). Fuchs (1968) estimates $\alpha =$ 1.05 for services generally, whereas Houthakker and Taylor (1966) obtain income elasticities for a wide variety of individual services in the range .5 to as high as 2.2. Most services had $\alpha$ values near 1.0. Inman (1978b) surveys the estimates of the income elasticity for government services and the values fall in the range from .6 to 1.2. Price elasticity estimates for government services range from – .2 to – .8 [Inman (1978b)] and for private services from – .4 to –1.6 [Houthakker and Taylor (1966)].

6. The share grew from .40 in 1929 to .55 in 1965, which implies a compounded annual growth rate in this share of .008 per annum (Fuchs, 1968, p. 21).

7. Fuchs estimated that the exogenous shifts in service demand accounted for no more than 10% of the growth in the service share (Fuchs, 1968, p. 4). But Fuchs's procedure used interindustry input–output tables and thus misses any important exogenous shifts in the demand by the household sector. Fuchs recognized this point in his 1968 book (he emphasizes *intermediate* demand for services in his discussion) and in his essay for this volume he stresses the important role of changing service demands with the reorganization of household activity.

8. Baumol's general equilibrium analysis has been applied to specific subsectors of the service economy as well. For example, Spann (1977) finds the Baumol model does an accurate job of tracking the growth in government's share of employment

over the decades 1950–70. Baumol and Bowen (1966) have the Baumol model in mind when discussing the relative decline of expenditures and employment on the performing arts. They do not apply the model directly in their analysis, however.

9. I have replicated the analysis at equation (2) using the more recent estimates of the rates of productivity growth in manufacturing and services as provided in Kendrick (this volume). Compounding each of Kendrick's rates of productivity growth over the period 1966–81 implies an estimate of the annual rate of growth in labor productivity in goods production of .0133 ( $= r_m$ ) and of the annual rate of growth in service labor productivity of .0062 ( $= r_s$ ). From Leveson's Figure 3.2 we can estimate the annual rate of growth in the service sector's share of labor as .0083 per year ( $= \dot{l}_s$ ). Setting $\alpha = 1.05$ and $\beta = -.6$ as before, we obtain from equation (1):

$$.0083 = (1.05 - 1)(.0113) + \Delta + (.0113 - .0062)(1 - .6),$$

which implies a value of $\Delta = .0057$. Exogenous demand shocks ($\Delta$) have therefore accounted for 69% of the annual growth in services' share in employment ( $= .0057/.0083$) for the period 1966–81. This is to be contrasted to $\Delta$'s 31% contribution to annual share growth over the period 1929–65. Fuchs (1981) argues that an important component of the exogenous demand shock ($\Delta$) in recent years is the increased labor force participation of women. Stanback et al. (1981) argue that the shift to producers' services explains the large value of $\Delta$.

10. Tacitly, at least, Leveson accepts the evidence of Fuchs (1968) for the United States and of Summers (this volume) for world economies that the income elasticity of demand for services is approximately 1. Thus the first term in equation (1) drops away, and Leveson rightly focuses his attention on exogenous effects and relative productivity.

11. See Saxonhouse (this volume) and Leveson (this volume).

12. Summers (this volume).

13. See, for example, *Economic Report of the President*, 1984, Chapter 3, "Industrial Policy"; the opening paragraph reads: "Should the United States adopt an industrial policy? Proponents argue that such a strategy is necessary to revitalize our manufacturing sector."

14. The theoretical foundation of service sector productivity analysis will likely prove to be the multicharacteristic approach to consumer demand pioneered by Lancaster (1966) and discussed more recently in Deaton and Muellbauer (1980). Services are commodities that often have several aspects that provide consumer utility. If these aspects are measurable, then we can estimate multioutput production functions for these services. There have been several recent studies that have estimated multioutput production functions or cost schedules for services – see [Inman (1978a, road travel), Merewitz (1971, mail service), Brueckner (1981, fire protection), Getz (1979, fire protection; 1980, library services), Carr–Hill and Stern (1977, police protection), Braeutigam, Daughety, Turnquist (1982, railroad services)]. Interesting single-output production function or cost function studies of service industries include Gapinski (1982, cultural events), Summers and Wolfe (1977, elementary/secondary

education), McGuckin and Winkler (1979, higher education), Jansson and Shneerson (1978, shipping).

The work on service industry productivity is just beginning, but the theoretical and econometric methodologies are available as are many excellent examples of how such studies might be done.

15. Lest I leave the impression that the "goods" market does not suffer from the problem of asymmetric information, I need only remind readers of the difficulty of judging automobile quality and the problem auto "lemons" create for the used car market. Both Holmstrom and his discussant, Andrew Postlewaite, make an important comment in this regard. Services are not inherently "shoddy" commodities. In fact, many services arise to correct the problems created by shoddy merchandise – for example, auto mechanics, consultants and, when all else fails, lawyers. Many services are offered to help the market for goods work more efficiently.

16. It is important to note, however, that something other than effort must be unobserved, e.g., service quality or another determinant of service quality besides effort. If quality is observed and only effort determines quality, there will be no market failure, for we can judge effort by quality. When service quality is observed, but there are other random and exogenous determinants of quality besides effort, then the transaction between buyer and seller will necessarily entail some risk sharing. The transaction will have to balance risk protection and the incentives to provide good effort.

17. The empirical results are reported in Pauly and Satterthwaite (1981).

18. The existing health care literature contains several studies that do treat the consumer as a participant on both sides of the market; see, for example, Inman (1976), Goldman and Grossman (1978), and Wilcox–Gok (1983).

19. For some initial speculations on this question, see Stanback et al. (1981). What is required are careful social and economic histories of service organizations; again health care services provides an example – see Starr (1982). Also see Arrow (1963) who, in a provocative essay on the medical marketplace, argues that trust relationships may become as important as exchange relationships in a service economy where informational asymmetries predominate. Titmuss (1971) presents an analysis of the possible advantages of such a change in his study of the market for blood transfusion services.

# References

Arrow, Kenneth (December 1963), "Uncertainty and the Welfare Economics of Medical Care," *American Economic Review,* 53, 941–73.

Baumol, William (June 1967), "Macroeconomices of Unbalanced Growth," *American Economic Review,* 57, 415–26.

Baumol, William, and William Bowen (1966), *Performing Arts: The Economic Dilemma,* Cambridge, Mass.: MIT Press.

Braeutigam, R., A. Daughety, and M. Turnquist (August 1982), "The Estimation of a Hybrid Cost Function for a Railroad Firm," *The Review of Economics and Statistics,* 64, 394–404.

Brueckner, Jan (February 1981), "Congested Public Goods: The Case of Fire Protection," *Journal of Public Economics,* 15, 45-58.

Carr-Hill, R., and N. Stern (1977), "Theory and Estimation in Models of Crime and Its Social Control and Their Relations to Concepts of Social Output," in M. S. Feldstein and R. P. Inman (eds.) *Economics of Public Services,* 194-232, London: Macmillan.

Clark, Colin (1957), *The Conditions of Economic Progress,* New York: Macmillan.

Deaton, Angus and J. Muellbauer (1980), *Economics and Consumer Behavior,* New York: Cambridge University Press.

Fuchs, Victor (1968), *The Service Economy,* New York: Columbia University Press, 221-420.

(1981), "Economic Growth and the Rise of Service Employment," in H. Giersch (ed.) *Towards an Explanation of Economic Growth,* Tubingen, J. C. B. Mohr.

Gapinski, James (November 1982), "The Production of Culture," *The Review of Economics and Statistics,* 62, 578-86.

Getz, M. (1979), *The Economics of the Urban Fire Department,* Baltimore: The Johns Hopkins University Press.

(1980), *Public Libraries: An Economic View,* Baltimore: The Johns Hopkins University Press.

Goldman, Fred, and M. Grossman (April 1978), "The Demand for Pediatric Care: A Hedonic Approach," *Journal of Political Economy,* 86, 259-80.

Haig, B. D. (February 1975), "An Analysis of Changes in the Distribution of Employment between Manufacturing and Service Industries, 1960-1970," *The Review of Economics and Statistics,* 57, 35-42.

Houthakker, H. and L. D. Taylor (1966), *Consumer Demand in the United States, 1929-1970,* Cambridge, Mass.: Harvard University Press.

Inman, R. P. (1976), "The Family Provision of Children's Health: An Economic Analysis," in R. Rosett (ed.) *The Role of Health Insurance in the Health Services Sector,* 215-54, New York: Neale Watson Academic Publication.

(January 1978), "A Generalized Congestion Function for Highway Travel," *Journal of Urban Economics* 5, 21-34.

(1978), "The Fiscal Performance of Local Governments: An Interpretative Review," in P. Mieszkowski and M. Straszheim (eds.) *Current Issues in Urban Economics,* 270-321, Baltimore: The Johns Hopkins University Press.

Jansson, J. O. and D. Shneerson (May 1978), "Economies of Scale of General Cargo Ships," *The Review of Economics and Statistics,* 60, 287-93.

Lancaster, K. (April 1966), "A New Approach to Consumer Theory," *Journal of Political Economy,* 74, 132-57.

Marshall, Alfred (1929), *Principles of Economics,* London.

McGuckin, Robert H. and D. R. Winkler (May 1979), "University Resources in the Production of Education," *The Review of Economics and Statistics,* 61, 242-48.

Merewitz, Leonard (September 1971), "Cost and Returns to Scale in U.S. Post Offices," *Journal of the American Statistical Association,* 66, 504-9.

Pauly, M. V. and M. A. Satterthwaite (Autumn 1981), "The Pricing of Primary Care Physicians' Services: A Test of the Role of Consumer Information," *Bell Journal of Economics* 12, 488-506.

Spann, R. (December 1977), "The Macroeconomies of Unbalanced Growth and the Expanding Public Sector," *Journal of Public Economics* 8, 397-404.

Stanback, T. M. and associates (1981), *Services: The New Economy,* Totowa, N.J.: Allanfeld, Osmun, and Co.

Starr, Paul (1982), *Social Transformation of American Medicine,* New York: Basic Books.

Stigler, G. (1956), *Trends in Employment in the Service Industries,* Princeton, N.J.: Princeton University Press.

Summers, A. and B. Wolfe (September 1977), "Do Schools Make a Difference?" *American Economic Review* 67, 639–52.

Titmuss, Richard M. (1971), *The Gift Relationship: From Human Blood to Social Policy,* New York: Random House.

Wilcox-Gok (May 1983), "The Determination of Child Health: An Application of Sibling and Adoption Data," *The Review of Economics and Statistics* 65, 266–73.

# Role of services in world economies

# CHAPTER 1

# Services in the international economy*

ROBERT SUMMERS

## I    Introduction

Approximately 50 percent of all U.S. expenditures on its gross domestic product (GDP) in 1975 were spent on services, up from about 46 percent in 1970.[1] Other countries, facing different economic and social conditions, in 1975 and in other years allocated their total expenditures between services and commodities in quite different proportions. (For example, India's proportion in both years was about 20%.) Drawing on data from the United Nations International Comparison Project (ICP), this paper systematically compares the experience of a number of countries at different times with that of the United States to illuminate the interspatial and – with greater difficulty – the intertemporal factors associated with the service–commodity split. Attention will be devoted exclusively to output phenomona – and final output at that. The equally interesting input phenomona, employment in service activities, will not be studied here,[2] though an important motivation for being concerned with service outputs is directly related to the nature of service production. Service production usually being more labor intensive than commodity production implies certain structural changes are in store for an economy with a changing share of service output. Furthermore, since it is commonly believed that improvements in productivity take place more slowly in service production than in commodity production, a changing share of an economy's service output has implications for the economy's growth rate.

Consider two different research strategies for this investigation. Sherlock Holmes has enunciated the following approach: "...It is a capital mistake to theorize before one has data. Insensibly one begins to twist facts to suit theories instead of theories to suit facts..."[3] In sharp contrast Tjalling C. Koopmans in a famous review of a major empirical investigation of

* This paper draws heavily on work done on this subject jointly with Alan Heston and Irving B. Kravis. The present paper involves some aspects of services that go beyond the results previously reported, however, so mistakes of omission or commission here are not to be attributed to them. Particular acknowledgement should be given though for useful discussions with Heston about aspects of intertemporal service share measurement. Martin Shanin and Ju-Yong Park provided indispensable computational assistance. Portions of the research benefited from the support of the National Science Foundation.

business cycle fluctuations recommends a diametrically opposed alternative: "...Fuller utilization of the concepts and hypotheses of economic theory...*as a part of the process of observation and measurement* promises to be a shorter road, perhaps even the only possible road, to understanding..."[4]

The economics profession has endorsed the general Koopmans position, but in many quarters there is still strong support for avoiding imposing too much structure too early in an investigation. In the spirit of Holmes, this paper will begin by simply laying out the facts. The treatment of the subject begins in Section II with a discussion of the distinction between services and commodities and a description of the data under analysis. Raw information above disaggregated service outlays for thirty-four different countries is presented for 1975. Summary statistics are computed to display the basis for the conventional wisdom on how service shares rise with the level of economic development.

In Section III the data on service expenditures are presented in a way that takes account of the variation in price structures in the various countries. Expenditure proportions for services and commodities in all countries are converted to real quantity proportions by revaluing all final product with a common set of so-called international prices, which reflect average relative prices around the world. This makes real service quantities as a proportion of total real output directly comparable across countries. The introduction of price considerations leads to a very different perception of how a country's choice between services and commodities depends upon its level of income.

Tracing out in Section III the consequences of differences in price structures across countries is as Holmesian an approach as the exploratory data analysis of Section II. However, Section IV refers to the economic theory Koopmans calls for to explain why price structures are as they are. In addition, in Section IV the role of prices as partial determinants of opportunities available to countries is investigated by means of elementary demand regressions.

Unfortunately, the scanty ICP data on real service shares for years other than 1975 provide only a limited basis for inferring what intertemporal changes can be expected in service shares. The evidence, such as it is, is reviewed in Section V. The concluding Section VI summarizes the empirical findings of the paper and suggests further avenues of research.

## II     The data and first cut

The classification of final products as either final commodities or final services is fairly straightforward. Commodities can be stored; services cannot. For example, items of food, clothing, or furniture; automobiles and gallons of gasoline; and baseball bats and television sets clearly are all commodities. On the other hand, the benefits flowing from the existing housing stock, clothing and automobile repairs, visits to a physician's office or a hospital, air transport, educational instruction, and police direction of traffic unambiguously are all services. Certainly, awkward classification cases abound. What part of a restaurant meal should be called a commodity, if any? Is a textbook bought by a student a commodity or should it be regarded as part of the range of educational services the student absorbs? Are individually prescribed and purchased drugs to be regarded as commodities or should they be classified as services along with the services of physicians, since they are just a part of the physician's treatment? The final product benefits derived from the activities of government employees are all services, unless the product of the employee's labor is delivered explicitly in the form of a commodity. (But surely the receipt of a letter containing a check for a social pension payment does not represent the acquisition of a commodity.) However, what about the government's purchases of commodities? In this paper, they are regarded as intermediate products used as inputs to the production of services supplied to the public by government. As such, the benefits of government output derived from them are valued as services. [5]

Most of these and other service-versus-commodity distinctions can be resolved satisfactorily if final product can be disaggregated finely enough. The data analyzed in this paper are drawn from the multicountry investigations of the United Nations International Comparison Project, a joint undertaking of the United Nations Statistical Office and the International Comparison Unit of the University of Pennsylvania. [6] The 151 detailed categories of GDP in the ICP data base cover 108 categories of consumption, 38 categories of capital formation, and 5 categories of government. Of these, 29 consumption and all 5 government categories have been classified as services; all capital formation categories are treated as commodities. [7] In conformity with the System of National Accounts (SNA), all public as well as private capital formation expenditures appear in the capital formation account. In a departure from the SNA, however, the ICP treats all government expenditures on medical care and education as part of consumption, along with private spending in these two areas. The ICP has collected expenditure data, along with price information, on all of these categories for each of 16 countries in 1970, 1973, and 1975, and for 18 additional countries in 1975. The nature of the ICP data makes comparisons across countries within any year much more reliable than comparisons for any particular country across years.

Before following Sherlock Holmes's admonition to get the facts in hand prior to theorizing, some minimal amount of speculation is appropriate about the point of this whole exercise.[8] Quite possibly, countries at different levels of economic development or enjoying different levels of affluence wish to absorb different proportions of their national output in the form of services. Whether any observed pattern arises from differences in taste or differences in the conditions of production should be explored. But the diverse nature of services is such that a common *economic* characteristic of all services is not easy to pin down.[9] The production and consumption of services are *necessarily* simultaneous, so inventories of services cannot be maintained. Final product services are different from final product commodities in this respect, but not universally in any other. As previously indicated, they are likely to be produced in a more labor-intensive way than commodities but this is not *necessarily* so (e.g., electric and communication utilities and public transport). Furthermore, identical outputs of the same production process could be classified either as a service or part of a commodity, depending upon the stage at which the production takes place (e.g., the repainting of an old car vs. the painting of a new one – or to make the intermediate good aspect stand out, the repainting of the car by a used car dealer[10]). Nor can services be distinguished from commodities by the types of tastes they each satisfy. One might conjecture that the consumption of classical music is income elastic, but a greater-than-one elasticity does not necessarily carry over to classical music *services*. If the music is purchased through concert performances, yes; but if purchased through high-fidelity sound equipment and records or tapes, no. (If 98% of the cost of listening to recorded music was attributable to payments to the orchestra, would it be more reasonable to classify the record and tape expenditures for classical music as a service? How much of the value of a pension payment must be embodied in the physical envelope and check before the payment should be called a commodity?) In the last part of Section IV an attempt is made to determine whether increased consumption in some broad area, such as recreation, disproportionately takes the form of services rather than commodities.

The simplest possible representation of how nations absorb services is a display of the percentage of GDP each country expends on services in each of six major areas of spending. In a concession to Koopmans even at this stage, Table 1.1 lists the thirty-four countries of the ICP's Phase III in order of their GDP per capita in 1975. Columns (2) through (7) give the countries' proportions of GDP devoted to services within each of six major groupings. [Government spending in providing final services is shown in terms of both the ICP and SNA concepts which appear respectively in Columns (7) and (8).] The share of all services in GDP appears in Column (9). Visual inspection of the columns suggests that service shares of each type and in the aggregate go up with country income.

Table 1.2 confirms this by giving the results of regressing service shares against per capita GDP for each of the major groupings and for total services. The simple regression equation designed to summarize Table 1.1 is:

$$\ln Sh_{ij} = \alpha_i \ln r_j + \beta_i + u_{ij} \qquad \begin{aligned} i &= 1, \dots, 6 \\ j &= 1, \dots, 34 \end{aligned} \qquad (1.1)$$

$$\ln Sh_j = \alpha \ln r_j + \beta + u_j \qquad j = 1, \dots, 34 \qquad (1.1')$$

where $Sh_{ij}$ is the $j$th country's expenditure share devoted to the $i$th major service grouping, $Sh_j$ is the $j$th country's total service share, $r_j$ is the $j$th country's real per capita GDP relative to the United States, expressed as a percentage, and both $u_{ij}$ and $u_j$ are disturbance terms.

All $\tilde{\alpha}_i$ and $\tilde{\alpha}$ values are positive, and five of the eight are significantly different from zero, four of them highly so. (Before knowing what to expect of the relationship between services and income, it was prudent to use two-tail tests here.) Only in the Transportation, Communication and Government (under both ICP and SNA concepts) groupings is $\tilde{\alpha}$ insignificant. (Education undoubtedly is contributing strongly to the significant slope coefficient of Recreation, Education. The Government SNA concept includes government outlays on education, but the Government ICP concept does not. It is to be expected then that the SNA concept slope would be greater than the ICP one.) Without doubt, service shares as measured in domestic prices go up with country income almost across the board. This appears to be in accord with a general belief that total services are income elastic.[11] In fact, it would appear that all of the major components of services are income elastic as well as the aggregate.

## III    Revaluing services to take account of price differences

But income elasticity is a partial derivative, ceteris paribis, concept. Moving down the columns of Table 1.1, the expenditure shares have an undeniable tendency to increase – though the inevitable "noise" in the share figures makes the tendency far from monotonic – but income is not the only variable changing as one goes to countries lower on the list. The systematic pattern of variation in country price structures as development takes place makes the changes in service expenditure shares down the columns a consequence of changes in the prices of services relative to commodities as well as changes in income. Table 1.3 displays the changing relative prices as one moves from poorer to richer countries. Observe in Column (10) that the price index for all services is less than half the index for commodities in the lowest income countries but it is about 80 percent as great in the high income countries. This implies that if services in all countries are revalued at

Table 1.1. *Percentage of gross domestic product expenditures devoted to various services, 1975*

| | Real GDP per capita (US=100) (1) | Housing (2) | Medical Care[b] (3) | Transportation, Communication (4) | Recreation, Education[c] (5) | Other Consumption Services[d] (6) | Government[e] (7) | Government[f] (8) | Total (9) |
|---|---|---|---|---|---|---|---|---|---|
| Malawi | 4.9 | 5.3 | 1.0 | 2.4 | 4.2 | 2.4 | 7.7 | 11.5 | 22.8 |
| Kenya | 6.6 | 9.3 | 3.3 | 3.8 | 7.7 | 3.0 | 9.9 | 18.4 | 37.0 |
| India | 6.6 | 2.5 | 0.7 | 3.9 | 2.8 | 1.9 | 7.8 | 9.9 | 19.6 |
| Pakistan | 8.2 | 7.5 | 1.3 | 1.4 | 3.6 | 2.3 | 9.2 | 10.9 | 25.2 |
| Sri Lanka | 9.3 | 3.6 | 1.5 | 3.8 | 3.7 | 1.5 | 6.4 | 10.2 | 20.5 |
| Zambia | 10.3 | 5.5 | 2.8 | 1.2 | 6.9 | 6.5 | 18.9 | 27.5 | 41.9 |
| Thailand | 13.0 | 3.2 | 1.0 | 3.3 | 5.2 | 4.5 | 7.3 | 10.4 | 24.6 |
| Philippines | 13.2 | 5.5 | 1.6 | 0.9 | 4.1 | 3.5 | 6.6 | 9.6 | 22.1 |
| Korea | 20.7 | 3.4 | 1.8 | 4.7 | 4.1 | 3.6 | 8.3 | 10.3 | 25.8 |
| Malaysia | 21.5 | 6.5 | 1.7 | 3.4 | 6.0 | 5.0 | 11.8 | 17.6 | 34.6 |
| Colombia | 22.4 | 6.3 | 2.7 | 6.3 | 7.0 | 7.9 | 2.8 | 7.4 | 33.1 |
| Jamaica | 24.0 | 8.1 | 2.2 | 5.1 | 5.5 | 7.0 | 13.0 | 18.4 | 40.8 |
| Syria | 25.0 | 6.1 | 0.9 | 2.0 | 3.2 | 2.5 | 18.9 | 21.2 | 33.5 |
| Brazil | 25.2 | 7.2 | 2.1 | 2.9 | 3.8 | 6.3 | 7.2 | 9.8 | 29.5 |
| Romania | 33.3 | 3.2 | 1.9 | 2.5 | 3.7 | 4.3 | 5.0 | 11.0 | 20.6 |
| Mexico | 34.7 | 7.7 | 2.5 | 3.3 | 4.9 | 3.9 | 5.0 | 10.3 | 27.4 |
| Yugoslavia | 36.1 | 3.7 | 3.1 | 2.3 | 5.6 | 4.1 | 11.3 | 20.8 | 30.0 |
| Iran | 37.7 | 6.9 | 2.0 | 1.3 | 3.9 | 2.8 | 18.5 | 23.3 | 35.4 |
| Uruguay | 39.6 | 8.8 | 3.1 | 5.6 | 4.8 | 5.2 | 10.0 | 13.3 | 37.6 |
| Ireland | 42.5 | 5.9 | 5.1 | 2.0 | 6.9 | 10.8 | 10.5 | 20.5 | 41.2 |

| | | | | | | | | | |
|---|---|---|---|---|---|---|---|---|---|
| Hungary | 49.6 | 3.6 | 2.2 | 2.0 | 5.4 | 5.1 | 7.8 | 15.4 | 26.1 |
| Poland | 50.1 | 4.2 | 2.0 | 2.0 | 5.1 | 3.4 | 7.2 | 14.1 | 23.8 |
| Italy | 53.8 | 8.2 | 4.5 | 3.2 | 5.8 | 4.8 | 11.7 | 15.9 | 38.2 |
| Spain | 55.9 | 8.9 | 3.6 | 2.8 | 4.1 | 7.1 | 4.1 | 9.2 | 30.6 |
| U.K. | 63.9 | 11.0 | 3.1 | 3.8 | 6.5 | 7.9 | 15.5 | 24.2 | 47.8 |
| Japan | 68.4 | 9.1 | 3.6 | 3.7 | 6.6 | 7.4 | 5.1 | 10.1 | 35.4 |
| Austria | 69.6 | 6.5 | 5.2 | 3.7 | 4.9 | 4.6 | 9.2 | 17.3 | 34.2 |
| Netherlands | 75.2 | 7.0 | 5.8 | 2.6 | 7.1 | 5.5 | 11.9 | 18.3 | 39.9 |
| Belgium | 77.7 | 9.0 | 3.8 | 2.7 | 6.0 | 6.9 | 11.1 | 16.5 | 39.4 |
| France | 81.9 | 8.9 | 5.2 | 3.7 | 4.5 | 5.9 | 10.9 | 14.5 | 39.2 |
| Luxembourg | 82.0 | 9.7 | 2.7 | 3.0 | 4.8 | 7.4 | 10.0 | 14.3 | 37.6 |
| Denmark | 82.4 | 11.2 | 2.6 | 3.1 | 8.7 | 4.1 | 15.5 | 26.7 | 45.1 |
| Germany | 83.0 | 9.0 | 6.0 | 3.4 | 5.2 | 5.3 | 10.8 | 14.5 | 39.8 |
| U.S.A. | 100.0 | 11.9 | 7.0 | 3.6 | 7.8 | 7.8 | 11.3 | 19.1 | 49.3 |

[a] Kravis, Heston, Summers (1982), Table 1.2, Column (6).

[b] All Medical Care service expenditures are combined, whether private or public.

[c] All Education service expenditures are combined, whether private or public.

[d] Clothing and footwear repairs are included in Other Consumption.

[e] Total compensation and purchases. ICP concept: All public expenditures on medical care and education are transferred to consumption. [Kravis, Heston, Summers (1982), Table 6.2: Government PFC].

[f] Total consumption and purchases. SNA concept: No transfers of public expenditures to consumption [Kravis, Heston, Summers (1982), Table 6.2: Government GFCE].

Source: All final service expenditures are calculated as the aggregate of expenditures of detailed categories within those major groupings in Kravis, Heston, Summers (1982), Table 6.1, which are identified in Appendix Table 2.1 as services.

Table 1.2. *The relationship between service expenditure shares (%) and real GDP per capita (US = 100): 34 countries, 1975*

(1.1)   $\ln Sh_{ij} = \alpha_i \ln r_j + \beta_i + u_{ij}$

(1.1′)   $\ln Sh_j = \alpha \ln r_j + \beta + u_j$

|  | $\tilde{\alpha}$ | $\tilde{\beta}$ | $\bar{R}^2$ |
|---|---|---|---|
| Housing | .244* | 1.015* | .236 |
|  | (.073) | (.259) |  |
| Medical Care | .486* | −.749* | .521 |
|  | (.080) | (.284) |  |
| Transportation, Communication | .086 | .754* | −.001 |
|  | (.087) | (.310) |  |
| Recreation, Education | .123* | 1.207* | .122 |
|  | (.052) | (.123) |  |
| Other Consumption Services | .333* | .380* | .375 |
|  | (.073) | (.260) |  |
| Government (ICP concept) | .073 | 1.962* | −.010 |
|  | (.088) | (.313) |  |
| Government (SNA concept) | .123 | 1.915* | .067 |
|  | (.067) | (.587) |  |
| Total Services | .178* | 2.859* | .334 |
|  | (.042) | (.151) |  |

*Note:* Standard errors appear in parentheses.
* Significantly different from zero at the .05 level (two-tail test).

a common set of prices, the *real* service share of the high income countries will be reduced and the share of the low income countries will be raised, relative to the nominal shares displayed in Table 1.1. The *real* shares, calculated to take account of the price effects, are given in Table 1.4. This table parallels Table 1.1 but takes account of the price adjustments, and Table 1.5 summarizes the pattern of Table 1.4 in the way Table 1.2 summarizes Table 1.1. The regression coefficients estimates in Table 1.5 are for the equations:

$$\ln \overline{Sh}_{ij} = \gamma_i \ln r_j + \delta_i + v_{ij} \qquad \begin{aligned} i &= 1, \dots, 6 \\ j &= 1, \dots, 34 \end{aligned} \tag{1.2}$$

$$\ln \overline{Sh}_j = \gamma \ln r_j + \delta + v_j \qquad j = 1, \dots, 34 \tag{1.2′}$$

where the bar of $\overline{Sh}_{ij}$ indicates *real* share.

Tables 1.4 and 1.5 turn the tables on Tables 1.1 and 1.2. The virtue of disaggregating total services into its components is now apparent. Because the gradient of relative price change varies across service groupings, the fairly uniform upward gradient in the nominal shares $(Sh_{ij})$ for the various groupings in Table 1.1 (all were positive, and only two were not statistically significant) is transformed into quite diverse gradients in Table 1.4. As indicated by the slope coefficient estimates reported in Table 1.5, in two groupings, Recreation, Education and Government, the gradient is actually reversed. Now the aggregate's slope is essentially flat, slightly negative but not significantly so. The conventional view of rising shares appears to be in trouble.

Could these revisionist findings be an accident of 1975, with the rising-share view holding up for other years? When a regression equivalent to the Total Services one of Table 1.5 is run for sixteen countries in 1970, the same kind of slope appears: $-.055$ with a standard error of .025. (Inexplicably, the equivalent coefficient for 16 countries in 1973 is much greater: over .3.)

## IV   Allowing for price in demand relationships [12]

The higher prices of services relative to commodities in richer countries gives a proximate explanation for why the larger observed percentage of GDP devoted to services in the richer countries is a misleading indicator of how changes in income affect the absorption of services. Just why a country's service prices vary with its level of income has been discussed elsewhere at length. [13] It is sufficient here to comment that the "differential productivity" model, developed for a rather different purpose, deals with the implications of labor productivity being more similar in rich countries and poor in the production of nontraded services than in the production of traded commodities. This differential in productivity leads to a systematic difference in the relative prices of services and commodities for countries at different incomes.

In addition to being useful as a deflator, service prices play (presumptively) an important role in determining how attractive services are relative to commodities for a nation. The price adjustments underlying the shift from Table 1.1 to Table 1.4, and the change in the regression coefficients between Tables 1.2 and 1.5, bring us closer to estimates of income elasticities but the Table 1.5 slope coefficients still fall short of measuring the partial effects of income. They indicate how income affects service shares but only when prices are increasing at the same time. Since the rising prices can be expected to have a dampening effect on the purchase of services – these ad hoc demand curves should have a negative slope whether they meet the formal conditions of demand theory or not – each of Table 1.5's

Table 1.3. *Price indexes for various services: 1975 (US = 100)*

| | GDP | Services | Commodities | Housing | Medical Care | Transportation, Communication | Recreation, Education | Other Consumption | Government | $P_s \div P_c$ (2) ÷ (3) |
|---|---|---|---|---|---|---|---|---|---|---|
| | (1) | (2) | (3) | (4) | (5) | (6) | (7) | (8) | (9) | (10) |
| Malawi | 39.3 | 22.0 | 54.1 | 43.8 | 7.8 | 61.5 | 9.4 | 40.4 | 22.6 | .406 |
| Kenya | 51.2 | 33.8 | 69.7 | 39.3 | 56.1 | 49.7 | 15.4 | 87.0 | 37.4 | .485 |
| India | 31.0 | 12.4 | 49.0 | 14.2 | 5.5 | 17.3 | 5.0 | 14.9 | 17.3 | .252 |
| Pakistan | 32.1 | 17.2 | 45.9 | 37.6 | 18.9 | 12.6 | 8.4 | 19.2 | 16.8 | .375 |
| Sri Lanka | 27.6 | 10.8 | 45.1 | 12.1 | 7.4 | 21.8 | 5.4 | 11.9 | 12.3 | .240 |
| Zambia | 67.0 | 47.9 | 87.1 | 67.5 | 50.4 | 66.0 | 32.0 | 69.8 | 47.6 | .550 |
| Thailand | 37.4 | 25.8 | 47.5 | 34.8 | 20.7 | 26.0 | 18.0 | 27.3 | 29.4 | .543 |
| Philippines | 39.7 | 17.2 | 62.6 | 22.0 | 9.0 | 19.5 | 9.7 | 26.4 | 19.7 | .274 |
| Korea | 39.3 | 25.7 | 51.1 | 58.9 | 18.2 | 27.7 | 13.5 | 24.2 | 30.3 | .502 |
| Malaysia | 50.6 | 36.6 | 64.2 | 40.2 | 18.9 | 43.6 | 23.4 | 37.8 | 48.5 | .570 |
| Colombia | 35.1 | 24.3 | 45.5 | 25.6 | 26.9 | 24.1 | 15.6 | 29.2 | 27.5 | .534 |
| Jamaica | 81.6 | 56.3 | 108.9 | 78.4 | 39.6 | 60.1 | 28.1 | 50.4 | 80.3 | .517 |
| Syria | 40.0 | 31.8 | 48.1 | 32.8 | 19.9 | 33.5 | 13.4 | 26.8 | 46.3 | .661 |
| Brazil | 63.4 | 44.2 | 81.0 | 67.7 | 29.9 | 51.4 | 21.1 | 62.9 | 42.2 | .546 |
| Romania | 73.0 | 36.0 | 104.4 | 20.9 | 12.7 | 96.7 | 27.3 | 67.7 | 56.0 | .345 |

| | | | | | | | | | |
|---|---|---|---|---|---|---|---|---|---|
| Mexico | 58.9 | 41.3 | 74.7 | 37.1 | 47.4 | 29.2 | 34.9 | 65.0 | 54.0 | .552 |
| Yugoslavia | 64.2 | 40.5 | 86.8 | 33.2 | 19.4 | 47.9 | 27.8 | 50.2 | 58.6 | .467 |
| Iran | 58.6 | 44.9 | 71.9 | 48.9 | 50.7 | 23.2 | 31.4 | 43.0 | 56.6 | .624 |
| Uruguay | 46.0 | 30.9 | 61.8 | 44.7 | 18.1 | 45.5 | 22.3 | 34.1 | 27.5 | .500 |
| Ireland | 86.3 | 68.1 | 103.9 | 73.6 | 35.9 | 82.0 | 56.2 | 72.7 | 88.0 | .655 |
| Hungary | 59.7 | 34.7 | 82.5 | 51.3 | 10.1 | 47.0 | 24.7 | 37.0 | 52.0 | .420 |
| Poland | 71.9 | 39.9 | 99.9 | 37.1 | 15.0 | 52.3 | 30.7 | 51.8 | 56.5 | .400 |
| Italy | 89.1 | 71.8 | 106.1 | 78.8 | 40.9 | 51.1 | 68.1 | 80.7 | 91.2 | .677 |
| Spain | 73.6 | 55.7 | 90.6 | 59.4 | 41.3 | 60.5 | 36.7 | 55.1 | 99.5 | .615 |
| U.K. | 90.2 | 71.9 | 107.3 | 89.7 | 23.7 | 92.2 | 72.9 | 77.8 | 82.7 | .671 |
| Japan | 91.2 | 83.3 | 102.5 | 109.0 | 34.9 | 67.3 | 65.3 | 104.3 | 109.0 | .813 |
| Austria | 100.3 | 82.8 | 118.4 | 60.2 | 48.0 | 103.8 | 70.9 | 128.7 | 117.9 | .700 |
| Netherlands | 112.3 | 116.6 | 117.1 | 91.2 | 82.4 | 84.9 | 121.1 | 130.7 | 158.1 | .996 |
| Belgium | 113.0 | 110.4 | 121.3 | 120.0 | 53.6 | 81.8 | 113.8 | 112.6 | 151.6 | .910 |
| France | 109.4 | 98.6 | 122.2 | 104.3 | 63.3 | 77.0 | 96.4 | 115.3 | 120.5 | .806 |
| Luxembourg | 109.4 | 96.3 | 124.3 | 108.4 | 38.7 | 77.6 | 123.0 | 88.3 | 143.9 | .775 |
| Denmark | 126.8 | 112.2 | 140.4 | 95.4 | 38.6 | 102.2 | 131.8 | 138.1 | 159.8 | .799 |
| Germany | 114.2 | 109.3 | 123.5 | 106.3 | 69.0 | 111.6 | 95.2 | 115.1 | 144.5 | .885 |
| U.S.A. | 100.0 | 100.0 | 100.0 | 100.0 | 100.0 | 100.0 | 100.0 | 100.0 | 100.0 | 1.000 |

[a] (Price index)$_{ij}$ = (Purchasing Power Parity)$_{ij}$ ÷ (Exchange Rate)$_j$
*Sources:* (i) (Purchasing Power Parity)$_{ij}$: Derived from aggregation over appropriate service category figures in Appendix Tables 6.1 and 6.5 of Kravis, Heston, Summers (1982). (ii) (Exchange Rate)$_j$: Table 1, Column (2), Kravis, Heston, Summers (1982).

Table 1.4. *Real shares (%) of Gross Domestic Product expenditures devoted to various services, 1975*

| | Real GDP per capita (US = 100) [a] | Housing | Medical Care [b] | Transportation, Communication | Recreation, Education [c] | Other Consumption Services [d] | Government [e] | Government [f] | Total [g] |
|---|---|---|---|---|---|---|---|---|---|
| | (1) | (2) | (3) | (4) | (5) | (6) | (7) | (8) | (9) |
| Malawi | 4.9 | 4.2 | 2.5 | 1.2 | 9.7 | 2.0 | 12.1 | 22.9 | 31.8 |
| Kenya | 6.6 | 10.7 | 1.6 | 3.1 | 14.4 | 1.5 | 12.4 | 25.0 | 43.6 |
| India | 6.6 | 4.9 | 1.9 | 5.5 | 9.8 | 3.4 | 12.7 | 19.9 | 38.1 |
| Pakistan | 8.2 | 5.6 | 1.1 | 2.8 | 7.7 | 3.4 | 15.9 | 20.0 | 36.5 |
| Sri Lanka | 9.3 | 7.2 | 2.8 | 3.8 | 10.7 | 3.1 | 13.1 | 24.6 | 40.7 |
| Zambia | 10.3 | 4.9 | 1.9 | 1.0 | 8.1 | 5.5 | 24.2 | 33.2 | 45.6 |
| Thailand | 13.0 | 3.0 | 1.0 | 3.8 | 6.1 | 5.5 | 8.5 | 12.7 | 27.8 |
| Philippines | 13.2 | 8.8 | 3.6 | 1.4 | 9.4 | 4.7 | 12.0 | 19.2 | 39.9 |
| Korea | 20.7 | 2.0 | 2.0 | 5.2 | 6.6 | 5.2 | 9.7 | 12.9 | 30.7 |
| Malaysia | 21.5 | 7.3 | 2.4 | 3.1 | 7.3 | 5.9 | 11.2 | 18.1 | 37.2 |
| Colombia | 22.4 | 7.7 | 1.8 | 7.2 | 8.8 | 8.4 | 3.3 | 9.2 | 37.2 |
| Jamaica | 24.0 | 7.5 | 2.3 | 5.4 | 8.9 | 9.9 | 12.0 | 20.7 | 46.0 |
| Syria | 25.0 | 6.7 | 0.9 | 1.8 | 5.3 | 3.2 | 14.8 | 18.8 | 32.8 |
| Brazil | 25.2 | 6.0 | 2.3 | 2.8 | 6.5 | 5.5 | 9.9 | 14.9 | 32.9 |
| Romania | 33.3 | 9.9 | 5.6 | 1.5 | 5.5 | 4.1 | 5.9 | 17.3 | 32.5 |
| Mexico | 34.7 | 0.9 | 1.6 | 5.2 | 4.6 | 3.1 | 5.0 | 9.5 | 30.4 |
| Yugoslavia | 36.1 | 6.3 | 5.2 | 2.4 | 7.2 | 4.6 | 11.2 | 24.9 | 37.0 |
| Iran | 37.7 | 7.3 | 1.2 | 2.6 | 4.1 | 3.3 | 17.4 | 21.9 | 36.0 |
| Uruguay | 39.6 | 8.1 | 4.1 | 4.4 | 5.5 | 6.2 | 15.2 | 19.6 | 43.5 |
| Ireland | 42.5 | 6.1 | 6.2 | 1.7 | 6.0 | 11.3 | 9.4 | 19.1 | 40.6 |

| | | | | | | | | |
|---|---|---|---|---|---|---|---|---|
| Hungary | 49.6 | 3.7 | 6.5 | 2.0 | 7.3 | 7.3 | 8.1 | 21.3 | 34.9 |
| Poland | 50.1 | 7.2 | 5.0 | 2.1 | 6.7 | 4.1 | 8.3 | 19.9 | 33.3 |
| Italy | 53.8 | 8.2 | 5.0 | 4.3 | 4.3 | 4.7 | 10.4 | 13.5 | 36.9 |
| Spain | 55.9 | 9.7 | 3.3 | 2.7 | 4.6 | 8.4 | 2.7 | 7.8 | 31.4 |
| U.K. | 63.9 | 9.8 | 6.0 | 2.9 | 4.5 | 8.1 | 15.3 | 25.2 | 46.6 |
| Japan | 68.4 | 6.7 | 4.8 | 3.9 | 5.1 | 5.7 | 3.9 | 7.0 | 30.1 |
| Austria | 69.6 | 9.7 | 5.5 | 2.8 | 3.9 | 3.1 | 7.1 | 14.6 | 32.2 |
| Netherlands | 75.2 | 7.6 | 4.1 | 2.7 | 3.7 | 4.1 | 7.7 | 10.7 | 29.9 |
| Belgium | 77.7 | 7.5 | 4.1 | 2.9 | 3.4 | 6.1 | 7.5 | 10.4 | 31.3 |
| France | 81.9 | 8.3 | 4.6 | 4.1 | 2.9 | 4.9 | 9.0 | 11.2 | 33.8 |
| Luxembourg | 82.0 | 8.7 | 3.9 | 3.3 | 2.4 | 8.1 | 6.9 | 8.7 | 33.2 |
| Denmark | 82.4 | 13.2 | 4.3 | 3.0 | 4.7 | 3.3 | 11.2 | 2.3 | 39.7 |
| Germany | 83.0 | 8.6 | 5.1 | 2.7 | 3.5 | 4.6 | 7.8 | 8.9 | 32.3 |
| U.S.A. | 100.0 | 10.5 | 3.6 | 2.8 | 4.4 | 6.9 | 10.2 | 14.8 | 38.4 |

[a] Kravis, Heston, Summers (1982), Table 1.2, Column (6).

[b] All Medical Care service expenditures are combined, whether private or public.

[c] All Education service expenditures are combined, whether private or public.

[d] Clothing and footwear repairs are included in Other Consumption.

[e] Total compensation and purchases. ICP concept: All public expenditures on medical care and education are transferred to consumption. [Kravis, Heston, Summers (1982), Table 6.5: Government PFC].

[f] Total consumption and purchases. SNA concept: No transfers of public expenditures to consumption [Kravis, Heston, Summers (1982), Table 6.5: Government GFCE].

[g] These numbers differ from the entries of Column (2) of Table 6.10 Kravis, Heston, Summers (1982) by the share of GDP devoted to government purchases.

Source: All final service expenditures are calculated as the aggregate of expenditures of detailed categories within those major groupings in Kravis, Heston, Summers (1982), Table 6.5, which are identified in Appendix Table 2.1 as services.

Table 1.5. *The relationship between the shares of real services and real GDP per capita for various major groupings: 34 countries, 1975*

| (1.2) $\ln \overline{Sh}_{ij} = \gamma_i \ln r_j + \delta_i + v_{ij}$ |
| (1.2') $\ln \overline{Sh}_j = \gamma \ln r_j + \delta + v_j$ |

|  | $\tilde{\gamma}$ | $\tilde{\delta}$ | $\bar{R}^2$ |
|---|---|---|---|
| Housing | .197* | 1.272* | .168 |
|  | (.071) | (.253) |  |
| Medical Care | .420* | −.343 | .384 |
|  | (.090) | (.321) |  |
| Transportation, Communication | .060 | .855* | −.017 |
|  | (.092) | (.325) |  |
| Recreation, Education | −.395* | 3.119* | .701 |
|  | (.045) | (.158) |  |
| Other Consumption Services | .231* | .777* | .179 |
|  | (.081) | (.286) |  |
| Government (ICP concept) | −.219* | 2.996* | .138 |
|  | (.087) | (.310) |  |
| Government (SNA concept) | −.229* | 3.555* | .233 |
|  | (.069) | (.245) |  |
| Total Services | −.036 | 3.700* | .023 |
|  | (.027) | (.097) |  |

*Note:* Standard errors appear in parentheses.
* Significant at the .05 level (two-tail test).

slope coefficients added to unity is a lower bound for the actual corresponding income elasticity. Now we have left Sherlock Holmes behind, even if we have not fully embraced the Koopman call for a full-scale model, when we pass to equations (1.3) and (1.3'):

$$\ln q_{ij}^s = \alpha_i \ln \left( \frac{p_{ij}^s}{p_j^{\text{GDP}}} \right) + \beta_i \ln r_j + \gamma_i + \epsilon_{ij} \qquad \begin{aligned} i &= 1, \dots, 6 \\ j &= 1, \dots, 34 \end{aligned} \qquad (1.3)$$

$$\ln q_j^s = \alpha \ln \left( \frac{p_{ij}^s}{p_j^{\text{GDP}}} \right) + \beta \ln r_j + \gamma + \epsilon_j \qquad j = 1, \dots, 34 \qquad (1.3')$$

where $q_{ij}^s$ is the quantity of services purchased in the $i$th major grouping by the $j$th country; $p_{ij}^s/p_j^{\text{GDP}}$ is the price of services, relative to the price of all GDP goods, in the same group in the same country; $r_j$ is the real GDP per capita of the country expressed as a percentage of United States; and the

Table 1.6. *Price and income elasticities for various services:*
*34 countries, 1975*

$$(1.3) \quad \ln q_{ij}^s = \alpha_i \ln\left(\frac{p_{ij}^s}{p_j^{GDP}}\right) + \beta_i \ln r_j + \gamma_i + \epsilon_{ij}$$

$$(1.3') \quad \ln q_j^s = \alpha \ln\left(\frac{p_j^s}{p_j^{GDP}}\right) + \beta \ln r_j + \gamma + \epsilon_j$$

|  | Price Elasticity | Income Elasticity | $\bar{R}^2$ |
|---|---|---|---|
| Housing | $-.474^*$ <br>(.166) | $1.219^*$ <br>(.065) | .914 |
| Medical Care | $-.586^*$ <br>(.119) | $1.458^*$ <br>(.069) | .931 |
| Transportation, Communication | $-.605^*$ <br>(.235) | $1.076^*$ <br>(.084) | .827 |
| Recreation, Education | $-.365^*$ <br>(.141) | $.794^*$ <br>(.084) | .870 |
| Other Consumption Services | $-.682^*$ <br>(.104) | $1.301^*$ <br>(.076) | .900 |
| Government (ICP concept)[a] | $-.448$ <br>(.402) | $.912^*$ <br>(.146) | .708 |
| Total Services | $-.063$ <br>(.141) | $.977^*$ <br>(.141) | .973 |

*Note:* Standard errors appear in parentheses.
* Significantly different from zero at the .01 level (one-tail test).
[a] Relative prices are available for Government only on the basis of the ICP concept.

$\alpha$'s and $\beta$'s are price and income elasticities. The spirit underlying the quantification of (1.3) and (1.3') is to introduce price primarily for the purpose of "noise screening" to sharpen the income-elasticity estimates. Table 1.6 gives the price and income elasticity estimates for the six major groupings and total services based upon the 1975 data covering thirty-four countries. The income elasticities of services in Housing, Medical Care, and Other Consumption Services are all significantly greater than unity; the elasticity is significantly less than unity for Recreation, Education; and neither Transportation, Communication nor Government have elasticities significantly different from unity. (Comparisons of empirical estimates of elasticities across research studies typically show greater variability than can be rationalized by differences in research technique.[14] When the entries in Table 1.6

for Housing, Transportation, Communication, Recreation, Education, and Other Services are compared as best one can with the price and expenditure elasticities of Lluch, Powell, and Williams (1977), Tables 3.12 and 3.13, one finds the price elasticities remarkably similar but the income elasticities are less in line.) For Total Services, the income elasticity is an insignificant trifle short of one. So much for the view that development brings a rising share of services!

### Changing share of services within major groupings

It was remarked previously that it is not possible to infer the income elasticity of demand for services in a major grouping from the income elasticity of demand for the major grouping. Recall that even if the income elasticity for classical music was greater than one, the extra music purchased out of extra income might be obtained through services such as concerts, or through commodities such as a high-fidelity sound system and records or tapes. As a family's income goes up, it might well wish to purchase freedom from coping with dirty dishes. But will its purchase bring into the kitchen a dishwasher or a washer of dishes (that is, a Kitchenaid or an aid in the kitchen)? Clearly, the relative prices of services and commodities will help to determine the answer to these questions, but there is an empirical question that goes beyond relative prices. Consider an equation relating the services proportion of expenditure on a major grouping to the price of such services relative to the price of commodities also within the major grouping and to the total expenditure on the major grouping:

$$
\ln \left( \frac{\bar{E}_{ij}^2}{\bar{E}_{ij}} \right) = \alpha_i \ln \left( \frac{p_{ij}^s}{p_{ij}^c} \right) + \beta_i \ln \bar{E}_{ij} + \gamma_i + \xi_{ij} \qquad \begin{matrix} i = 1, \dots, 6 \\ j = 1, \dots, 34 \end{matrix} \qquad (1.4)
$$

where $\bar{E}_{ij}^s$ and $\bar{E}_{ij}$ are the real expenditure of country $j$ on the services component, and the total, respectively, for the $i$th major grouping; and $p_{ij}^s / p_{ij}^c$ is the relative price of services and commodities in the $i$th major grouping.

Table 1.7 gives the regression estimates of the coefficients of (1.4) for the six major groupings. (In the case of government, which includes no commodities to contrast with services – in this investigation both compensation and government purchases are considered services – the equation is meant to throw light on an aspect of government make-or-buy policies rather than service-vs.-commodity purchases.) In every case, the price coefficients are negative and highly significant. The relative prices of services and commodities must be an important determinant of whether wants within a major grouping will be satisfied with services or commodities. The evidence for a uniform shift toward or away from services when expenditure on one

Table 1.7. *Spending on services vs. commodities within a major
grouping when spending on the major grouping changes*

| $(1.4) \quad \ln\left(\dfrac{\bar{E}^s_{ij}}{\bar{E}_{ij}}\right) = \alpha_i \ln\left(\dfrac{p^s_{ij}}{p^c_{ij}}\right) + \beta_i \ln \bar{E}_{ij} + \gamma_i + \xi_{ij}$ | | | |
|---|---|---|---|
| | $\tilde{\alpha}^a$ | $\tilde{\beta}^b$ | $\tilde{\gamma}^b$ | $\bar{R}^2$ |
| Housing | −.312* | .199* | 4.843* | .389 |
| | (.066) | (.100) | (.325) | |
| Medical Care | −.168* | .186 | 4.539* | .135 |
| | (.095) | (.124) | (.449) | |
| Transportation, Communication | −.492* | −.090 | 5.926* | .654 |
| | (.073) | (.086) | (.232) | |
| Recreation, Education | −.303* | −.034 | 5.436* | .823 |
| | (.026) | (.076) | (.214) | |
| Recreation only | −.784* | −.108 | 6.885* | .537 |
| | (.144) | (.124) | (.521) | |
| Other Consumption Services | −.217* | .121* | 5.083* | .475 |
| | (.040) | (.053) | (.178) | |
| Government[c] | −.304* | −.260* | 5.897* | .308 |
| | (.079) | (.101) | (.453) | |

[a] One-tail test.
[b] Two-tail test.
[c] In all other parts of this paper, government purchases are treated as services.
Here, however, government purchases of commodities are treated as a substitute
for government compensation. (NB: Public capital formation is not included in
government spending.)
*Note:* Standard errors appear in parentheses.
* Significant at the .05 level.

of the five major grouping other than Government goes up is mixed. In
three cases, the shift is toward services, but in the remaining two, the shift
is away from them. The strongest effects are associated with the shifts
toward them, however. (See Housing, Other Consumption Services, and,
though not statistically significant, Medical Care.) Recreation has been
examined separately from Education to see if the low and negative $\tilde{\beta}$ obtained for the joint grouping was a result of Education diluting a possibly
important "income" effect present for Recreation alone. (Education, as one
would expect, is nearly entirely made up of services, so the scope for substitution there is very slight.) The $\tilde{\beta}$ coefficient remains quite insignificant,
however.

A striking finding for public finance specialists to puzzle over is the strong tendency even after taking account of relative prices for increased government to be accompanied by an increasing share of government purchases and a reducing share of government compensation. The dependent variable, the proportion of total government expenditures devoted to services – that is, compensation – goes down with total government expenditure. See $\tilde{\beta} = -.260$ for Government. (NB: Public capital formation is not contained in the government spending category.)

## V      Intertemporal considerations

Table 1.8 assembles the available ICP evidence on service shares of sixteen countries in 1970 and 1975. Making the 1970 and 1975 estimates of the country shares comparable is difficult for technical reasons arising out of the way the ICP develops its quantity comparisons among countries, but the numbers in Table 1.8 for those years probably give a fair indication of what has happened over the five-year period.

The simplest intertemporal comparison that can be made between the real shares as recorded by the ICP for 1970 and 1975, is given in Columns (1) and (5) in Table 1.8. Of the sixteen changes between 1970 and 1975, nine were upward, five were downward, and two remained about the same. If the ratio of the 1975 share to the 1970 share is regressed against the level of 1970 income and the rate of increase of income over the five-year period, the empirical relationship is:

$$\frac{\overline{Sh}_{75}^{\text{ICP}}}{\overline{Sh}_{70}^{\text{ICP}}} = \underset{(.094)}{-.154} \; r_{j,70} \underset{(.108)}{-.264} \; \frac{r_{j,75}}{r_{j,70}} \underset{(.157)}{+1.445} \qquad \bar{R}^2 = .22 \qquad (1.5)$$

The relationship is quite weak but it appears the share has increased less in rapidly growing countries than in slow-growing ones and also in richer countries than in poorer.

Unfortunately, there are difficulties with these share comparisons of 1970 and 1975. In each of its benchmark studies the ICP estimates a set of international prices, $\pi_i^{(t)}$, which reflect the world average of relative prices of all final goods in the current year. $[\pi_i^{(t)} : t = 1970, 1975; \; i = 1, \dots, 153 \text{ goods}]$. The service share reported by the ICP for the $j$th country in the $t$th year is computed as $\overline{Sh}_{jt}^{(t)} = \sum_{i=1}^{N_s} \pi_i^{(t)} q_{ij}^{(t)} / \sum_{i=1}^{153} \pi_i^{(t)} q_{ij}^{(t)}$ where $i = 1, \dots, N_s$ covers all categories of goods classified as services. Thus the 38.4 figure given for the United States in column (9) of Table 1.4 represents

$$\overline{Sh}_{\text{US},75}^{(75)} = \sum_{i=1}^{N_s} \pi_i^{(75)} q_{ij}^{(75)} \left/ \sum_{i=1}^{153} \pi_i^{(75)} q_{ij}^{(75)} \right. .$$

The corresponding number provided by the ICP for 1970 was

Table 1.8. 1970 and 1975 service shares of real gross domestic product, valued at 1970 and 1975 international prices

| | (1) $\overline{Sh}_{70}^{(70)}$ | (2) $\overline{Sh}_{75}^{(70)}$ | (3) (2) ÷ (1) | (4) $\overline{Sh}_{70}^{(75)}$ | (5) $\overline{Sh}_{75}^{(75)}$ | (6) (5) ÷ (4) | (7) (4) ÷ (1) | (8) (2) ÷ (5) |
|---|---|---|---|---|---|---|---|---|
| Kenya | 37.9 | 49.0 | 1.291 | 35.5 | 43.6 | 1.230 | .937 | 1.124 |
| India | 33.4 | 44.5 | 1.330 | 30.1 | 38.1 | 1.266 | .901 | 1.168 |
| Philippines | 35.2 | 42.1 | 1.196 | 33.9 | 39.9 | 1.177 | .963 | 1.055 |
| Korea | 31.6 | 34.7 | 1.099 | 29.1 | 30.7 | 1.058 | .921 | 1.130 |
| Malaysia | 33.2 | 40.6 | 1.223 | 30.8 | 37.2 | 1.210 | .928 | 1.091 |
| Colombia | 37.3 | 41.0 | 1.098 | 34.3 | 37.2 | 1.085 | .920 | 1.102 |
| Iran | 39.2 | 38.0 | .968 | 38.6 | 36.0 | .932 | .985 | 1.056 |
| Hungary | 37.2 | 34.0 | .915 | 38.5 | 34.9 | .909 | 1.035 | .974 |
| Italy | 31.3 | 37.4 | 1.196 | 30.7 | 36.9 | 1.202 | .981 | 1.014 |
| U.K. | 35.9 | 44.6 | 1.243 | 37.0 | 46.6 | 1.261 | 1.031 | .957 |
| Japan | 29.0 | 31.0 | 1.067 | 28.7 | 30.1 | 1.050 | .990 | 1.030 |
| Netherlands | 31.2 | 29.7 | .951 | 32.0 | 29.9 | .933 | 1.026 | .993 |
| Belgium | 35.3 | 31.4 | .889 | 35.7 | 31.3 | .878 | 1.011 | 1.033 |
| France | 30.7 | 34.6 | 1.127 | 30.5 | 33.8 | 1.109 | 1.000 | 1.024 |
| Germany | 30.7 | 31.8 | 1.033 | 30.7 | 32.3 | 1.052 | 1.000 | .985 |
| U.S.A. | 37.7 | 36.6 | .972 | 39.6 | 38.4 | .969 | 1.050 | .953 |

*Sources:* $\overline{Sh}_{j,70}^{(70)}$: Kravis, Heston, Summers (1978) revised.

$\overline{Sh}_{j,75}^{(75)}$: Kravis, Heston, Summers revised.

$\overline{Sh}_{j,70}^{(75)}$: Estimated by author from U.S. Bureau of Labor Statistics and Department of Commerce price data.

$\overline{Sh}_{j,75}^{(70)}$: Estimated by author from U.S. Bureau of Labor Statistics and Department of Commerce price data.

$$\overline{Sh}_{US,70}^{(70)} = \sum_{i=1}^{N_s} \pi_i^{(70)} q_{ij}^{(70)} \Bigg/ \sum_{i=1}^{153} \pi_i^{(70)} q_{ij}^{(70)}.$$

but unfortunately this number, 37.7, is not precisely comparable with the 38.4 because the international prices (the $\pi$'s) were not the same in the two years. The individual international prices for each year are not actually known, so a special estimating procedure drawing on a set of U.S. price indexes for 1975 relative to 1970 was employed to reprice the 1970 service shares in 1975 international prices and the 1975 service shares in 1970 international prices.

Columns (1) and (2) of Table 1.8 give the service shares of the sixteen countries for 1970 and 1975 each based upon 1970 international prices, and Columns (4) and (5) give the shares each based upon 1975 international prices. Column (7) shows how much difference it makes in estimating the 1970 shares. Clearly the differences are negligible for affluent countries but are sizable in a few cases for poor countries.

But Columns (3) and (6) provide the story the ICP has to tell about intertemporal changes in service shares. The difference between using 1970 or 1975 international prices is trivial. In eleven of the countries the shares went up and in five the share went down. The simplest generalization, from visual inspection of the table, is that the shares went up in poor countries but stayed about the same in the rich. Looking more closely in order to see how rapidity of growth affects the rate of increase of shares, the following regression result is obtained:

$$Avge\ \Delta\ \overline{Share}_j = -.340\ r_{j,70}^{ICP} - .296\ \frac{r_{j,75}^{ICP}}{r_{j,70}^{ICP}} + 1.599 \qquad \bar{R}^2 = .44 \qquad (1.6)$$
$$\phantom{Avge\ \Delta\ \overline{Share}_j = }(.096) \qquad (.111) \qquad\quad (.161)$$

where $Avge\ \Delta\ Share = [(\overline{Sh}_{75}^{(70)}/\overline{Sh}_{70}^{(70)}) + (\overline{Sh}_{70}^{(75)}/\overline{Sh}_{70}^{(75)})]/2$. The relationship is stronger than the previous one but it has the same general character. The rate of growth in income is a statistically significant variable but is unimportant substantively. Low income countries' shares grew more than high income countries; in fact, on average high income countries' shares did not change perceptibly. It should be clear that these results are not entirely consistent with the interspatial results above.

## VI    Conclusion

Patterns of service absorption over space and, to a limited extent, time have been illuminated through the use of expenditure and price data of the International Comparison Project. By taking account of the variation in the price of services relative to commodities in countries at different levels of income, it was possible to examine *real* patterns. It was found that in 1975 service shares were essentially unrelated to income, but an investigation of changes in shares over time found shares rising in poor countries and remaining essentially constant in rich ones.

The disaggregated share patterns have not been analyzed in detail here, but their diverse pattern suggests that services as an aggregate may be an excessively large category for serious study. Particularly, the constancy of the Government share over the income spectrum is intriguing and deserving of further study.

An agenda for further research would include tapping other data sources to get more time-series readings, and other variables, notably demographic, should be introduced.

### Notes

1. These percentages and the corresponding ones for India are calculated from the data of Appendix Table 4.1 of Kravis, Heston, Summers (1978) and Appendix Table 6.1 of Kravis, Heston, Summers (1982). (See Notes 5 and 7.)
2. See Kravis, Heston, Summers (1983) and the references cited there for a discussion of service industry employment and a documentation of various propositions about labor intensity and labor productivity in the production of services vs. commodities.
3. Doyle (1967), pp. 349–50.
4. Koopmans (1947), p. 162.
5. This is a change in concept from previous International Comparison Project treatments where government purchases were considered commodities.
6. The results of the three phases of the ICP's work are reported in Kravis, Kenessey, Heston, Summers (1975), Kravis, Heston, Summers (1978) and Kravis, Heston, Summers (1982).
7. Kravis, Heston, Summers (1982), Appendix to Chapter 2, including Appendix Table 2.1, but see Note 5. (Typographical errors in Appendix Table 2.1 make it difficult but not impossible to identify which detailed categories are classified as services.) The columns of Table 1 below list the broad summary groupings within which the service categories are contained.
8. After all, even the most complete empiricist would be guided by some casual theory. Would it be worthwhile to see if the countries' service expenditure percentages are keyed to the position of the country on an alphabetized list (in English) of the countries? One would think not. (It is reassuring that in the regression of service percentage on alphabetical order the slope coefficient is not statistically significant!)
9. For an extended discussion of the nature of services see Hill (1977) and Kravis, Heston, Summers (1982), Chapter 5.
10. A difference between how services and commodities are produced in the United States can be seen in the U.S. input–output tables. Consider the relative proportions of inputs taking the form of commodities and services entering into the

production of final commodities and final services. More commodity inputs than service inputs enter into the production of final commodities, and the opposite is true for final services. Furthermore, the ratio of value-added to the value of purchased inputs in service industries is much higher than in commodity industries. See Kravis, Heston, Summers (1983), Table 1.

11. This conventional wisdom is sometimes attributed to Colin Clark but in fact Clark's view (Clark 1951) is that the share of *employment* devoted to production of services goes up with income.

12. It is an act of boldness to omit quotation marks around the word "demand" in this heading. Do the peoples of the 34 countries studied here have the same tastes? Are the shares observed the consequence of choices made on the basis of opportunities defined by prices and income? By relegating these remarks to a Note, I avoid facing into this factor. But see the extensive review of the "commonality of tastes around the world" theme in Chapter 9 of Kravis, Heston, Summers (1982). Some readers might prefer the use of total consumption, private and public, as the income variable instead of GDP in some parts of this analysis.

13. Kravis, Heston, Summers (1982), pp. 332–5; Kravis, Heston, Summers (1983), pp. 202–7 and Appendix.

14. Time-series results for three countries are reported in Kravis, Heston, Summers (1983), which are in rough agreement with the cross-section results given here.

## References

Clark, C. (1951), *The Conditions of Economic Progress.* London: Macmillan (First edition 1941).

Doyle, A. Conan (1967), "A Scandal in Bohemia," in W. S. Baring-Gould (ed.) *The Annotated Sherlock Holmes,* Vol. 1., 349–50. New York: Clarkson N. Potter.

Hill, T. P. (1977), "On Goods and Services," *Review of Income and Wealth,* December, 315–38.

Koopmans, Tjalling C. (1947), "Measurement Without Theory," *Review of Economic Statistics,* Vol. XXIX, No. 3, August, 161–72.

Kravis, I. B., Z. Kenessey, A. Heston, and R. Summers (1975), *A System of International Comparisons of Gross Product and Purchasing Power.* Baltimore, Maryland: The Johns Hopkins University Press.

Kravis, I. B., A. Heston, and R. Summers (1978), *International Comparisons of Real Product and Purchasing Power.* Baltimore, Maryland: The Johns Hopkins University Press.

(1982), *World Product and Income: International Comparisons of Real Gross Product.* Baltimore, Maryland: The Johns Hopkins University Press.

(1983), "The Share of Services in Economic Growth," in F. G. Adams and B. Hickman (eds.) *Global Econometrics: Essays in Honor of Lawrence R. Klein,* 188–218. Cambridge, Massachusetts: MIT Press.

Lluch, C., A. A. Powell, and R. A. Williams (1977), *Patterns in Household Demand and Saving.* New York, New York: Oxford University Press.

# Comment: Services in the international economy

## JERE R. BEHRMAN

This paper reads like the first part of a good mystery. A number of clues are uncovered, leading to a clearer understanding of the comparative role of services in different economies characterized by different degrees of economic development. Though the paper provides some clarification, however, the mystery of the relation of services to development is not resolved definitely. As Detective Summers notes in his conclusion, the agenda for future research still is extensive.

Why is the relation of services to development a mystery worth investigating? The answer to this question is that services obviously are an important part of total economic activity, whether measured by output or labor shares, and understanding services better might help to elucidate the nature of the basic structural changes that characterize the development process. But the association of services with development is but little understood. This is so because of the heterogeneity of services (encompassing the services of both Dacca shoeshiners and Philadelphia lawyers), the influence of materialistic and Marxian views that goods are what really count, and the inherent greater measurement difficulties for services than for goods. Nevertheless there is considerable emphasis on the important role of services in the development process. For example, the commercialization of agricultural products markets and eventually the labor and financial markets play an important role in the Fei–Ranis dualistic view of the development process. The prevalent view based on a priori assumptions and on Clark–Kuznets–Chenery type cross-country aggregate associations is that the share of services in the economy increases in the development process, though Chenery (p. 12) suggests there is a maximum at middle-income levels.

Summers examines the cross-country association between service shares in final demand and per capita income in the Clark–Kuznets–Chenery tradition. His contribution is fourfold. (1) His comparison is for more recent years than used in earlier studies. (2) His investigation is for a more disaggregated representation of services, and his estimates suggest that such disaggregation is important since they differ across his six service subsectors. (3) He utilizes ICP data to obtain the real shares of services instead of just the nominal shares, and his estimates suggest that in some sectors (e.g., recreation and education, government, total services) the real share

49

estimated income elasticities are significantly less than those for nominal shares (cf. Tables 1.2 and 1.5). (4) He utilizes ICP data to introduce relative prices into what he calls demand relations, with results suggesting that such relative prices significantly discourage service subsector consumption as they increase with development, though the income elasticities do not appear affected much by the inclusion of the relative prices (cf. Table 1.6 vs. 1.5). Perhaps the most important single number that comes out of this analysis is a unitary income elasticity for total real services (whether or not relative prices are included), which contrasts with the traditional belief noted previously that the service share rises with development. In the words of Summers: "So much for the view that development brings a rising share of services."

The detective work of Summers does represent progress. Why does it not solve the mystery of the relation of services to development? The reasons are several, as the following three sets of questions indicate.

First, Summers follows the tradition of identifying the cross-country associations as dynamic demand relations. But in the spirit of Koopmans, it occurs naturally to ask of this tradition: Given the quite different demographic compositions of these countries and the systematic association of age structures with development, shouldn't demographic factors be incorporated explicitly into the analysis? If children are relatively service intensive due to schooling, child care, and so forth, for example, might not the failure to control for demographic factors mean that the true income elasticities are higher than Summers claims? How are the demand relations identified from supply relations? Might not real per capita product be representing supply factors such as productivity and not just the demand considerations that are emphasized? What is the role of international trade in services in this analysis? Why should we be comfortable with the dynamic interpretation of these cross-country relations? Would not more explicit specification of the relevant economic structural relations be illuminating for answering such questions?

Second, even with the improvements made possible by the use of the ICP data, some questions occur about the nature of the data. Several of these questions focus on dimensions of the economy not covered by standard data, including household production and the underground economy. If there is substantial home production of goods at low levels of economic development that are eliminated with development as Hymer and Resnick claim, for example, might not existing data understate goods production at low levels of development and thus understate the growth of the service share with initial development? If expanded leisure time results in more do-it-yourself activities in high income countries, might not there be the opposite bias at the high-income end of the spectrum? If in the process of development, food preparation for the middle and upper class shifts from that performed by hired domestic servants to nonmarket household production to restaurant preparation, won't the probable underrepresentation of household production in the data result in an apparent U-shaped share of food preparation services even if they in fact have a constant share? If underground economic activities are largely services and are induced by high marginal tax rates, might they not be particularly underrepresented in data from high marginal tax rate more developed countries – once again causing the data to underrepresent the relative growth of services with development?

Other data questions pertain to the problem of measuring service output in the public sector in particular. In the development literature, for example, there are frequent characterizations of governments hiring workers at wages above true marginal products for political reasons, particularly at lower levels of development. If this is the case, might not existing data based on factor payments overstate service product at low levels of development and thus understate the growth of the service share with development? Another feature that is thought to be of concern in many developing countries, particularly middle income ones with extensive restrictions on international trade, is what Krueger calls "rent-seeking" or Bhagwati and Srinivasan call "directly-unproductive, profit-seeking (DUP) activities." Might not the increase in such activities in the initial stage of development cause increase in measured relative goods shares (since the payments for these activities often are intermediate inputs for traded goods), thus causing in this income range an upward bias in the goods share as development occurs?

Third, the Clark–Kuznets–Chenery–Summers approach concentrates on characterizing the share of services in final demand, but some of the critical issues about services and development may pertain to the role of services as an intermediate input. Does this role increase substantially in the development process? Is it an important components of the development process?

Thus there remain many important questions about services and the development process. Hopefully Sherlock Tjalling Summers and others will be inspired to investigate them.

### References

Bhagwati, Jagdish N., and T. N. Srinivasan (August 1982), "The Welfare Consequences of Directly-Unproductive, Profit-Seeking (DUP) Activities: Price Versus Quantity Distortions," *Journal of International Economics* 13, 33–44.

Chenery, Hollis B. (1979), *Structural Change and Development Policy*. New York: Oxford University Press for the World Bank.

Fei, John C. H., and Gustav Ranis (1964), *Development of the Labor Surplus Economy: Theory and Policy*. Homewood, IL: Irwin.

Hymer, Stephen, and Steven Resnick (September 1969), "A Model of an Agrarian Economy with Nonagricultural Activities," *American Economic Review* 59, 493–506.

Krueger, Anne O. (June 1974), "The Political Economy of the Rent-Seeking Society," *American Economic Review* 64, 291–303.

# CHAPTER 2

# Services in the Japanese economy

GARY R. SAXONHOUSE

## Introduction

By the familiar standards of the rate of economic growth and productivity change and even price stability, among the major industrialized economies, the economic performance of Japan over the course of the twentieth century must be considered distinctively successful.[1] By virtue of its success, the Japanese economy becomes the appropriate historical laboratory within which at least a number of the central questions regarding the past, present character, and future of the multifaceted services industry can be examined. In the next section, the performance and role of the services industry in the pre-1945 Japanese economy will be explored. A succeeding section will look at those same questions for the four decades of the postwar period with particular interest in assessing the future growth and productivity performance of Japan's services industries and how this may relate to the future growth and productivity performance of the Japanese economy as a whole. In the final section the performance of important elements of Japan's services industries will be considered in an explicit comparative context. In particular, the distinctively large size of Japan's distribution system and the distinctively small Japanese exports of technology services will be carefully interpreted. The implications of these findings for U.S.–Japanese economic relations will also be considered.

## The services sector in Japan in the prewar period

Simon Kuznets in his landmark review of economic growth in the twentieth century found that historically "the share of the services sector in country-wide produce, when measured in current prices, remained constant or declined whereas its share in countrywide labor force rose" in most major industrialized countries.[2] As shown in Table 2.1, Japanese services' share of output experience conforms to Kuznets's generalization. The share of services in total Japanese output when measured in current prices is more or less constant between 1887 and 1930, after which it falls rather sharply. When services and net domestic product (NDP) are measured in constant prices, as might be expected, this decline begins earlier and is much steeper.

53

Table 2.1. *Services share of net domestic product in current and constant prices*

|  | Current prices (% of NDP) | Constant prices (% of NDP) |
|---|---|---|
| 1887 | 37.5 | 48.2 |
| 1889 | 35.1 | 51.4 |
| 1904 | 36.4 | 49.3 |
| 1911 | 33.4 | 43.9 |
| 1919 | 31.8 | 48.3 |
| 1930 | 36.7 | 40.6 |
| 1938 | 36.0 | 34.3 |

*Source:* K. Ohkawa and M. Shinohara, *Patterns of Japanese Economic Development* (New Haven, Conn.: Yale University Press, 1979), Table 6.7. Services as measured here includes trade (wholesale and retail), finance (banking, real estate, and insurance), personal services (professionals and servants) and public administration.

Table 2.2. *Services sector share of Japanese labor force and rate of increase in size of services labor force*

|  | Services labor force share (%) |  | Rate of increase of services labor force (average annual change) |
|---|---|---|---|
| 1892 | 14.9 | 1888–96 | 0.30 |
| 1904 | 17.0 | 1897–1912 | 0.54 |
| 1916 | 21.9 | 1913–20 | 0.50 |
| 1925 | 23.0 | 1921–31 | 0.63 |
| 1936 | 26.4 | 1932–40 | 0.52 |

*Source:* Ohkawa and Shinohara, Table 6–8; Services Labor Force Share calculated from a five year moving average centered on year shown. Definition of services is the same as in Table 2.1.

The role of services in employing Japan's pre-1945 labor force also conforms to Kuznets's generalization. Between 1888 and 1940 there is a steady increase in the share of the Japanese labor force employed in the services sector. (Refer to Table 2.2.) The rapid increase in the services sector share in employment even while the services sector's share in output remained constant or declined can only imply that in this time period in Japan, as in so many other instances, the services sector's rate of productivity increase

Table 2.3. *Services sector share of Japanese labor force and rate of increase in size of services labor force*

|  | Services labor force share (%) |  | Rate of increase of services labor force (average annual %) |
|---|---|---|---|
| 1952 | 27.1 | 1949–54 | 3.13 |
| 1961 | 34.0 | 1955–61 | 1.71 |
| 1969 | 39.5 | 1962–70 | 2.24 |

*Source:* See Table 2.2.

was relatively low. Between 1902 and 1938 there is a modest secular decline in the level of services sector productivity in Japan. During these thirty-six years, productivity declined at an average annual rate of 0.03.[3]

### The services sector in Japan in the postwar period through 1970

The postwar services sector in Japan reversed important elements of its prewar behavior. In current prices, the services sector's share of total output rose continually through the postwar period. By 1953, the services sector's share in total output surpassed the previous high of 37.5 percent in 1887 and kept rising until 1969 when it absorbed 45.4 percent of total output. When the services sector's share in total output is measured in constant prices, performance is somewhat different. The postwar peak in the services sector's share was reached in 1953 when the services sector accounted for almost half of total output produced. Following 1953, the services sector's share in total output declines until in 1969 it reaches 38.9 percent of total output.[4]

Unlike shares in total output postwar services sector shares in total labor force are an acceleration of prewar trends. The services sector's share of total labor force rises to 39.5 percent in 1969. As a comparison of Table 2.2 with Table 2.3 indicates, in the postwar period, there is a dramatic acceleration in the growth rate of the services industries labor force. Between 1949 and 1970, the services sector labor force grew at four to five times its prewar rate.[5]

Despite the very rapid increase in the postwar services sector labor force, there is also a coincident rapid improvement in this sector's labor productivity. Between 1955 and 1968, labor productivity in the services sector grew at 4.25 percent a year. Given this performance it is difficult to characterize the services sector as a residual employer in the postwar Japanese economy.[6]

Inasmuch as Japan's services sector share trends in output and labor conform to Kuznets's generalization, it is not surprising that Japan's services sector productivity performance also conforms to international patterns. Despite the very rapid growth of Japanese services sector productivity in the postwar period, as in the prewar period, industrial sector productivity performance in Japan far outstrips it. As seen in Table 2.4, when measured in constant prices, Japan's services sector's productivity growth lagged behind industrial sector productivity growth by an annual average rate of almost 3 percent over the eighty years between 1885 and 1965. This is about twice as great as the services sector's lag behind industry performance in most other major economies. As might be expected, when international comparison is made on the basis of current price rather than constant price volumes, the differential performance of Japan's services sector no longer looks so pronounced.

## The role of services in the future of Japanese economic growth

For at least the past ten years, most of the official and semiofficial "visions" of the future of the Japanese economy have projected that an increasingly important share of Japanese output would be produced by the services sector.[7] The most recent Ministry of International Trade and Industry "vision" projected that the services sector (trade, finance, personal and professional services, and public administration) would increase its share of total Japanese output, when evaluated in current prices, from the 41.0 percent that was characteristic of the late 1970s, to 42.8 percent in 1990.[8]

Regardless of whether these specific projections are extrapolations of past trends, which might not be found in the data if more appropriate methods of deflation, or any deflators at all were used, or otherwise, there is reason to believe that the relative role of services in the Japanese economy is more likely to increase than decline. Although there is no trend in the share of services, when properly deflated, as a proportion of NDP for a cross section that includes both developed and Third World countries, when cross-national evidence is restricted to relatively high-income countries, a pattern does emerge. When the International Comparison Project data are examined, it is found that Japan's share of services in real output is below that of all economies with a higher gross domestic product per capita.[9] This does suggest that regardless of the mechanical character of the Japanese government projections it is not unreasonable to expect some increase in the role of the services sector in the future Japanese economy.

If the services sector will play a more important role in the Japanese economy over the next two decades, what impact might this have on the future performance of the Japanese economy? In particular, what impact

Table 2.4. *Output per worker, industrial sector and services sector in developed countries*

| | | Ratio of services sector productivity to industrial sector productivity | Average annual rate of relative change (%) |
|---|---|---|---|
| *A. In constant prices* | | | |
| Germany[a] | 1850–59 | 3.10 | – 1.58 |
| | 1935–38 | 0.73 | |
| Sweden[b] | 1861–70 | 1.60 | – 0.57 |
| | 1963–67 | 0.89 | |
| Italy[c] | 1861–70 | 3.79 | – 1.34 |
| | 1963–67 | 0.99 | |
| United States | 1839[d] | 0.67 | – 1.21 |
| | 1899 | 0.47 | |
| | 1899[e] | 0.98 | – 1.24 |
| | 1929 | 0.69 | |
| Japan[f] | 1885–89 | 3.71 | – 2.74 |
| | 1960–65 | 0.46 | |
| *B. In current prices* | | | |
| Great Britain | 1801–11 | 2.03 | – 0.26 |
| | 1907 | 1.56 | |
| | 1907 | 1.46 | – 0.77 |
| | 1963–67 | 0.96 | |
| Sweden | 1861–70 | 1.14 | – 0.24 |
| | 1963–67 | 0.86 | |
| Italy | 1861–70 | 2.33 | 0.75 |
| | 1881–1900 | 2.72 | – 1.20 |
| | 1963–67 | 1.04 | |
| United States | 1839 | 0.46 | 0.39 |
| | 1899 | 0.81 | – 0.21 |
| | 1929 | 0.76 | – 0.40 |
| | 1963–65 | 0.66 | |
| Japan | 1885–89 | 3.71 | – 0.91 |
| | 1960–65 | 0.46 | |

[a] 1913 prices.  [b] 1959 prices.  [c] 1963 prices.
[d] 1859 prices.  [e] 1929 prices.  [f] 1934–36 prices.
*Source:* Ohkawa and Shinohara, Table 2.16.

will this have on the future aggregate growth and productivity performance of the Japanese economy?

Despite the continuing, and even accelerating good repute of Japanese economic performance, the past decade has witnessed the sharp deceleration of the previous Japanese trends in growth and productivity performance. The average annual rate of growth of real GNP (gross national product), which was 10.5 percent between 1960 and 1973, slowed to 3.8 percent between 1973 and 1981. [10] During the same time periods, the average annual rate of productivity improvement fell from 9.9 percent to 3.6 percent. [11] Also, during the past decade the continuing high rate of Japanese household saving, which in previous decades had financed an equally high rate of corporate investment, underwrote instead a burgeoning Japanese government deficit and foreign purchases of Japanese products. Unhappily much of the very large potential increase in foreign claims, which should have been built up by the combination of Japanese thrift on the one hand and superb Japanese export performance on the other, was eaten up by a 43.8 percent deterioration in the Japanese terms of trade over the past decade. [12]

In the context of the slower growth now envisioned for a Japanese manufacturing sector finally on the technological frontier, it is doubtful that a relatively more important services sector in Japan will act as a drag on aggregate Japanese productivity performance. In the postwar period, the Japanese services sector has regularly demonstrated a capacity for productivity improvement comparable to what the manufacturing sector is expected to achieve in the next two decades. As pointed out earlier, between 1955 and 1968 services sector productivity increased by an annual average rate of 4.25 percent. Much of this increase in productivity was the result of a rapid increase in services sector capital formation. Between 1955 and 1968, services sector net capital stock grew at an average annual rate of 7.6 percent. Since during this same period services sector labor force grew at an average annual rate of 4.6 percent, the resulting capital deepening must have been responsible for a substantial proportion of the observed increase in labor productivity. [13]

Japan successfully substituted capital for labor in services and rapidly increased labor productivity in this sector during one substantial segment of the postwar period. This demonstrates that, taken as a whole, the services sector does have the same possibilities for capital deepening stimulated labor productivity improvement, more conventionally associated with factory work. There is ample reason to believe that such possibilities continue to exist for Japan's services sector. A recent study by the Japan Productivity Center, summarized in Table 2.5, found that although Japanese productivity levels in manufacturing were close to the U.S. and best Western European levels, in services Japan continues to lag substantially behind. In 1979 Japanese manufacturing labor productivity was some 94 percent of the U.S. level. By contrast, labor productivity in Japanese services remained less than two-thirds the U.S. level.

Table 2.5. *Comparisons of labor productivity in manufacturing and services, 1979*

|  | Japan | U.S.A. | West Germany[a] | France | United Kingdom[a] | Belgium |
|---|---|---|---|---|---|---|
| Manufacturing | 100 | 107 | 99 | 98 | 53 | 104 |
| Commerce & services | 100 | 154 | 144 | 136 | 87 | 124 |

[a] Japan Productivity Center, *International Comparison of Labor Productivity* (Tokyo, 1982).

Table 2.6. *Employment in wholesale and retail activities as a % of total economically active labor force*

|  | Japan[a] | U.S.A. | England[b] | West Germany | France |
|---|---|---|---|---|---|
| 1960 | 15.8 | 16.3 | 10.3 | 12.4 | – |
| 1970 | 19.3 | 19.1 | 11.9 | 14.6 | 15.8 |
| 1975 | 21.4 | 20.6 | 12.2 | 11.9 | 15.5 |
| 1982 | 22.9 | 20.9 | 12.9 | 12.0 | 16.3 |

[a] Japan data for 1983.
[b] English data for 1983.
Source: Sōrifu (Prime Minister's Office), *Nihon tōkei nenkan 1982 (Japan Statistical Yearbook, 1982)*. Nihon ginkō (Bank of Japan), *Kokusai hikaku tōkei 1983 (Comparative International Statistics 1983)*.

## The Japanese distribution system and Japan's international trade in services in comparative perspective

### The distribution system

It is apparent that although the performance of the Japanese services sector does conform to Kuznets's generalizations, there are many elements in the structure of this performance that differ quite markedly from experiences in other economies. As indicated in Table 2.6, one of the most distinctive and important elements in Japanese services sector performance is the relatively large share of Japan's economically active labor force that is engaged in distribution activities.

It is hardly surprising to discover that the size of the Japanese distribution system is unusual by international standards. For at least the past eleven years, U.S. government trade negotiators have attempted to link the very low share of imported manufactures as a proportion of total Japanese GNP or as a proportion of total imports to the special character of the Japanese distribution system and the government regulation maintaining that system.[14] Indeed, the apparent inefficiency of the Japanese distribution system is often exaggerated by American critics. As the House Ways and Means Committee suggests[15]

Basically, Japan is a nation of small shopkeepers – and wholesalers. There is often at least one more level of wholesalers in the distribution system than exists in the U.S. system. In Japan, with a population about half that of the United States, there were 340,000 wholesalers in 1974, compared with 370,000 in the United States in 1972. Further, there are more retail establishments in Japan than in the United States (1.61 million as opposed to 1.55 million). Inventories are kept small because of space problems – deliveries must be frequent – special services must be offered – mark-ups multiply.

In fact, the number of establishments are a poor proxy for the resources actually devoted to distribution in Japan and the United States. As Table 2.6 does make clear, the proportion of the American labor force working in distribution is almost as high as in Japan. The average size of retail and wholesale establishments in Japan may be half that found in the United States, but this is hardly an index of relative efficiency.

Although the different organization, but very similar resource-using consequences of the U.S. and Japanese distribution systems will be examined later, for the present, a comparison between the Japanese and European systems is probably more instructive. The Japanese and the European economies have similar resource endowments and transportation systems and neither Europe nor Japan was the initiator of the "distribution revolution." For all this similarity, however, none of the more industrialized European economies devotes anywhere near the Japanese proportion of the labor force to distribution. Indeed, the West Germans devote barely half the Japanese share of labor resources to distribution.

If the Japanese organization of wholesale and retail trade is anomalous either because of establishment size or resources committed, how can its peculiarities be explained? Through the early 1970s the role of larger stores in the Japanese distribution system greatly expanded. In retailing, stores with fifty or more employees (characteristically supermarkets, but carrying a larger percentage of nonfood items than their American counterparts) rose from 9.1 percent of total sales in 1954 to 21.2 percent in 1974. Similarly, wholesale firms with fifty or more employees increased from 35.7 percent of all wholesale trade in 1954 to 57.0 percent of this trade twenty years later.[16]

These significant changes in structure in Japan came with the encouragement of the Japanese government. During the 1950s small retailers were given some protection through legislation such as the Department Store Law, which acted to restrict the expansion of department stores. In the

Table 2.7. *Employees and sales in Japanese wholesaling and retailing*

| Number of Employees | Share of employees (%) | | | Share of sales (%) | | | Annual sales per employee (index) | | |
|---|---|---|---|---|---|---|---|---|---|
| | 1970 | 1974 | 1982 | 1970 | 1974 | 1982 | 1970 | 1974 | 1982 |
| *Wholesale* | | | | | | | | | |
| 1- 2 | 3.2 | 3.1 | 4.3 | 0.9 | 0.8 | 1.3 | 26.2 | 29.1 | 28.5 |
| 3- 4 | 7.1 | 7.2 | 9.1 | 2.9 | 3.0 | 4.0 | 39.6 | 43.1 | 42.1 |
| 5- 9 | 16.5 | 16.7 | 19.0 | 8.6 | 9.2 | 10.7 | 59.8 | 56.5 | 53.6 |
| 10-19 | 19.0 | 18.4 | 19.6 | 12.3 | 16.1 | 12.9 | 62.8 | 67.4 | 62.7 |
| 20-49 | 22.7 | 22.3 | 22.1 | 18.4 | 17.7 | 17.7 | 78.2 | 81.2 | 76.6 |
| 50-99 | 12.9 | 13.0 | 11.5 | 13.3 | 12.7 | 12.0 | 100.0 | 100.0 | 100.0 |
| >100 | 18.7 | 19.2 | 14.4 | 43.5 | 44.3 | 41.4 | 224.4 | 236.1 | 273.9 |
| *Retail* | | | | | | | | | |
| 1- 2 | 30.1 | 28.7 | 26.2 | 15.5 | 15.1 | 14.0 | 40.6 | 40.9 | 47.1 |
| 3- 4 | 22.4 | 22.8 | 21.8 | 18.9 | 19.0 | 18.9 | 66.4 | 65.0 | 76.1 |
| 5- 9 | 17.9 | 18.4 | 18.2 | 21.2 | 21.1 | 22.0 | 93.2 | 89.0 | 105.8 |
| 10-19 | 10.3 | 10.2 | 11.1 | 12.9 | 12.4 | 12.5 | 98.8 | 95.3 | 99.2 |
| 20-49 | 8.7 | 8.8 | 11.0 | 11.1 | 11.3 | 12.6 | 100.0 | 100.0 | 100.0 |
| >50 | 10.6 | 11.1 | 11.6 | 20.3 | 21.2 | 20.1 | 151.2 | 148.1 | 152.0 |

*Source:* Chūshō kigyōchō (Small and Medium Enterprise Agency), *Chūshō kigyō hakushō 1984 (Small and Medium Enterprise White Paper 1984)* (Tokyo, 1984).

1960s the policy of overt protection shifted to one of encouraging small wholesalers and retailers to merge, to form voluntary chains or to join in cooperative shopping centers so that they might better compete with department stores and supermarkets. This policy led to a rapid increase in labor productivity in distribution. In the 1970s, however, there was another dramatic reversal in policy with the passage in 1974 of the Large-Scale Retail Store Law. This law, as originally passed, required government approval in order to open any retail establishment of more than 1500 square meters. In 1978 this law's impact was greatly enhanced when government approval was extended to all new retail establishments of greater than 500 square meters. As can be seen from Table 2.7, this law has had an almost immediate impact. Between 1974 and 1982 the employee and sales shares of the smaller scale firms in wholesaling and retailing stopped declining and even increased modestly, reversing twenty-year trends in the other direction. [17]

It is clear that during the past ten years government policy has had a major role in maintaining the role of small-scale retailers and wholesalers in the distribution of goods. Quite apart from the Large-Scale Retail Store Law, there are many other regulations affecting trade associations, *keiretsu* (industrial groups), resale price maintenance, and transportation, which might also help to explain the large commitment of Japanese resources to this area. However, there are also explanations for the character of the Japanese distribution system that do not rely primarily on the impact of government policy. Some Japanese economists view the Japanese distribution system as a suitable accommodation to Japanese taste, Japanese population density, and the Japanese transportation system. Just as the *kanban* system of inventory control in the automobile industry in Japan relies on a multiplicity of suppliers carefully tailoring their production and deliveries to the needs of the Japanese automobile assembler, so also it is argued does the Japanese distribution system work to carefully meet the needs of the Japanese household. [18]

### Japan's international trade in services

The large size and apparently low productivity of Japan's distribution system is not the only facet of Japan's services economy that is internationally distinctive. The logic of comparative advantage suggests that Japan, which has been so successful in the export of manufactured goods, might find itself distinctively successful in the import of services. Indeed, during the late 1970s and early 1980s, among modern industrial economies, Japan, together with West Germany, has seen the international economic system's largest deficit on international transactions in services. As Table 2.8 indicates, in 1981 Japan ran a deficit of $14 billion on international services transactions totaling over $95 billion. Whereas the large West German deficit in services is built almost entirely of tourist expenditures, the structure of the still larger Japanese deficit is entirely different. The distinctive features of the Japanese services account include large deficits on the lines labeled Other Transportation and Other in Table 2.8. As explained in Table 2.9, Other Transportation includes passenger fares for ocean-going vessels and aircraft, ocean-going vessels and aircraft charters, and port disbursement. Other, by contrast, includes management and license fees, patent royalties, advertising, film rentals, and nonmerchandise insurance. The large Japanese deficit on Other Transportation clearly reflects Japanese geography and the related Japanese import of bulky raw material inputs and the export of finished products. The large deficit on royalties and license fees, however, merits further investigation.

Table 2.10 presents ten industrialized countries' receipts from and expenditures on patents, invention processes, and copyrights. In common with Japanese performance on the services account overall, Japan has the largest imbalance between receipts and expenditures in what can be considered trade in technology. It is not simply that the absolute imbalance is large, it is also that receipts as a proportion of expenditures are so very low. Further light on this subject can be shed by examining Table 2.11, which

Table 2.8. *1982 services account balance for Japan and six other major industrialized countries (million SDR)*

| | Japan | | United States | | United Kingdom | | West Germany | | France | | Italy | |
|---|---|---|---|---|---|---|---|---|---|---|---|---|
| | Recpts | Paymts | Recpts | Paymts | Recpts | Paymts | Recpts | Paymts | Recpts | Paymts | Recpts | Paymts |
| Balance on services | — | 8,900 | 30,770 | — | 8,563 | — | — | 9,110 | 7,703 | — | 1,402 | — |
| Freight and insurance | 6,760 | 3,420 | 3,810 | 5,710 | 3,277 | 3,020 | 4,230 | 4,550 | 1,105 | 2,287 | 2,467 | 3,721 |
| Other transportation | 5,290 | 11,730 | 10,140 | 9,160 | 6,278 | 6,467 | 3,980 | 4,580 | 8,576 | 8,391 | 1,931 | 1,607 |
| Travel | 690 | 3,730 | 10,220 | 11,250 | 5,041 | 5,779 | 5,000 | 14,680 | 6,308 | 4,649 | 7,522 | 1,571 |
| Investment income | 16,600 | 15,020 | 76,250 | 51,510 | 17,381 | 14,904 | 12,080 | 12,900 | 21,100 | 21,007 | 5,152 | 8,710 |
| Government | 2,120 | 300 | 13,170 | 12,189 | 1,983 | 1,962 | 5,960 | 1,510 | 912 | 812 | 318 | 305 |
| Other | 5,770 | 11,950 | 10,620 | 3,650 | 11,263 | 4,529 | 13,380 | 15,500 | 20,830 | 14,912 | 6,489 | 6,563 |
| Total | 37,230 | 46,130 | 124,210 | 93,440 | 45,222 | 36,659 | 44,610 | 53,220 | 59,831 | 52,128 | 23,879 | 22,477 |

*Source: International Monetary Fund Yearbook;* SDR (IMF Standard Drawing Rights) averaged 1.104 $ U.S. in 1981.

Table 2.9. *The structure of Japan's services deficit 1979–1983 ($ million)*

| | 1979 | | 1980 | | 1981 | | 1982 | | 1983 | |
|---|---|---|---|---|---|---|---|---|---|---|
| | Recpts | Paymts | Recpts | Paymts | Recpts | Paymts | Recpts | Paymts | Recpts | Paymts |
| *Other transportation* | | | | | | | | | | |
| Port disbursements | 2,770 | 4,891 | 3,661 | 6,652 | 4,792 | 7,254 | 3,809 | 6,617 | 3,454 | 6,253 |
| Passenger fares | 514 | 1,511 | 524 | 1,488 | 548 | 1,713 | 555 | 1,711 | 551 | 1,704 |
| Time charters | 951 | 3,452 | 1,136 | 4,696 | 1,291 | 5,324 | 1,106 | 4,340 | 856 | 3,406 |
| *Other* | | | | | | | | | | |
| Management fees | 567 | 968 | 573 | 1,190 | 730 | 1,487 | 854 | 1,708 | 886 | 1,793 |
| Patent royalties | 321 | 1,274 | 354 | 1,328 | 482 | 1,712 | 559 | 1,754 | 569 | 1,982 |
| Fees (including agents' fees) | 1,687 | 3,146 | 2,020 | 4,147 | 2,001 | 5,405 | 1,913 | 4,991 | 1,814 | 4,444 |
| Advertising | – | 386 | – | 504 | – | 491 | – | 536 | – | 553 |
| Film rentals | – | 115 | – | 105 | – | 79 | – | 76 | – | 145 |
| Nonmerchandise insurance | 715 | 819 | 57 | 309 | 38 | 280 | –28 | 179 | –235 | 183 |

*Source:* Nihon Ginkō (Bank of Japan), *Kokusai shushi tōkei nenpō* (*Balance of Payments Yearbook*). Unlike Table 2.8, this table evaluates the Japanese balance of payments in dollars.

Table 2.10. *Selected industrial countries' receipts from and expenditure on patents, invention processes, and copyrights (DM million)*

| Country | | 1977 | 1978 | 1979 | 1980 |
|---|---|---|---|---|---|
| Austria | Receipts | 59 | 57 | 61 | 66 |
| | Expenditure | 242 | 238 | 249 | 279 |
| | Balance | − 183 | − 181 | − 188 | − 213 |
| Belgium and | Receipts | 304 | 292 | 320 | 336 |
| Luxembourg[b] | Expenditure | 572 | 578 | 642 | 826 |
| | Balance | − 268 | − 286 | − 322 | − 490 |
| France[a] | Receipts | 659 | 698 | 783 | 902 |
| | Expenditure | 1,267 | 1,364 | 1,475 | 1,866 |
| | Balance | − 608 | − 666 | − 692 | − 964 |
| Germany[a] | Receipts | 826 | 922 | 961 | 1,101 |
| | Expenditure | 2,268 | 2,387 | 2,517 | 2,624 |
| | Balance | − 1,462 | − 1,465 | − 1,556 | − 1,523 |
| Italy[b] | Receipts | 1,055 | 1,079 | 1,277 | 1,565 |
| | Expenditure | 1,879 | 1,884 | 1,862 | 2,365 |
| | Balance | − 824 | − 805 | − 585 | − 800 |
| Netherlands[a] | Receipts | 536 | 585 | 680 | 760 |
| | Expenditure | 834 | 894 | 1,019 | 1,166 |
| | Balance | − 298 | − 309 | − 339 | − 406 |
| Sweden[a] | Receipts | 173 | 143 | 166 | 168 |
| | Expenditure | 306 | 289 | 341 | 400 |
| | Balance | − 133 | − 146 | − 175 | − 232 |
| Japan[a] | Receipts | 474 | 564 | 588 | 643 |
| | Expenditure | 2,289 | 2,348 | 2,335 | 2,411 |
| | Balance | − 1,815 | − 1,784 | − 1,747 | − 1,768 |
| United | Receipts | 1,714 | 1,772 | 1,921 | 2,185 |
| Kingdom[a] | Expenditure | 1,329 | 1,402 | 1,380 | 1,681 |
| | Balance | + 385 | + 370 | + 541 | + 504 |
| United | Receipts | 10,970 | 11,791 | 11,350 | p 12,698 |
| States[a] | Expenditure | 1,008 | 1,225 | 1,294 | p 1,375 |
| | Balance | + 9,962 | + 10,556 | + 10,056 | p + 11,323 |

[a] Excluding film business.
[b] Including film business.
[c] Including film business, consultancy fees, etc. p = Provisional.
*Sources:* Belgium and Luxembourg, Italy, Sweden: IMF Balance of Payments Yearbook. United Kingdom: British Business. United States: Survey of Current Business. Other countries: publications of the respective central banks.

Table 2.11. *Japanese technology payments and receipts by industry 1983 (¥ million)*

| | Receipts | | | Payments | | |
|---|---|---|---|---|---|---|
| | Total | New Programs | Continuing Programs | Total | New Programs | Continuing Programs |
| All Industry | 184,921 | 63,336 | 121,585 | 282,613 | 44,439 | 238,174 |
| Agriculture, forestry, and fisheries | 326 | – | 266 | – | – | – |
| Mining | 821 | 49 | 771 | 293 | 92 | 201 |
| Construction | 19,145 | 17,833 | 1,312 | 2,298 | 213 | 2,085 |
| Manufacturing | 164,058 | 45,139 | 118,920 | 278,075 | 42,475 | 235,601 |
| Food processing | 4,720 | 1,962 | 2,757 | 11,286 | 1,168 | 10,118 |
| Textile products | 6,256 | 540 | 5,716 | 2,821 | 293 | 2,528 |
| Pulp and paper | 1,158 | 444 | 713 | 1,220 | 133 | 1,087 |
| Publishing and printing | 91 | – | 64 | 1,066 | 22 | 1,044 |
| Chemicals | 29,409 | 7,956 | 21,453 | 45,860 | 8,984 | 36,876 |
| Textile fibers | 18,069 | 6,234 | 11,835 | 22,807 | 7,948 | 14,859 |
| Oils and paints | 2,280 | 159 | 2,121 | 2,478 | 104 | 2,375 |
| Pharmaceuticals | 6,638 | 787 | 5,857 | 13,009 | 830 | 12,179 |
| Other chemicals | 2,422 | 775 | 1,647 | 7,556 | 102 | 7,464 |
| Petroleum and coal products | 4,576 | 3,337 | 239 | 2,909 | 639 | 2,269 |
| Rubber products | 2,094 | 69 | 2,025 | 3,473 | 219 | 3,254 |
| Ceramics | 6,271 | 1,680 | 4,592 | 10,759 | 704 | 10,055 |
| Iron and steel | 29,047 | 8,983 | 20,064 | 7,800 | 934 | 6,867 |
| Nonferrous metals | 3,034 | 1,741 | 1,292 | 3,396 | 344 | 3,052 |
| Fabricated metals | 1,862 | 1,211 | 652 | 3,057 | 45 | 3,012 |
| General machinery | 5,249 | 1,553 | 3,696 | 27,405 | 1,717 | 25,688 |

| | | | | | | |
|---|---|---|---|---|---|---|
| Electric machinery | 35,484 | 6,682 | 28,802 | 89,158 | 15,530 | 73,627 |
| Electric machinery and household equipment | 9,861 | 998 | 8,862 | 29,682 | 4,611 | 25,071 |
| Communications and electronic equipment | 25,623 | 5,683 | 19,940 | 59,475 | 10,919 | 48,556 |
| Transportation equipment | 28,698 | 9,696 | 19,002 | 56,413 | 8,872 | 47,541 |
| Automobiles | 15,469 | 968 | 14,501 | 16,094 | 4,702 | 11,392 |
| Other transportation | 13,230 | 8,729 | 4,501 | 40,319 | 4,170 | 36,148 |
| Precision equipment | 2,418 | 308 | 2,110 | 3,515 | 1,247 | 2,268 |
| Other manufacturing | 7,692 | 1,950 | 5,742 | 7,938 | 1,623 | 6,315 |
| Transportation, communication, and public utilities | 571 | 255 | 316 | 1,946 | 1,660 | 286 |

*Source:* Sōrifu (Prime Minister's Office), *Kagaku gijutsu kenkyū hōkoku 1983 (Report on the Survey of Research and Development, 1983)* (Tokyo, 1984).

breaks down Japanese technology transactions by industry and by whether the transaction reflects new or continuing programs.[19] Although patterns differ strikingly by industry, it is very clear that data on total transactions do not bear a close relationship to new transactions. Where comparative advantage is rapidly changing, this might be expected. Table 2.11 suggests that in programs commenced just last year, Japan is a large net exporter of technology. Such an interpretation, however, may outrun the quality of the survey data base. As long ago as 1973 receipts from new programs for technology exports exceeded payments for new programs of technology imports. This suggests heavy net receipts for new programs may reflect a long-standing relative Japanese preference for up-front payments over higher royalties and license fees when selling technology. Furthermore, many sales of new technology take place within the context of continuing programs. To the extent that this is important, this would heavily bias in Japan's favor the receipts/payments ratio for new programs. For these reasons, it cannot be confidently predicted that at any time in the near future Japan will become an overall net exporter of technology services. Japan's new technology agreements do not appear to be good predictors of changes in overall trade technology.

In common with interpretations of the large Japanese commitment of resources to distribution, distinctive Japanese government policies can again be pointed to as an explanation of the distinctively low Japanese export of technology. For example, unlike most foreign patent laws, Japanese Patent Law requires the unanimous consent of all co-patent holders before a foreign or domestic license can be given. Perhaps, because Japanese firms have so often been charged with patent and copyright infringement by their foreign competitors, the Japanese courts have also given quite restrictive interpretations of the rights of patent holders. This, in turn, may have made Japanese companies quite reluctant to license foreign or domestic companies for fear their own patents gave them insufficient standing to protect them against abuse by licensees of proprietary information.

### Explaining sectoral allocation of resources and trade in technology services

Japanese commitment of resources to distribution services and Japanese trade in technology services have just been adjudged globally distinctive on the basis of relatively simple criteria. Before concluding that Japanese government policy has been responsible for these politically significant outcomes, it is appropriate to explore whether Japanese behavior really looks so distinctive if more sophisticated criteria are actually applied.

Japanese behavior in distribution and technology trade has been considered distinctive among the class of highly industrialized countries.

Highly industrialized countries, however, differ markedly with respect to natural resource endowments, geography, labor force skills, scientific base, and the character of plant and equipment. It is quite possible that if due allowance is made for distinctive Japanese endowments and geography, less weight might be given to the role of government policy.

Following Hollis Chenery's early work, it is possible to develop standards for normal industrial and international trade structure by empirically implementing cross-nationally a version of the Hecksher–Ohlin theory of comparative advantage.[20] Unlike Chenery's work, this work will concentrate on output structure as it relates particularly to services and on trade structure, particularly as it relates to trade in technology services. Also, unlike Chenery's work and appropriate to a consideration of Japan's special position, this analysis involves an extensive treatment of the role of natural resources and the differing qualities of factor inputs. By drawing directly on modern production theory it is possible to obtain an explicit functional form within which the Hecksher–Ohlin framework can be implemented.[21] Indeed, provided the much debated Law of One Price and the Factor Price Equalization Theorem hold, then (as shown in the Appendix to this chapter) it is possible to derive equations (A.2.6) and (A.2.8), which respectively explain sectoral domestic output and sectoral trade in goods and services as simple linear functions of aggregate endowments.

$$X_i(L) = \sum_{s=1}^{K} Q_{is} a_s L_s \qquad\qquad (A.2.6)$$

where $\qquad Q_{is} \equiv \sum_{j=1}^{H} d_{ij}(\tfrac{1}{2} P_i^2 + \tfrac{1}{2} P_j^2)^{-1/2} P_i + c_{is}$

$a_s \equiv$ quality of $s$th factor of production

$L_s \equiv s$th factor of production

$X_i \equiv i$th good or service

$P_i \equiv$ price of $i$th good or service

$c_{is}, d_{is} \equiv$ parameters of the profit function $\pi$

$$E_i(L) = \sum_{s=1}^{K} B_{is} a_{is} L_{s'} \quad (i = i, \dots, N) \qquad\qquad (A.2.8)$$

where $\qquad B_{is} \equiv G_{is} - Q_{is}$ and $G_{is} \equiv \dfrac{w_s \sum_{j=1}^{N} b_{ij} P_i^{-1/2} P_j^{1/2}}{\sum_{k=1}^{N} \sum_{m=1}^{N} b_{km} P_k^{1/2} P_m^{1/2}}$

$E_i(L) \equiv$ export of $i$th good

$w_s \equiv s$th factor reward

$b_{ij} \equiv$ parameter

Equations (A.2.6) and (A.2.8) are to be estimated for $H$ and $N$ sectors, respectively, from international cross-section data. Were it not for unknown

Table 2.12. *Estimates of Japan specific constants*

| | Japan-specific constants for gross domestic product originating by sector | Japan-specific constants for sector trade in technology |
|---|---|---|
| Agriculture, forestry, and fisheries | $268 \times 10^2$ $(685 \times 10)^*$ | $-.313$ (4.15) |
| Mining | $233 \times 10$ $(451 \times 10)$ | $-10.3$ (31.1) |
| Construction | $645 \times 10^2$ $(318 \times 10^3)$ | $158.0$ (142.0) |
| Food processing | $174 \times 10^2$ $(909 \times 10)$ | $-37.5$ (29.6) |
| Textiles | $812 \times 10$ $(969 \times 10)$ | $-21.7$ (10.5) |
| Pulp and paper | $794 \times 10$ $(358 \times 10)^*$ | $-1.89$ (8.88) |
| Publishing and printing | — | $-.362$ (1.75) |
| Chemicals | $105 \times 10^2$ $(784 \times 10^2)$ | — |
| Industrial chemicals | — | $20.1$ (1.50) |
| Oils and paints | — | $-.276$ (.564) |
| Pharmaceuticals | — | $-15.2$ (13.4) |
| Other chemicals | — | $-33.1$ (42.7) |
| Petroleum and coal products | $978 \times 10$ $(513 \times 10)^*$ | $7.29$ $(2.66)^{**}$ |
| Rubber products | — | $4.67$ (7.81) |
| Ceramics | $490 \times 10$ $(217 \times 10)^{**}$ | $-31.1$ (24.9) |
| Primary metals | $346 \times 10^2$ $(351 \times 10^2)$ | — |
| Iron and steel | — | $-20.6$ (35.7) |
| Nonferrous metals | — | $-5.80$ (10.3) |
| Fabricated metals | $-268 \times 10$ $(253 \times 10)$ | $-5.98$ (5.74) |
| General machinery | $115 \times 10^2$ $(384 \times 10^2)$ | $-107.0$ (76.2) |
| Electrical machinery | $178 \times 10^2$ $(163 \times 10^2)$ | $-214.0$ (16.9) |
| Communications and electronic equipment | $-^b$ | $-71.7$ (62.8) |
| Transportation equipment | $286 \times 10^2$ $(323 \times 10^2)$ | — |
| Automobiles | — | $40.1$ (34.0) |
| Other transportation equipment | — | $-116.0$ $(47.4)^*$ |
| Precision equipment | $437 \times 10$ $(180 \times 10)^{**}$ | $4.22$ (31.7) |
| Other manufacturing | $-251 \times 10^2$ $(685 \times 10^2)$ | $-2.13$ (6.66) |
| Transportation, communication, and public utilities | — | $-1.50$ (14.3) |
| Electric, water, and gas utilities | $871 \times 10$ $(982 \times 10)$ | — |
| Transportation and communication | $214 \times 10^2$ $(618 \times 10^2)$ | — |
| Wholesale and retail trade | $591 \times 10^2$ $(501 \times 10^2)$ | — |
| Finance and insurance | $-915 \times 10$ $(621 \times 10)$ | — |
| Real estate | $257 \times 10^2$ $(794 \times 10^2)$ | — |
| Other nongovernment services | $515 \times 10^2$ $(684 \times 10^3)$ | — |
| Government services | $-241 \times 10^2$ $(236 \times 10^2)$ | — |

variations in the quality of inputs across countries, estimation of (A.2.6) might proceed using ordinary least squares methods. Formally, this estimation of (A.2.6) and (A.2.8) with $a_s$ differing across countries and unknown is a multivariate errors in variables problem.[22] Instrumental variable methods will allow consistent estimation of the $B_{is}$ and the $Q_{is}$.[23] For any given good and services cross section, $a_s$ will not be identified. In the particular specification adopted now, however, at any given time, there are $i$ cross sections that contain the identical independent variables. This happy circumstance will permit estimation of the $a_s$ for each economy. These estimates of $a_s$ can then be used to obtain new Aitken efficient estimates of $B_{is}$ and $Q_{is}$.

Equations (A.2.6) and (A.2.8) are estimated with data taken from eleven countries on gross domestic product originating in twenty-three industrial sectors and on technology trade in twenty-five industrial sectors for the years 1965, 1973, 1975, 1977, and 1979. The eleven countries include Australia, Canada, France, Germany, Italy, Japan, Korea, the Netherlands, Sweden, the United Kingdom and the United States. The seven factors treated as central to the explanation of industrial and technology trade structure include directly productive capital stock, labor, educational attainment, distance from major trading partners, petroleum resources, iron ore resources, and arable land.[24]

In estimating (A.2.6) and (A.2.8) using a time series of cross sections, it is assumed that with the exception of input quality and disembodied technology time trends, the preferences and technology underlying (A.2.6) and (A.2.8) do not change. Even so, because prices and wages will change over time, in (A.2.6) and (A.2.8), $B_{is}$ and $Q_{is}$ will not be time invariant. The $a_s$ will also change from cross section to cross section.

Each equation in (A.2.6) and (A.2.8) will also contain a set of country-specific dummy variables that are also assumed to be time invariant. These variables are meant to allow for those characteristics not otherwise provided for in the analysis. Such variables might reflect national policies regarding the protection and/or disencouragement of particular industries. A positive, statistically significant country term for Japan in the equation explaining gross domestic product originating in the wholesale and retail trade might well signify a distinctive policy of protection. In this case, Japan would be producing more distribution services than might otherwise be expected,

---

Notes to Table 2.12

[a] numbers in parentheses to the right of Japan specific constants are standard errors
[b] blanks reflect differences in sectoral definition for gross domestic product originating data and track in technology data
*Note:* ** significant at 1% level
* significant at 5% level

Table 2.13. *Country specific constants for domestic output by sectors*

| Part A | Japan | Italy | France | Canada | West Germany | U.K. |
|---|---|---|---|---|---|---|
| Agriculture, forestry, and fisheries | * | — | * | — | — | — |
| Mining | — | — | — | — | — | — |
| Construction | — | — | * | * | — | — |
| Food processing | * | * | * | — | * | * |
| Textiles | — | * | * | — | * | * |
| Pulp and paper | * | * | — | — | — | * |
| Chemicals | — | — | * | * | * | * |
| Petroleum and coal products | * | — | — | — | — | — |
| Ceramics | * | * | — | * | — | * |
| Primary metals | — | — | — | * | — | * |
| Fabricated metals | — | — | * | — | — | — |
| General machinery | — | * | — | * | * | * |
| Electrical machinery | — | * | — | — | — | * |
| Transportation equipment | — | — | * | — | — | — |
| Precision equipment | * | — | — | * | — | — |
| Other manufacturing | — | — | * | — | — | — |
| Electric, water, and gas utilities | — | — | — | — | — | — |
| Wholesale and retail trade | — | — | — | — | — | — |
| Finance and insurance | — | — | * | — | * | — |
| Real estate | — | * | — | — | — | — |
| Other nongovernment services | — | — | — | — | — | — |
| Government services | — | * | — | — | — | — |

| Part B | Netherlands | S. Korea | Australia | Sweden | $\bar{R}^2$ |
|---|---|---|---|---|---|
| Agriculture, forestry, and fisheries | — | * | — | — | .62 |
| Mining | — | — | — | — | .71 |
| Construction | — | — | — | * | .56 |
| Food processing | — | — | — | * | .51 |
| Textiles | * | — | — | * | .84 |
| Pulp paper | * | * | — | — | .72 |
| Chemicals | * | * | — | — | .77 |
| Petroleum and coal products | — | * | — | — | .86 |
| Ceramics | — | * | — | — | .53 |
| Primary metals | * | * | * | — | .85 |
| Fabricated metal | — | — | * | — | .75 |
| General machinery | — | * | * | — | .78 |

Table 2.13 (cont.)

|  | Netherlands | S. Korea | Australia | Sweden | $\bar{R}^2$ |
|---|---|---|---|---|---|
| Electrical machinery | − | − | − | − | .82 |
| Transportation equipment | − | * | * | − | .88 |
| Precision equipment | − | * | − | − | .80 |
| Other manufacturing | − | * | * | − | .63 |
| Electric, water, and gas utilities | − | − | − | * | .74 |
| Wholesale and retail trade | − | − | − | − | .65 |
| Finance and insurance | − | * | − | * | .43 |
| Real estate | − | − | − | − | .58 |
| Other nongovernment services | − | − | − | − | .67 |
| Government services | * | * | − | * | .64 |

Note: * = Coefficient is statistically significant for 5% or 1% level.

given the quantity and quality of its natural resources, labor force, capital, and its consumption priorities. A statistically insignificant country variable in any given equation does not mean that the development of an industry necessarily conformed to liberal domestic and international canons. If all countries facing comparable imperatives with respect to distribution services resorted to comparable protective practices, the country variables would be, in all likelihood, statistically insignificant. Given that this investigation is interested only in examining whether Japan's high share of distribution services and small export of technology really are evidence of distinctive Japanese behavior and practices this limitation by no means undermines the interest of the results here. The Japanese government may make it difficult to export technology, but, within the limits of this type of evidence, a statistically insignificant country term would suggest Japanese behavior is no different from other comparably situated economies. Of course, the research being undertaken here has taken special pains to define comparably situated in a theoretically defensible fashion.

In actual estimation, as reported in Tables 2.13 and 2.14, relatively few of the Japanese country terms are statistically significant. In the forty-eight sectoral equations for domestic industrial structure and trade in technology only nine Japanese country terms are statistically significant. The six Japanese industrial sectors with statistically significant country constants include agriculture, forestry and fisheries, food processing, pulp and paper, petroleum and coal products, ceramics and precision equipment. Whereas some of these sectors are significant and do account for nontrivial shares of

Table 2.14. *Country specific constants for technology trade*

| Part A | Japan | Italy | France | Canada | West Germany | U.K. |
|---|---|---|---|---|---|---|
| Agriculture, forestry, and fisheries | – | – | – | – | – | – |
| Mining | – | – | – | – | – | – |
| Construction | – | – | – | – | – | – |
| Food processing | – | – | * | – | – | – |
| Textiles | – | – | – | – | – | * |
| Pulp and paper | – | – | * | – | – | – |
| Publishing and printing | – | * | – | – | – | * |
| Industrial chemicals | – | – | – | – | * | – |
| Oils and paints | – | * | – | – | * | – |
| Pharmaceuticals | – | – | * | – | * | * |
| Other chemicals | – | – | – | * | – | – |
| Petroleum and coal products | * | – | – | – | – | – |
| Rubber products | – | * | – | – | – | – |
| Iron and steel | – | – | – | * | – | * |
| Nonferrous metals | – | – | * | – | – | – |
| Fabricated metals | – | – | – | – | – | * |
| General machinery | – | – | – | * | * | – |
| Electrical machinery | – | – | – | – | – | – |
| Communications and electronic equipment | – | – | * | – | – | – |
| Automobiles | – | * | – | * | – | – |
| Other transportation equipment | * | * | – | – | – | * |
| Precision equipment | – | – | – | * | * | – |
| Other manufacturing | – | – | – | – | – | – |
| Transportation, communication, and public utilities | – | – | – | – | – | – |

| Part B | Netherlands | S. Korea | Australia | Sweden | $\bar{R}^2$ |
|---|---|---|---|---|---|
| Agriculture, forestry, and fisheries | – | – | – | * | .47 |
| Mining | * | * | – | * | .36 |
| Construction | * | * | – | – | .41 |
| Food processing | * | – | – | * | .28 |
| Textiles | – | – | – | – | .48 |
| Pulp and paper | * | * | – | * | .46 |
| Publishing and printing | – | – | – | – | .28 |
| Industrial chemicals | – | – | – | – | .53 |
| Oils and paints | – | – | – | – | .37 |
| Pharmaceuticals | – | – | * | – | .59 |
| Other chemicals | – | – | – | – | .67 |

Table 2.14 *(cont.)*

| | Netherlands | S. Korea | Australia | Sweden | $\bar{R}^2$ |
|---|---|---|---|---|---|
| Petroleum and coal products | — | * | — | — | .59 |
| Rubber products | — | * | — | — | .32 |
| Iron and steel | — | * | * | — | .66 |
| Nonferrous metals | — | — | * | — | .57 |
| Fabricated metals | — | * | — | — | .71 |
| General machinery | — | — | * | * | .68 |
| Electrical machinery | — | — | — | — | .73 |
| Communications and electrical equipment | — | * | — | * | .78 |
| Automobiles | — | * | * | — | .73 |
| Other transportation equipment | — | * | * | — | .82 |
| Precision equipment | * | — | — | — | .67 |
| Other manufacturing | * | — | — | — | .28 |
| Transportation, communication, and public utilities | — | — | — | — | .44 |

*Note:* * = Indicating constant term is statistically significant at 1% or 5% level.

Japanese gross domestic product, none of these sectors are predominantly services related. Neither wholesale and retail trade nor any of the conventionally defined Japanese services sectors are found to have statistically significant country terms. The level and structure of services in Japan, given the level of Japanese development and geography do not appear unusual by international standards. Despite the repeated involvement of the Japanese government in shaping the character of the distribution sector, the basic evolution of this sector's role in the Japanese economy is consistent with international patterns in ways that make it doubtful that the impact of the government policies has been ultimately distinctive. The lag in performance in Japanese services relative to Japanese manufacturing appears developmental and not the result of special Japanese government policies directed to either sector.

As is clear from Table 2.13, none of the other economies examined have statistically significant country constants for the distribution sector. Unlike Japan, however, a number of the other economies do have significant country constants for some of their other services sectors. Italy has positive country constants for real estate and for government services; France and West Germany have negative country constants for finance and insurance; the

Netherlands has a negative country constant for government services; South Korea has a negative country constant for financial services and a positive country constant for government services; and finally Sweden has a positive country constant for financial services and a positive country constant for government services. Overall, of fifty services sector country constants, only nine are statistically significant. Because of the relatively large share in the major industrialized economies that government services occupies these constants do explain a nontrivial proportion of the level and structure of gross domestic product in a number of important economies. Although the definition of services, the sample of economies used, the time period covered, and the empirical framework used are rather different, this result is consistent with other studies that have attempted to explain cross-national variation in government services.[25]

In common with the empirical results for domestic industrial structure, Japanese trade in technology services, by and large, does conform to international patterns. The same theories stressing national resource endowments and geography that have proven useful in explaining both domestic industrial structure and the international commodity structure of trade are also useful for explaining trade in technology.[26] The only Japanese sectors with statistically significant country constants in their technology trade equations are Petroleum and Coal Products (positive) and Other Transportation Equipment (negative). By gross value, these two sectors have averaged 12 percent of Japanese trade in technology over the sample period. In general, it does not appear that the character of the Japanese Patent Law or other intervention by the Japanese government has worked to keep Japanese exports of technology low and Japanese imports of technology high. Rather, the still largely derivative character of Japanese technology during the sample period seems a more plausible explanation.

*Finale*

The analyses presented suggest that the development of the Japanese services sector appears to be remarkably consistent with international patterns. This appears to be true both during the entire last century generally and, in particular, during the past twenty years. It also appears true not only for services in aggregate but also for the various services subsectors. Although the Japanese government has exhibited high profile concern with the Japanese services economy, there is rather little evidence suggesting that from a comparative perspective this concern has made much difference.

If the pattern of Japan's services economy development is consistent with the general development of the Japanese economy and Japan's distinctive geography, there remains the matter of explaining the speed of the development process. The rapid changes identified in the service sector reflect the rapid changes in the economy as a whole. Explaining changes in the services sector in the postwar period, for example, is in large measure a matter of explaining the rapid growth in Japan's aggregate capital stock and to a lesser extent the rapid improvement in quality of Japanese labor and of the education embodied in that labor. Whereas Japanese government policy had little differential impact on the sectoral allocation of resources, there is more reason to believe that Japanese financial regulations and Japanese government educational policies have had an important influence on the growth of the Japanese capital stock and in the improvement of the quality of postwar labor. [27]

## Appendix: A general equilibrium explanation of output and trade structure

*Formal framework* [A1]

*Supply:* Suppose the technology of an economy may be summarized by a variable profit function. [A2] Further suppose that this profit function is approximated by

$$\pi(P, L) = \sum_{i=1}^{N} \sum_{j=1}^{N} \sum_{s=1}^{K} d_{is} (\tfrac{1}{2} P_i^2 + \tfrac{1}{2} P_j^2)^{1/2} a_s L_s$$

$$+ \sum_{i=1}^{N} \sum_{s=1}^{K} c_{is} P_i a_s L_s$$

$$+ \sum_{i=1}^{N} \sum_{s=1}^{K} \sum_{r=1}^{K} f_{sr} (a_s L_s^{1/2})(a_r L_r^{1/2}) P_i \qquad (A.2.1)$$

where    $d_{is} = d_{si}$

$f_{sr} = f_{rs}$

$d_{ii} = 0$ for $i = 1, 2, \ldots, N$

$f_{ss} = 0$ for $s = 1, 2, \ldots, K$

$\pi \equiv$ profit function

$P \equiv$ price

$L \equiv$ factor of production

$a \equiv$ quality of factor

$c_{is}, d_{is} \equiv$ parameters of the profit function

Using Hotelling's lemma, (A.2.1) may be differentiated with respect to each of the output prices to obtain a system of derived supply functions. [A3]

$$X_i(P,L) = \sum_{j=1}^{N} \sum_{s=1}^{K} d_{ij}(\tfrac{1}{2}P_i^2 + \tfrac{1}{2}P_j^2)^{-1/2}P_i a_s L_s$$

$$+ \sum_{s=1}^{K} c_{is} a_s L_s + \sum_{s=1}^{K} \sum_{r=1}^{K} f_{sr}(a_s L_s^{1/2})(a_r L_r^{1/2}) \qquad i = 1, 2, \ldots, N$$

$$= \sum_{s=1}^{K} Q_{is} a_s L_s + \sum_{s=1}^{K} \sum_{r=1}^{K} f_{sr}(a_s L_s)^{1/2}(a_r L_r)^{1/2}$$

$$= \sum_{s=1}^{K} Q_{is} a_s L_s + \sum_{s=1}^{K} \sum_{r=1}^{K} f_{sr}(a_s a_r)^{1/2} L_s^{1/2} L_r^{1/2} \qquad i = 1, 2, \ldots, N$$

$$\text{(A.2.2)}$$

where $\quad Q_{is} \equiv \sum_{j=1}^{N} d_{ij}(\tfrac{1}{2}P_i^2 + \tfrac{1}{2}P_j^2)^{-1/2}P_i + c_{is}$

$X_i \equiv i$th good or service

Provided the much debated Law of One Price holds and the price of a particular good is everywhere the same, the $Q_{is}$ may be treated as constant and (A.2.2) can be used as a framework to explain cross-national sectoral economic activity. Sectoral economic performance is in this way tied to aggregate factor availability. If it is also assumed that the Factor Price Equalization Theorem holds up to a multiplicative quality differential, then by using Hotelling's lemma the second partial derivatives of the profit function with respect to factor endowments must be zero if factor price equalization is to occur.[A4] Applying Hotelling's lemma

$$a_s w_s = \partial \pi(P,L) / \partial \pi(a_s L_s) \qquad s = 1, \ldots, K \qquad \text{(A.2.3)}$$

where $\quad w_s \equiv s$th factor reward

$$\frac{\partial a_s w_s}{\partial(a_s L_s)} = \frac{\partial^2 \pi(P,L)}{\partial(a_s L_s)^2} = 0 \qquad s = 1, \ldots, K \qquad \text{(A.2.4)}$$

or from equation (A.2.1)

$$\tfrac{1}{2}f_{rs}(a_s L_s)^{-1/2}(a_r L_r)^{-1/2}\left( \sum_{i=1}^{N} P_i \right) = 0 \qquad \text{(A.2.5)}$$

This, in turn, implies $f_{rs} = 0$ and

$$X_i(L) = \sum_{s=1}^{K} Q_{is} a_s L_s \qquad \text{(A.2.6)}$$

*Demand:* The framework for obtaining trade structure as opposed to just output structure requires a demand side. Assume an indirect trade utility exists that expresses the maximum level of utility an open economy can obtain as a function of a vector of prices for commodities, a vector of factor endowments and the balance of trade.[A5] The indirect trade utility can be defined concretely in terms of the ordinary trade utility function and the variable profit (or GNP) function in (A.2.1). When this is done and following the approach taken in the previous section, an extension of Roy's Identity can be developed that allows the easy generation of net export functions by differentiation. If it is assumed as in the previous section that commodity prices are equalized by trade and that technology is homogeneous and identical across economies up to multiplicative quality differentials in inputs and if, in addition, it is assumed that national preferences are homothetic, but not necessarily identical, then the net export function can be written analogously to (A.2.2) in a form that is linear in the parameters and that can be estimated econometrically. If the generalized Leontief form is imposed not only on the supply side, as in (A.2.1), but also on the demand side, the following general form of net export function emerges:

$$E_i = \sum_{s=1}^{K} B_{is}(a_s L_s) + \sum_{s=1}^{K} \sum_{r=1}^{K} H_{irs}(a_s L_s)^{1/2}(a_r L_r)^{1/2} \qquad i = 1, \ldots, N \qquad (A.2.7)$$

where    $E_i \equiv$ net exports of $i$th good or service

$$B_{is} \equiv G_{is} - Q_{is} \text{ where } G_{is} \equiv \frac{w_s \sum_{j=1}^{N} b_{ij} P_i^{-1/2} P_j^{1/2}}{\sum_{k=1}^{N} \sum_{m=1}^{N} b_{km} P_k^{1/2} P_m^{1/2}}$$

$$H_{irs} \equiv f_{rs}$$

As in the previous section, if it is also assumed that the Factor Price Equalization Theorem holds up to a multiplicative quality term, then international trade will equalize factor prices per unit of factor quality and, as before, the $H_{irs}$ in (A.2.7) will equal zero. This simplifies (A.2.7) to the extent that[A6]

$$E_i = \sum_{i=s}^{K} B_{is}(a_s L_s) \qquad i = 1, \ldots, N \qquad (A.2.8)$$

(A.2.7) or (A.2.8) can be used as a framework to explain structural change in an economy's international trade.

*Estimation:*   In this study, (A.2.6) and (A.2.8) are estimated from international cross-section data on sectoral trade in technology and industrial structure. Were it not for unknown variations in the quality of inputs across countries, estimation of (A.2.6) and (A.2.8) might proceed using ordinary least squares methods. Formally, the estimation of (A.2.6) and (A.2.8) with $a_s$ differing across countries and unknown is a multivariate errors in variables problem.[A7] Instrumental variable methods allow consistent estimation of $B_{is}$ and $Q_{is}$. For any given commodity cross section, however, $a_s$ will not be identified. In the particular specification adopted here, at any given

80     Gary R. Saxonhouse

time, there are $i$ cross sections that contain the identical independent variables. This happy circumstance will permit consistent estimation of the $a_s$ for each economy.[A8] These estimates of $a_s$ can then be used to obtain new Aitken efficient estimates of $B_{is}$ and $Q_{is}$.

## Notes

1. S. Kuznets, *Modern Economic Growth: Rate Structure and Spread* (New Haven, Conn.: Yale University Press, 1966) contains summary material on pre-1945 economic performance. R. Summers, I. Kravis, and A. Heston, "International Comparison of Real Product and Its Compositions: 1950–77," *Review of Income and Wealth* (March 1980) contains related post-1950 data.
2. Kuznets, p. 146.
3. K. Ohkawa and M. Shinohara, *Patterns of Japanese Economic Development* (New Haven, Conn.: Yale University Press, 1979), p. 126.
4. Ohkawa and Shinohara, p. 129.
5. Ohkawa and Shinohara, p. 131.
6. Ohkawa and Shinohara, p. 126.
7. See, for example, Nihon keizai kenkyū senta (Japan Economic Research Center) *Sekai no naka no nihon keizai – 1980-nen (Japan in the World Economy – 1980s)* (Tokyo, 1972); Sangyō kōzō shingikai (Industrial Structure Council), *Sangyō kōzō no chōki bishon (Long-Term Vision of Industrial Structure)* (Tokyo, 1978) and Ministry of International Trade and Industry, *Background Data on the Vision of MITI Policies* (Tokyo, 1980).
8. The definition of services and output used by the Ministry of International Trade and Industry is somewhat different from what is used earlier in this paper.
9. Robert Summers, "Services in the International Economy," this volume.
10. Organization for Economic Cooperation and Development, *Economic Outlook* (various issues).
11. John W. Kendrick, "International Comparisons of Recent Productivity Trends," in William Fellner (ed.), *Essays in Contemporary Economic Problems* (Washington, D.C.: American Enterprise Institute, 1981) and Organization of Economic Cooperation and Development.
12. Masaru Yoshitomi, "An Analysis of Current Account Surpluses in the Japanese Economy," in Edward R. Fried, Philip H. Trezise, and Shigenobu Yoshida, *The Future Course of U.S.–Japan Economic Relations* (Washington, D.C.: Brookings Institutions, 1983) p. 16.
13. The data on Japanese services sector capital for stock and labor force growth are taken from Ohkawa and Shinohara, p. 126.
14. See Commercial Section, U.S. Embassy, Tokyo, "The Japanese Distribution System" (Unclassified A-1065, October 1972). See also G. Saxonhouse, "Employment, Imports, the Yen and the Dollar," in H. Rosovsky (ed.), *Discord in the Pacific* (Washington, D.C.: Columbia Books, 1972). More recent criticism appears in Subcommittee on Trade, Committee on Ways and Means, U.S. House of Representatives, United States–Japan Trade Report (Washington, 1980).

15. Subcommittee on Trade, Committee on Ways and Means.
16. Chūshō kigyōchō (Small and Medium Enterprise Agency), *Chūshō kigyō hakushō 1982 (Small and Medium Enterprise White Paper, 1982)* (Tokyo, 1982).
17. More recent evidence, when it becomes available, should give a rather more startling indication of the impact of this legislation. Since October 1981 the Ministry of International Trade and Industry, which is charged with administering this legislation, has not approved a single application for a large-scale supermarket to open a new store.
18. Japanese writers sympathetic with this view include Hiroshi Mori in "Ryutsu kakurei ron (The Distribution System)," in *Gendai sangyō ron* (Modern Industry): Vol. 1 *Sangyō kōzō (Industrial Structure)* (Tokyo: *Nihon keizai shimbun sha*, 1973) and Yukichi Arakawa, *Ryūtsu seisaku e no shikaku (Distribution Policy and its Rationale)* (Tokyo: Chigura Shobo, 1973).
19. The data in Table 2.10 have been collected from balance of payments sources, whereas the Japanese data in Table 2.11 are the by-product of a regular sample survey on research and development conducted by the Statistics Bureau, Prime Minister's Office.
20. Hollis B. Chenery, "Patterns of Industrial Growth," *American Economic Review* Vol. 50 (September 1960). In later work, such as Hollis B. Chenery and Moises Syrquin *Patterns of Development 1950–1970* (New York: Oxford University Press, 1975) Chenery abandons any attempt to provide a theoretical framework for his comparative empirical work.
21. The modern production theory made use of is described in Michael Intriligator and David A. Kendrick (ed.), *Frontiers of Quantitative Economics* Vol. 2 (New York: Elsevier, 1974).
22. See Appendix footnote A8.
23. See Appendix footnote A8.
24. The capital, labor, and educational data are adapted from materials assembled by L. Christensen, D. Cummings, and D. Jorgensen and reported in "Economic Growth, 1947–1973: An International Comparison," in J. W. Kendrick and B. Vaccara (eds.), *New Developments in Productivity Measurement and Analysis* (Chicago: University of Chicago Press, 1980) pp. 595–698, in "Relation Productivity Levels, 1947–1973: An International Comparison," *European Economic Review* 16, May 1981, pp. 61–94, in "Productivity Growth, 1947–1973: An International Comparison," in W. Dewald (ed.), *The Impact of International Trade and Investment on Employment* (Washington, D.C.: Government Printing Office, 1978) pp. 211–33, and in D. Jorgensen and B. M. Fraumeni, "The Role of Capital in U.S. Economic Growth, 1948–1976" and "Accounting for Capital" in G. von Furstenberg (ed.), *Capital Efficiency and Growth* (Cambridge, MA: Ballinger, 1980) pp. 9–25 and pp. 51–319, and from the associated projects of D. Jorgensen and M. Kuroda, "Energy and Economic Growth in the United States and Japan: A Progress Report to the National Science Foundation 1981" (mimeo) and M. Kuroda and K. Imamura, "Productivity and Market Performance: Time Series Analysis in the Japanese Economy 1960–1977," *Keio Economic Observatory Discussion Paper* No. 2, 1981. The industrial structure data is also adapted from the above sources and from data reported to the United

Nations. The United Nations is also the source for natural resources data whereas the arable land are taken from the Food and Agricultural Organization. The data on trade in technology are taken from Japan, Sōrifu (Office of the Prime Minister), Tōkei kyoku, *Kagaku gijutsu kenkyū chōsa hōkoku (Report on the Survey of Research and Development in Japan)* (Tokyo, various issues), Australia, Department of Manufacturing Industries, *R&D in Manufacturing Industries* (Canberra, various issues), France, Ministere du Developpement Industriel et Scientifique, *Statistique des echanges internationaux* (Paris, various issues), Germany, Deutsche Bundesbank, *Patent and License Transactions with Foreign Countries* (Bonn, various issues, Sweden, National Bureau of Statistics, *Research Statistics* (Stockholm, various issues) and Korea, Ministry of Science and Technology, *Science and Technology Annual* (Seoul, various issues). After sectoral specific national price indices are used to deflate the various dependent and independent variables used in this analysis, exchange rates are then used to put all constant national currency figures on a common basis. The deflation and conversion procedures used here make no explicit allowance for systematic international price differences among nontraded goods. Indeed, by assuming that the Law of One Price and the Factor Price Equalization Theorem hold up to multiplicative differences in the quality of factors this possibility cannot be treated explicitly. Given, however, that the analytical framework used here attempts to explain the evolution of trade and industrial structure, it can be expected that systematic deviations from the Law of One Price will be embedded in the various time-varying, country-specific parameters estimated.

25. See Summers, this volume. Of the six service sectors, whose cross-national variation Summers attempts to explain, the government services equation has by far the poorest fit.

26. A framework similar to that outlined here is used to explain the commodity structure of trade in Gary R. Saxonhouse "The Micro- and Macroeconomics of Foreign Sales to Japan," in William Cline (ed.), *Trade Policy for the 1980s* (Cambridge, Mass.: MIT Press for the Institute of International Economics), pp. 259–304, and in Gary R. Saxonhouse, "Evolving Comparative Advantage and Japan's Imports of Manufactures," in Kozo Yamamura (ed.), *Policy and Trade Issues of the Japanese Economy* (Seattle, WA: University of Washington Press, 1982) pp. 239–70. Technology trade levels, of course, are not determined independently of trade in commodities. Econometrically speaking, however, since the independent variables used here to explain trade in technology are identical to those which would be used to explain trade in commodities, efficient estimation will not be compromised by ignoring trade in commodities. See Arnold Zellner, "An Efficient Method of Estimating Seemingly Unrelated Regressions and Tests for Aggregation Bias" *Journal of the American Statistical Association* 57, (June 1962), pp. 348–68. Note also that Sapir and Lutz in a paper which treats trade in services at a more highly aggregated level than that used here comes to broadly similar conclusions regarding the utility of theories of international trade in goods for explaining international trade in services. See A. Sapir and E. Lutz, "Trade in Services: Economic Determinants and Development Related Issues," *World Bank Staff Working Paper No. 480,* August 1981.

27. See the discussion in Gary R. Saxonhouse, "The Micro- and Macroeconomics of Foreign Sales to Japan."

A1 A framework similar to what is proposed here has been used to explore international trade in goods. See Gary Saxonhouse, "The Micro- and Macroeconomics of Foreign Sales to Japan," in William Cline (ed.), *Trade Policy for the 1980s* (Cambridge, Mass.: MIT Press for the Institute of International Economics, 1983) and Gary Saxonhouse, "Evolving Comparative Advantage and Japan's Imports of Manufactures," in Kozo Yamamura (ed.), *Policy and Trade Issues of the Japanese Economy* (Seattle, Wash.: University of Washington Press, 1982).

A2 The concept of a variable profit function was first suggested by Paul A. Samuelson, "Price of Factors and Goods in General Equilibrium," *Review of Economic Studies* 21, June 1953.

A3 Hotelling's lemma is discussed in W. M. Gorman, "Measuring the Quantities of Fixed Factors," in J. N. Wolfe (ed.), *Value Capital and Growth* (Chicago, 1968).

A4 In what follows empirical work will proceed as if $N = K$, despite the number of inputs for which data are available being almost 100 less than the number of goods. Given the rather arbitrary aggregation and disaggregation in goods and factors in empirical work of this kind, it is appropriate to assume that the number of goods and input are many and that included and excluded dependent and independent variables have properties such that exclusion of relevant variables does not bias estimation of the coefficients for included variables.

A5 This formulation rests critically on the existence of direct community utility functions. For the conditions under which this might be true see Paul A. Samuelson, "Social Indifference Curves," *Quarterly Journal of Economics,* February 1956, and E. Eisenberg, "Aggregation of Utility Functions," *Management Science,* July 1961. Applications upon which the current analyses are built include Gary R. Saxonhouse, "Evolving Comparative Advantage and Japan's Imports of Manufactures," in Kozo Yamamura (ed.), *Policy and Trade Issues of the Japanese Economy* (Seattle, Wash.: University of Washington Press, 1982), and Gary R. Saxonhouse, "The Micro- and Macroeconomics of Foreign Sales to Japan," in William Cline (ed.), *Trade Policy for the 1980s* (Cambridge, Mass.: MIT Press for the Institute of International Economics, 1983).

A6 The estimation of a version of (A.2.7) is discussed in Gary R. Saxonhouse, "Evolving Comparative Advantage and Japan's Imports of Manufactures." The estimation of (A.2.8) is discussed in Gary R. Saxonhouse, "The Micro- and Macroeconomics of Foreign Sales to Japan."

A7 In actual estimation an additive error term for equations will also be assumed.

A8 For example, let $a_s = 1 + a_s'$. Using instrumental variable techniques in the presence of multiplicative errors allows consistent estimation of the $B_{is}$. Using these estimates, for each economy an $N \times 1$ vector $[v_i']$ of commodity equation residuals can be formed for each time period. Consistent estimates of the quality terms for each country for each time period can then be obtained from

$$\{[B_{is}L_s]'[B_{is}L_s]\}^{-1}\{[B_{is}L_s]'[v_i]\}.$$

# Comment: Services in the Japanese economy

## HUGH PATRICK

Professor Saxonhouse's approach is explicitly comparative, theoretically rigorous, and quantitative – notable strengths in the analysis. It both provides answers and insights and raises questions that merit further research.

The review of the prewar and more recent role of the services sector – defined as trade, finance, personal services, and public administration – provides a useful general setting. One major puzzle emerges from the prewar data: There was a very small but absolute decline in labor productivity in the services sector between 1902 and 1938. I find an absolute decline difficult to accept. This was a period of considerable innovation, with technical and institutional improvement throughout the economy, including services. Real wage rates increased, albeit modestly; there was capital deepening. It is true, as implied in Table 2.2, that the labor force grew slowly; the population growth rate was low and the labor force participation rate declined from initially high levels. The services sector, especially so-called traditional components such as distribution and personal servants, was a contra-cyclical residual absorber of labor. This cyclical pattern has persisted even as labor abundance ended and wages began to rise rapidly from the early 1960s.

Thus, the problem may be one of fallacy of composition: Whereas productivity may have remained constant or increased in all services subsectors, employment may have grown more rapidly in low productivity services. More likely, however, is that the data are inaccurate. Japanese historical series are quite good in comparison with other countries; and the estimates are less accurate as one goes back in time. Direct data on services – output, value-added, prices, even employment – are scanty and partial; Ohkawa and his colleagues had to utilize indirect methods of estimation (ratios to real output and the like), especially for earlier years. They are forthright in assessing the lower reliability of estimates for services as compared to real goods. Clearly the historical role of the services sector in Japan's economic development merits further research.

Interestingly, Saxonhouse predicts that the services sector share in real as well as nominal Japanese output will rise in the future, and that productivity growth will persist rapidly enough not to be a drag on aggregate productivity performance – in part because industrial productivity growth has decelerated sharply in the past decade, in part because relatively rapid capital formation will continue. (Saxonhouse evidently believes, as do I, that there is no iron law whereby services sector productivity growth will always be $X$ percent below that of the industrial sector.) He argues that since Japanese manufacturing productivity is comparable to the United States, West Germany, and France but services sector productivity is substantially lower (Table 2.5), considerable room exists for further productivity improvement in Japanese services. I accept the implicit assumption that demand for services will continue to be income elastic.

The major and most original and interesting part of the paper comes from the author's estimation of a Hecksher–Ohlin general equilibrium model to determine whether Japan's sectoral structure of production and trade is significantly different from that of a sample of other industrial economies. Saxonhouse's model is described in the Appendix to this chapter and in his other recent publications. It is not my assignment to evaluate the model in detail. It has the virtues of a general equilibrium formulation, comparison of Japan with a group of other relevant countries, and relatively undemanding data requirements. It resolves the problem of the Law of One Price for factor inputs, especially labor, both by disaggregation (labor into several categories by level and type of education) and by assuming cross-national quality differences within categories, and then deriving estimates of changes in those quality levels.

This model provides evidence for a wide range of production and trade questions. Saxonhouse applies it here specifically to the service sector and to net imports or exports of technology by sector to determine to what degree and where Japan differs from other countries. Saxonhouse derives a number of broader conclusions from the data (reported in Tables 2.12, 2.13, and 2.14) though they are not particularly highlighted in the text. Thus, the most important source of postwar growth in the service sector has been the increase in Japan's aggregate capital stock, with significant capital deepening in services as well as other sectors; improvements in the educational level and (within-category) quality of labor have also been of some importance. Taking into account factor endowments and distance, the structure of Japanese production and technology trade – for services and indeed for all productive activity – is not unusual in international comparison. This is important because it has been alleged that in services, especially distribution, as in other sectors Japanese government policy has provided a protective barrier. Saxonhouse's conclusion is that although that may be true, Japan does so no more or less than other countries; it adheres to average behavior. Its policies are not significantly different, or at any rate they do not have a significantly different impact on the structure of production and trade, in services and generally. There are exceptions of course, but the number of cases is no greater, and often fewer, than for the Western European nations (Tables 2.13 and 2.14).

Saxonhouse obtains these conclusions by first noting that in two sectors – distribution, and foreign trade in technology – Japan is distinctive in terms of relatively simple criteria. He then asks whether this distinctiveness is a result of government policy or of underlying economic conditions. As I have noted previously, he finds it to be true for the latter explanation. I find this a congenial conclusion, and my remaining comments are designed to consider some further points about these sectors.

Japan and the United States have a much larger, and more rapidly rising, share of their labor force in wholesale and retail trade than do the Western European countries. Japan has a far larger number of establishments relative to population, and of much smaller average size, than in the United States. The larger the size the greater is labor productivity in Japan (though the measures do not take into account adequately the quality of services – locational convenience, hours, delivery, credit – especially important for small urban neighborhood retail shops). Most retail establishments in Japan are family owned and operated, typically based on older, often female, family labor and on ownership of a small urban plot that is used to house both the store and the family. Land prices are extremely high in Japan, having risen rapidly over the postwar period. This encourages substitution of labor for land, and lower labor productivity, which is offset by relatively higher prices to meet the opportunity cost of labor. High land costs mean there are few suburban shopping malls with huge parking lots. Car dealers have small lots and salepersons call on potential customers rather than waiting for them to come in; the number of sales per employee is substantially lower than in the United States. With space so expensive it pays to economize on inventories and to replenish them frequently. With sharply rising costs of land and labor and modestly declining costs of capital, distribution like other sectors in Japan has been in an ongoing long-run process of structural change. That takes time, often generational, because of the structure of urban land ownership and the nature of labor markets. We need to sort out the relative importance of labor quality and labor markets, land costs, and adjustment lags in assessing Japanese productivity/efficiency in distribution.

Whereas Saxonhouse shows that, given factor endowments, the size of the distribution sector in Japan or indeed any of the countries in the sample is not atypical, he also points to the evolving importance of Japanese government policy for retail trade. Earlier policy was ameliorative for smaller establishments in responding to the economic forces encouraging growth of department stores, discount chains, and supermarkets. Since 1974, and especially since 1978, government policy has become protective of small establishments by greatly restructuring entry of large floorspace competitors. The data (Table 2.7) show less of a change between 1974 and 1979 than the author suggests, but he probably has caught an important turning point in the late 1970s in government policy regarding the trade-off between efficiency and income distribution in retail business. This reflects the growing political power and activism of small business in Japan generally. It remains to be seen to what degree these policy shifts will (adversely) affect labor productivity growth (and employment, especially of older persons). The recent burgeoning growth of Japanese Mom and Pop owned Seven-Eleven Stores with centralized ordering, inventory control, brand name, and other services is one innovative response.

Japan, like West Germany, has a large deficit on international trade in services. A half of Japan's deficit is a consequence of shipping costs for imports and exports, and roughly another 15 percent is due to payments for technology net imports. The shipping deficit is not surprising. With high Japanese labor costs the Japanese merchant marine is not particularly competitive. However, as the Saxonhouse data on charters imply, Japanese shipping companies do carry almost half of Japan's trade in part by chartering foreign vessels and crews (typically Japanese built, Hong Kong owned and manned, ships). Even so, Japan earns a net surplus on freight and insurance. Japan has a well-developed marine insurance industry that works closely with the large (and small) Japanese trading companies.

Of greater analytical interest is the distinctive Japanese pattern of both imports and exports of technology. On the import side, Japan is second only to West Germany, though Italy is close behind and rising whereas Japan's payments appear to be leveling off. More distinctive is Japan's low level of technology exports: Japan ranks below the United States, the United Kingdom, West Germany, France, even the Netherlands. Accordingly, on a net basis Japan is the largest importer of technology, with West Germany a close second. Saxonhouse shows this is consistent with its factor endowment, even more so by sector for Japan than Western Europe. He argues that Japan's pattern reflects the "still largely derivative character of Japanese technology." He points out that in terms of new technology contracts exports have come to exceed imports; comparative advantage is changing rapidly.

Saxonhouse also surmises that technology exports and more sophisticated manufactured goods have become complements; they are both increasing in the same sectors. I suspect that at the margin they may already be substitutes, which Saxonhouse sees as a future possibility. A more micro analysis would (inevitably) show a more complex pattern. Technology payments are probably closely related to Japanese foreign direct investment, which in turn may be either a complement to or substitute for exports. Sample evidence for the mid-1970s suggests that only about a quarter of Japanese repatriation of revenues from foreign direct investments is as dividends; much is for technology licenses and management fees. I suspect technology receipts are significantly related to Japanese investment abroad in textile products, textile fibers, electrical machinery, automobiles, and ship repair dockyards, among others. On the other hand, Japanese steel companies have licensed technology to (potential and in some cases now actual) foreign competitors in Brazil, South Korea, Taiwan, China, and more recently the United States. Although this has been a controversial decision within the management of Japanese steel firms, the prevailing (and correct) view is that if their firm does not export the technology some other firm will – whether Japanese or (horror of horrors) foreign.

# CHAPTER 3

# Services in the U.S. economy

IRVING LEVESON

## Introduction

The growing interest in service industries derives from many concerns. Services now account for two-thirds or more of all employment, depending on how defined. Employment in service industries and white collar occupations continues to greatly outpace the growth of employment in industry (Figure 3.1). With that growth has come an intensification of myths and unfounded concerns just at a time when service industry performance appears to be on the forefront of solving, far more than adding to, problems in the economy.

Increasingly, there are questions about whether a service economy can grow rapidly and raise productivity sufficiently to contribute to price stability, whether it can give us strength in international trade, and how it affects our national security. The growth of service employment also raises many questions about the future of society and the nature of work, and even of how well we will measure, understand, and respond to the changes that are taking place.

There are rising concerns about the potential ability of service industries to absorb labor of women, youth, minorities, and immigrants; the role of services in economic stability; the adaptability of workers displaced from goods production to a service environment; implications of reductions in the role of government, not-for-profit organizations, and social service functions; and even questions about the effectiveness of monetary controls in a service dominated economy. At the same time there is growing evidence that service industries are undergoing an unprecedented amount of innovation. With these changes we will have to understand new structures of industry, whole new industries and production systems, and potentially far-reaching implications of a climate of rapid service productivity growth. The new realities can be expected to challenge misconceptions and even require a complete reversal of thinking on a number of critical issues.

## The roles of service industries in the U.S. economy

### Myths and realities

Services have commonly been viewed as a lagging sector, exerting a drag on economic growth. Yet, even in the post–World War II period as a whole,

89

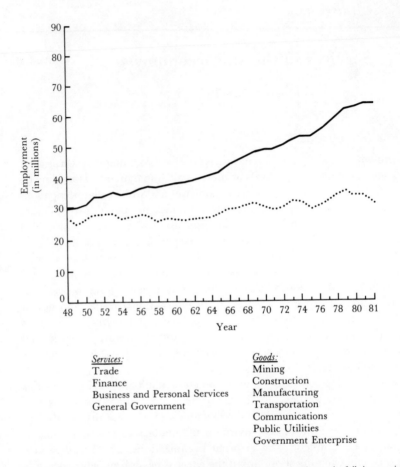

Year

| Services: | Goods: |
|---|---|
| Trade | Mining |
| Finance | Construction |
| Business and Personal Services | Manufacturing |
| General Government | Transportation |
| | Communications |
| | Public Utilities |
| | Government Enterprise |

*Note:* Employment and persons engaged in production, defined as employees in full-time equivalents, plus proprietors. Services include trade, finance, and business and personal services and general government.

*Source:* Bureau of Economic Analysis, Department of Commerce, *National Income and Product Accounts of the United States, 1929-1976,* pp. 250-52, 255-57, 264, 267-69; idem, *Survey of Current Business,* July 1982, pp. 83, 84, 86, 87, and July 1983, pp. 73 & 74.

Figure 3.1.  Employment in goods and services, 1948-1982

studies by Kendrick, Fuchs, and others, for the United States have shown that the difference in productivity growth between goods producing and service industries has been far smaller than appears in series on output per man-hour, when allowance is made for the faster rate of growth of capital per worker and other inputs in the goods sector (Kendricks, 1973; Fuchs, 1968).

The extreme rejection of the value of services occurs in Marxist ideology, which considers them unproductive. Service industries are not even included in the official Soviet GNP. This value judgment is reflected in exaggerated complaints about the service industries in the major cities of developing countries. These industries are often viewed as a dumping ground for underutilized workers displaced from the farms. This perspective fails to recognize that in most large cities of developing countries there is sizable employment in service industries, which benefits economic development. Even the more marginal service industries play a significant role in the process of small business development and intergenerational mobility to higher economic status.

There is no shortage of myths about the role of services in the United States, either. The service economy is sometimes thought of as being a collection of low-paying jobs, incapable of providing upward mobility. Yet, service industries have fostered tremendous mobility through the establishment and growth of small business, flexible movement between firms, creation of new occupations, and growth of markets. Service industries now provide the main avenue for absorbing the large supplies of labor of women and youth and offer growing opportunities for minorities, immigrants, and displaced workers.

The remark is often made that the United States cannot be militarily strong if it is *only* a service economy. This view fails to recognize that although most employment is in services, nearly half of U.S. output is in goods production, that there are tremendous opportunities for trade in services, and that services are making a great contribution to the revitalization of the economy as a whole. Such thinking in part reflects a machismo attitude in which concrete, easy-to-understand products are thought of as better targets for economic expansion or more deserving of special treatment to salvate them from the process Joseph Schumpeter called creative destruction, which accompanies economic growth. The reality of service industries is quite different.

*Functions of service industries*

Service industries have always played a major role in making the products of the goods-producing sector available to business users and consumers. Producer services, which include such professional areas as accounting, law, and advertising, provide important inputs into the production of goods and other services. Some distribution services channel goods to businesses and could be counted as part of producer services. Some producer services are used for the development and maintenance of physical capital.

In 1952, Kurt Vonnegut, Jr., wrote a book called *Player Piano,* in which a future, highly automated society consisted of three groups – managers and technicians, the Reconstruction and Reclamation Corps, and the army. The "reeks and wrecks," as they were called, were a huge cadre of repair people. Since 1978, the fastest-growing occupation in the United States is what the Bureau of Labor Statistics calls "other repair services," as anyone who has a live-in copier repair person will attest.

Many consumer services can be viewed not so much as direct objects of consumption – such as seeing a movie – but as services that facilitate life-styles – such as financial services, travel agent services, tax preparation, and various social services. They relate to personal business in much the same way as producer services relate to activities of business firms. Personal business services include what Victor Fuchs has called validation services in health services (Fuchs, 1972), and the comparable functions of testing and credentialing in education. They also include services that maintain household durable goods.

There is also a huge industry that creates human capital. This includes much of the formal education industry and much of the health industry, which also adds to productive capability. It includes other services linked to learning, such as the operation of conference centers and running business seminars. Some of these activities represent a mix of consumption for present enjoyment and investment for future benefit; the two are almost impossible to separate from one another.

An important newcomer to the human capital-producing and capital-maintaining industries is the computer services industry. According to Jerome Dryer, President of Association of Data Processing Service Organizations, the computer services industry came from being virtually non-existent fifteen years ago to an output of more than $22 billion in 1981. It is growing at more than 20 percent per year and will soon reach 1 percent of GNP. Although some of the activities of the industry support ongoing functions, a large part involves the development of systems and programs that will provide service for many years. Human capital embodied in computer systems and software has taken on a particularly powerful form, capable of wide distribution. This *programmed human capital* incorporates sophisticated knowledge in a way that often can be used easily by those with limited computer skills or those interested only in applications.

Consumer services that are desired in their own right have been called "quaternary services" by Herman Kahn (Kahn, 1979). In this formulation, which I favor, the combination of producer services and personal business services might be relabeled the "tertiary sector." This tertiary sector serves an enabling function rather than providing direct utility. To some observers, such as Daniel Bell and Herman Kahn, quaternary services are the essence of a postindustrial society. However, Bell's formulation is close to Gottman, who wonders:

Whether a new distinction should not be introduced in all the mass of nonproduction employment: a differentiation between *tertiary* services – transportation, trade in the simpler sense of direct sales, maintenance, and personal services – and a new and distinct *quaternary* family of economic activities – services that involve transactions, analysis, research or decision making, and also education and government. (Gottman, 1959)

One could also consider a significant part of the underground economy in the service sector. Gambling and prostitution, a portion of the activities of illegal aliens, and part of the unreported activity of the aboveground economy – especially of independent agents such as waiters and waitresses and proprietors of small businesses (i.e., self-employed people) – are clearly of a service nature. Of course, some activities, such as drug traffic, would be valued at far less if aboveground. The largest part of underground services are quaternary services, products of an affluent, pleasure-seeking society.

Services play a critical role in the adjustment of the economy to a difficult period of structural change. For example, innovations in financial instruments, money management, and financial service delivery systems facilitate adjustment to inflation and raise productivity in the economy as a whole. Similarly, accounting services adapt to a new tax climate, computer services facilitate meeting environmental regulations, and new services assist in energy development and conservation.

At the same time as service industries are growing rapidly, there is rapid growth in service-type functions within the goods-producing sector. This development of an "internal service sector" within goods industries is apparent in the growth of white collar occupations as a share of goods sector employment as managerial and professional employees and their staffs oversee ever more efficient production operations, and in other changes in the structure of goods-producing industries.

### The demand for services

*Factors influencing demand*

The demand for services has grown only slightly faster than the demand for goods. The long-term growth of service demand has been spurred by rising incomes. Offsetting much of this effect has been the impact of slower productivity growth in service industries. With less productivity growth in services than goods, prices rise more rapidly, slowing the rise in consumption of services. This slower productivity growth, in the face of relatively strong demand for output based on income, appears to have been the major reason for continuing rapid service employment growth, according to the studies by Fuchs (Fuchs, 1982 and 1968).

A number of other factors have contributed to movements in service output and employment in recent years. Changing roles of women have been an increasingly important factor. Demands for services have been generated by the rising role of government with economic development. In recent years that tendency has been modified.

Since the mid-1960s, high costs of energy, environmental restrictions, effects of inflation, and rising effective tax rates have acted disproportionately to discourage capital-intensive industries and, by making their output more costly, to shift demand to services. Services also benefited from rising tax rates because of pressure for the growth of tax-exempt fringe benefits. Fringe benefits other than employee contributions for social insurance increased from 2 percent of wages and salaries in 1947 to 10 percent in 1982. With this rise came the growth of various forms of insurance and other services. Because tax rates were so high, dental insurance continued to grow rapidly right through the 1981 recession, contrary to the experience of health insurance in previous downturns. Inflation has contributed to increased demands for financial services. Extensive nonprice competition in banking after the imposition of deposit interest rate ceilings led to a rapid expansion of branches and services. Services also grew because of a need to take care of the large stock of housing and automobiles built up in the 1950s and 1960s.

Service employment is far less sensitive to the business cycle than goods employment because compensation tends to be more flexible in service industries. Thus, the service share of employment rises especially rapidly in recession. Similar influences arise when major structural changes depress the output of goods-producing industries for longer duration.

There are indications that the growth of the service share of employment may not be as rapid in the 1980s as in the past. Growth of general federal government and nonprofit organization activities will not provide the same stimulus. Defense spending will encourage goods production. There will be cutbacks and slower growth in government at the state and local level. Greater restrictions will be placed on expenditures for medical care. The factors that have hurt capital-intensive industries are partially reversing. A larger than usual proportion of the population at nesting age will raise demand for housing and consumer durables, as will improvements in real interest rates. School enrollment will continue to ebb with changes in the age distribution.

*A simple model*

In order to examine the aggregate effects of these forces, a very simple model was fit to describe the share of services in nonfarm employment

from 1952 to 1981. The model is in reduced form, influenced by both supply
and demand factors. No attempt was made to use real output as a dependent variable or price as an independent variable because of lack of confi-
dence in the validity of the data.

Employment is measured by the Department of Commerce series on persons engaged in production, which counts employees on a full-time equivalent basis and includes proprietors. Services are delineated according to
Fuchs's definition, as in Figure 3.1. The service share of nonfarm employment was estimated based on real GNP per capita, and the ratio of actual to
potential GNP, a measure that takes into account both utilization of physical capacity and unemployment. The equation is:

$$S = 77.97 + .0036 \left( \frac{\text{GNP}}{P} \right) - 39.70 \left( \frac{\text{Act. GNP}}{\text{Pot. GNP}} \right) \qquad (3.1)$$
$$\phantom{S = }(14.94) \quad (24.46) \qquad\qquad (7.69)$$

(*Note: t* values are in parentheses, $R^2 = .934$, and *SEE* = .762.)

Actual and predicted values of the service share of employment are
shown in Figure 3.2. Note that in spite of the aggregation and simplicity of
the variables, the equation provides a very good fit. GNP per capita reflects
rising incomes and other associated developments such as urbanization and

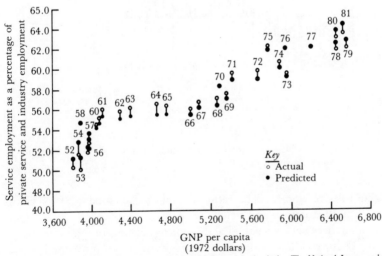

Source: U.S. Department of Commerce, Bureau of Economic Analysis, *The National Income and Product
Accounts of the United States 1929–1976*; idem, *Survey of Current Business*, July 1982, U.S. Bureau
of the Census, *Statistical Abstract of the United States*, various issues.

Figure 3.2. Share of services in nonfarm employment by level of real GNP per
capita, 1952–1981

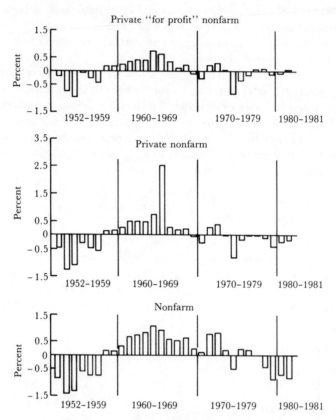

*Source:* U.S. Department of Commerce, Bureau of Economic Analysis, *The National Income and Product Accounts of the United States 1929–1976*; idem, *Survey of Current Business*, July 1982, U.S. Bureau of the Census, *Statistical Abstract of the United States*, various issues.

Figure 3.3. Difference between actual and predicted service sector share of nonfarm employment, 1952–1981

changing roles of women. The ratio of actual to potential GNP picks up both cyclical fluctuations and structural shifts.

The differences between actual and predicted values show an interesting pattern. These residual values from equation (3.1) are presented in the bottom panel of Figure 3.3. Note that the service share of employment is lower than expected from 1952 to 1957 and from 1977 to 1981 and higher during all but one year from 1958 to 1976. This could potentially be explained by the strong role of government during the middle years. In order to separate the changing role of government, the same variables were used to predict the share of services in nongovernment, nonfarm employment. The differences between actual and predicted values for this equation are shown in the middle panel of Figure 3.3. The differences are much smaller. However, evidence of the kind expected from a thirty-year social cycle is present here too (Molitor, 1979).

The upper panel repeats the procedure, also excluding not-for-profit organizations. Here the fit is even closer. The coefficient of determination is .981 and the standard error of the estimate is .422. The larger of the deviations that remain coincides with the 1954, 1958, and 1974 recessions and the effects of the Kennedy tax cuts in 1964 and 1965, and largely appear to reflect imperfect cyclical adjustment.

The outstanding fit of a simple real GNP per capita plus cycle model does not necessarily mean that other demand factors are unimportant. The variables chosen reflect complex collections of forces and although offsetting one another in one period, may not do so in another. An acceleration of productivity growth may have slowed the rise in the service share of private, for-profit, nonfarm employment. However, shifts from the public and not-for-profit sectors may have increased the share of the private service sector at the same time, offsetting part of the productivity effect. This shift to the private sector could continue, with far-reaching consequences. New forces will be operating as well.

## Gauging the performance of service industries

"The best of our production indexes give inadequate representation to new industries, to services as compared with commodities, to 'secondary' production, to the utilization of by-products, and to improvements in the quality of product." That observation was made by Wesley Mitchell fifty years ago in his summary of Arthur Burns's treatise, *Production Trends in the United States since 1870* (p. xxiii). Although vast improvements have been made since that time, the state of information continues to be accurately described by Wesley Mitchell's remarks. Moreover, the very trends Arthur Burns observed compound the difficulties of measurement in modern society.

Professor Mitchell goes on to summarize Arthur Burns's study:

A growing share of production is assuming the form of luxuries, superfluities, and style goods; the demand for such products has no such stability as the demand for staples. Hence, an increase in the birth-rate of new products means an increase in the death-rate of old products and a decline in the average life-span of individual industries. (p. xviii)

This tendency is especially true in the present environment. The U.S. economy of the 1980s is characterized not only by evolutionary development in the tertiary economy, but also by continuing major structural changes and adjustments, the beginnings of a powerful new wave of technological innovation, and by a revolution in the ways services are distributed as well as produced.

Determining performance of service industries hinges on a number of extraordinarily difficult questions. The task of measuring output cannot be accomplished by counting physical units since services are so heterogeneous. In many service industries, this has led to assuming that percentage changes in outputs are equal to percentage changes in inputs such as man-hours. Another approach is to convert sales, net of purchased inputs, into a measure of real output by dividing by a price index. Usually, however, the price index is little more than a price of inputs and does not take into account changes in the efficiency with which those inputs are used.

Various hybrids exist. In retailing, for example, the GNP series assumes that gross margins are a constant percent of sales even though improvements in efficiency and changes in levels of service could shift margins dramatically. The rationale given in this case is that studies show margins to be relatively stable over time. However, modest differences in margins between periods, which cannot be separated from measurement error, can imply rather substantial variations in annual rates of output growth. Potentially even more important is that constant margins may reflect opposing trends. Increases in efficiency with which a given amount of service is provided could reduce the spread between retail sales and costs of inputs. Increases in the level of service with demands from rising incomes or female labor force participation could provide an offsetting increase in spreads.

The problems of measuring the quality of output are pervasive. The introduction of videotapes in place of a large university lecture class loses some of the personal nature of the process and the vibrancy of live theater (which many would doubt ever existed). However, it may bring to the student the best curriculum development and the best lecturer, allow viewing at the most convenient times and locations, facilitate review, and free up time of lecturers for productive small group discussions. How are we to capture these changes in any set of output, quality, or price measures?

The issue of output measurement is confounded by the many levels at which activity can be assessed. A CAT scanner, which takes thousands of pictures, dramatically reduces the cost per X-ray. But it greatly increases the cost per patient day, per hospital stay, or per treatment.

Quality problems are especially difficult to handle. The resolutions of the first CAT scanners were poorer than conventional X-rays, but now they are much better; specialized machines for mammography and other purposes have been developed, and there is a body of experience that makes the information far more available. The Consumer Price Index has improved its treatment of health care (Layug, 1978), but numerous problems remain.

In a rapidly changing environment new products are constantly being introduced. Yet, present methods are almost entirely incapable of taking their benefits into account. Changes in product prices are counted after the products have established a place in the market, but the often dramatic effective decline in the price of accomplishing a task made possible by the new product's use is ignored. In fact, the GNP accounts show no change in the price of computers despite persistent declines in the cost of computing from 20 to 30 percent per year. Similar measurement issues arise with shifts away from problems. If Post Office inefficiencies in package delivery cause patrons to shift to Express Mail or to private delivery services, the higher cost of the new service is not reflected as a price rise or productivity decline.

The measurement of outcomes is especially intractable. There is very little usable information on the contribution of services to health, learning, or utility. Important strides in health have been made in the last ten years by attention to side effects of drugs and drug combinations. Now gains are being made by recognizing the effects of diet on drug effectiveness. Healthy outcomes from developments such as these are not included in the output of the health care industry even when the changes in health status are clearly the result of resources devoted to and actions taken by that industry.

Complexities also arise in allowing for the role of the consumer in the production process. The shift to self-service, evident in the growth of department stores and laundromats, continues with the introduction of fast-food restaurants, teller machines, and new technologies for home learning, health testing, shopping, and entertainment. The consumer's time is an important input in the production of many services, and the quality, outcomes, and efficiency of time use may be influenced by the consumer's education, initiative, and time behavior and the way these features are matched with characteristics of the production process (Leveson, 1983).

The structure of industry also creates numerous problems for measurement. We know too little about franchises and other interfirm arrangements. The present distinction between production and supervisory workers in service industries in Bureau of Labor Statistics data has little meaning in small organizations or in professional services (teachers, nurses, and doctors are production workers). Information on the self-employed continues to be spotty because of incentives for nonreporting and misreporting. Flexible compensation and work arrangements are also poorly measured and understood.

## Accelerating productivity growth in services

Two pieces of aggregate data support the conclusion that service productivity growth has accelerated. Between 1976 and 1981 the price deflators for trade and miscellaneous services rose less rapidly than prices in the economy as a whole. This implies that output per unit of total factor input – that is, man-hours adjusted for use of capital, and so forth – grew more rapidly than in goods production. The improved price performance in services relative to the entire economy is in marked contrast to the experience for the postwar period as a whole, and to the impression given by data on output per full-time equivalent employee. The recent better price performance of some services reflects many things, including productivity declines in mining and construction associated with increased regulation, greater productivity losses in capital-intensive industries with increased energy prices, and rising costs of transportation with railroad deregulation. There are other indications of accelerating service productivity growth that suggest there has been improved relative performance in service industries.

Increases in productivity tend to expand demand for product and lead to higher wages in the short and intermediate run. Figure 3.4 shows that wage rates of private production workers in finance and insurance and in general services soared in 1980 and 1981, passing the growth rates of the total private economy.

Services were always thought of as being less capable of achieving rapid productivity gains because they were not as amenable to mechanization and mass production. I believe that with a growing share of resources devoted to services, incentives to find ways of improving efficiency increased as well. As some progress was made, the image of services as being incapable of progress weakened. Modern management techniques and new technologies began to be applied more widely to service production. Standardization and the spread of technology were encouraged by new organizational forms such as the growth of franchises, and techniques began to adapt rapidly to service applications. Then the nature of the techniques themselves changed so that not only did technological advance accelerate, but it grew particularly rapidly in forms such as distributed computing that have special immediate benefits for service industries.

New organizational forms have begun to develop that will facilitate the use and spread of new technologies and product innovations, such as networking in financial and other services (Leveson et al., 1982). The study of organizational arrangements, tied in with case studies of product and process innovations, is a particularly promising avenue for insights about the new environment of rapid change.

*Source: U.S. Department of Labor, Bureau of Labor Statistics, Handbook of Labor Statistics, December 1980, table 90, idem, Monthly Labor Review, March 1981, p. 96; and ibid., September 1982, p. 65.*

Figure 3.4. Annual percent change in average hourly earnings of production or nonsupervisory workers in finance and nondurable goods manufacturing, 1966–1981

## Concluding comment

At a time of potentially enormous growth of productivity in services we must carefully consider the policies that the nation chooses to foster economic growth. Infatuation with technology is beginning to produce a balance between ideas about aid to distressed sectors and ways of encouraging new industries as a route to higher employment and standards of

102     **Irving Leveson**

living. Yet both traditional industry and high-tech industrial strategies tend to ignore the growing opportunities for the entire economy to benefit from developments in service industries. It would be unfortunate if those opportunities were curtailed by increases in tax rates, interest rates, and government intervention in economic processes that ignored the service revolution.

## References

Fuchs, Victor R. (1968), *The Service Economy*, National Bureau of Economic Research, N.Y.
  (1972), "The Contribution of Health Services to the American Economy," in *Essays in the Economics of Health and Medical Care*, Victor R. Fuchs, ed., pp. 3–38, National Bureau of Economic Research, N.Y.
  (March, 1982), *Economic Growth and the Rise of Service Employment*, National Bureau of Economic Research, Reprint #257, N.Y.
Gottman, Jean (1959), *Megalopolis*, Twentieth Century Fund, N.Y.
Kahn, Herman (1979), *World Economic Development*, Westview Press, Boulder, Colorado.
Kendricks, John W. (1973), *Postwar Productivity Trends in the United States, 1948–1969*, Columbia University Press, N.Y.
Layug, John (August 31, 1978), "An Examination of the Revised and Unusual Consumer Price Indexes after Six Months," presented at annual meeting of the Industrial Relations Research Association.
Leveson, Irving, with contributions by Jane Newitt (April 1983), *Financial Service Innovation and the American Consumer*, Hudson Strategy Group, Croton-on-Hudson, N.Y., through the Corporate Communications Department of American Express Company.
Leveson, Irving, et al. (February 1982), *The Future of the Financial Services Industry*, Hudson Institute, Croton-on-Hudson, N.Y.
Molitor, Graham (1979), "Sweden, A Bellwether of Future Policy Trends," in *Critical Food Issues of the Eighties*, Marylin Chou and David P. Harmon, eds., pp. 66–90, Pergamon Press, N.Y.

# Comment: Services in the
# U.S. economy

DUNCAN MANN

Irving Leveson's paper on services in the U.S. economy sheds light on several aspects of the service sector. Common misperceptions about the role of services in a modern economy are clarified. A simple, yet powerful model of the growth in demand for services in the U.S. economy is presented. Many problems associated with measuring performance in the service sector are highlighted with specific examples.

In several sections of his paper, Leveson mentions the role of government in the service sector. An important area of government involvement in the service sector is regulation. Government regulatory involvement in markets for services affects conditions of supply in these markets. In particular, the structure of many service industries has been importantly influenced, if not determined by regulatory intervention. This has implications for the performance of these service industries and may be important to understanding the effects of deregulation on service industries.

The list of U.S. industries that either currently are, or historically have been, regulated include a disproportionate number of service industries. Airline transportation, banking, and telecommunications are examples of service industries that have been heavily regulated and are now in various stages of deregulation. Ground transportation, parts of the health care sector, and communications (radio, television) are other service industries that are also regulated. An interesting question is, why? An important area for research concerns the evidence and prospects for improved performance in these industries under continued regulation or deregulation.

The traditional economic justification for regulation is technological in nature. It may be more efficient to regulate entry and price in an industry characterized by natural monopoly than to allow additional entry and competition or unconstrained monopoly behavior. More generally, other types of market failure, such as externalities and information failures, may lead to resource allocations that can be improved upon, to some degree, by regulation. It appears that technological change and demand growth are eliminating many of the natural monopolies of the past. The remaining economic arguments for regulation of service industries pertain primarily to informational problems.

All of the industries noted earlier have experienced the close regulation of entry into the market. Airlines, telecommunications, ground transportation, health care, and communications have all had entry directly restricted by regulatory agencies. Changes in the structure of service industries such as airlines, banking, telecommunications, and health care are attributable to the government's relaxation of entry regulation. Competitive pressure itself, can sometimes circumvent regulations restricting entry. New sports leagues have sprung up when government-sanctioned leagues have not allowed additional teams to enter. The outlook for improved performance and consumer welfare in these markets due to increased competition is good. The prospects for improved economic performance in other service markets via allowing entry should be studied carefully.

Regulation of many services based on information problems also should be examined. The market mechanism is becoming more and more sophisticated. Franchises can be important in establishing a reputation for quality in an otherwise transient and uncertain environment. Advertising can be a source of valuable information. Recent experience in the optometry market is a leading example of this benefit. Quantity rationing by firms can be a supplier device to deal with poor information about customers. Loan limitations by banks is an example. Guarantees and warranties may provide valuable information to consumers in addition to their assurance role.

Innovations in the delivery of services are both solving some regulatory problems and creating new issues. The entertainment and information industries are two examples where new service technologies pose problems. The video and copy revolution is upon us, and information and entertainment producers are faced with replication industries that could siphon off the producers' benefits. On the other hand, health maintenance organizations hold some promise for improving the extent of competition in the medical field as a medical service delivery option.

In summary, there are several service markets where the prospects for increased competition and improved performance are good. With changing technology and delivery, other service industries that are now regulated may also benefit from deregulation and competition. Policy analysis and legislators must examine the service economy for such opportunities for reform.

# Part I: Role of services in world economies

Mr. Baumol began the discussion and complimented the presentation by Mr. Summers as "one of the most illuminating papers I have heard in years." Taking off from the Sherlock Holmes quotes of Mr. Summers, Mr. Baumol paraphrased a line of Leonard Silk defining "an economist as someone who takes something that works very well in practice and worries whether it works in theory." Mr. Baumol, however, took the reverse approach and proceeded to offer a theory to explain the riddle of the data supplied by Mr. Summers.

The theory relied on the premise that there are certain classes of services that inherently resist productivity improvement. He used an example to illustrate his ideas. Consider an economy that consists of two perfectly competitive sectors, string quartet concerts and pinball machines. The change in string quartet productivity over time is assumed to be zero. (In reality productivity may well be positive, because of transportation, communication, and other advances.) The string quartet that Mozart wrote for a half-hour performance in 1780 still takes two person-hours of labor today. Pinball productivity, on the other hand, is assumed to double every forty years. If we look at the changes in economic variables over a forty-year period three facts will stand out. First, the relative price of string quartets must precisely double. Second, assuming that price and income effects offset each other (noting that real income must be going up due to the increase in pinball productivity), demand for actual output will be in the same proportion. Therefore, the proportion of dollars spent on string quartets will double in relation to dollars spent on pinball. Lastly, the share of the labor force in string quartet production must double relative to the share of the labor force in pinball production.

Mr. Baumol then tied these theoretical observations back to the data of Mr. Summers. Analysis of this data showed a shift to services in terms of labor and expenditures, yet each sector's share of real output was constant. These are the same shifts identified by theory in Mr. Baumol's example. The theory and data go hand in hand; there was a shift toward services in two senses and no shift to services in another sense. Mr. Baumol

105

emphasized that it is important to recognize the clear differences in these three changes as well as their inherent compatibility with each other.

Mr. Leveson was concerned with the impact of changes in quality on the theory proposed by Mr. Baumol. Overadjustment may result when quality varies with income, as in international price comparisons. He referenced Mr. Baumol's own 1967 paper in the *American Economic Review.* "Macroeconomics of Unbalanced Growth," in questioning how to reconcile this theory with the modernization of the service industries. He proposed that the large amount of resources tied up in service industries create an induced innovation effect. Firms have an incentive to economize on these resources and apply new technology and management technologies to service provision. This modification of the theory is more complex but also more hopeful.

Mr. Summers added that the current paper was an outgrowth of earlier work on the International Comparison Project. The earlier paper is more complete and examines the determinants of changes in employment patterns. The conclusion was that the primary determinants are differential productivity improvements and differences in income elasticities for the various final products. The current paper is only concerned with the latter factor.

Ms. Norwood asked a clarifying question concerning exactly what services were included in the analysis done by Professor Summers. Mr. Summers responded that his data pertained to final product services. These included consumption services such as recreation or medical services, capital formation services, and government services but did not include intermediate product services. The usual national income accounts were manipulated to transfer government capital formation to investment. The rest of the government account then was basically services provided to people. His working definition of a service was essentially a commodity that is consumed and produced simultaneously.

Following an answer by Mr. Summers, Ms. Norwood pointed out that intermediate product services are an important missing piece of the picture. They need to be studied. Mr. Summers agreed.

Mr. Gruenstein made two points. First, highlighting Ms. Norwood's point, growth in intermediate product services has been one of the fastest expanding subsectors in services. Second, an issue touched upon by Mr. Behrman in his discussion needed elaboration. The choice between internalization of services within an organization and the external specialization of services in other firms must be examined. The secular increase in services relies on what can be observed with existing external specialization. This, however, misses a crucial dimension, the decision of firms regarding internalization or externalization of services. He noted that there is no necessary implication that externalization is the preferred choice and examples could be found representing movement in both directions of service delivery. Mr. Behrman agreed the issue was an important one. Mr. Leveson suggested that one approach would be to look for systematic patterns of organization across various types of services and firms.

Mr. Kravis raised several points pertinent to Mr. Saxonhouse's paper. U.S. firms are free to license technology in other countries and maximize their own profit. In competing among themselves it is doubtful that these firms are also maximizing the national return on technology. On the other hand, Mr. Kravis asserted, Japan has a more cohesive policy with central control over decisions concerning patent licensing, investment, and the like. Whereas U.S. foreign investments often compete with U.S. exports, Japan has made investments abroad that supplement its domestic economy. This has recently been changed after U.S. insistence on domestic assembly. In Japan the foreign licensure of technological developments that are difficult to copy has effectively been restricted, whereas those likely to be imitated soon are more freely licensed. Mr. Kravis believed this sort of policy program would not be feasible for the United States. However, these policy differences could help explain some of the observations in the balance of payments tables.

Mr. Saxonhouse thought Mr. Kravis's conclusions regarding the differences in government policy toward technology and foreign investment were somewhat overstated. He was not aware of any grand conception of industrial strategy that dealt with the fine detail of what is licensed abroad. Although some of this may have occurred in the past, recently there has been extensive Japanese overseas investment and licensing activity. He added that many important flows of technology, such as information, are difficult to stop. As an example, he pointed to nineteenth century England, which tried, unsuccessfully, to stop the transfer of industrial technology by prohibiting the export of machinery and the emigration of trained mechanics.

Mr. Campbell closed the discussion by recalling the empirical and theoretical observations made by Mr. Summers and Mr. Baumol. The increase in the proportion of the labor force in the service sector, the increase in the proportion of GNP accounted for by the service sector, and the lack of change in the service sector's share of real output are important changes to ponder, both in isolation and in their interrelationships.

# Service productivity, trade, and market structure

# CHAPTER 4

# Measurement of output and productivity in the service sector

## JOHN W. KENDRICK

The measurement of productivity in service industries is the focus of this paper, with particular reference to the problems of measuring output. In principle, the measurement of inputs poses much the same problems in all industries, but I shall devote some space to this subject as well in order to summarize some of the major issues and to point up several measurement problems peculiar to the service sector. Productivity in the service sector is an increasingly important issue for policymakers and economists. The productivity of labor in services is a key to economic growth as the economy becomes more service intensive. This trend toward services may also influence the effectiveness of macroeconomic policy directed at shifting the aggregate supply curve. Finally, labor income and wages in the service sector tend to follow labor productivity. This influences the welfare of a majority of U.S. workers.

### Productivity concepts and measures

In this section I first explain the basics of the productivity concept for the benefit of those who may not be familiar with it. A little simple algebra is used to help clarify the definitions. Then I describe productivity trends in the U.S. business economy since 1948, looking separately at the service sector, by major industry group, as distinguished from the tangible goods producing sector.

#### The basics of productivity accounting

Productivity is the relationship of output to associated inputs, in "real" physical volume terms, usually expressed in index numbers of ratios for successive time periods. The problems of converting current dollar estimates of outputs (production values) and of inputs (costs) to real, constant dollar estimates are treated in subsequent sections. Here the discussion relates to real values representing physical volumes of outputs and inputs, in which current dollar unit values are used only as "weights" to indicate the relative importance of each component for purposes of combining into aggregates.

111

The broadest measure may be called *total productivity* (*TP*) or the ratio of total output (*TO*) to total inputs (*TI*) of the factors of production (*F*), consisting of labor (*L*) and capital (*K*) including natural resources as well as structures, equipment and inventories; and "intermediate products" (*M*) consisting of materials, components, supplies, energy, and services purchased from other producers. Thus

$$TP = \frac{TO}{TI} = \frac{TO}{L + K + M}$$

Changes in total productivity reflect the net saving of inputs (real costs) per unit of output achieved over time as a result primarily of innovations in the technology and organization of production.

The ratios of total output to any one set of inputs, such as the familiar "output per labor hour" measure, are called *partial productivity* ratios. Changes in the partial ratios reflect factor substitutions, such as increases in capital goods per unit of labor, as well as changes in productive efficiency generally. Index numbers of *TP* can be viewed as a weighted average of index numbers of the several partial productivity ratios, the weights for each ($w_l$, $w_k$, and $w_m$) representing the shares of each in the base-period value of total output. Thus:

$$TP = \frac{TO}{TI} = w_l \frac{TO}{L} + w_k \frac{TO}{K} + w_m \frac{TO}{M}$$

Total productivity estimates are particularly useful at the company or plant level. Management is interested in saving on all cost elements, and the *TP* and associated partial productivity ratios enable direct analysis of the savings achieved in use of energy and other purchased goods and services as well as of factor inputs per unit of output.

In the entire economy and in the predominant business sector, however, interindustry sales and purchases of intermediate products cancel out, and gross national or business product consists only of *final* products, the value of which is equal to gross factor costs, labor and property inclusive of capital consumption allowances.[1] In other words, GNP is the value of total output less the costs of intermediate products. The latter are excluded to avoid double counting since their costs are already included in the value of final products. So, in order to measure total factor productivity (*TFP*) real gross product originating (GPO) in the nation, business sector, or industry must be related to the factor inputs (*FI*), labor and capital. Thus,

$$TFP = \frac{TO - M}{L + K} = \frac{GPO}{L + K} = \frac{GPO}{FI}$$

The advantage of dealing with *TFP* estimates for industries and sectors is that *TFP* for the national economy or the business sector is a weighted average of *TFP* in each of component industries, the weights being the base-period proportions that each industry's GPO is of total gross product.[2] As with *TP*, *TFP* is a weighted average of each of the partial productivity ratios:

$$TFP = \frac{GPO}{TI} = w_l \frac{GPO}{L} + w_k \frac{GPO}{K}$$

Although intermediate product inputs do not appear explicitly, savings of these costs per unit of final product increase *TFP* since *M* decreases and GPO rises as percentages of *TO* under those circumstances. Thus, changes in *TFP* reflect changes in productive efficiency as a result of net savings in real factor costs per unit of final products. Changes in each partial factor productivity ratio GPO/*L* and GPO/*K* reflect factor substitutions as well. From an economic welfare viewpoint, changes in *TFP* are more meaningful than changes in *TP* since the former reflect changes of efficiency in producing the final goods and services that satisfy present and future wants. In the description of U.S. productivity trends that follows I use estimates of real gross product, *TFP* and the component partial factor productivity ratios since I am interested in comparing the services and goods sectors, and both with the business economy as a whole.

## Measuring output, or real product

Folklore has it that it is very difficult, if not impossible, to measure service outputs. In principle, they are no more difficult to measure than tangible goods. Like tangibles, services can be classified by type, and the number of times services of each type are rendered can be counted – haircuts, tooth extractions, appendectomies, wills executed, and so forth. The numbers in each category then can be weighted by the average price or unit cost in a base period for aggregation purposes. Or, the units can be priced over time and index numbers prepared that can be used to deflate service values.

Even if types of services are specified narrowly, it is probable that there is somewhat more variation in quality of units than is true of standardized goods. But over large numbers of service units of a given type, average quality should not vary much over time. If quality changes due to technological or other factors, there is the same problem of adjusting units to provide continuity that is present for commodities. A minimal adjustment followed by the Bureau of Labor Statistics is to adjust quantity and price for the difference in unit cost of the new relative to the old model output. There are also the problems of custom services, nonmarket services, and new offerings, but all of these problems are present in the case of tangible goods as well, and the solutions or conventions suggested to handle them can be applied to both categories.[3]

In theory it is immaterial whether values are deflated by appropriate price indexes or physical units are weighted by prices if value, price, and quantity data are equally available and reliable. As a practical matter, value data are available as part of the economic accounts, and there are many more price series available for deflation than there are quantity series for extrapolating base-period values – particularly in the service industries. Consequently, the Bureau of Economic Analysis (BEA) generally relies on price-deflation to obtain real product estimates, whether for final expenditures or for gross product originating (GPO) by industry. There is the further advantage to price deflation when there is incomplete coverage of quantities and prices for a category. It is more probable that prices of uncovered items move with those that are covered than would be the case with quantities of various items. Actually, price data collection can use sample designs based on research determining which items are representative of product families. Further, price deflation has the advantage that deflated values reflect shifts among product qualities assuming that relative prices of differing quality products of the same type reflect different degrees of consumer satisfaction and of resource inputs. This could not be accomplished using physical quantity data unless it were available by detailed quality classes of goods or services.

It is generally agreed that for purposes of production and productivity analysis, it is better to weight or deflate by unit costs rather than prices, which also reflect indirect business taxes less subsidies. Results of the alternative procedures do not usually differ much. In any case, when value and price data both reflect market prices and price deflation is used, the resulting real product series can be used to extrapolate real product at factor cost. This is desirable when real GPO of several industries is being combined to estimate total factor productivity for a broader sector. The weighting system will be discussed a bit further in the section on inputs. Suffice it to say here that the weighting schemes for outputs and for inputs should be consistent. It is my own view that weights should be changed at least occasionally to reflect changes in the structure of production and associated changes in relative prices.

As background for more specific commentary on service output measurement, I shall summarize the general methods used by BEA to estimate real GPO in the service industries. Almost 80 percent of total GPO in the private service sector is estimated using price deflators or output volume indicators. The remainder is estimated essentially through extrapolating base-period GPO by components by labor input indicators. Including general government and government enterprises, the ratio drops to about 65 percent, since GPO in government, except for a major part of federal government enterprises, is obtained by use of labor extrapolators.

When BEA judged that the current dollar GPO estimates were better than the total revenue estimates, the price deflators for revenues were applied directly to the gross product numbers. Generally the price deflators implicitly incorporated changing quantity weights, since revenue components were deflated separately and the real aggregate divided into the current dollar aggregate and the ratio multiplied by 100.0.[4]

This procedure is based on the assumption that prices of intermediate purchases have the same movements as output prices, or that the intermediate expenses are so small that it makes little difference if the movements of the two sets of prices are not parallel. This may be true, but the GPO deflator would be more accurate if BEA adjusted it for input prices. A true implicit price deflator for GPO obtained by the double-deflation method is a weighted difference between the output and intermediate input price indexes. Using base-year input–output tables, the composition and weights for input prices, including energy, could be determined, applied to appropriate input price indexes, and the present deflators based on output prices adjusted accordingly.

When it was judged that total sales revenue estimates were better than those for GPO, base-period GPO was extrapolated by deflated revenues or by physical volume indicators. The revenues were generally deflated by components, and component physical volume indicators were aggregated by appropriate base-period value weights. This procedure involves the assumption that movements of real intermediate inputs and of outputs are parallel in the several industries, or that the intermediate costs are so minor that real GPO is little affected by divergences. These assumptions could be tested by reference to input–output tables in constant prices for a succession of years. If the technical coefficients for total intermediate inputs had changed significantly, corresponding adjustments to the real gross output estimates should be made in converting them into real GPO estimates. Unfortunately, the adjustments could only be done for past periods given the present data base, and current estimates would be based on the most recent technical coefficients unless there were good reason to extrapolate past trends as a basis for interim adjustments.

In the private industries and general government, in which base-period GPO was extrapolated by employment, hours, or deflated labor compensation, the assumption is that there was no change in labor productivity. Actually, the labor input indicators were applied to various categories of labor and weighted, in effect, by base-period average compensation. Thus, shifts among categories with different rates of compensation are reflected in the aggregate measures. Generally the shifts have been toward higher-pay classifications, reflecting increases in average education and training of workers. Once real capital estimates are available for two-digit industries from BEA in a year or so, capital as well as labor input should be used in the extrapolators. If returns on capital are not included in GPO, as in the case of households, private nonprofit institutions, and general governments, imputations should be added. Since real capital per worker has increased in almost all industries and sectors, real GPO would rise by more if total factor input were used as an extrapolator rather than labor input alone.

Clearly, the important thing is to try to develop true output measures for uncovered industries. Some have now been constructed by others for some of the BEA industries for which labor extrapolators are still used. Notably, the Bureau of Labor Statistics (BLS) has just completed output and productivity estimates for commercial banking.[5] The "liquidity" approach to banking output formerly used by BEA was abandoned since it implied declining productivity. The BLS has implemented the alternative transactions approach, outlined by John A. Gorman some years ago.[6]

Given the progress made by BLS in recent years in estimating output per civilian employee-year in federal general government, I also think BEA should now seriously consider using the BLS measure as a basis for imputing productivity changes to all federal civilian employees as a basis for obtaining output measures for that sector.[7] BLS now has more than four thousand output measures representing the work of around two-thirds of all federal civilian government employees, classified by twenty-eight functions. For other sectors and major industry groups, background papers on the problems and possibilities of developing useful measures for output, input, and productivity are needed. Task forces could then be assembled with members from the industries concerned, academia, and government to try to clarify the conceptual issues, and outline the further practical steps required to produce productivity estimates and analyses. Service industries for which estimates are now made should not be excluded from purview if it were felt that the present output measures have serious shortcomings. This is probably true of insurance, and the issue of changes in service quality in retail trade needs further investigation, for example.[8]

### Measuring inputs of factor services

Most of the problems involved in measuring real factor costs or inputs relate to the entire economy, and these will be discussed briefly since they have been treated elsewhere.[9] There are a few special problems in the service sector, however.

Productivity specialists generally agree that labor input should be measured in terms of hours worked by all persons engaged in production – proprietors, self-employed, and unpaid family workers, as well as employees at all levels. Some analysts, such as Dale Jorgenson, weight labor hours by average hourly compensation by industry, occupation, and other significant classifications, including levels of education and experience, if data permit.[10] By this procedure relative shifts of labor to higher paid categories represent an increase in labor input. Other analysts, including BLS, prefer to use unweighted labor hours, in which case the shifts are an element in productivity change. The important thing is that shift effects are measured, whether they are called input changes or part of the explanation of productivity growth.

Statistically, a major problem has been that data on average hours worked by nonproduction and supervisory workers have not been directly available. Further, official measures of employee hours relate to hours paid for rather than hours spent at the work place, although it is well known that hours paid for but not worked have risen substantially since World War II. Other problems include unpaid household work and the possibility that there is a considerable amount of remunerated time of part-time workers in sales, education, or instruction, repair, and other kinds of personal services that are not picked up in the employment and hours data. Yet the value of the resulting services may be included in the GPO and other output estimates. This entire area, which merges with some of the issues posed by the underground economy, requires much more research.

With regard to fixed capital, I agree with those who would measure its services by applying a base-period rate of return, gross of depreciation allowances, to real stocks gross of depreciation reserves, but net of retirements. Since the real stocks are not adjusted for changes in rates of utilization of capacity, those changes are part of the explanation of short-term cyclical changes in productivity. Since output-producing capacity (as distinct from net income-producing capacity) may decline somewhat as plant and equipment age, changes in the average age of fixed capital goods may also have some productivity effect.

In industries in which the actual rate of return on total capital deviates significantly for extended periods from the opportunity cost of capital, consideration should be given to using the latter in the weighting scheme.

Fortunately, BEA hopes to complete its estimates of real gross and net capital stocks by two-digit industries within the coming year. For many of the service industries, great reliance has been placed on data from the plant and equipment survey as input into the perpetual inventory calculations. This underlines the need to strengthen that survey, by broadening the sample for the service sector and by improving the response rate.

*Productivity trends since 1948*

The rates of change in output, inputs, and productivity ratios shown in Table 4.1 are calculated from estimates currently prepared by Elliot Grossman of Pace University for the American Productivity Center in Houston. They represent an extension of the estimates developed by Grossman and myself. [11] The sources and methods are described in that volume, and represent an updating of those I had developed for the National Bureau of Economic Research beginning in the mid-1950s. [12] The chief differences from my earlier estimates are (1) for output, we are now using the BEA annual estimates of real GPO and (2) the real capital stock estimates on which the capital input estimates are based are net of retirements but gross of depreciation, and are weighted by base-period rates of return gross of depreciation. This is to provide symmetry with the labor estimates, which are also gross of depreciation on human capital, and with the real gross product numbers.

It is interesting to first review what the estimates show with respect to trends since 1948 by subperiod. Even though the estimates are confined to the business economy, the service sector output and productivity growth numbers are probably biased downward, particularly in the finance and private services industry groups. Over the 33-year period from 1948 to 1981 total factor productivity in the service sector increased at an average annual rate of 1.3 percent compared with 2.2 percent in goods production, averaging 1.8 percent in the business economy as a whole. As shown in Table 4.1, productivity growth decelerated in both sectors after 1966, but by somewhat less in services through the subperiod from 1973 to 1979 as productivity increases in the real estate industry remained strong. In the final subperiod from 1979 to 1981, during which there was little net gain in real product due to the aborted recovery between 1980 and 1981, total factor productivity in services declined 0.4 percent compared with 0.2 percent in goods.

The difference between the sectors in growth of output per labor hour also averaged almost one percentage point a year from 1948 to 1981, since the growth of the capital/labor ratio also diverged by about 1 percent a year, on the average. But after 1973 the growth of capital per unit of labor decelerated more in services than in goods production, so labor productivity growth also decelerated more in services relative to the total factor productivity measure. But even in services labor productivity growth was a modest plus from 1979 to 1981.

Although productivity grew less in services than in goods production, both labor and total inputs grew by proportionately more in services. As a consequence, real product grew by an average 3.6 percent a year between

Table 4.1. *Output, inputs, and productivity ratios; average annual percentage rates of change, 1948–81 by subperiod; U.S. business economy by major sector and industry*

**Real gross product**

|  | 1948–81 | 1948–66 | 1966–73 | 1973–79 | 1979–81 |
|---|---|---|---|---|---|
| Business economy | 3.3 | 3.7 | 3.6 | 2.7 | 0.6 |
| Goods production | 2.8 | 3.5 | 3.0 | 1.7 | −0.9 |
| Services production | 3.6 | 3.7 | 4.1 | 3.4 | 1.7 |
| Trade | 3.6 | 3.9 | 4.4 | 2.7 | −0.0 |
| Finance/Insurance | 4.0 | 4.2 | 4.5 | 3.4 | 2.8 |
| Real estate | 2.9 | 3.3 | 2.7 | 3.1 | 0.2 |
| Services | 3.7 | 3.5 | 3.5 | 3.9 | 4.7 |

**Total factor input**

|  | 1948–81 | 1948–66 | 1966–73 | 1973–79 | 1979–81 |
|---|---|---|---|---|---|
| Business economy | 1.5 | 1.1 | 1.9 | 2.3 | 1.0 |
| Goods production | 0.6 | 0.5 | 0.7 | 1.3 | −0.7 |
| Services production | 2.2 | 1.8 | 2.9 | 2.9 | 2.1 |
| Trade | 1.6 | 1.4 | 1.9 | 2.1 | 0.6 |
| Finance/Insurance | 3.6 | 3.0 | 4.3 | 4.3 | 4.2 |
| Real estate | 1.8 | 1.5 | 2.7 | 1.9 | 1.3 |
| Services | 3.4 | 3.1 | 3.8 | 3.8 | 3.6 |

**Labor input**

|  | 1948–81 | 1948–66 | 1966–73 | 1973–79 | 1979–81 |
|---|---|---|---|---|---|
| Business economy | 0.9 | 0.5 | 1.3 | 1.9 | 0.1 |
| Goods production | −0.0 | −0.2 | 0.2 | 0.8 | −1.8 |
| Services production | 1.7 | 1.2 | 2.2 | 2.7 | 1.4 |
| Trade | 1.2 | 1.0 | 1.4 | 1.9 | 0.1 |
| Finance/Insurance | 3.1 | 2.7 | 3.2 | 3.6 | 3.0 |
| Real estate | 2.6 | 1.7 | 3.4 | 4.6 | 1.1 |
| Services | 3.0 | 2.5 | 3.3 | 3.9 | 3.9 |

**Capital/Labor ratio**

|  | 1948–81 | 1948–66 | 1966–73 | 1973–79 | 1979–81 |
|---|---|---|---|---|---|
| Business economy | 2.2 | 2.4 | 2.4 | 1.3 | 2.9 |
| Goods production | 2.5 | 2.7 | 2.1 | 2.0 | 4.2 |
| Services production | 1.7 | 1.9 | 2.2 | 0.6 | 1.9 |
| Trade | 3.6 | 4.2 | 3.9 | 1.6 | 3.5 |
| Finance/Insurance | 4.2 | 2.9 | 6.2 | 5.1 | 6.5 |
| Real estate | −0.9 | −0.3 | −0.7 | −2.9 | 0.1 |
| Services | 1.3 | 2.1 | 1.4 | −0.5 | −0.8 |

Table 4.1 (cont.)

| | Output/Labor ratio | | | | | Total factor productivity | | | | |
|---|---|---|---|---|---|---|---|---|---|---|
| | 1948–81 | 1948–66 | 1966–73 | 1973–79 | 1979–81 | 1948–81 | 1948–66 | 1966–73 | 1973–79 | 1979–81 |
| Business economy | 2.4 | 3.2 | 2.3 | 0.8 | 0.5 | 1.8 | 2.6 | 1.7 | 0.4 | −0.4 |
| Goods production | 2.8 | 3.7 | 2.8 | 0.9 | 1.0 | 2.2 | 3.0 | 2.3 | 0.4 | −0.2 |
| Services production | 1.9 | 2.4 | 1.9 | 0.7 | 0.3 | 1.3 | 1.9 | 1.1 | 0.5 | −0.4 |
| Trade | 2.3 | 2.9 | 2.9 | 0.8 | −0.1 | 1.9 | 2.5 | 2.4 | 0.6 | −0.7 |
| Finance/Insurance | 0.9 | 1.4 | 1.0 | −0.1 | −0.2 | 0.4 | 1.1 | 0.3 | −0.9 | −0.3 |
| Real estate | 0.3 | 1.5 | −0.7 | −1.4 | −0.9 | 1.1 | 1.8 | 0.0 | 1.2 | −1.0 |
| Services | 0.6 | 0.9 | 0.2 | 0.0 | 0.8 | 0.2 | 0.4 | −0.3 | 0.1 | 1.0 |

Source: American Productivity Center, Houston.

120

1948 and 1981 in the service sector compared with 2.8 percent in goods and 3.3 percent in the business economy as a whole. The rate of growth in the goods sector began to slow after 1966, but in services deceleration first began after 1973, with a major slowing only after 1979. Even in the period from 1979 to 1981, however, real gross product continued to increase at a 1.7 percent average annual rate compared with a decline of almost 1 percent in goods production. Real GPO of private services even accelerated, and finance/insurance also grew substantially over the 2-year subperiod. It was real estate and trade that showed little or no growth reflecting the anemic gains in the business economy as a whole.

### The productivity outlook

What is the outlook for productivity in the business economy generally, and the service sector in particular? Elsewhere, I have argued that the slowdown of productivity growth in the U.S. business economy after 1966, and especially after 1973, was temporary, associated with the down phase of a long wave in rates of growth, and that we can look forward to a rebound during the 1980s. [13] The reacceleration cannot be expected to bring productivity gains back to the rates experienced in the golden age of U.S. economic growth in the first two decades following World War II, which were marked by special factors, such as the accumulation of innovational and investment opportunities carried over from depression and war. But it is likely that the average rate of total factor productivity growth could return to around 2 percent a year, and labor productivity to near 2.5 percent. The figure for goods production would be a bit higher, and that for services a bit lower.

The chief depressing forces had been a slowdown in the growth of real capital stocks after 1973, and in capital per worker since 1966; a slowing in the rate of cost-reducing technological innovations since 1966; unfavorable changes in the age–sex mix of the labor force after 1966; deteriorating quality of natural resources; less favorable impacts of interindustry labor shifts; reduced opportunities for economies of scale and lower average rates of utilization of capacity after 1973; possibly lesser labor efficiency as such; and negative effects of increased government regulations beginning around 1970 that increased real costs and inputs but not outputs as measured.

In the decade ahead, some of the negative forces will have played out or reversed. Further, the net effect of tax legislation and regulatory reforms of the last several years should be to stimulate investment and technological progress, once the effects of the economic contraction between 1981 and 1982 have lifted. This should mean stronger growth with attendant increases in scale economies, and increased rates of utilization of capacity that will reinforce the productivity rebound. In making my projections for the 1980s I quantified the expected contributions of the various causal forces to the growth of productivity using a Denison-type growth accounting model.[14]

The acceleration of productivity growth rates in services will be somewhat less than in goods production since the slowdown had been less in services that were less vulnerable to a number of the depressing forces. I would expect total factor productivity growth in services to somewhat exceed 1 percent a year on the average during the next decade, and for growth of output per labor hour to approach 2 percent. This assumes use in the future of the same real GPO estimates that are used at present with the same downward biases discussed earlier.

## Notes

1. The item "indirect business taxes less subsidies," added to gross factor costs to reconcile with the market valuation of gross product, may be ignored for productivity analysis. It is not matched by a corresponding input, and the factor costs of government services are already included in gross national income.
2. The business economy *TFP* estimates can be obtained from the industry *TP* estimates only if the weights sum to more than one, equaling the ratio of value of production to value-added (GPO) for each industry. There is a systematic divergence of industry *TP* from *TFP* measures in rates of growth on the down side, the divergence being larger the smaller the ratio of GPO to the value of gross production.
3. See John W. Kendrick, *Economic Accounts and Their Uses* (New York: McGraw-Hill Book Co., 1972), Chapter 6.
4. The weights are, of course, the real dollar volumes of the revenue components classified by service categories. A summary of BEA methodology used for estimating real GPO in the service industries will be supplied until such time as BEA publishes its planned volume on sources and methods underlying the national income and product accounts. Please address requests to Professor John W. Kendrick, Department of Economics, The George Washington University, Washington, D.C. 20052.
5. Jerome A. Mark, "Measuring Productivity in Service Industries," *Monthly Labor Review*, June 1982, pp. 3–8.
6. John A. Gorman, "Alternative Measures of the Real Output and Productivity of Commercial Banks," in *Production and Productivity in the Service Industries*, Victor Fuchs, Ed., in *Studies in Income and Wealth*, Vol. 34 (New York: National Bureau of Economic Research, 1969), pp. 155–88; and the "Discussion" by Donald R. Hodgeman, pp. 189–98.
7. See Allen D. Searle and Charles A. Waite, "Current Efforts to Measure Productivity in the Public Sector: How Adequate for the National Accounts?" in *New Developments in Productivity Measurement and Analysis*, John W. Kendrick and Beatrice Vaccara, Eds., *Studies in Income and Wealth*, Vol. 44 (Chicago: The University

of Chicago Press, 1980), pp. 333-50, and "Comment" by Jerome A. Mark, pp. 351-6.

8. With regard to insurance, see my comments in Volume 34 of Income and Wealth series.

9. *The Measurement and Interpretation of Productivity*, Report of the Panel to Review Productivity Statistics (Washington: National Research Council, National Academy of Sciences, 1979).

10. See Frank M. Gollop and Dale W. Jorgenson, "U.S. Productivity Growth by Industry, 1947-73," in *New Developments in Productivity Measurement and Analysis*, op. cit., pp. 17-124.

11. See Multiple Input Productivity Indexes, Vol. 3, No. 1 (Houston: American Productivity Center, September 1982, and subsequent issues); also John W. Kendrick and Elliot S. Grossman, *Productivity in the United States: Trends and Cycles* (Baltimore: Johns Hopkins University Press, 1980).

12. The last of those monographs, which contains references to the earlier ones, is John W. Kendrick, *Postwar Productivity Trends in the United States, 1948-1969* (New York: National Bureau of Economic Research, 1973).

13. See John W. Kendrick, "The Coming Rebound in Productivity," *Fortune*, June 28, 1982, and "Productivity Trends and the Recent Slowdown: Historical Perspective, Causal Factors and Policy Options," in *Contemporary Economic Problems, 1979*, William Fellner, Ed. (Washington: American Enterprise Institute, 1979), especially Table 4, pp. 33-4.

14. "Productivity Trends and the Recent Slowdown," ibid., pp. 33-4, and 49.

# Comment: Measurement of output and productivity in the service sector

WILLIAM J. BAUMOL

Professor Kendrick's paper raises some important issues related to measurement of productivity in service industries. Although there is a great deal of truth to the widespread view that the outputs of services are more difficult to observe and measure than those of manufacturing and agriculture, there are noteworthy exceptions. Concerts can be measured in terms of number of performances or number of persons in the audience; education can be measured in terms of number of persons completing each grade level and telephone calls can be measured as number of messages, message-miles or message-minute-miles. Of course, the quality of two concerts can differ markedly and a 1920 education year is not the same as one in 1982, but watches also differ in quality and a 1920 automobile, too, is very different from a 1982 model.

My first observation on quality measurement, then, is that quality changes cause output measurement problems for *all* economic sectors; the services are distinguishable here only in degree. My second observation is that although quality changes do constitute an obstacle to the measurement of output and productivity, they are less fatal an impediment than is sometimes suggested. I will argue this on three levels, first by pointing out that measurement efforts do nevertheless succeed in practice, second, by showing that for many applications they are irrelevant and, third, by indicating that for some purposes an exact measure of quality change is available, certainly in theory, and to some degree in practice.

The feasibility of measurement of service outputs despite the quality change problems is demonstrated conclusively by the fine papers presented to this conference by Professors Summers and Kendrick. The clear relationships and suggestive results surely show beyond any doubt that the quality problem, though real, is hardly fatal.

To make my second point let me introduce a bit of terminology, distinguishing between *crude productivity,* that is, productivity measurement without any attempt at adjustment for quality changes, and *quality-adjusted productivity.* I shall now argue a point that seems rarely to have been recognized – that *for many applications it is crude productivity and not quality-adjusted productivity that constitutes the pertinent datum.* To see why this is so we must digress briefly to deal with the analysis of the productivity record of the services and some of its implications that are brought out so beautifully by

124

Professor Summers's analysis. Although, as will emerge in the subsequent discussion, the services' productivity record is far from uniform, it is true nevertheless that some services (notably those in which quality is directly dependent on time devoted to their performance and those that resist standardization) do not lend themselves to rapid productivity growth and have in fact shown little such growth in practice. *Live* performance in the performing arts is my oft-repeated example. A quintet written in 1800 for a half-hour performance, required 2.5 person-hours per performance then and still requires it today. If, say, the time needed to produce a watch has meanwhile fallen to 1/20th of its value in 1800 (undoubtedly a most conservative estimate) two conclusions follow almost tautologically:

1. If prices are roughly proportional to labor cost, today a concert will be 20 times as expensive in comparison with a watch as it was in 1800.
2. If the ratio of concert performances to watches produced had remained unchanged the ratio of the labor force engaged in performance to that in watchmaking must have increased twentyfold.

Notice that the preceding observations are expressed *exclusively* in terms of crude productivity. We have taken no note of the improved accuracy and compactness of watches (or of the decreased amount of engraving found in their interior) nor has anything been said about the alleged improvement in quality of violin playing.

This immediately indicates two very pressing applications of productivity measurement for which *crude* productivity growth is the pertinent productivity datum. First, in issues involving planning for the composition of the labor force, for example, construction of training facilities, teacher training, planning relating to future size of union membership, it is clear that we must investigate prospective demands for watches and concerts and, in addition, one must estimate crude productivity growth (but not quality-adjusted productivity growth). Second, in determining how much must be budgeted for outlays on the two, for example, by the Department of Defense on watches and by the National Endowment for the Arts on concerts, crude productivity growth is, once again, the pertinent piece of productivity information. Of course, quality changes do enter into these matters by affecting demand, but to take this into account one must measure shifts in demand. No attempt to quantify quality changes is required.

Having thus shown that for at least some significant purposes crude productivity gives the requisite information and obviates any need to measure quality changes, let me turn to my last observation on quality changes, arguing that the quality measurement problem is not quite the obstacle it is usually taken to be. For I will suggest now that even where such changes are of direct relevance we sometimes have ways of dealing with them directly.

The point is that to the economist a quality change should not be interpreted as a modification of a product's specifications but as a contribution to the welfare of consumers (and, perhaps, producers). A 1980 automobile is better (or worse) than one of 1920 only to the extent that it yields an increment in consumers' utility. It does not matter whether this is achieved by changed styling, safety features, economy, or a combination of these.

Thus, to measure the change in a product's quality the one correct way to go about it is to measure the associated change in consumers' utility. But this we do know how to do, at least in principle. Here we have two options. First, we may concern ourselves with the change in the marginal utility of the product, that is, with the increment in marginal utility measured in money terms – in its marginal rate of substitution for money. But that we can surely observe directly from the price of the item. If after the quality improvement its price (in real terms) rises 20 percent, we need know no more, for that *is* the rise in marginal utility for all utility-maximizing consumers.

However, there is good reason to argue that the proper measure of quality change involves not marginal utility but the consequent rise in consumers' and producers' surplus. Clearly, that is a far more difficult undertaking. But we do know how to do it in theory, given demand and production functions and their behavior, whereas we do not know how to evaluate changes in the physical attributes of a product, even in theory. In practice, measurement of surpluses is, of course, much more difficult, but estimation procedures have been devised and used for the purpose; indeed, there is a significant literature on the subject. Certainly, it takes us well beyond the pursuit of the chimera of "direct" measurement of quality changes.

# Comment: Measurement of output and productivity in the service sector

CHARLES R. HULTEN

The paper by John W. Kendrick provides an interesting and highly relevant insight into the growth of the service-producing sectors.[1] The output of the service sectors is shown to have grown more rapidly than the output of the goods-producing sectors over the period from 1948 to 1981, but it is also shown that the growth rate of total factor productivity was much lower in the former than in the latter. The growth dynamics of the two sectors was thus quite different: Growth in the goods-producing sectors was largely driven by improvements in technical and economic efficiency, whereas services grew primarily through an increase in capital and labor input.

These growth trends imply some potentially unpleasant consequences for the economy as a whole. If these trends continue and the service sectors account for an increasingly large fraction of GNP, the growth rate of the entire business sector will converge to the growth rate of the service sector component. In this extreme and unlikely case, Kendrick's numbers imply that the growth rate of real gross product would fall from 3.3 percent per year (its historical rate for the years 1948–81) to 2.8 percent in the future. This occurs because the business sector is "stuck" with the low rate of total factor productivity growth historically prevailing in the service sectors. (Refer to the following table based on Kendrick's data.)

*Economic growth in the U.S. business economy (past and hypothetical future)*

|  | Average annual growth rates | |
|---|---|---|
|  | Actual[a]<br>1958–81 | Hypothetical future,<br>with an all-service economy |
| Total factor input | 1.5% | 1.5% |
| Total factor productivity | 1.8% | 1.3% |
| Real gross product | 3.3% | 2.8% |

[a] *Source:* Kendrick's Table 4.1.

This scenario is very improbable, but it does point to an important implication of Professor Kendrick's estimates: The continued growth of the

127

service economy – a sign of its health and success – relative to the goods-producing sectors will tend to lower overall growth if the service sectors continue to experience a relatively low rate of productivity increase.

This conclusion depends crucially on the observation, based on official statistics, that total factor productivity growth in the service sectors is relatively low. However, as Kendrick notes, estimates based on official statistics are probably biased downward. The output of the service sectors is largely intangible, and it is thus difficult to separate the value of services purchased in any year into price and quantity components. The Bureau of Economic Analysis therefore (generally) extrapolates a base-year value of output (gross product originating) using various measures of labor input, such as employment or hours worked. Since the use of labor input to extrapolate real output treats labor productivity growth as constant, the resulting estimates of real output cannot be used to produce independent estimates of productivity change. When they are, the growth rate of labor productivity is biased toward zero and the growth rate of total factor productivity biased downward.[2]

The need for better measures of service sector output is widely recognized. Although one can argue with Kendrick's view, the measurement of service sector output is in principle no more difficult than the measurement of output in the goods-producing sectors, it should be noted that practical measurement problems have proved exceedingly difficult to solve. The main difficulty arises because services are typically intangible and embody a large quality component. The output of doctors, lawyers, and barbers, for example, depends at least as much on the quality of the product as on the hours spent in its production. Quality differentials typically show up as price differentials, and it is difficult to know (in practice) how much of an observed price increase is due to an improvement in product quality and how much is due to inflation.[3]

The problem of quality measurement and its implications for productivity analysis can be illustrated by the following example. Suppose that in one industry, G, one unit of output is produced from one unit of labor and one unit of R&D. Suppose, further, that the R&D effort leads to a yearly doubling of the quantity of output that can be produced from one unit of labor. In this industry, total factor productivity will appear to grow at 100 percent a year, if labor input is constant. Compare, now, this industry with another, S, in which one unit of output is produced using one unit of labor and one unit of R&D, but in which R&D is used to double the *quality* of output every year, leaving the quantity constant. If our measurement techniques permit us to measure only quantity increases, we will be led to the erroneous (from the standpoint of consumer welfare) conclusion that sector S is stagnant whereas sector G is highly progressive.

The problem of quality measurement is, of course, relevant to both goods- and service-producing industries. The problem, however, is likely to be greater in the latter than in the former because the intangible nature of services can make quality differences difficult to observe, and because product differentiation is a more central aspect of competition in many service industries ("repair shop X is more reliable than Y," "Doctor W is more sympathetic to my problems than Doctor Z").

An effort is made to account for quality change in many productivity studies, and a number of techniques can be brought to bear on the problem. In measuring public sector productivity, for example, the output of selected services can be estimated using such indicators as the number of garbage collections per week, the number of arrests by the police force, the number of students enrolled in a school system, and so on. However, although such measures are generally recognized to be superior to labor input as a measure of output, they are also recognized to be inadequate for precisely the same reason that the number of haircuts is not a good measure of barbering: They fail to account for the quality, or "effectiveness," of the service as it is perceived by the recipient.

The use of "price hedonics" is another way to account for quality differentials in goods and services. This method is based on the view put forward by Lancaster that consumers choose among goods in order to obtain the characteristics embodied in those goods.[4] Goods and services are thus seen as bundles of characteristics, and quality differentials may be defined in terms of different combinations of characteristics. This approach can be operationalized using the price hedonic method, in which various observed characteristics are used to explain observed price differentials, and the estimated price differentials used to infer the corresponding quality differential.

My own research into the productivity of state and local governments is based on a variant of the Lancaster approach. Instead of using price hedonics, the state–local government sector is treated as though it were a household, and Becker's model of household production (a close relative of the Lancaster model) is used to obtain an estimated rate of total factor productivity change for the sector.[5] This estimate is obtained without explicit reference to sectoral output, and can be shown to embody quality differentials as perceived by the recipient public.[6]

Further research using the Becker–Lancaster model will doubtless yield further progress. Other approaches – perhaps unique to the specific industry under study – are also likely to be of great importance in improving the quality of service sector output measures.

### Notes

1. Recall that the service-producing sectors are defined by Kendrick as Trade, Finance/Insurance, Real Estate, and Services. The goods-producing sectors are

Agriculture, Mining/Construction, Manufacturing, and Transportation/Utilities. This classification is used in this Comment.

2. The standard growth accounting relationship allocates the growth rate of output among the growth rates of total factor productivity, capital, and labor (the latter weighted by their income shares). When labor input is used to extrapolate output, the growth rates of the two series are equal. This implies that the growth rate of the output/labor ratio is zero, and that the growth rate of total factor productivity equals the negative of the growth rate of the capital/labor ratio, weighted by capital's share in income.

3. The extrapolation of output using labor input implicitly assumes that output quality does not change, i.e., that the growth rate of barbering services equals the growth rate of barbering hours.

4. Lancaster, K. J., "A New Approach to Consumer Theory," The *Journal of Political Economy* (1966): 132–57. For a recent contribution to the quality measurement debate which summarizes the issues, see Triplett, J. E., "Concepts of Quality in Input and Output Price Measures: A Resolution of the User-Value Resource-Cost Debate," in M. F. Foss, ed., *The U.S. National Income and Product Accounts: Selected Topics,* National Bureau of Economic Research, Chicago, 1983.

5. Becker, G. S., "A Theory of the Allocation of Time," *The Economic Journal* (1965): 493–517.

6. The estimated rate of state–local productivity is found to be approximately unchanged over the period 1959–79. This estimate must, however, be understood to combine the productive efficiency of the capital and labor used in the production of state–local services with the changing urban environment into which the services were introduced.

# Comment: Measurement of output and productivity in the service sector

JANET L. NORWOOD

Many of the issues raised in Professor Kendrick's paper underline the special challenge the service sector presents to those of us who are responsible for measuring economic trends. In the Bureau of Labor Statistics, service sector measurement issues are especially important in the development of estimates of employment, prices, and productivity.

### Employment

The service sector – by its very nature – has many more small establishments than the manufacturing sector. In manufacturing, for example, the number of establishments with 250 or more employees is about equal to the number with less than 250 employees. In the service sector, however, 70 percent of the establishments have less than 250 employees. The fact that the service sector has a large proportion of relatively small establishments is important in measuring employment trends. Small establishments seem to have much greater labor turnover than large ones and must be carefully measured to produce accurate changes in employment.

Another data collection problem is caused by the fact that there are a much larger number of small establishments than large ones that start up or go out of business. We adjust for these "births" and "deaths" through an annual benchmark to the universe of establishments providing State Unemployment Insurance tax reports. Since these U.I. tax reports cover 98 percent of all nonagricultural establishments, we can be sure that the benchmarked employment estimates are accurate. We have not yet, however, found an adequate method for benchmarking the hours and earnings data.

### Prices

The basic price measurement problem in services relates to identification and quantitative measurement of quality change. Since measurement of a particular quantity of a service produced is not easily accomplished with precision, isolation of that part of price change due to the change in the quality of the services becomes extremely difficult.

Perhaps the problem of quality measurement of services may be better understood if we assume that a given service is a package of specific products,

131

which varies in composition from one firm to another and from one time period to another. Consumer banking services are a good example. There are a large number of different accounts and types of loans. There are automatic teller services, safe-deposit boxes, and a variety of other nonfunding services. Very little data are available on this product mix. Although data collectors for the Consumer Price Index are able to sample these service types, the individual characteristics of these services and changes in their quality are extremely difficult to identify.

Another problem in price measurement of services involves the conceptual level at which the output is defined. Should the service be defined by its characteristics as transacted in the market or should the service be defined by how well it achieves the desired effect? Medical care, for example, could be defined as the package of products for which an individual has been billed. On the other hand, medical care could be defined in accordance with the degree to which the treatment brings about the better health of the patient. The practical problems of measurement argue for the market-transacted characteristics approach, although I must admit the "desired effects" approach has considerable appeal.

### Productivity

All of the measurement issues discussed previously have implications for productivity measurement. The need to produce a single index of quantity of service provided further complicates the productivity measurement problem. Clearly, such an overall measure has to be found before it can be determined if the output level has increased faster or slower than the level of inputs used in producing the service.

### Conclusion

I have mentioned some of the serious conceptual problems in measuring quality change, output, and employment, hours and earnings in the service sector. But an even more overriding problem, which I have not touched on, is that of data availability. The U.S. statistical system has reasonably good coverage of the goods-producing sector; a vast array of statistical series are available. But the service sector, unfortunately, is covered in only a very limited way and then often not very comprehensively.

We must recognize, however, that in the current period of budget cutting, the likelihood is that we will produce *less* rather than *more* statistical series. At a time when seven out of ten American workers is employed in the service sector, it is clear that more and better data on services are needed. But we need to do a better job of setting priorities. Too often those engaged in analytic studies tell us in government that more and more data are required. What we need is a sifting of priorities. Tell us where the data need to be expanded or improved. And then, tell us which data series can be eliminated to accomplish the desired increases.

# CHAPTER 5

# Services in world transactions*

IRVING B. KRAVIS

A new interest in the role of services in world transactions has been generated by the current efforts of the U.S. government to reduce barriers to
international trade in services. The services that are the focus of this attention are not the same as those often spoken of in discussions of the "service
economy." Yet generalizations based on definitions of services in the
domestic context are sometimes drawn upon to support policy proposals in
the international area.

This paper has two objectives. One is to sort out these various congeries
of services and to assess their importance in international transactions. The
second is to examine the implications of the empirical findings for current
U.S. policy with regard to international trade.

## Introduction

It seems like a natural extension of the concept of an evolving service
economy to conceive of a relative expansion of international transactions in
services. Yet when an effort is made to assess these prospects in the trade of
nations, a large stumbling block is posed by the uncertainty that clouds the
identity of the "services" involved. There are different congeries of services,
each based on a different cross cut of economic activity. In the domestic
economy there is a difference between services defined as final-demand
products (e.g., public passenger transport)[1] and service industries in the
sense of those that add value mainly by means of the use of capital and
labor with relatively little intermediate inputs of physical things (e.g., finance). For the distinction between services and commodities based on the
relative importance of physical inputs in total output see Kravis, Heston,
and Summers, 1983, Table 1. Other conceptual aspects of services are discussed there and in other papers in this volume. When it comes to inter-

* This paper originated in a discussion of Helena Stalson's paper for the ARA/Wharton Conference on the Future of the Service Economy, November 19–20, 1982. The work of expanding the original discussion was supported in part by the Wharton School's Fishman-
Davidson Center for the Study of the Service Sector and in part by NSF Grant PRA-8116459
to the National Bureau for Economic Research for International Economic Policy Research.
The author is indebted to Robert P. Inman, Robert E. Lipsey, and Helena Stalson for helpful
comments. The statistical work for this paper was performed by Martin Shanin.

national transactions, still other classifications are used. A major difference from the usual domestic concepts is that incomes from factors of production operating abroad, particularly capital in the case of the United States, are often grouped with services in international classifications, regardless of the type of output produced by these factors. Another difference, recently emphasized in U.S. trade-negotiating policy, is that the concept of trade in services is extended to include services rendered within foreign host countries by affiliates of U.S. parent companies.

## The U.S. policy initiative

Similar problems of classification do not arise with respect to commodities even though the obverse character of the definitions of commodities and services as two mutually exclusive but exhaustive sets of economic activities might be expected to lead to common difficult border areas.[2] Indeed, the analysis of international commodity trade flows has a long history, relatively untroubled by definitional questions. In recent years the issues of commodity composition, country origins, and destinations of trade have been investigated by many analysts. This work has been instigated by claims and counterclaims about the role of trade in stimulating or curbing employment in the United States or other industrialized countries and in promoting or retarding economic growth in developing countries. This attention has been almost entirely focused on the merchandise component of international trade. Trade in services has been largely neglected.

Now, however, this neglect is being replaced, especially in the United States, by an increasing degree of attention to the role of services in the international business activities of American firms and in the world economy.[3] The reasons for this change are probably to be found among the following factors:

1.  The widely perceived growth of the service sector in the domestic economy of the United States and other countries was likely sooner or later to turn attention to the role of services in world transactions.
2.  The unprecedented growth of the world economy between World War II and the onset of the slowdown of the 1980s (as measured by real world GDP[4]) was accompanied by an even more rapid expansion of international commerce and investment, which brought concurrent demands and opportunities for expansion in service transactions.
3.  In the United States, the Reagan Administration has launched a diplomatic campaign to remove obstacles to the exports of services by U.S. firms and, equally vigorously, to reduce barriers to the establishment and operation of U.S.-owned affiliates in service industries in foreign countries.[5]

We do not attempt to delve further into these motivations, and we leave it to the Stalson paper in this volume to describe the institutional and other details of the Administration's program for liberalizing international business in the service industries. We are interested primarily in examining the role of services in U.S. international business activities, and in world transactions.

## The background: services in the domestic economy

The role of services in the domestic economy has been written about extensively, and summaries and further contributions appear elsewhere in this volume. However, it will be useful in considering international transactions in services briefly to highlight some salient features of services in the domestic setting.

### The expansion of spending on final demand services

A hypothesis that is frequently advanced is that the demand for services is income elastic – that is, that at any relative price of services the quantity absorbed rises more than the quantity of commodities as real income per capita increases. Sometimes this notion is at the root of the perception that services may be expected to expand rapidly in international transactions. The appropriate concept of services for considering the underlying economic proposition is in terms of service categories of final demand (e.g., haircuts, medical care).

The most important final-product or final-demand services are government, housing, and education; they account for roughly 60 to 65 percent of service spending in both poor and rich countries. (See Table 5.1, columns 1 and 2.) The addition of medical care and hotels and restaurants raises the proportion of service spending accounted for to the 80–85 percent range.

The similarities of the aggregate proportions in low and high income countries do not extend to the individual components. For example, public transport absorbs a higher share in poor countries and housing a lower share. There is a difference also in that the share of aggregate service spending in total spending on GDP is much lower in the poor countries. However, this is due to much lower service prices in the low income countries. When a common set of average international prices is used to value the quantities of all components of GDP (Table 5.1, columns 4 and 5), the resultant "real" share of spending on aggregate services is not very different between poor and rich countries. However, some compositional differences (government, housing, education, and medical care) become greater.

Table 5.1. *Shares of various services in final expenditures on GDP for countries with different income levels, at own prices and at international prices, 1975*

| | In own prices | | | In international prices | | |
|---|---|---|---|---|---|---|
| | Low income countries[a] (1) | High income countries[b] (2) | United States (3) | Low income countries[a] (4) | High income countries[b] (5) | United States (6) |
| Share of spending on services | | | | | | |
| Housing | 19.8 | 22.8 | 24.1 | 16.0 | 27.1 | 27.4 |
| Gross rent | 14.9 | 18.1 | 20.3 | 9.8 | 24.5 | 22.6 |
| Medical care[c] | 6.8 | 10.6 | 14.2 | 5.5 | 15.3 | 9.3 |
| Education[c] | 15.4 | 12.5 | 12.9 | 20.9 | 8.8 | 8.7 |
| Hotels and restaurants | 9.8 | 10.4 | 7.2 | 4.1 | 12.6 | 8.6 |
| Other consumption | 17.0 | 15.6 | 18.8 | 16.5 | 18.5 | 19.3 |
| Public transport | 6.7 | 2.9 | 1.1 | 6.3 | 2.3 | 0.9 |
| Communication | 0.7 | 1.6 | 2.6 | 0.4 | 1.7 | 3.0 |
| Recreation[c] | 4.0 | 2.8 | 3.0 | 3.0 | 3.4 | 2.8 |
| Barber and beauty shops | 0.4 | 1.3 | 0.7 | 1.0 | 1.3 | 0.5 |
| Government[d] | 31.2 | 28.1 | 22.8 | 37.0 | 17.7 | 26.7 |
| Total | 100.0 | 100.0 | 100.0 | 100.0 | 100.0 | 100.0 |
| Service spending as share of GDP | 26.8 | 39.8 | 49.3 | 38.1 | 34.1 | 38.4 |

[a] Eight countries with 1975 real per capita GDP below 15% that of the United States (Kravis, Heston and Summers, 1982, p. 18).
[b] Nine countries with 1975 real per capita GDP between 60 and 90% that of the United States. Ibid.
[c] Includes both public and private spending.
[d] Excludes spending on medical care, education, and recreation. Includes both employee compensation and government purchases of goods and services.
*Source:* Kravis, Heston, and Summers (1982).

Two inferences may be drawn from these similarities and differences in the use of GDP for the provision of final-demand services in poor and rich countries. (1) For the aggregate of services in GDP, the cross-country income elasticity of demand is near unity. (2) For individual kinds of final-demand services, income elasticities can be very different.

On the first point, a study based on data from the U.N. International Comparison Project (Kravis, Heston, and Summers, 1983, Table 7) produced an income elasticity for the aggregate of final-demand services of .99, virtually identical with the elasticity of 1.00 for aggregate commodity final demand. This tendency toward constant service shares for countries with different income levels was also reported in each of the three International Comparison Project (ICP) studies (Kravis, Heston, and Summers, 1982, pp. 21–3 and references there to the earlier ICP reports). On the second point, the ICP-based study shows a wide range of income elasticities for twenty-six detailed service categories with a few less than 0.5 and about a third in excess of 1.5[6], and Summers's paper in the present volume shows income elasticities for six major subdivisions of services ranging from 0.79 (recreation and education) to 1.46 (medical care). Reasons for this combination of overall unitary elasticity and component diversity have been explored in Kravis, Heston, and Summers, 1983, and need not be repeated here.

When services are viewed in terms of final demand, they become more expensive relative to commodities and absorb larger fractions of current spending as income grows, but there is no support in the cross-country data for the view that the physical quantities of services as a whole will on the average expand more than the physical quantities of commodities.

### The contribution of service industries to GDP

Another and more common way to identify and classify service activities is in terms of the industries that produce them. A more or less standard classification of the main service industries in these terms is set out in Table 5.2. In this classification the key is the intangibility or nonstorability of the output without regard to the nature or motive of the purchaser; intermediate as well as final-demand services are included.

The table shows the contribution the main service industries make to total production in developing countries, developed countries, and the United States.[7] In these terms the service industries are of even larger importance in rich countries relative to poor ones than in terms of the final-demand figures of Table 5.1. The difference between the 46-percent share for developing countries and the 61-percent share for industrialized countries is more than fully accounted for by the larger shares of finance and

Table 5.2. *Shares of various service industries in producing GDP at own current prices, various groups of countries, 1979*

|  | 20 developing countries (1) | 10 industrialized countries (2) | United States (3) |
|---|---|---|---|
| Commodities | 53.7 | 39.1 | 34.7 |
| Services | 46.3* | 60.9 | 65.3 |
| Electricity, gas, water | 1.7 | 2.6 | 2.6 |
| Trade | 18.7 | 14.6 | 16.9 |
| Transport, storage, communication | 6.1 | 6.5 | 6.3 |
| Finance, insurance, real estate | 3.8 | 16.3 | 19.4 |
| Personal services | 7.5 | 8.9 | 7.9 |
| Government services | 6.5 | 12.0 | 12.2 |
| Total GDP | 100.0 | 100.0 | 100.0 |

*Note:* Countries include all those in each category for which sources cited below gave the necessary data.
* Subdivisions shown add to 44.3. "Ownership of dwellings" and "other branches," not separately given in the source for all countries, constitute the remaining 2%.
*Sources:* Column 1: IBRD, *World Tables, 1980.* Columns 2 and 3: OECD, *National Accounts, 1963–80,* Vol. II, Detailed Tables.

government in the latter. We know from the cross-country data of Table 5.1 that the larger share of government in the rich countries is attributable mainly to higher compensation of government employees rather than to larger numbers of them,[8] and similar differences in the compensation of employees in other labor-intensive services probably increase shares of other service sectors in the industrialized countries relative to those in the developing countries. The large role of wholesale and retail trade in the developing countries accounting for nearly one-fifth of gross production and over one-third of service output, despite low wages, raises questions about the efficiency of this sector in these countries.

The relative roles of price and quantity changes in changing the share of service industries in domestic production over time are examined in Table 5.3. For the "world" consisting of forty-nine market economies[9] the share of service expenditures in own-currency current prices rose by 6 percentage points between 1960 and 1975. Half of the increase was attributable to price increases and the other half to real quantity increases. Similar changes occurred in the industrial countries, but in the developing countries the expansion in real terms was larger than that in current prices.

Table 5.3. *Shares of GDP originating in service industries, in current and constant prices, 1960 and 1975, world and selected areas*

|  | No. of countries | Current prices | | 1975 prices | |
|---|---|---|---|---|---|
|  |  | 1960 | 1975 | 1960 | 1975 |
| World | 49 | 51 | 57 | 54 | 57 |
| Industrialized countries | 13 | 55 | 62 | 58 | 62 |
| United States | 1 | 60 | 67 | 66 | 67 |
| Developing countries | 36 | 40 | 43 | 39 | 44 |

*Source:* IBRD, *World Tables, 1980.*

Thus the time-series data for service industries point to a small rise in their shares in the production of GDP. This expansion of service shares over time seems to be in conflict with the stability of final-demand service shares in the cross-section data considered earlier. Each set of service classifications encounters great difficulties in factoring out price and quantity changes, and in the time-to-time data these problems are not met in the same way by all countries.

There is a high correlation ($\bar{r}^2 = .71$) between the share of final-demand services in expenditures on GDP and the share of service industries in the production of GDP (1975 data for 27 ICP countries), but the a priori grounds for expecting such concordance are not strong. The reason is the factors affecting the changes in the relative importance of service industries in the production of GDP are different in some important respects from those that influence the share of final-demand services in the absorption of GDP. All or almost all final-demand services are produced by service industries[10] and the forces that lead changes in the consumption of final-demand services produce matching changes in the production of the relevant service industries. However, the important group of intermediate services produced by service industries rises or declines relative to commodity production in response to entirely different sets of influences. Some of these influences such as those affecting the relative importance of trade, transportation, and finance are linked to the general expansion of economic activity and wealth. But these services and others are often necessary concomitants of commodity production. In this context, they may either be carried on as ancillary operations of firms whose primary function is to produce some given commodity, or they may be contracted out to specialized service firms. The relative size of service industries thus depends not only on the volume of services (accounting, delivery, etc.) that are necessary to bring a commodity to the buyer, but also on the extent of internalization by commodity-producing firms. In general, the mechanization of ancillary services probably promotes contracting out. Factors favoring the use of the market and those favoring internalization are treated in the literature on the transaction approach to industrial organization (Williamson, 1981).

The conclusion of this examination of the behavior of the service shares in final demand and in the production of GDP suggests that the expansion of the service shares in real terms is not nearly as dramatic as is sometimes portrayed in the literature on the shift to a "service economy." The widely noted shift in employment to service industries is attributable at least as much to different average productivity trends as to differences in the response of demand to rising incomes. However, the wide dispersion of individual services around these average tendencies must be borne in mind in considering their implications for the role of services in world transactions. There are as noted some service activities that are experiencing rapid growth in both current and constant prices.

### Services in world transactions

The classification of services usually presented in statistics of international transactions includes factor and nonfactor services. The former represent direct services rendered by the factors of production such as interest payments for the use of foreign capital or wages to a foreign worker, regardless of the nature of the output. Nonfactor services, on the other hand, are those which require the addition of intermediate inputs to labor and/or capital for their production. [11]

#### Services in the U.S. balance of payments

In balance of payments terms, services inclusive of direct factor services and nonfactor services accounted for over one-third of the U.S. exports of "goods and services" in 1980 and nearly 25 percent of U.S. imports (see Table 5.4). However, policy-oriented discussions often concentrate on nonfactor services which constitute only 9 percent of the export total and 11 percent of the import total. In some contexts only investment income is excluded in order to obtain the total for nonfactor services. The treatment of royalties and fees in services does not change the picture very much; if as in the table they are regarded as (direct factor) services, the share of total exports counted as services is only a couple of percentage points higher than would otherwise be the case.

These classifications, it should be borne in mind, are not without their arbitrary elements. The same kind of activity may wind up with its trans-

Table 5.4. *Factor and nonfactor services in the U.S. current account transactions*

| | 1980 (in millions of $) | | Ratio (1980/70) | |
|---|---|---|---|---|
| | Exports | Imports | Exports | Imports |
| Goods and services | 344,667 | 333,888 | 5.25 | 5.56 |
| Merchandise[a] | 228,664 | 253,199 | 5.26 | 6.20 |
| Services[b] | 116,005 | 80,689 | 5.22 | 4.20 |
| Direct factor services | 84,685 | 44,593 | 5.86 | 7.43 |
| Capital | 82,801 | 43,943 | 5.88 | 7.66 |
| Investment income | 75,936 | 43,174 | 6.46 | 7.83 |
| Royalties and fees | 6,865 | 769 | 2.95 | 3.42 |
| Labor[c] | 1,884 | 650 | 5.01 | 2.42 |
| Nonfactor services[d] | 31,320 | 36,096 | 4.04 | 2.74 |
| U.S. government transactions[e] | 3,895 | 8,624 | 4.67 | 1.88 |
| Private nonfactor services | 27,425 | 27,472 | 3.97 | 3.20 |
| Transport[f] | 24,102 | 24,900 | 4.02 | 3.10 |
| Other[g] | 3,323 | 2,572 | 3.62 | 4.58 |

[a] Includes U.S. defense equipment and supplies.
[b] Excludes U.S. defense equipment and supplies.
[c] Includes contractors' fees.
[d] Services that require addition of intermediate inputs to labor and capital.
[e] Mainly defense expenditures excluding equipment and supplies.
[f] Includes transportation, travel, and passenger fees.
[g] Includes reinsurance, communication, film rentals, and "other."

Source: Reclassification of data in Anthony J. DiLullo, "Services Transactions in the U.S. International Accounts, 1970–80," *Survey of Current Business*, November 1981, pp. 30–9.

actions value in one category or another according to the accounting convenience of different reporters or the practices of the statistical authorities. For example, the income derived by a U.S. parent from a foreign service affiliate may appear in balance of payments statistics as investment income, as a royalty or fee,[12] or as a payment for a professional or a managerial service.

Among the nonfactor services, transport (including freight, passenger fees, and travel) accounts for around 70 percent of the total. Government transactions make up a good part of the balance. The private services other than transportation, such as communications and data processing, that appear to be the main concern of current U.S. policy are found mainly in the "other" category, which constitutes about 10 percent of nonfactor services and 1 percent of trade in goods and services.

### Service activities of U.S. foreign affiliates

However, account must be taken of the important role of U.S.-owned foreign affiliates in rendering private nonfactor services in order to round out the picture of the role of services in U.S. international business activity. Foreign service revenues earned through majority-owned affiliate sales are larger than those earned from a U.S. base. Thus, for 1977, the most recent date for which official data on affiliate sales are available, sales of U.S. affiliates abroad amounted to close to $280 billion (see Table 5.5), far in excess of private nonfactor service exports of $19 billion.[13] The service affiliates accounted for over 40 percent of the income of all affiliates and over 25 percent of their employment. The categories of "petroleum related services" and "trade" accounted for over 70 percent of service income and nearly 60 percent of service industry employment. The remaining service sectors, where the service activities on which U.S. policy efforts seem to be concentrated are found, thus account for about one-eighth of total affiliate income and employment.

Reliable and comprehensive estimates of income, sales, and employment are not available for subsequent years. However, the U.S. direct investment position abroad (book value of direct investors' equity and net loans to affiliates) increased by about 50 percent in service industries between 1977 and 1981, and, if past experience is any guide, sales probably increased by a larger percentage.[14]

### Growth of U.S. foreign service transactions

The behavior of service industry shares in domestic transactions, considered earlier, would lend some support to expectations for above-average

Table 5.5. *Income and employment of all foreign affiliates of all U.S.*
*parents, by commodity producing and service industries, 1977*

| | Total income[a] (bil $) | Employment (1,000) |
|---|---|---|
| All industries[b] | 680.1 | 7,342 |
| Commodity producing | 399.9 | 5,404 |
| Services | 280.2 | 1,938 |
| Petroleum related[c] | 97.2 | 140 |
| Trade | 104.4 | 991 |
| Banking | 23.2 | 135 |
| Finance, insurance, real estate[d] | 17.4 | 97 |
| Finance (excl. banking) | 4.2 | 27 |
| Insurance | 10.4 | 62 |
| Real estate | 0.2 | 2 |
| Construction | 10.1 | 179 |
| Transportation | 3.5 | 48 |
| Water | 2.0 | 17 |
| Air | 0.3 | 5 |
| Related services[e] | 1.3 | 26 |
| Communication, public utilities | 9.9 | 40 |
| Communication | n.a. | 28 |
| Public utilities | n.a. | 12 |
| Other services | 12.6 | 308 |
| Hotels and other lodging places | 1.6 | 66 |
| Advertising | 1.4 | 32 |
| Motion pictures (incl. TV tape) | 1.1 | 12 |
| Engineering, architectural | 3.2 | 40 |
| Accounting | 0.4 | 9 |
| Other personal and business sources | 4.9 | 149 |

[a] Sales data were not available in the same degree of industry detail as the figures for income and employment given above. However, sales make up the preponderance of income. For nonbank affiliates of nonbank parents, 1977 sales were $648 billion and income $656 billion (U.S. Department of Commerce, 1981, pp. 137 and 139).
[b] The data are classified according to the industry of the affiliate. They include commodity income and employment of affiliates in service industries and exclude service income and employment of affiliates classified as commodity producing.
[c] Oil and gas field services, petroleum wholesale trade, tanker operations, pipeline transmissions, gasoline service stations, etc.
[d] Excludes banking.
[e] Includes warehousing, terminal facilities, travel agents, etc.
*Source:* U.S. Department of Commerce, 1981, pp. 10–11.

Table 5.6. *Sales of U.S. majority-owned foreign affiliates, by industry, 1957, 1966, and 1977 (in billions of dollars)*

|  | 1957[a] | 1966[b] | 1977[c] |
|---|---|---|---|
| All industries | 40.3[d] | 97.8 | 507.0 |
| Mining | 2.0 | 3.3 | 5.1 |
| Petroleum | 14.5 | 27.5 | 198.6 |
| Manufacturing | 18.3 | 47.4 | 194.2 |
| Trade | 1.3[e] | 14.1 | 77.4 |
| Finance, insurance (excl. banking) | 0.8[e] | —[g] | 10.0 |
| Other | 3.3[f] | 5.6[h] | 21.7 |
| Agriculture | 0.9 | — | 1.2 |
| Construction | — | — | 7.9 |
| Transportation, communication, public utilities | 1.2 | 1.4 | 3.6 |
| Services | — | — | 9.1 |
| Addendum: |  |  |  |
| GDP | 440.5 | 750.3 | 1894.9 |
| Exports | 20.87 | 30.43 | 121.23 |
| Imports | 14.62 | 27.79 | 160.41 |

[a] Includes affiliates for which at least 25% of voting stock was owned by affiliated U.S. residents or 50% by nonaffiliated U.S. residents.
[b] Includes affiliates for which a single U.S. reporter's ownership interest was at least 50%.
[c] Includes nonbank affiliates of nonbank parents with at least 50% ownership by single U.S. reporter.
[d] Includes total costs rather than sales for trade and finance.
[e] Total costs.
[f] Includes "miscellaneous."
[g] Less than $0.1 billion.
[h] Includes "other industries."
*Source:* U.S. Department of Commerce, 1960, 1975, and 1981; IMF, 1983.

growth rates for trade by service industries, if it could be assumed that growth in domestic and international transactions are likely to go hand-in-hand. This does not, however, appear to be the case. The 1980/1970 expansion ratios (i.e., the ratios of the 1980 values to those of 1970) shown in Table 5.4, are lower for services than for commodities and lower still for nonfactor services. However, international transactions of the United States expanded more rapidly over the decade than the domestic economy, and trade in both services and in its nonfactor component increased at a faster rate than U.S. GDP.[15]

Table 5.7. *Expansion ratios*$^a$ *for affiliate sales*

|                                      | 1966/57 | 1977/66 |
|--------------------------------------|---------|---------|
| All industries                       | 2.43    | 5.18    |
| Commodity producing$^b$              | 2.22    | 5.04    |
| Mining and petroleum                 | 1.86    | 6.61    |
| Manufacturing                        | 2.59    | 4.10    |
| Services                             | 4.04    | 5.80    |
| Trade and finance                    | 6.71    | 6.20    |
| Transportation, communication,       |         |         |
| public utilities                     | 1.17    | 2.57    |
| Other                                | 2.38    | 5.45    |

$^a$ Ratio of terminal-to-initial-year sales.
$^b$ Includes agriculture with an interpolated figure of $1 million for 1966.

Comprehensive data for the other and larger component of international business services, foreign sales by U.S.-owned foreign affiliates, are available for the period from 1957 to 1977. The most reliable data are from major surveys for 1957, 1966, and 1977. (See Table 5.6). There are serious incomparabilities in the three data sets in the definitions of the foreign affiliates covered and in the industrial classifications, the latter bearing especially on "service" industries. The summary of the Table 5.6 expansion ratios (terminal year sales as ratios of beginning year sales) relating to the relative growth of service sales is set out in Table 5.7. Due to the difficulties with the statistics discussed previously, these should be regarded as very approximate. Here a relationship opposite to that found for exports emerges: The sales of service affiliates expanded more rapidly than those of commodity-producing affiliates, and this was true in both periods. Trade and finance were the fastest growing sectors in both periods, whereas transportation, communication, and public utilities sectors had the lowest expansion. Other private nonfactor services such as lodging places, advertising, engineering, and accounting are in the "other" service category, which has intermediate expansion ratios. The "other" service ratios were higher than the commodity ratios, and both sets were substantially above the expansion ratio for the domestic economy.[16]

Direct investment in service industries did not expand more rapidly than in commodity-producing industries between 1977 and 1981, although it seems clear that at least some sectors in the "other" set expanded very rapidly. A U.S. International Trade Commission (ITC) survey that elicited responses from 143 international service firms in 14 selected service industries[17] concluded that between 1980 and 1982 foreign revenues increased by more than 50 percent, rising from 12.9 to 14.9 percent of the total foreign and domestic revenues.

By way of summary, the dominant components of U.S. international business in services are transport in the private nonfactor export category and trade- and petroleum-related services in the foreign sales of service affiliates. There is evidence that a selected set of private nonfactor services that are the focus of U.S. trade policy have been growing rapidly in foreign affiliate sales, but there is not much reason to believe that service exports have increased relative to commodity exports in any general way. The services to which most policy attention is being given still constitute modest shares both of exports and of affiliate sales.

### Role of services in world trade

A picture of the role of services in world transactions that is broader in country coverage is provided in Table 5.8. The source does not permit a decomposition into factor and nonfactor services.[18] When "services" are taken to include investment income as payment for a direct factor service, services constituted about one-quarter of world transactions in merchandise and services in 1980. The U.S. service share in exports of goods and services was larger than the world average whereas that for developing countries was smaller. On the import side, the main deviation from the world average was the large share of the developing countries.

When the more usual procedure of excluding investment income is followed, the service share in world trade in goods and services drops to 17 or 18 percent, of which 10 or 11 percent represents transport and travel. The U.S. share of services less investment income is below the world average due mainly to a lower proportion for transportation.

Further comparisons of the recent U.S. balance of payments position in services are found in Table 5.9. The bulk of the U.S. balance of payments in services surpluses is due to payments for factor services. The U.S. is not a dominant exporter of private nonfactor services although it has had modest surpluses in this category.[19] Furthermore, the U.S. share in both world exports and industrial country exports of transport and other nonfactor services declined during the 1970s.[20] Developing countries are the dominant debtor nations in all the categories of trade in services shown in Table 5.9.

### The growth of world service transactions

The decade of the 1970s was not only marked by rapid economic growth but by rapid growth that was widely dispersed throughout the world economy.[21]

Table 5.8. *Share of services in world transactions of goods and services, world and subdivisions: 1970, 1980*

A. Exports (in billion SDRs)

| | World | | Industrial countries | | United States | | Developing countries | |
|---|---|---|---|---|---|---|---|---|
| | 1970 | 1980 | 1970 | 1980 | 1970 | 1980 | 1970 | 1980 |
| Total merchandise and services | 365.2 | 1747.0 | 309.1 | 1299.7 | 65.7 | 264.9 | 56.2 | 429.9 |
| Merchandise | 267.6 | 1288.4 | 222.2 | 925.3 | 42.5 | 172.1 | 45.4 | 348.0 |
| Services[a] | 97.6 | 458.6 | 86.9 | 374.4 | 23.2 | 92.8 | 10.8 | 81.9 |
| Investment income | 26.4 | 168.2 | 25.1 | 145.5 | 11.9 | 58.3 | 1.3 | 22.0 |
| Transportation[a,b] | 43.5 | 173.8 | 37.9 | 133.8 | 5.9 | 18.6 | 5.7 | 38.9 |
| Other official[c] | 7.8 | 22.1 | 6.1 | 19.1 | 1.8 | 7.8 | 1.7 | 3.0 |
| Other private[d] | 19.9 | 94.5 | 17.8 | 76.0 | 3.6 | 8.1 | 2.1 | 18.0 |
| Share in total merchandise and services | | | | | | | | |
| Services | 26.7 | 26.3 | 28.1 | 28.8 | 35.3 | 35.0 | 19.2 | 19.1 |
| Services less investment income | 19.5 | 16.6 | 20.0 | 17.6 | 17.2 | 13.0 | 16.9 | 13.9 |

Table 5.8 (*cont.*)

B. Imports (in billion SDRs)

| | World | | Industrial countries | | United States | | Developing countries | |
|---|---|---|---|---|---|---|---|---|
| | 1970 | 1980 | 1970 | 1980 | 1970 | 1980 | 1970 | 1980 |
| Total merchandise and services | 364.2 | 1780.4 | 298.0 | 1328.8 | 59.9 | 256.2 | 66.2 | 433.6 |
| Merchandise | 258.8 | 1283.6 | 215.0 | 976.5 | 39.9 | 191.6 | 43.8 | 292.2 |
| Services | 105.4 | 496.8 | 83.0 | 352.3 | 20.0 | 64.6 | 22.4 | 141.5 |
| Investment income[a] | 28.4 | 175.3 | 19.7 | 126.8 | 5.3 | 33.1 | 8.7 | 47.8 |
| Transportation[b] | 48.1 | 200.1 | 39.3 | 142.6 | 7.8 | 19.2 | 8.8 | 55.7 |
| Other official | 9.9 | 33.6 | 8.4 | 16.9 | 5.9 | 9.2 | 1.5 | 16.7 |
| Other private | 19.0 | 87.8 | 15.6 | 66.0 | 1.0 | 3.1 | 3.4 | 21.3 |
| Share in total merchandise and services | | | | | | | | |
| Services | 28.9 | 27.9 | 27.9 | 26.5 | 33.4 | 25.2 | 33.8 | 32.6 |
| Services less investment income | 21.1 | 18.1 | 21.2 | 17.0 | 24.5 | 12.3 | 20.7 | 21.6 |

[a] "Other goods, services and income" in source. Includes investment income.

[b] Includes freight, merchandise insurance, port services, passenger fees, and expenditures of travelers.

[c] Mainly diplomatic and military personnel and installations.

[d] Includes labor and property incomes of nonresidents, insurance (other than freight insurance), communication, advertising, brokerage, management, operational leasing (other than charters), subscriptions to periodicals, and professional and technical services (including surveys, research, and provision of instruction and know-how).

*Source:* IMF, *Balance of Payments Statistics,* Vol. 32, Yearbook, Part 2, 1981; and *Balance of Payments Yearbook,* Supplement to Vol. 28, 1970–76.

Table 5.9. *Balance of payments in services, selected areas and countries, 1980 (in billion SDRs)*

| | World | Industrial countries | United States | Germany | France | United Kingdom | Japan | Developing countries |
|---|---|---|---|---|---|---|---|---|
| **Services**[a] | | | | | | | | |
| Credit | 458.6 | 374.4 | 92.8 | 39.7 | 40.8 | 41.9 | 24.2 | 81.9 |
| Debit | 496.8 | 352.3 | 64.6 | 48.3 | 34.4 | 35.3 | 32.9 | 141.5 |
| Net credit | -38.2 | 22.1 | 28.2 | -8.6 | 6.4 | 6.6 | -8.7 | -59.6 |
| **Nonfactor services**[b] | | | | | | | | |
| Credit | 290.5 | 229.0 | 34.4 | 29.6 | 25.6 | 27.4 | 20.1 | 54.5 |
| Debit | 321.5 | 225.4 | 31.6 | 39.5 | 21.9 | 20.8 | 25.0 | 93.8 |
| Net credit | -31.0 | 3.6 | 2.8 | -9.9 | 3.7 | 6.6 | -4.9 | -39.3 |
| **Private nonfactor service**[c] | | | | | | | | |
| Credit | 268.4 | 209.9 | 26.6 | 24.8 | 25.2 | 25.5 | 19.0 | 51.5 |
| Debit | 287.9 | 208.5 | 22.4 | 38.1 | 21.1 | 18.7 | 24.8 | 77.1 |
| Net credit | -19.5 | 1.4 | 4.2 | -13.3 | 4.1 | 6.8 | -5.8 | -25.6 |
| **Transportation**[d] | | | | | | | | |
| Credit | 173.7 | 133.7 | 18.5 | 12.9 | 14.5 | 16.2 | 10.5 | 38.9 |
| Debit | 200.1 | 142.7 | 19.1 | 24.5 | 13.2 | 14.8 | 16.9 | 55.9 |
| Net credit | -26.4 | -9.0 | -0.6 | -11.6 | 1.3 | 1.4 | -6.4 | -16.8 |
| **Other private nonfactor**[e] **services** | | | | | | | | |
| Credit | 94.7 | 76.2 | 8.1 | 11.9 | 10.7 | 9.3 | 8.5 | 12.6 |
| Debit | 87.8 | 65.8 | 3.3 | 13.6 | 7.9 | 3.9 | 7.9 | 21.4 |
| Net credit | 6.9 | 10.4 | 4.8 | -1.7 | 2.8 | 5.4 | 0.6 | -8.8 |

[a] "Other goods, services, and income" in source. Includes investment income.

[b] "Other goods, services, and income" less investment income.

[c] "Other goods, services, and income" less investment income and less "other official goods, services, and income." The last category refers mainly to services rendered to diplomatic and military personnel and installations.

[d] Freight, insurance, passenger services, port services, tourism.

[e] Private nonfactor services less transportation. For inclusions see note *d* of Table 5.5.

*Source:* IMF, *Balance of Payment Statistics*, Vol. 32, Yearbook, Part 2, 1981.

Table 5.10. *Expansion ratios (1980/1970) for GDP and trade (based on current prices)*

|  | World | Indus-trialized countries | United States | Developing countries |
|---|---|---|---|---|
| GDP | 3.9 | 3.6 | 2.6 | 5.4 |
| Trade, total | 4.8 | 4.2 | 4.0 | 7.6 |
| Merchandise | 4.8 | 4.2 | 4.0 | 7.7 |
| Services | 4.7 | 4.3 | 4.0 | 7.6 |
| Excluding investment income | 4.1 | 3.7 | 3.1 | 6.3 |
| Private | 4.7 | 4.3 | 2.2 | 8.6 |

*Note:* GDP based on aggregate GDP of 94 developing market economies and 21 industrialized countries, converted to dollars by exchange rates. "Expansion ratios" are obtained by dividing 1980 current values by 1970 current values.

Trade based on IMF export data. See Table 5.8 for source.

Growth was accompanied by a rise in the proportion of world production that was traded. Thus Table 5.10 shows a more rapid expansion in trade than in GDP for the world, industrialized countries, developing countries, and the United States. The expansion of service exports was not very different from that of merchandise exports. However, if investment income is excluded the expansion ratio for services is notably smaller than in commodities. It is interesting to note that growth during the decade for both GDP and all the trade categories including private services was higher for the developing countries than for the industrialized countries.

*Assessment*

How then shall we assess the relative importance of private nonfactor services in the international business activities of the United States? Growth in service exports and in sales of foreign service affiliates has been greater than domestic growth, but service exports have not expanded as rapidly as merchandise trade. Revenues from the sales of foreign affiliates are much larger than export proceeds. Service industry affiliates accounted for about 40 percent of total affiliate sales, but much of this was in trade- and petroleum-related services, which do not seem to be the focus of policy attention. Sales of foreign service affiliates have been more dynamic than sales of foreign commodity affiliates, at least until the last few years.

However, if the actual or potential growth rate is to be the criterion for policy attention, the classification of an industry as a service or commodity

Table 5.11. *Service industries involved in U.S. trade liberalization efforts, crudely classified by motivations of foreign restrictions*

| Restrictions related to cultural or regulatory motivations | In-between situations | Restrictions not clearly related to regulatory motivations and mainly protective in purpose |
|---|---|---|
| Banking (FS, NS) | Accounting (NS) | Construction |
| Health (PP) | Advertising (CI) | Franchising |
| Information (PP, NS) | Business, professional services (CI) | Leasing |
| Insurance (FS, PP) | Education (CI) | Lodging |
| Transportation (PP, NS) | Employment services (PP, CI) | Tourism |
|  | Motion pictures (CI) |  |

*Note:* CI: cultural identity.
  FS: financial stability.
  NS: national sovereignty or security.
  PP: protection of public from monopoly power, fraud or other undesired practices not easily discerned by consumers.

activity becomes irrelevant. The data we have examined and the hetero-geneity of services stressed earlier suggest that there are some (many?) private nonfactor services not characterized by rapid growth. On the other hand, a search into the commodity sectors would doubtless produce some industries characterized by rapid growth in affiliate sales.

Some types of services may warrant special attention for reasons other than their direct quantitative importance or growth potential. For example, telecommunications and data transfers are areas to which importance is sometimes attached not only owing to their growth potential, but to their high technological character and their strategic importance to other inter-national business activities. But here again the commodity–service dichot-omy is not the key element.

### International services in current U.S. commercial policy

The kinds of services that are the focus of U.S. commercial policy are represented by the sixteen industries found in Table 5.11[22]. The industries all fall under the heading of private nonfactor services found in balance of transactions statistics. However, no effort has been made in the U.S. list to provide a comprehensive classification of all private nonfactor services. The criterion of inclusion seems to have been services about which the con-cerned U.S. government agencies (mainly the Office of the U.S. Trade

Representative and the Department of Commerce) learned through receipt of complaints or through surveys of U.S. business firms of the existence of barriers to foreign service sales. A second major difference is that the focus is not on exports but on service transactions carried out in a host country by a U.S. affiliate. The fact that the ITC reported that most of the foreign service revenue of the responding firms were produced by foreign affiliates, joint ventures, and franchising and licensing suggests that the main targets are investment rather than trade restrictions. (Incidentally, the liberalization of the imports from the U.S. of the commodities and services necessary to support service sales are also included in U.S. policy objectives.)

The economic characteristics of the industries included in the U.S. list can only be treated impressionistically. A number including information services, accounting, advertising, and the engineering and design features of construction services are probably intensive in human capital. Some of these and others such as leasing and franchising are industries in which firms have developed special managerial techniques that can be exploited abroad with relatively limited additional development effort on the part of the firm [Caves's public goods analogy applies here (1971).] Human capital intensity and advanced managerial methods in these industries probably confer a comparative advantage on the U.S. companies. However, the list also includes industries such as tourism and transportation, where comparative advantage rests with other countries having lower wages and sunnier climes. Even in the latter cases, of course, a U.S. firm may have a company-specific comparative advantage, leading, for example, to the establishment of U.S. hotel affiliates in tropical climates.

With respect to growth prospects also, the industries seemed to vary widely. Some, such as information and data processing services, seem to be strong growth points of great strategic importance whereas others such as transportation appear to be tied to a slower pattern.

The U.S. emphasis on the investment-related sales relative to exports is also suggested by a classification of the barriers offered in an official briefing paper.[23] The barriers in this document can be grouped under three main headings: restrictions on rights of residents to import services from a foreign country, limitations on right of establishment, and discrimination against operations of foreign-owned firms once they are established. Examples of more specific barriers under the first classification are quotas or license requirements and restrictions on availability of foreign exchange. Outright prohibition or impediments to establishment of local operations and local ownership requirements are particular barriers in the second group. The last category includes a varied collection of examples of barriers restricting management control, such as controls on reinvestment or repatriation of profits and discriminatory taxes on earnings, and barriers that interfere with marketing and support facilities, such as discriminatory regulatory procedures and government procurement policies.

This classification invites several comments relating to the similarity and dissimilarity of these restrictions compared to those that might be found on a list focused on commodities. The similarities are obvious; there are few if any items in the service classification that would not be found also in a similar survey of restrictions on commodities, although the commodity list might well include more numerous references to restrictions on exports.

The dissimilarities are not inherent in the restrictions per se but rather in the political context in which they are found. With respect to restrictions on commodity trade, GATT provides a set of rules and some sort of surveillance mechanism that is entirely absent for services.[24] When it comes to investment there is no worldwide code like GATT either for commodities or services. The disagreements among countries about the investment provisions of the Charter for an International Trade Organization (ITO) were among the main causes that led to the failure of that document to receive ratification. It is hardly likely that it will be easier today than it was then for capital exporting and capital importing countries to reach a meaningful agreement on an investment code.

The other important difference between commodity and service restrictions is the extensive degree to which restrictions on foreign service activities are bound up with social, political, and economic objectives that transcend the merely protective motivations of the restrictions. In a number of service industries domestic firms are subject to various restraints and regulations designed to protect the public from monopoly power, fraud, deception, or the invasion of privacy. The regulation of banking and of foreign exchange markets to promote financial stability are almost universal. Similar motivations, particularly those related to the protection of public health and safety, lead to regulation of some commodity-producing industries (e.g., drugs, electric appliances), but they are probably less pervasive.

Not only is it to be expected that foreign-controlled firms will also be subject to such regulations and restrictions, but foreign ownership often raises special fears and problems. The concentration of financial power in foreign hands and the foreign control of advertising stereotypes are illustrations. A crude and rather arbitrary classification of the sixteen service industries according to the extent to which discrimination against foreign firms may be based on or reinforced by such social motivations is presented in Table 5.11. The classification is meant to be suggestive; it is not based on any effort to assess the nature and strength of foreign attitudes. Nor is it intended to deny that a protective motivation may often enter into barriers that are justified on social grounds. What seems very likely, however, is that strongly held positions in support of barriers to foreign control in certain services are deeply embedded in the domestic values and institutions of many countries. It is important to add that these objections to foreign control do not necessarily apply to the same industry in each actual or potential host country. The inference for negotiations is that an industry-by-industry, country-by-country approach is called for.

## Conclusion

In considering the policy implications of the findings of the previous sections, due regard has to be taken of our concentration on the empirical aspects of a very complicated subject. Only limited attention has been devoted to the political and diplomatic context in which the U.S. service initiative must be placed. With this caveat, the following points emerge from our considerations:

1. Services probably represent a relative growth sector in the domestic economies. Measurement problems abound, but as a rough approximation it may be taken that something like half of the growth in service industry shares in the production of GDP tends to reflect a relative increase in prices and only the other half an increase in real quantities.

2. There is little evidence of rapid growth in private nonfactor services relative to world trade in commodities or as a share of trade in commodities and services. This may represent inadequate measurement. Also, trade in both commodities and services has expanded more rapidly than the world GDP of market economies. However, a policy based on a sweeping view of the entire category of private nonfactor services as an area of great future trade growth relative to commodity trade does not seem warranted. If growth prospects are to be the criteria for special negotiations of trade barriers, the commodity–service dichotomy is not very relevant.

3. Trade in many services does not have characteristics that provide any justification for their exclusion from the GATT regimes. Trade in nonfactor services, amounting to something like 10 or 15 percent of world trade in commodities and services appears to have been omitted from the GATT rules more by oversight and lack of knowledge than for any compelling reason. An effort to extend the GATT rules to trade in nonfactor services seems warranted.

4. In the case of U.S. firms, nonfactor service sales by affiliates, or branches, in host countries are much more important than service sales made from the United States (i.e., exports). Thus, though much of the language of U.S. policy statements is cast in terms of trade, what is really at stake is the treatment of U.S. direct investment in foreign host countries. Service activities do not seem to warrant special treatment related to direct foreign investment. The general case for the removal of restrictions on the

right of establishment and on the business operations of a foreign affiliate is not different for commodity- and service-producing industries (unless it is argued that restrictions on direct investment should be more lenient for services because they cannot be exported).

5. With the exception of a general extension of the GATT, there appear to emerge strong reasons for industry-by-industry, country-by-country negotiations. One set of reasons rests in the often deeply embedded objections to equal treatment for foreign suppliers of services in certain industries, particularly ones that are domestically regulated in pursuit of nationally accepted objectives. The strength of these attitudes and the industries upon which they focus vary from one country to another. An effort to include all countries in a broad coverage negotiation might produce a very low common denominator. Also, a more selective approach will enable the U.S. negotiators to concentrate on situations (industries and countries) where the payoff from the relaxation of restrictions would be high.

6. The evaluation of the prospects of a program that is based on so many unknowns and so many uncertainties is hazardous. However, the size of the industries included, the subset for which a large expansion in U.S. exports could be expected even with the relaxation of barriers, and a realistic appraisal of the extent to which barriers are likely to be negotiated down, all suggest that the potential gains to the U.S. balance of payments from the present program are not likely to be large. A similar evaluation seems appropriate for U.S. sales of services from foreign-based affiliates and branches. The prospects for gains are enhanced by the greater importance of such sales and by the rapid growth of some sectors, but the difficulty of reducing obstacles to direct investment is an offsetting factor. However, particular industries and firms may benefit substantially.

All this is not to denigrate any U.S. initiative for lower trade and investment barriers. Such a policy initiative does identify and attack restrictions on international business. If the restrictions it seeks out are foreign ones, our trade partners can be relied upon to identify ours. In any case, considering the growing speed with which imitation overtakes innovation in world markets, any improvement in the U.S. balance of payments or other U.S. gains may turn out to be mainly of a transient character. Nonetheless, the program provides a modest counterweight on the side of liberalization in a world in which restrictions are growing.

### Notes

1. "Final" demand refers to purchases for own use; that is, they are purchases not intended for resale, with or without further processing.

2. In domestic production and consumption, services and commodities are usually defined so that together they exhaust the GDP. In the balance of payments, however, flows of capital assets form another important component.

3. See Helena Stalson's paper in this volume. Also Sapir and Lutz (1980 and 1981), DiLullo (1981), Balassa (1983), U.S. ITC (1982), Sapir (1982) and Schott (1982).

4. See Kravis and Lipsey (1984).

5. Among the service categories that are the focus of attention in the U.S. efforts are communication, computer and data processing, construction and engineering, consulting and management, educational services, equipment leasing, financial services, franchising, health services, hotel–motel services, insurance, motion pictures, air transportation, and maritime transportation. [U.S. ITC (1982). See also the largely overlapping list in Table 22 infra.]

6. Income elasticities were computed for 26 detailed service and 77 detailed commodity categories (Kravis, Heston, and Summers, 1983, Table 8).

7. The underlying figures doubtless suffer from serious incomparabilities for the two sets of countries and even for countries within each set, but the main outlines of the service sector are probably correctly reflected.

8. However, government services in Table 5.2, unlike the corresponding Table 5.1 entry, includes public spending on health, education, and recreation.

9. All the countries are included for which data were available on a revised World Bank tape corresponding to *World Tables 1980*. The 49 countries accounted for 67% of the population of all market economies and 73% of their aggregate real GDP in 1975. The period 1960–75 is taken because the number of countries for which data are available shrinks for earlier and later years. For the experience of France, the United Kingdom and the United States over time see Kravis, Heston, and Summers, 1983, Table 5.

10. A few in which individuals proffer their labor directly to households may or may not be regarded as "industries."

11. In the domestic economy classifications virtually all services are nonfactor services. Purchases of these services involve payments for some distinct form of production or output rather than a payment made solely for the services of a factor of production. (This is true even when the service output is measured by the input of the factor, as is often done in national accounting.) Nonfactor services in balance of payments classifications include a mixture of categories found in the final-demand and industry-of-origin classifications. For example, transportation is a standard category in the industry-of-origin classification, where it includes both final and intermediate purchases. Components such as passenger fees would be found on a sufficiently detailed list of final-demand expenditures. On the other hand, some categories found in standard classifications of domestic service industries are not found in the classifications used for international transactions. Trade, for example, is an important domestic service industry, but the value of distributive services in international transactions is included in the value of the commodity or service traded. The difference is related to the fact that the contribution of service industries to the production of GDP is measured from a value-added approach, whereas the value of nonfactor

services in international transactions is measured in terms of gross sales revenue or purchase values.

12. In the U.S. statistics royalty and fees include compensation of U.S. employees temporarily assigned to foreign affiliates of U.S. parents.

13. The $19-billion-dollar figure includes $1.2 billion in contractors' fees. DiLullo, 1981, p. 31.

14. As Helena Stalson points out in her paper in this volume, widely varying estimates of revenues from foreign service sales have been offered. An estimate by the U.S. International Trade Commission (ITC, 1982) covering 14 service categories that accounted for a large part but not for all of the service sector placed 1981 service revenues from foreign sources at $105.5 billion.

15. The 1980/70 expansion ratio for GDP (in current prices) was 2.63 (IMF, 1983). Here and elsewhere, relative quantitative evaluations about services must be hedged with reservations about the comprehensiveness of statistical coverage for service transactions relative to that for merchandise. It is possible that both the relative level and growth of services may be understated.

16. The GDP expansion ratios were 1.70 and 2.53 for the two periods, whereas those for merchandise exports were 1.46 and 3.98.

17. The 143 responses came from a questionnaire mailed to 479 "known international service companies in 14 categories of services."

18. The difficulty is with the category "other private goods, services, and income" given in the source. The category includes payments to labor and for royalties as well as for nonfactor services such as communications and nonmerchandise insurance. "Other official goods, services, and income" seems to be constituted mainly of nonfactor services; it is dominated by payments for diplomatic representation and joint military arrangements abroad. IMF (1977a).

19. The International Monetary Fund (IMF) classification "other private goods, services, and income" shows gradually rising U.S. surpluses for the years 1970–80. The U.S. classification, private nonfactor services excluding transportation (Table 5.4) gives the same results though with smaller absolute magnitudes.

20. IMF, *Balance of Payments Statistics,* Vol. 32, Yearbook, Pt. 2, (1981).

21. Kravis and Lipsey (1984).

22. This list, which is not intended to be exhaustive, is based on industries that appear in the documents produced by and for the Office of the U.S. Trade Representative. The list overlaps substantially with the 14 industries included in the ITC study cited previously.

23. U.S. Office of the U.S. Trade Representative (1982). An inventory of over 800 cases of barriers was compiled.

24. Except for motion pictures, which are included in the GATT.

## References

Balassa, B. (1983), "New Issues in Trade Policy in the 1980s," in W. R. Cline (ed.), *Trade Policy in the 1980s,* Washington, D.C.: Institute for International Economics.

Caves, R. E. (February 1971), "International Corporations: The Industrial Economics of Foreign Investment," *Economica* 38, 1–27.

DiLullo, Anthony J. (November 1981), "Service Transactions in the U.S. International Accounts, 1970–80," *Survey of Current Business* 61, 29–47.

International Bank for Reconstruction and Development (1980), *World Tables 1980,* Second Edition, Washington, D.C.: IBRD.

International Monetary Fund (1977a), *Balance of Payments Manual,* Fourth Edition, Washington, D.C.: IMF.

(1977b) *Balance of Payments Yearbook,* Supplement to Vol. 28, 1970–76, Washington, D.C.: IMF.

(1981) *Balance of Payments Statistics,* Vol. 32, Yearbook, Part 2, Washington, D.C.: IMF.

(1983) *International Financial Statistics Yearbook, 1982,* Washington, D.C.: IMF.

Kravis, I.B., A. Heston, R. Summers (1982) *World Product and Income: International Comparisons of Real Gross Product,* Baltimore: The Johns Hopkins University Press.

(1983) "The Share of Services in Economic Growth" in F. G. Adams and G. Hickman (eds.), *Global Econometrics: Essays in Honor of Lawrence R. Klein,* Cambridge, Mass.: M.I.T. Press.

Kravis, I. B., and R. E. Lipsey (1984), "The Diffusion of Economic Growth in the World Economy, 1950–80," in J. W. Kendrick (ed.), *International Comparisons of Productivity and Causes of the Slowdown,* Cambridge, Mass.: Ballinger Publishing Co.

Leveson, Irving (1985), "Services in the U.S. Economy," Chapter 3 in this book.

Organization for Economic Cooperation and Development (1982), *National Accounts, 1963–80,* Vol. II, Detailed Tables, Paris: OECD.

Sapir, Andre (Fall 1982), "Trade in Services: Policy Issues for the Eighties," *Columbia Journal of World Business,* 17, 77–83.

Sapir, A., and E. Lutz (August 1980), "Trade in Non-Factor Services: Past Trends and Current Issues," World Bank Staff Working Paper No. 410.

(August 1981), "Trade in Services: Economic Determinants and Development-Related Issues," World Bank Staff Working Paper No. 480.

Schott, Jeffrey J. (1982), "International Trade in Services," Carnegie Endowment for International Peace.

Stalson, Helena (1985), "U.S. Trade Policy and International Service Transactions," Chapter 6 in this book.

Summers, Robert (1985), "Services in the International Economy," Chapter 1 in this book.

U.S. Department of Commerce (1960), *U.S. Business Investments in Foreign Countries,* by Samuel Pizer and Frederick Cutler, Office of Business Economics, Washington, D.C.: USDC.

U.S. Department of Commerce (1975), *U.S. Direct Investment Abroad, 1966,* Bureau of Economic Analysis, Washington, D.C.: USDC.

U.S. Department of Commerce (1981), *U.S. Direct Investment Abroad, 1977,* Bureau of Economic Analysis, Washington, D.C.: USDC.

U.S. International Trade Commission (September 1982) Publication 1290, *The Relationship of Exports in U.S. Service Industries to U.S. Merchandise Exports,* Washington, D.C.: USITC.

U.S. Office of the U.S. Trade Representative (1982), Briefing Packet: *International Trade in Services, #4, What Are the Different Kinds of Barriers Service Industries Encounter in Their Foreign Operations?* Washington, D.C.: U.S. Office of the U.S. Trade Representative.

Whichard, Obie G. (August 1982), "U.S. Direct Investment Abroad in 1981," *Survey of Current Business* 62, 11–29.

Williamson, Oliver E. (December 1981), "The Modern Corporation: Origins, Evolutions, Attributes," *Journal of Economic Literature* 19, 1537–70.

# CHAPTER 6

# U.S. trade policy and international service transactions*

## HELENA STALSON

The role of services in the U.S. domestic economy has been the subject of a number of major investigations since World War II; their role in international trade and investment has received little attention until the last decade. In both cases the investigators have been plagued by serious problems of definition and measurement, and policy makers have been slow to take account of the contribution of services and to place service issues on their agenda. The result has been delay in understanding a sector that is rapidly growing at home and internationally. A short description of services in international trade will be followed by a discussion of trade restrictions faced by U.S. service firms and the rationales offered for these impediments to trade. International and U.S. action on trade in services is surveyed next. The final sections of the paper address United States policy, recent policy proposals, and their fate in the international arena. The ongoing debate concerning the direction and strategy that U.S. policy should take is outlined.

Both domestically and internationally services are characterized by their range and complexity. The pattern of domestically traded services, however, is very different from that of those traded internationally. Two sectors that figure prominently in the U.S. domestic economy are government and a broad range of social services, such as education and health activities. They are minor items in the international picture where transportation, financial services, and tourism are relatively more important – estimated at 55 percent of the total – than they are at home. And it is expected that the newer, high-technology sectors, especially communications and data processing, could soon account for a significantly greater proportion of service revenues from abroad than their share in total sales of services in the domestic market.

A complicating development in the way services are produced and recorded in the United States is also taking place in the international sphere:

* The author has greatly benefited from comments and suggestions made on a draft of this chapter by William Diebold, Jr., former Senior Fellow at the Council on Foreign Relations, who was a member of the Services Policy Advisory Committee of the U.S. Trade Representative's office.

a blurring of the distinction between goods and service producers. In the trend toward diversification some domestic manufacturers have purchased service firms as additional profit centers that will help to smooth out fluctuations in income from goods sales; others have replaced in-house service operations with outside suppliers who can provide the services more efficiently and cheaply. Similarly, U.S. manufacturers are selling their goods abroad and at the same time making service contracts for maintenance and repair, or providing an engineering service to start with and then supplying the equipment and materials once the designs are accepted. Faced with the threat of nationalization or ownership-sharing requirements, some U.S. firms with foreign manufacturing plants are giving up their equity positions, or separating them from service operations, and are turning to contracts that provide more lucrative and certain returns in the form of management, consulting, and research fees. The common thread in all these cases is a rearrangement of functions that, although resulting in the same production of goods and services, are classified in a different way.

Finally, in what has been called an "inconspicuous" export of services,[1] some portion of the administrative, financial, and technical talent in U.S. home offices and laboratories supports the formal transactions across national borders or the sales of U.S. subsidiaries abroad but is not recorded as an export of services. If we allow for the contributions of services to the domestic output of goods or services that are themselves destined for export, we are obliged to question the definition of services as activities that must be performed where they are consumed.

### Foreign restrictions on U.S. services

The present situation in world trade in services is one of rapid change. As the United States relinquishes its commanding lead in world trade in manufactured goods, it looks to international markets as an outlet for its services, in many of which it has a competitive advantage. Although it is risky to say that international service transactions are growing faster than goods trade – given the unsatisfactory data available – all indicators seem to suggest that the United States is the world's largest exporter of services and that there has been significant growth in the nontraditional services, whereas tourism and transportation have suffered from the effects of worldwide recession.

The special nature of some services has galvanized governments into taking action. Often services have a special relation to cultural and political objectives as well as to security requirements. Some services provide an essential contribution to economic activities. The extent to which barriers or at least restrictive regulations have gone up is attested to in a voluminous inventory compiled by the Office of the U.S. Trade Representative. Many services that are traded internationally are regulated by governments, with responsibilities widely dispersed among official agencies. When a government wants to differentiate its treatment of domestic and foreign firms, a few services can be controlled by measures similar to tariff barriers for goods, such as licenses, fees, and special taxes. Most of the restrictions, however, resemble nontariff barriers, and because of their flexibility they lend themselves to the great range of activities that services represent. Administrative barriers take the form of delays in granting licenses, failure to certify professional services, discriminatory implementation of statutory regulations, inadequate access to local judicial bodies. Most of the barriers can be adapted to the regulation of any service, although financial or personnel requirements tend to affect certain sectors more than others.[2]

Both developed and developing, market-oriented and centrally planned countries resort to restraints on foreign services, and there is no clear pattern that emerges. In the U.S. government's inventory of complaints by American firms against foreign barriers, more cases of restriction showed up in developing countries. But this does not provide a weighted picture of obstacles to trade in services and, of course, reflects only the experience of those firms that responded to the survey. Furthermore, there is no industry pattern of how discriminatory practices are applied. In some countries the government may rely chiefly on procurement policies to give support to a domestic service industry; in others there is greater selectivity, with financial controls applied in some sectors, personnel restrictions in some, and licensing or performance requirements in others.

Restrictions include restraints on services that are both traded and provided by subsidiaries operating within a country and also on those that are solely investment related.[3] Among the former are denial of access to a market by imports and of right of establishment to perform the service within the country; limitation on the level of sales permitted to a foreign service firm or requirements that it use local sales organizations; discriminatory fees or licensing arrangements; government procurement practices and subsidies to local firms that limit the competitive opportunities for a foreign firm; limitation on importation of goods needed to perform a service; failure to make information on local standards and legal requirements available to a foreign supplier.

Among the barriers that are investment related are employment requirements that control the personnel practices of the foreign firm; restrictions on the extent of foreign ownership permitted; government regulations that bear more heavily on a foreign firm than on its local competitors; restrictions on the level of profits and royalties that may be transferred to the parent firm; limitation of the foreign firm's access to advertising and communications facilities; discriminatory practices against specific service industries, for example, higher reserve requirements for foreign bank subsidiaries, special capital requirements for foreign insurance firms.[4]

## Major issues in service transactions

International competition in services affects employment in both importing and exporting countries. As in trade in goods, foreign suppliers of services may both substitute the work of employees back home for that of host-country workers and at the same time provide local jobs in distribution, maintenance and repair, and other supporting activities. The net gain or loss in terms of job creation will depend on the type of activity, how far it is conducted by a subsidiary office of the foreign parent, and its relationship to other activities with which it is closely linked.

Access to technology has led to a number of government regulations. Some require an unbundling of the various parts of a multinational's operations, a separation of some of the services it performs from its other activities. Others require the inclusion of certain services in addition to the activities that the firm would normally have undertaken abroad. By selective application of licensing fees, royalty arrangements, data-processing restrictions, and exchange controls on remittance of profits, a government may be able to gain greater access to those aspects of the foreign firm's business that it believes will contribute to, or fill a gap in, its own technology.

In many cases this approach closely resembles the historical infant-industry policy of protecting a domestic activity until it is strong enough to stand up to foreign competition. It has found favor in both developed and developing countries and is most prominent in regulation of data flows and financial activities. Comparative advantage in one service or another is also a goal of governments, one that is closely related to protection of an emerging industry. It can be acquired – in a sense artificially – by (1) nurturing a domestic industry, by means of subsidies, government procurement contracts, or tax treatment, so that it can offer a better price than foreign competitors, or (2) by granting entry to a foreign firm on the condition that it meet certain performance requirements, such as a minimum level of exports to third markets.

Foreign services, even if they are supplied by foreign affiliates within a country, tend to be seen as less an integral part of the economy than a branch plant of a foreign manufacturer. Because of the nature of many services, there seems to be a closer tie to the foreign parent; the host government has less leverage, and the foreign-controlled operation is perceived to be more of a potential threat to national welfare. More than most goods, many services carry with them the overtones of national values and customs and are likely to collide with the social objectives of another country. The control of professional services, such as legal, accounting, advertising, and education and health, is the basis for many regulations, and the protection of the cultural identity of the nation underlies a wide range of restrictions in the world of entertainment and the arts.

Broad security issues weigh more heavily in services than they do in most goods. All governments regulate their financial sectors to ensure the safety of their monetary systems as well as the protection of their citizens. They also regulate their aviation, shipping, and motor transport sectors as vital areas for the nation's economy and defense. Communications systems are highly regulated if private, and many are government owned.

These commercial, social, and defense objectives move a government to set up barriers to international transactions. The motivation of those who oppose the barriers is predominantly economic. They argue that, like goods, services that are allowed to flow freely bring benefits to the consumer because competition is encouraged and the range of services available is increased. They recognize the merits of protection for national defense purposes, for meeting social needs, and even for maintaining cultural values, but they are concerned about the costs of trade and investment restraints in achieving these goals, and they question the efficacy of any policy that blocks the flow of technologically advanced services when they can contribute to progress in other sectors.

### International action on services

For many decades certain services have been the object of international arrangements that provide machinery for cooperation on regulations and technical procedures. The oldest, the International Telecommunications Union, came into being in 1934, replacing the International Telegraph Union of 1865. Banking regulations are reviewed by the Bank for International Settlements, set up in Basel in 1930. Aviation has been handled by the International Civil Aviation Organization since 1947, and shipping by the International Maritime Organization (1958) and the Intergovernmental Maritime Consultative Organization (1959). A major service in international trade, insurance, has never been subject to rules of an international body.

The articles of the General Agreement on Tariffs and Trade (GATT) refer, with one exception, to goods, although some claim that they can be interpreted as applying equally well to services. (The exception is motion pictures, a service industry that was given an article of its own, permitting a host country to impose quotas on foreign films in order to reserve screen time for the domestic industry.) At the end of the Tokyo Round of multilateral negotiations in 1979, three of the codes dealing with nontariff barriers referred specifically to services: (1) the government procurement code, which sets out rules for official purchases and includes purchases of services that are incidental to the supply of tangible goods, but does not include service contracts per se; (2) the subsidies code, which in a round-about way also refers to services since the annex to the code gives, for illustrative purposes, a number of subsidy situations, including subsidies to services; and (3) the code on civil aircraft, which provides for repair services as well as trade.

The Organization for Economic Cooperation and Development (OECD) has since the early 1960s administered two codes – on Liberalization of Current Invisible Transactions and on Capital Movements – which apply to services as well as to goods; progress in eliminating barriers to service trade under the codes has been circumscribed by the ease with which member states may without penalty acquire exceptional status for their industries. A 1975 pledge by OECD members to assure foreign-owned firms in services and manufacturing the same treatment as that provided to domestic firms has not brought noticeable improvement in opportunities for the foreigners. The OECD is reviewing this pledge and expanding the invisibles and capital movements codes, with special attention to the right of establishment as the most urgent problem. In addition, the Organization is giving special attention to a few industries – financial services, insurance, tourism, telecommunications, construction/engineering, and maritime transportation. By pursuing these parallel activities, the OECD hopes to combine the conclusions from industry-specific work (which may indicate problems that are common to other industries) with the broader study of procedures for general liberalization and international cooperation in the service sector.

The United Nations Conference on Trade and Development (UNCTAD) is the international forum where developing countries' concerns with trade issues receive major attention. These countries are heavily dependent on trade in commodities and merchandise. They account for two-thirds of the world's exports transported by sea but only 10 percent of the world's fleets. Accordingly, they have put their primary attention on shipping, with secondary attention to insurance, another service essential to commodity production and trade. The UNCTAD Committee on Shipping has been responsible for a series of innovative – or calamitous (depending upon one's point of view) – proposals for reshaping world shipping arrangements, and UNCTAD's initiative for a code governing liner shipping has been approved by a majority of the members, the United States voting against it. Ratification by countries representing 25 percent of the world's merchant fleets will bring into force the code's cargo-sharing stipulation for a

40-40-20 ratio, that is, 40 percent of a country's merchandise trade to be carried in its own ships, 40 percent in the partner country's ships, and the remainder available to third-country shipping. The United States has refused to sign the code, but the American Seafarers International Union and many U.S. shipping companies support the provisions of the code, believing that they will be assured of more jobs and contracts under it.

The UNCTAD strategy on insurance has been to work for greater domestic control over local markets. In a Special Program on Insurance, the Committee on Invisibles and Financing Related to Trade is paying particular attention to crop insurance and marine hull and aviation insurance.

## U.S. public and private action on services

With very few international agencies capable of dealing with service sector matters, complaints by U.S. firms of unfair treatment abroad have, for the most part, been handled bilaterally. Section 301 of the U.S. Trade Act of 1974 (amended in 1979) permits action against a foreign government that discriminates against or restricts U.S. commerce, including commerce in services, and the President is authorized to take retaliatory action on a unilateral basis if negotiations with the foreign government are unsuccessful. Section 102 of the 1974 Act offers possibilities of negotiating but apparently more problems than opportunities; so far no complaints have been lodged under Section 102 and only five under Section 301.

There are problems with the Trade Act approach. When the executive branch of the government sets out to negotiate a reduction in foreign barriers against American firms, its jurisdiction in assuring comparable treatment of foreign service firms in the United States must be shared with national regulatory agencies such as the Interstate Commerce Commission and the Federal Communications Commission and with state governments in the case of insurance and some banking. The federal government is therefore limited in exchanging concessions with other countries by its ability to persuade the autonomous national and state regulators to go along.[5] Furthermore, since the application of the Trade Act specifically to services is so new, there is some question about the President's authority to retaliate. Although a number of state laws permit the restriction of foreign financial services if the foreign government discriminates against U.S. firms, so far no state has taken action, and the problem is one of coordinating federal and state policies, not easily done where 51 statutes and regulatory charters might have to be taken into account.

Other difficulties in applying the Trade Act to foreign barriers to services are (1) the risk that retaliation or the threat of it – the only course available if negotiations fail – would do more harm than good by jeopardizing the existing situation for the U.S. firm abroad, and (2) related to this risk, the fact that in so many service areas the United States doesn't have much to trade off since its presence abroad in services is already so much greater than the foreign presence in the United States.

U.S. federal legislation applying to international operations of specific service industries includes:

1. *Aviation.* The Civil Aeronautics Board authorizes the entry of a foreign airline if it is considered to be in the public interest, and the Board may order reciprocal treatment for an airline whose government denies access to its market by a U.S. airline.

2. *Shipping.* The Federal Maritime Commission supervises domestic and foreign water transport and is authorized to retaliate against foreign carriers.

3. *Trucking.* The Interstate Commerce Commission certifies all firms, domestic and foreign, engaging in motor carrier transportation. A 1980 act easing the requirements for entry has led to strong protests from the American industry that deregulating the U.S. market has given Canadian truckers an advantage in competing here not available to U.S. truckers in Canada.

4. *Communications.* The Federal Communications Commission regulates domestic and foreign communications and limits the extent to which aliens may own and operate facilities. It has interpreted its Congressional mandate as including the right to require reciprocal action by foreign governments.

5. *Banking.* The Federal Reserve System's policy of granting charters to foreign banks seeking entry into the United States is one of national treatment, that is, the foreign applicant who meets the requirements is given the same status as a domestic bank, regardless of the treatment that a U.S. applicant meets in the home country of the foreign bank. (Some states, however, apply standards of reciprocity.)

Services have been perceived as a heterogeneous collection of activities, many highly regulated by official agencies zealous in protecting their authority, all of them difficult to measure, many closely linked to the production or distribution of goods, many sensitive to political and cultural goals, some facing government-owned entities abroad. The result has been the neglect of services as a sector and a lack of domestic institutions and procedures for treating them more broadly than as individual industries. However, the recent upsurge of interest has been accompanied by the creation of a number of public and private agencies and organizations specifically devoted to trade in services. The U.S. Trade Representative's Office is the major agency formulating policy proposals on services in general and individual services as well; reporting to it are a number of service sector advisory committees made up of private citizens. The U.S. Department of Commerce, where the work on data collection and analysis is concentrated, has established an Office of Service Industries, with specialists handling ten major sectors. The International Trade Commission has analyzed the effects of restrictions on services on the export of goods. The President's Export Council has a Subcommittee on Trade in Services. In the private sector the U.S. Council for International Business, the U.S. Chamber of Commerce, and the Committee for Economic Development have set up service sections; twenty large companies have organized a Coalition of Service Industries to make sure their case is heard, and Georgetown University has set up a Panel on Services and U.S. Trade Policy, made up of representatives from nine U.S. firms with large overseas organizations. (A major study abroad has been undertaken by the Trade Policy Research Center in London.)

## U.S. proposals and the foreign response

The long-term objective of the U.S. government, strongly supported by major business groups, is a far-reaching commitment to liberalization of trade in services and equal treatment of domestic and foreign investors in services – by all countries. As originally conceived, this ambitious goal was to be worked toward in a series of what were regarded as manageable stages, in the expectation that a decade would pass before a comprehensive liberalization of service transactions could be achieved. Meanwhile, it was hoped that progress could be made in establishing general rules and principles, preferably in GATT because it is the only international agency where nations can exchange concessions of a binding nature. In addition, however, the United States believed that multilateral negotiations could and should be carried out simultaneously with bilateral efforts. Each approach, it was thought, complements the other. Bilateral talks can keep the pressure on governments to abstain from new restrictions; they also may bring to light problems that need examination in a broader forum. Multilateral talks are necessary to give shape and substance to broad concepts that apply to services generally and to provide a framework of procedures for dealing with a wide range of industries.

At the November 1982 meeting of GATT the United States proposed that its members undertake a work program consisting of three major parts:

1. An inventory and analysis of existing barriers to services, both in general and in individual sectors.
2. A study of the applicability to services of GATT principles and procedures; of its basic concepts of national treatment, nondiscrimination, dispute settlement; and of the codes dealing with nontariff barriers, especially those concerned with subsidies, government procurement, licensing, and standards.
3. An examination of national objectives and the role of services in achieving them.

The overtures of the United States to its trading partners met with responses ranging from lukewarm to hostile, with no other country prepared to grant the subject the priority that the United States felt it warranted. The most supportive GATT members were the United Kingdom, West Germany, Sweden, and Japan. The most negative were France, Italy, and the Third World countries. Canada, Australia, and the remaining European countries were somewhere in between. Most foreign governments regarded U.S. service industries as more advanced than their own, and the benefits from liberalizing the terms of entry seemed much slighter than the costs of exposing their own service sectors to the kind of aggressive competition attributed to the Americans, particularly in a period of severe recession when national income and employment might be adversely affected.

More generally, many developed country representatives abroad and some observers in the United States argued against a major initiative on services at the time, on the grounds that relations in traditional areas of trade in goods were so bad that there should be no attempt to negotiate international understandings in new sectors until problems in the old ones had been straightened out. In their view a shift to a focus on services would be a way of dodging the responsibilities incurred in earlier rounds of negotiations. They went on to note that there has been very little experience with the GATT codes on nontariff barriers and that an adequate period of testing their applicability to goods should precede any resort to them for services.

The developing countries were, for the most part, even more resolutely opposed to the U.S. initiative. They were skeptical of U.S. official motives, and they regarded U.S. service firms with the same suspicious eye they turn on multinationals engaged in manufacturing and mining, charging them with the same business practices that they believe are denying their countries an opportunity to develop in these other sectors: pricing policies and employment practices that are disadvantageous to the host country, excessive transfer of earnings to the parent, lack of adequate training and technical assistance for host-country workers and firms. Furthermore, they were not eager to enter an international agreement requiring them to subject their own service sectors to the scrutiny of GATT members, and, as in other matters, they preferred to negotiate in UNCTAD.

The outcome of the 1982 GATT conference was regarded as a disaster by some and as a miraculous staving-off of total defeat by the more optimistic. Although services were on the GATT agenda for the first time, they had to compete with a number of thorny nonservice issues, notably procedures for safeguards, dispute-settlement mechanisms, agricultural support programs, and trade with developing countries. The atmosphere at the conference was tense, the debate acrimonious, and the achievements minimal.

The industrial countries, for the most part, offered little help on services, and the developing countries tried to make the matter a North–South issue. Instead of the modest work program the United States hoped that GATT members would adopt, it had to settle for an arrangement under which those countries *interested in services* would examine their national policies and pool their information. No GATT working group was set up, and no funds were made available for collecting and analyzing the national data. No study was authorized on how GATT principles and codes could apply to services or how trade versus investment issues should be handled. At best, the subject of services would be reviewed at the 1984 session of GATT when the members, it was agreed, would consider whether multilateral action should be taken.

### Policy issues for the future

The assertions and assumptions of the advocates of service trade liberalization are being debated and challenged in an ever-widening circle of interested parties. The advocates, in both the private and public sectors, make a persuasive case:

1. Benefits from trade liberalization in services can be defended by the same logic that applies to trade in goods. A freer flow of services will mean a better allocation of economic resources, lower prices of services to consumers and, by making possible a reduced cost of service inputs in manufacturing operations, lower prices of goods as well.

2. An increasing proportion of world trade is represented by services,[6] and a number of them (especially transport, insurance, communications, and banking) are the essential underpinning of trade in goods, so that restriction or distortion of one automatically restricts the other.

3. Most of the barriers to services now in place or being contemplated are similar; even when they are not, general principles and rules can be established and subsequent sectoral agreements can handle differences in treatment.

4. The United States has a competitive advantage in most services, and trade in services offsets the balance-of-payments deficit in merchandise trade. The future of the United States rests on the health and growth of the service industries, and their foreign operations make a significant contribution to these industries' well being, whether they are conducted from this country or from affiliated offices abroad.

5. We need to negotiate an international agreement on services because at present there is no place to bring grievances or settle disputes. If we don't achieve some kind of agreement to reduce restrictions, or at least an understanding not to erect new ones, we will find ourselves facing the same kind

of wall of barriers that faced us before the reciprocal trade agreements program went into effect in 1934 and that has taken so long to whittle down.

6. The freer flow of trade and investment in services will facilitate the transfer of needed technologies to other countries – new kinds of insurance policies, more efficient ways of banking and, of course, the dazzling possibilities in data processing and transmission – thus contributing to economic development and general welfare of the world's people. Indeed, a good case can be made for the view that an unimpeded transfer of services can do more to raise standards of living than the free exchange of goods.

7. The very danger of backsliding in traditional trade areas lends support to the view that the liberalizing impulse might be revived and strengthened by energetic, well-organized action in a new area.

8. Even though a global agreement may not be feasible in the near term, a compact among like-minded countries will make investment decisions far easier under an established regime than are possible in the uncertain atmosphere today.

Those who recommend a wait-and-see approach believe that the issues are being thrust upon us for solution before we have arrived at any clear sense of the basic aspects of international transactions in services. They emphasize that we have not resolved conceptual problems of the size and composition of this sector or the relationship between its international and domestic operations. These critics reflect the views of a wide range of observers: old trade hands who are programmed to think in terms of goods and who are wary of demands by upstart sectors; students of the structural changes taking place around the world who are uncertain about the validity of applying old concepts to new situations; those who argue in pragmatic terms and question, not the need to consider service transactions on a global basis, but rather the desirability of lumping them together. Some of their concerns are:

1. No body of theory exists to support the free-trade argument for services. Because of their great diversity and their intimate association with national values and goals (reflected in the fact that many are controlled by regulatory bodies rather than by law), services cannot be treated in the same way as goods, even though both may be subjected to the same kind of nontariff restrictions.

2. The U.S. federal government restricts foreign activities in domestic air transport and shipping, banking, communications, and mineral and hydroelectric power development. The states regulate insurance and some sections of the banking industry. Although at present there is no threat to these industries from foreign services, have we thought through the consequences of opening them to international competition? Are there domestic objectives that are served by current control over alien participation, or are

the regulations only outmoded vestiges of measures adopted to meet earlier needs? Does the United States want free movement of people (immigration) and information (data flows)? A free international exchange of services may involve the transfer of workers, whether they are manual laborers on a construction site or lawyers and doctors who apply for licenses, and they may be opposed by unions and professional associations. Commitments to a free flow of information may conflict with national sentiments about individual and corporate rights to privacy. Are we fairly sure of how we would respond to foreign demands for free access?

3. Of more concern from a political point of view, how representative of American service industries are the firms in the forefront of the U.S. initiative? Are they opening the way for the medium-sized and smaller U.S. firms that don't have the knowledge of foreign markets but that are often preeminent in certain service sectors? Is there a consistency of view even among the major firms in an industry on the merits of liberalization? Or is there a vast base of domestic activity that will press the government to provide protection against foreign competition? (It is not unlikely that some of the reluctance of foreign governments to commit themselves to freer entry of outsiders can be explained by a vocal opposition of their nonmultinational firms.) Is it wise for the United States to push for international agreement when it cannot guarantee that it has the support of its own constituencies back home?

4. Almost from a logistical point of view, some critics wonder about the dangers of what might be a truly Procrustean operation, trying to fit such special services with long organizational traditions as shipping, aviation, and banking into an overall agency such as GATT or a special agency for services. Should any international body, old or new, be asked to digest such a mix of formidable prior arrangements as though these sectors were ordinary members of a series?

5. Finally, on the matter of digestion, some observers of recent unwillingness to honor global trade commitments question whether it is wise to put new burdens on a weakened international system. Until we can assure support for GATT principles as they relate to goods, we should not load the system with a new set of applicants. This view was well expressed by Jan Tumlir, Director of Economic Research and Analysis of GATT, who wrote:

It is important to be forward looking and such issues ["new to the trade policy areas, such as trade in services"] clearly have a place on the agenda of a meeting that will set the direction of the GATT's work for the remainder of the decade. But they must not be used as a tactic for avoiding discussion of the root causes of the current threats to the trading system. To use a homely analogy, it would be a mistake to focus on plans for new additions to a building without first taking steps to ensure that the foundation is healthy and, moreover, capable of supporting both the existing structure and likely future additions.[7]

It is clear that many important issues need to be examined in formulating future U.S. policy for trade in services. The efforts of both government and business will be required in this process. A good case can be made for a thoroughgoing study of the following questions.

1. What sort of bargaining position does the United States have? Since this country has a competitive advantage in so many services and is relatively free of barriers against foreigners, what do we have to offer in return for concessions by other countries? Are we prepared to make trade-offs in different sectors of services (e.g., data processing against shipping) or a service sector and a goods sector (e.g., insurance against textiles)? Have we taken account of the views of the firms and the labor employed in the sectors that might be traded off? If we are not reasonably sure of the answers to these questions, what leeway do we have in entering international negotiations?

2. If the United States is to offer a coherent, defensible program for international liberalization of services, it must first have some idea of how it will handle potentially disruptive domestic situations. How can conflicting views in various constituencies be reconciled? Are there sunset industries in services, as there are in goods, that will resist being exposed to foreign competition? What policies can ensure that inefficient members of an industry are not propped up at the expense of the efficient?

3. What role for regulatory agencies, federal and state, do we foresee? The postwar practice of merging manufacturing and service firms presents fewer problems than the increasing tendency to combine a number of different services under one corporate management. Regulatory agencies in the future may have difficulty determining the reach of their authority. Consider the combinations that have resulted from recent mergers of U.S. firms engaged in service activities:

> Insurance with investment banking.
> Commercial banking with savings and loan institution.
> Consumer credit corporation with a brokerage house.
> Retail sales chain with securities and real estate.
> Commodity trader with investment banking.

Although the United States has taken the lead in this kind of merging of services, a similar pattern is appearing elsewhere. If American regulators can reorganize their procedures to take account of the new hybrids, they may contribute to the credibility of U.S. proposals for international negotiations and even provide a model to foreign regulators facing similar problems.

4. How far is it in the U.S. interest to push for liberalization of investment in services? The lack of clarity when terms such as "right of establishment" and "market access" are used indicates a fundamental uncertainty about what we are asking for abroad. More important, it reflects the absence

of adequate analysis of the U.S. reaction to a foreseeable request for reciprocal concessions under an international investment code.[8]

5. Perhaps the most important aspect of services is their potential development in the long term, and here we need to leap into the unknown for insights into policy options. The experts tell us that we are becoming an information-based, knowledge-based society, which must, however, still maintain an adequate base of manufacturing in order to support an expanding service sector.[9] The futurists describe a post-industrial society for the United States in which the mobility of high-level business executives and professionals will far surpass the mobility of other factors of production. New technologies will enable decision-makers of the future to perform their services in any part of the world.[10] Not all services will partake equally in this grand new design, but the dynamic sectors surely will. What are the implications for the United States? Here one must turn to the specialists in many fields besides economics – labor, technology, finance, education – for help in analyzing the role of services, the comparative value added by those performed at home and abroad, the prospects for exchange of services with countries at different levels of development, the expectations for technological and other incentives that may provide for movement of domestic labor and financing into new kinds of services.

6. Finally, although trade policies can be formulated and international understandings on services arrived at without the kind of statistical underpinning that we have for the exchange of goods, it is important to make progress on the methodology behind measurements of services in international transactions. We need better data on (a) U.S. exports to affiliates and to unaffiliated firms abroad, (b) sales of services by U.S. affiliates abroad to customers in the host country, in third countries, and even back in the United States, (c) the relationship between U.S. foreign trade and investment in goods and services trade and investment, (d) the effect of service transactions on U.S. gross national product and employment, and (e) the reverse of these four items – the sales of foreign services in the United States, by whatever means they are made.

## Conclusion

Even if one is inclined to agree with those who fear the consequences of a strong, early policy initiative on services, there is no reason for advocating a freeze on discussions of the subject. Exploratory talks within GATT and bilaterally with foreign governments can proceed simultaneously with a comprehensive domestic inquiry into the place and contribution of internationally traded services in the U.S. economy. If we need services to support essential goods-producing industries as well as for their own sake, we will want to ask questions similar to those we ask about the future of various manufacturing sectors: What are the national security and economic efficiency aspects of various degrees of dependence on imports; should we require that some minimum supply be provided by domestic firms; should the government be a partner, as it frequently is abroad, in operating certain service industries; should we adopt a policy of selective protection or support for those services we wish to foster and, if so, how do we decide which ones to select? These are questions that other governments have already been asking themselves, and some of their hesitation in moving at present to international negotiations undoubtedly stems from the fact that they haven't yet arrived at all the answers. Because of its preeminence as a producer and exporter of most services, the United States has not started asking itself these questions, and it would be foolhardy to predict what the results will be when it does. But the process of probing these issues will be enlightening, and the outcome may suggest new ways to secure the benefits of international cooperation and adjustment that can be applied to transactions in goods as well as services.

## Notes

1. Raymond Vernon, "A Skeptic Looks at the Balance of Payments," *Foreign Policy*, No. 5, Winter 1971–72, p. 64.
2. In a report on responses from 143 U.S. service firms, the U.S. International Trade Commission found that three types of foreign restrictions were most frequently mentioned: (1) restrictions on right of establishment in the host country; (2) restrictions on exports from parent U.S. firms – complete prohibition, requirements for a proportion to be supplied locally, and discriminatory taxes; and (3) foreign exchange controls. U.S. International Trade Commission, *The Relationship of Exports in Selected U.S. Service Industries to U.S. Merchandise Exports* (Washington, D.C.: U.S. International Trade Commission, 1982), p. 5. This report has valuable analyses of competitive conditions encountered abroad by 14 service industries. See also Irving Kravis's paper in this volume.
3. For a comprehensive survey of foreign regulations, see Ronald K. Shelp, *Beyond Industrialization: Ascendancy of the Global Service Economy* (New York: Praeger, 1981), Chapter 5.
4. In a report on the situation in insurance, an industry with a large number of restrictions applied to it, the U.S. General Accounting Office pointed to the difficulty of measuring the effect of foreign barriers and concluded that, without more evidence, "the significance and economic effect of barriers are unknown." *International Insurance Trade – U.S. Market Open: Impact of Foreign Barriers Unknown* (Washington, D.C.: U.S. General Accounting Office, August 1982), p. iii. The GAO did not assert, however, that lack of evidence meant that there was no problem.
5. The federal government faces a similar problem in international negotiations on trade in goods when procurement and subsidy policies of state governments discriminate against foreign suppliers.

6. The argument that world trade in services has for many years maintained a steady relationship to trade in goods depends upon what is included in each category. If services provided by foreign affiliates are added to "exports" from the home country, it seems likely that the proportion of services is rising and will continue to rise.

7. "International Economic Order: Can the Trend Be Reversed?" *The World Economy* 5, March 1982, p. 38.

8. The hazards of tackling the problem of right of establishment are considered by Sidney Golt who regards the problem as "a central issue for the service industries. But the problems involved in international discussion of this subject go very much deeper and wider, and so far international effort has been singularly fruitless, on either the bilateral or multilateral fronts. The Council of Europe negotiated a Treaty of Establishment in the 1960s; only four countries signed it, and only Luxembourg has ratified it." "Towards Freer Trade in Services?" *The Banker* 132, May 1982, p. 125.

9. Ira C. Magaziner and Robert B. Reich point out that services supplied to domestic manufacturing firms are a necessary competitive base for overseas operations, and if we drop our manufacturing activities we will fail to maintain a competitive service sector. *Minding America's Business* (New York: Harcourt Brace Jovanovich, 1982), pp. 85–6.

10. Over a decade ago, Norman Macrae described a short, but not necessarily sweet, life for future practitioners in the knowledge-based services: "Eventually, the new mobility of people and ideas should lead to fairly equal wages and salaries for work of equal dexterity everywhere. Those undertaking rather boring or arduous or unpleasant jobs – defining unpleasant in Aristotelian terms as not making the full use of one's faculties along lines of excellence – will probably work for only brief periods a year, with long vacations. Those undertaking rather interesting or knowledge-processing and decision-making jobs may work for rather brief periods of their lives, because the rapid development of knowledge may drive so many of their attitudes out of date; they may usually retire very early." *The Economist* 242, January 22, 1972, p. xxxiii.

## References

Brock, William E. (November 1982), "A Simple Plan for Negotiating on Trade in Services," *The World Economy* 5, No. 3, 229–40.

Chamber of Commerce of the United States. International Service Industry Committee (April 1980), *Report 1978–1980*. Washington, D.C.: Chamber of Commerce of the United States.

Cohen, Michael, and Theodore Morante (1981), "Elimination of Nontariff Barriers to Trade in Services: Recommendations for Future Negotiations," *Law and Policy in International Business* 13, No. 2, 495–519.

Diebold, William, Jr., and Helena Stalson (1983), "Negotiating Issues in International Services Transactions," in William R. Cline, ed., *Trade Policy in the 1980s*, 581–609. Washington, D.C.: Institute for International Economics.

Economic Consulting Services, Inc. (June 1981), *The International Operations of U.S. Service Industries: Current Data Collection and Analysis*. Washington, D.C.: Economic Consulting Services, Inc.

Ginzberg, Eli, and G. J. Vojta (March 1981), "Service Sector of the U.S. Economy," *Scientific American*, 244:14, 48-55.

Golt, Sidney (May 1982), "Towards Freer Trade in Services?" *The Banker* 132, 115-25.

Lederer, Evelyn Parrish, Walther Lederer, and Robert L. Sammons (January 1982), *International Service Transactions of the United States: Proposals for Improvement in Data Collection*, prepared for the Departments of State and Commerce and the Office of the U.S. Trade Representative. Washington, D.C.: U.S. Department of State.

Organization for Economic Cooperation and Development (1977), *Policies for Innovation in the Service Sector: Identification and Structure of Relevant Factors*. Paris: OECD.

Samuelson, Larry (June 1981), "Toward a Service-Oriented Growth Strategy," *World Development* 9, 499-514.

Sapir, André (Fall 1982), "Trade in Services: Policy Issues for the Eighties," *Columbia Journal of World Business* 17, no. 3, 77-83.

     and Ernst Lutz (1981), *Trade in Services: Economic Determinants and Development-Related Issues*, World Bank Staff Working Paper No. 480. Washington, D.C.: World Bank.

Shelp, Ronald K. (1981), *Beyond Industrialization: Ascendancy of the Global Service Economy*. New York: Praeger.

Stanback, Thomas M., Jr. (1979), *Understanding the Service Economy: Employment, Productivity, Location*, Policy Studies in Employment and Welfare No. 35. Baltimore: Johns Hopkins University Press.

U.S. Department of Commerce (December, 1976), *U.S. Service Industries in World Markets: Current Problems and Future Policy Development*. Washington, D.C.: U.S. Department of Commerce.

     International Trade Administration (March 1980), *Current Developments in U.S. International Service Industries*. Washington, D.C.: U.S. Department of Commerce.

U.S. International Trade Commission (1982), *The Relationship of Exports in Selected U.S. Service Industries to U.S. Merchandise Exports*. Washington, D.C.: U.S. International Trade Commission.

Yochelson, John N., and Gordon J. Cloney, eds. (September 1982), *Services and U.S. Trade Policy*, a White Paper of the Panel on Services and U.S. Trade Policy. Washington, D.C.: Georgetown University Center for Strategic and International Studies.

# Comment: U.S. trade policy and international service transactions

## JOAN E. SPERO

The issues related to trade in services are complex, the analyses often divergent, and the data inadequate. Helena Stalson and Irving Kravis have done an excellent job of raising the many and complicated issues associated with the measurement and analyses of trade in services and the formulation of policy toward trade versus investment in services.

A theme, which I see as central to the services question, is the role of communication and information in trade in services. Communication and information services have become increasingly important as intermediate "producer" services for which demand is indirect – as opposed to "consumer" services, which are sold directly to retail customers. Producer services – for example, finance, insurance, law, advertising, consulting, data processing, and communication – form the most dynamic segment of the service sector. They are used in the intermediate production of manufactured goods and other services. Demand for these activities results largely from the economic transactions of other industries. Producer services are thus facilitators of other businesses. Moreover, they are commonly produced in one market and sold or consumed in another. Unlike consumer services, which must be purchased where they are produced, producer services are transportable from a seller in one location to a user in another location – thus, their importance becomes evident internationally.

The so-called information revolution has played an important role in service growth, productivity, and international exchange of services. During the past two decades, the revolution in the telecommunications and computer technologies has given producer services such as international banking and insurance a global reach on an almost instantaneous basis, supported by high-speed transaction processing. Not coincidentally, these industries are also leading earners of export revenues in U.S. services trade. The ability of service industries to continue to use automated, unhindered, cost-effective global communications networks is essential to their ability to operate, let alone compete, internationally. Communication and information are therefore a key issue in trade in services.

Communication and information technologies play a growing role in service businesses both internally and externally. Internally, service firms, like other businesses, use computer-communications in the international production process itself; for marketing coordination; planning, accounting,

179

and financial management; inventory control and sales coordination; communication of complex engineering and design computations; and as an indispensable tool for servicing customers and suppliers on a global basis. More than other businesses, however, services depend on international information flows in interacting with the public – for example, to move people (airline reservation systems), value (banking) or risk (insurance).

As information has become central to trade in services, it has also become the focus of public policy. Countries are understandably anxious about questions of sovereignty, jurisdiction, privacy, and the cultural consequences of unconstrained information exchange. Gradually, however, the motivation for national information policies is becoming openly economic, and information is becoming the subject of protectionism. One of the disturbing trends is the growth of arbitrary and discriminatory actions of governments that impede the flow of information, eliminate choice in the marketplace, and reduce the services that are available. This has the net effect of increasing costs, decreasing efficiency and making international users of communication and information less competitive. More often than not, restrictions resemble the classic tariff and nontariff barriers to trade discussed by Kravis and Stalson. From a business viewpoint, the United States is poorly equipped to respond because we have few remedies to counter arbitrary or discriminatory actions of other countries. The Executive Branch has few if any legislative tools; the FCC is without international negotiating authority; and international rules are inadequate. The principle of "free flow of information" on which U.S. policy is based is too often simply that – a principle, without teeth or force in international law.

In the multifaceted fields of communication and information, policymakers and experts in business, government, and academia are actively seeking cooperative approaches and understanding of the issues in the varied communication and information fora – the International Telecommunications Union, the United Nations Center for Transnational Corporations, the International Chamber of Commerce, the OECD, UNESCO, and others. On a parallel track, similar discussion is underway in the trade community. At the same time, the community of institutions and individuals engaged in the relatively new study of services would contribute greatly to our knowledge in this area by taking an in-depth look at the role of communication and information in the service sector. But better understanding of the issues and the protection of privacy, although important, are not enough. The international flow of data is moving rapidly from being a communication issue to becoming a trade issue. As a trade issue, it should be subject to international trade negotiations and a system of internationally agreed trade rules. Service industries require remedies for discriminatory treatment and negotiating authority within the U.S. government and internationally. By applying a trade approach that has served to liberalize the flow of goods for more than three decades, I believe it is possible to achieve liberalization – and some rules of the road – in the international flow of information.

CHAPTER 7

# The provision of services in a market economy*

BENGT HOLMSTROM

## 1    Introduction

Services are unlike goods in many regards. Some differences that appear economically relevant are the following: Services are not storable; service quality is difficult to measure or observe; the appropriateness of a service may be difficult to verify; service technology is more flexible. Character-istics like these suggest that the determinants of supply and demand in the service sector will be somewhat different from those in the goods sector and also that institutions facilitating economic exchange and production of ser-vices will exhibit idiosyncratic features.

How strong these differences are and what the overall significance is for the functioning of our economy is an important question in view of the rapid growth of the services sector. Measured by employment we are al-ready a service economy. Yet, our microeconomic theories remain strongly rooted in the industrial paradigm. It is time to start asking how well the market performs in matching the supply and demand of services, what the effects of market structure are, what theories help best explain service insti-tutions and whether and what kind of market intervention is desirable.

In this paper I will emphasize only a few features that are characteristic of services. My own comparative advantage dictates that these relate to information, although happily there is reason to believe they are generally significant. The most important one is the difficulty with which quality of a service can be observed or assessed. Paired with the flexibility with which quality can be varied over time, this informational asymmetry causes par-ticular problems for the service sector.

I will study how recent developments in the economics of uncertainty and information may help predict the consequences of such informational asym-metries. This leads to a study of various market responses to quality assur-ance. Use of explicit contracts such as contingent fee schedules or warran-ties is one remedy that theory is able to say quite a bit about. Unfortunately,

* I acknowledge helpful discussions with V. V. Chari, Andrew Postlewaite, Sherwin Rosen, Mark Satterthwaite, Carl Shapiro, Steven Shavell, Laurence Weiss, and Louis Wilde.

183

explicit contracts are often infeasible in service trade, because needed contingencies are either not observed or more often, not measurable in a verifiable way. Instead quality has to be assured by other means, perhaps most often by building a good reputation. The role of reputation appears indeed particularly relevant in the service context. Our understanding of how reputation mechanisms work is much less advanced than our understanding of contingent contracting, and therefore I will be somewhat more explicit about this subject.

The paper can be separated into two parts. In the first part (Section 2) I outline a general conceptual framework within which one might study the provision of services in the market place. It includes a discussion of equilibrium under full information, the sources of informational imperfections, the potential problems associated with information asymmetries, market remedies to these problems and the measurement of welfare in relation to market intervention. In the second part of the paper (Sections 3–5), I go on to discuss in more detail some selected issues within the general framework. My objective with the elaborations is not to offer firm conclusions either positive or normative regarding the service sector, but to be suggestive of what kinds of problems seem amenable to analysis and which research directions appear fruitful to probe in the near future. The last section reiterates my principal conclusions regarding further theoretical and empirical research in this field.

## 2    A general framework

### 2.1    *Symmetric information*

Although much of the ensuing discussion will be concerned with the ramifications of information imperfections in the service sector, it is useful to begin by taking a look at market outcomes in their absence. The analysis will bring out some differences between the production of services and the production of goods that are not information related, but rather consequences of the differences in technological flexibility and in the storability of the product. It will also be a convenient vehicle for introducing a formalization of service production.

For concreteness consider a particular kind of service, say, a legal service. A client wishes to hire an attorney so that his/her chances to win a case improve. Besides price, the client is concerned with one characteristic of the legal service: the probability of winning the case, or, if more than two outcomes are possible, the probability distribution over the various legal outcomes. The attorney provides his/her legal service using two inputs: one is the time and effort involved, denoted $a$, and the other is his/her ability and education, denoted $\eta$. The reason for this particular separation of inputs is that time and effort are variable in the short run, whereas ability and education may be viewed as fixed in the short run.

Formally the service can be represented as a function $x(a, \eta, \theta)$, which describes the relationship between inputs $(a, \eta, \theta)$ and service products, $x$. Here $\theta$ is an exogenous stochastic component (e.g., the mood of the judge) that cannot be controlled by either the client or the attorney but may influence the outcome of the case $x$. A probability distribution over $\theta$ will induce a corresponding distribution over outcomes $x$ as a function of the time and effort and the ability and education involved. Viewed in this way, $x(\cdot)$ is simply a stochastic production function that defines the service technology. Notice that the technology, including the probability distribution of $\theta$, is specific to the client–lawyer relationship. This is another important feature unique to a service. In other respects, though, the production technology looks formally much like that for goods. In the goods case, $\eta$ would represent long-term investments in capital, know-how, et cetera, and $a$ would represent variable factors that determine detailed characteristics of the good.

Mostly economic theory has explored how, given $a$ and $\eta$, goods are priced in equilibrium. Under a set of assumptions, convexity of preferences and technology in particular, an equilibrium price vector exists that equates supply and demand and allocates products efficiently. This does not address another important question: Do equilibrium prices also guide firms to produce the most desired set of products? Dreze and Hagen (1978) explore this question at some length and conclude that the answer is no in general. The reason is simple: There is a problem with the divisibility of a good. As an example, suppose a consumer desires one unit of a characteristic $A$ and one unit of a characteristic $B$ in a good, while another consumer desires one and two, respectively. The firm could produce two units of $A$ and three units of $B$ giving the right total, but if only one kind of product can be purchased there is no way both consumers can be satisfied simultaneously, since this single product would have $A$ and $B$ in the ratio two to three. This reflects a nonconvexity in the market that derives from an (assumed) inflexibility in the technology.

The reason I bring this up is to make the point that service technologies are generally much more flexible than goods technologies and can overcome the above problem. In the case of legal services for instance, if one client wants the attorney to put in a lot of effort in order to reach a high probability of winning and another client is content with less effort and a lower probability, both can be satisfied by the same lawyer. We may therefore expect that matching supply of service quality with service demand can be made efficiently absent informational problems. In a recent paper

(Begun, Easley and O'Hara, 1982) this has been proved correct. The efficient equilibrium is obtained simply by pricing service quality, or, in the attorney's case, effort and time. The problem of having to divide the service output in fixed proportions does not arise.

What about the choice of $\eta$? As far as ability is concerned, this component can presumably not be changed, but long term investments can. For a lawyer these include among other things the field in which he specializes and the location at which he decides to practice. On a general level, of course, the choice of $\eta$ merely defines the range of services that the lawyer may offer. In analogy with the previous discussion one may ask whether the market will guide suppliers to choose the right $\eta$'s. Will lawyers specialize and locate properly in response to market demand?

I have not explored this question fully, but the answer seems apparent. If inputs are being priced, which they presumably will be at least implicitly because of customer specific technology, maximization of market value minus investment cost will lead to optimal choices of $\eta$. In simpler terms, lawyers will specialize and locate correctly if they choose $\eta$ to maximize the return on their time and effort net of education and location costs. In stating this I am assuming that customers can use many lawyers at the same time and that their service contributions add up. If this is unrealistic it is only to avoid divisibility problems, which will disappear when the scale of service supply is large relative to individual demand.

These tentative conclusions ought to be checked by developing a proper equilibrium model of occupational choice. Such a model would be interesting also for another reason. Since services are nonstorable, markets in different locations are essentially separated. This raises the following question: How does demand at different locations relate to the degree of specialization? Presumably the old maxim that "the division of labor is determined by the extent of the market" will apply. This should be possible to analyze fruitfully in a particular context like the supply of physician services. The equilibrating force of the market requires physicians to be indifferent between both locations (assuming zero location costs) and specialties. From this should follow two predictions: the relationship between demand and degree of specialization and the relationship between wage and location. Both relationships ought to be testable empirically. What I find intriguing about such a research effort is that besides producing results of specific significance for the service industry it will permit a cross-sectional test of theories of labor division [see, e.g., Rosen (1982)] that normally would require time-series data.[1]

## 2.2    *Sources of market imperfection*

The previous section argued that under symmetric and complete information about the production technology, including the characteristics of a service (the level of care taken by the seller, the competence of the seller, etc.), a competitive market will lead to the right supply and distribution of services. In reality, of course, information about relevant variables are often severely limited and this will lead to market imperfections. The service sector appears particularly exposed to such problems, because of the difficulties with verifying quality.

Information economics provides a rather useful taxonomy for classifying problems arising from incomplete or asymmetric information. They are either called moral hazard or adverse selection problems, depending on the type of information asymmetry that is present.

*Moral hazard* refers to problems associated with the buyer's inability to observe actions taken by the seller ($a$). The level of care or effort is the canonical example of such an action. Since care is hard to measure there is an obvious temptation for the seller to undersupply it unless incentives are provided to assure proper care. It is important to recognize, though, that something in addition to care must be unobservable in order for moral hazard to cause difficulties. Otherwise one could simply set a standard for service quality (and other characteristics), which if not met, would be cause for nonpayment or cancellation of the service. With standards the knowledge about cars would be immaterial. This is the typical situation when goods are produced.

One of two additional information imperfections makes moral hazard a problem. The first possibility is that quality cannot be verified. In this case standards become useless, because they cannot be enforced. Notice here that even if the buyer can judge the quality after the service is delivered it is too late to cancel it because a service is generally irreversible. Thus, a buyer may be able to infer that improper care was taken because he/she received poor service quality, but there is nothing he/she can do about it if quality cannot be objectively determined. (Goods can always be returned in exchange for their price if the customer is dissatisfied.)

The other possible complication is that the service outcome is uncertain because of exogenous factors. Even if an attorney puts in the right amount of effort in a case, this does not assure that the case is won. Thus from the fact that a case is lost a client cannot be certain that it was due to insufficient effort on behalf of the attorney. The situation is similar for medical services. If responsibility is placed exclusively on the physician in these situations, he may have to carry undue risk. On the other hand, if he/she is relieved of all responsibility because exogenous factors influence the outcome, he will not have any incentive to supply costly care. There is a trade-off between risk protection and incentives and in general efficiency in both dimensions cannot be achieved. This is the cost of moral hazard.

*Adverse selection* refers to problems that are associated with the buyer's inability to observe either the seller's characteristics ($\eta$) or the contingencies under which the seller operates ($\theta$). Take the latter case first. The seller is often better informed about the customer's needs. This may be represented in the earlier formulation by the seller having superior information about $\theta$. When the customer observes the seller's actions, for instance the tests and treatments a physician undertakes, he/she cannot tell whether these actions were the appropriate ones for his medical needs. Consider another typical situation. My car is towed to the repair service because the engine does not start. Usually I would not know exactly what is wrong and diagnosing the problem is indeed part of the service I am buying. Once the car is fixed I get a description of what was done to it (and this can presumably be verified so actions are observed), but there may be little I can do to check whether in fact the service my car received was the minimal needed to fix it. The incentives to oversell repair service seem obvious, because of adverse selection.

The case where $\eta$, say a physician's competence, cannot be observed by the patient leads to another variant of adverse selection. Knowledge of competence would help predict the quality and value of the service including the risks for malpractice. When patients cannot distinguish between good and bad physicians, service needs cannot be matched correctly with service supply. Worse, quacks can enter the market and drive down the overall quality and price so that good physicians are unable to appropriate the returns from competence enhancing investments and have to leave. The potential costs associated with this type of adverse selection have been well described in Akerlof's seminal paper on the "Market for Lemons."

### 2.3     Market remedies to informational asymmetries

If nothing could be done about moral hazard and adverse selection phenomena, the service sector would look truly miserable. Only the lowest quality sellers would remain in the market and they would supply only minimal care. Fortunately, the market has a built-in flexibility, which permits it to respond to information related problems and alleviate, at least partly, their harmful effects. Institutions, both formal and informal, will develop that help overcome or circumvent informational asymmetries. Some prominent ones are detailed below.

*Contingent contracts:*   In some sectors of the service industry, it is possible to design contracts that are contingent upon variables that are both relevant to the delivery of the service and are observed so that contracts can be enforced. For instance, attorneys often sell their services on an outcome contingent basis. If they win their case they collect a share of the award, if they lose they may charge nothing. Obviously, a fee schedule of this form is partly designed to induce the attorney to pay proper attention to his case and thereby reduce moral hazard. But such contracts may also act as signals about the competence of the attorneys. An attorney who is willing to make his/her fee dependent on the outcome of a case is presumably more confident about his/her own ability than one who does not want to take such a risk. Therefore a contract, by signaling competence, reduces some of the informational gap between the attorney and his/her client.

The same would be true if physicians could design liability contracts against malpractice. In this case, however, the government has intervened by imposing liability laws uniformly over the profession. Moral hazard will be reduced and through self-selection of cases adverse selection will be affected.

Warranties constitute a third and most common example of contingent contracting. Theoretically, their form and function are similar to the above mentioned lawyer contracts. I will therefore be content with a description of the insights that the rather extensive literature on agency theory provides for understanding lawyer contracts, with the understanding that the discussion has broader scope.

*Reputation:* When contingent contracts cannot be used because they are not enforceable due to restrictions on observability, reputation may act as a powerful device in avoiding severe moral hazard and adverse selection problems. Reputation performs as an implicit contract, which is enforced by the seller's concern about future demand for his service. How close the performance of such a contract comes to an explicit contingent contract depends on the size of demand as well as how information about the service is disseminated among consumers. I will give some examples of models, which study the force of reputation, but generally speaking our understanding of this phenomenon is still limited, which is unfortunate in view of its importance in the service sector.

*Signaling:* I mentioned previously that explicit contracts may act as signals about ability or quality of the service supplier. There are a host of other signaling activities as well. The most common perhaps is education, which has been extensively treated in the literature [Spence (1973)], although not much in connection with service professions like law and medicine. Advertising and other firm specific investments provide alternative forms of signaling. All build on the idea that there is a differential cost of signaling as a function of quality or some other characteristic that is being signaled. Some of the examples later on will illustrate this important mechanism at work.

*Certification and monitoring:* A final recourse in reducing informational asymmetries is to have service qualifications certified. This way information about ability and long-term investments like specialization can be transmitted to consumers. Certification may involve either an explicit statement of some minimum qualities that the supplier possesses or it may be an indirect approval of his value. Examples include professional associations, partnerships, hotel or restaurant chains and similar organizational structures.

Another interesting aspect of certification is that this monitoring activity is frequently a service itself. Auditing, investment banking, and I presume to a large extent consulting in general involve elements of certification and third-party approval, which are conducted to reduce information asymmetries that otherwise would cause serious incentive problems. This perspective on certification raises a rich set of issues, few of which have been analyzed in the literature so far [see Wilson (1982)].

### 2.4     Intervention and welfare measurement

The institutions described previously are ingenious ways in which the market attempts to reduce transactions costs stemming from informational asymmetries. They permit beneficial trades which otherwise would be excluded due to uncertainty and accompanying incentive problems. The question is whether the market by itself exhausts all possibilities to enhance trade or whether there is scope for market intervention by the government. Judging from the abundance of regulatory clauses in the service sector, which include licensing, liability laws, forced disclosure and warranties, government intervention is believed to be welfare improving.

Welfare measurement is more difficult, though, in markets with asymmetric information. In standard economic theory we are used to the concept of Pareto optimality for welfare comparison. At a Pareto optimum, nobody's welfare can be improved without reducing the welfare of somebody else. But it is less clear how this optimality notion extends to situations with informational externalities. Obviously, using the same criteria that apply in the full information case is unreasonable. The government must be assumed to be limited by the same restrictions on observability that face the market, which means we are looking at second-best alternatives.

A certain consensus has been reached in the literature on information economics regarding the right normative efficiency criterion [for a detailed discussion, see Holmstrom and Myerson (1982)]. This criterion compares allocations that are contingent on all the private information in the economy and are feasible in the sense that individuals will have an incentive to tell the truth if asked about their private information for purposes of implementing a particular allocation. Among all these incentive feasible contingent allocations, those are efficient, which cannot be dominated in the sense that a social planner could guarantee for every individual, no matter what the individual's private information happens to be, a higher level of expected utility using another incentive feasible contingent allocation. In this definition, incentive feasibility reflects the restrictions on choice that have to be imposed on the government because it cannot control the individual incentives any better than the market. The notion of domination on the other hand, reflects the assumption that the government does not have any more information about individuals than is common knowledge in the economy, and this limits its ability to redistribute welfare.

This notion of efficiency (called incentive efficiency) is much weaker than the classical full information concept of Pareto optimality. Consequently, if employed it reduces considerably the scope for market intervention. To find contingent allocations, which are better for all participants in the market whatever their private information may be, is much harder. As an example, a regulation about compulsory licensing, which would make a single seller of services worse off (e.g., a quack), without being able to explicitly compensate him or her (because of informational problems in identifying the seller), would not be welfare improving by this criterion.

Of course, if one is comfortable with employing some explicit social welfare function in comparing contingent allocations, then a stronger ordering of such allocations will obtain. And this relates to the main point I wish to make: When discussing welfare in the context of informational asymmetries one is almost inevitably forced to make interpersonal utility comparisons without recourse to the standard arguments about redistribution of income.

## 2.5 Summary

In this section I have tried to provide a conceptual framework for assessing market performance in the service sector. At the center of the framework is a formalization of the service technology. I argued that through greater flexibility in this technology, the service sector has the potential to meet consumer needs even more efficiently than the goods sector, which allocates goods efficiently but does not necessarily produce the right characteristics. What limits the service sector more than the goods sector, however, is the extent of informational asymmetries particularly concerning quality. These asymmetries lead to problems of moral hazard and adverse selection. Markets try to overcome these afflictions by creating a variety of institutions that help reduce information gaps and control incentives.

As I see it, the research task ahead involves first building models which can explain service institutions from an informational perspective and next analyzing what market behavior they lead to in equilibrium. The rest of the paper is intended to give an idea of where we are in this research agenda by looking in more detail at market responses in particular instances.

## 3     Contingent contracts

I will use the lawyer–client relationship as my primary example of how contracts work to alleviate moral hazard and adverse selection. The insights that can be gained from studying lawyer fees apply in other contracting contexts as well. Overall, the importance of contingent contracts in the service sector may be small, because quality is difficult to verify. It should be noted, though, that the analysis of explicit contracts has some broader scope, because in some instances implicit contracts that are enforced by reputation can be expected to have similar features.

### 3.1     Lawyer fees

I will start by looking at lawyer fees from a pure moral hazard perspective. Problems concerning asymmetric information about lawyer competence or the potential of the client's case are presently suppressed.

Consider the simplest of situations: A lawyer is representing a client in a case where there are only two outcomes: Either the client wins and is awarded a million or he/she loses and gets nothing. Let the probability of winning be $p$. This probability is a function of the lawyer's effort and we may measure this effort simply in terms of $p$. The cost of effort is given by $c(p)$. The lawyer's utility is $v(x) - c(p)$ and the client's is $u(x)$, where $x$ is money. There are generally gains in sharing the risk associated with the outcome of the case. Fixing for a moment effort, optimal risk sharing involves equalizing the ratio of the lawyer's and the client's marginal utilities in each outcome state, that is, setting

$$u'(1 - s_1)/v'(s_1) = u'(- s_0)/v'(s_0) \qquad (3.1)$$

where $s_0$ is the lawyer's fee if the case is lost and $s_1$ is his/her fee if the case is won. This condition is nothing more than the standard condition for efficiency in economic exchange when we construe the transfers $s_1$ and $s_0$ as two separate goods. If (3.1) did not hold, then a small exchange of $s_1$ for $s_0$ (or conversely) would make both parties better off.[2] Notice that if either party is risk neutral, then (3.1) requires that party to carry all the risk. Thus, $s_1 = s_0$ if the client is risk-neutral and $s_1 = 1 + s_0$ if the lawyer is risk-neutral. On the other hand, if both are risk-averse there will be coinsurance and each side will share in the gains from winning the case.

Since effort cannot be observed, the lawyer may set it at any level he or she wants. Presumably he or she will choose a level that maximizes his/her expected utility. If the client is risk-neutral and the contract shares risk optimally, the lawyer is paid a fixed fee and will set effort at its minimum level. In this case the optimal risk-sharing solution will be very poor in terms of incentives. The situation can be improved by having the lawyer carry some risk. The key observation is that a marginal change in the risk sharing solution is costless in terms of increased risk (to a first-order, by definition of optimality), but it provides strictly better incentives. Thus, raising $s_1$ and lowering $s_0$ slightly (leaving the expected fee unchanged), will induce the lawyer to put out more effort with effectively no associated risk-sharing losses. Both parties will gain from the change.

This example illustrates the nature of the optimal solution to moral hazard. Going with optimal risk sharing will not provide adequate incentives. It will always be desirable to deviate somewhat from the risk sharing solution by increasing the lawyer's fee when the case is won and lowering it when the case is lost. The only exception is when the lawyer is risk-neutral. Then he/she will already carry all the risk in the optimal solution to the risk sharing problem and naturally choose the right level of effort in response.

Both the optimal risk-sharing solution and the moral hazard solution depend on the lawyer's and the client's attitudes to risk. The more risk-averse the lawyer is relative to the client, the less risk he/she will carry. Another factor that will influence the fee schedule is the sensitivity of the outcome to effort. If the outcome to a large extent depends on exogenous uncertainty, the lawyer's effort becomes a less decisive factor and the fee schedule will reflect more closely optimal risk sharing. It is instructive to view this in an alternative way. With much exogenous uncertainty, the outcome of the case tells little about whether the lawyer supplied proper effort or not and therefore there is less reason to make him heavily responsible by having him/her carry excess risk. In fact, the deviation from optimal risk sharing when moral hazard is present is in a rough sense proportional to how strongly the outcome indicates that the lawyer did what was expected of him/her (see Holmstrom, 1979). Furthermore, it can be shown that moral hazard costs are decreasing in the strength of this inference. This implies that any monitoring, which provides information about effort or about uncontrollable events that affect the outcome, is valuable and should be included in the contract. In reality we may not see that much information from monitoring explicitly included in contracts, but that is probably because such information is accounted for implicitly through reputation effects.

Finally, a third determinant of fee schedules is the cost of effort. It is worth noting that the opportunity cost of effort can be influenced in some instances, for example, if time spent on the case can be observed and used in determining the fee. The presumption is that a lawyer who invests time in a case because of contractural obligations, will have less incentives to cheat on effort. Once he/she is working on the case, the utility from reducing effort is small when it merely reflects the pleasure from day-dreaming instead of thinking productively. Thus, if the invested time can be verified, moral hazard considerations suggest that it will be included in the contract. In fact, the time rate will be set so that it will induce the lawyer to invest an excessive amount of time in the case relative to the effort supplied. This bias in observable factor inputs due to an inability to observe effort or care will reappear in various forms later.

The predictions from a theoretical analysis of moral hazard match the empirical evidence well in the sense that contracts do seem to vary both with case size, monitoring opportunities and lawyer–client risk preferences. Small clients with small risks employ fee schedules in which the lawyer's share is higher than when clients are large like firms. Firms also often contract based on a time rate only, because they are able to monitor the lawyer's input closely via their own legal staff. Of course, mere risk sharing (without moral hazard) could explain some of these features as well; in particular, the sensitivity of contracts to risk preferences and risk size. However, there is one reason to dismiss risk sharing as the only explanation for observed contracts, and that is the lack of outright insurance against adverse court decisions. The fact that lawyers, and not insurance companies, share the client's risk is revealing.

The market outcome under pure moral hazard is easy to describe if we make the (admittedly heroic) assumption that the client is informed about all available lawyers and their characteristics and can costlessly choose among them. Competition between lawyers will drive up the client's expected utility until only one lawyer is left, namely the one who is willing to offer the client the most favorable contract. This is an efficient outcome as one can readily check. The resulting match between lawyers and clients could not be improved by a social planner who is limited by the same moral hazard constraints as is the market, because no externalities are present. More realistically, though, one might expect that searching for the most suitable lawyer is more costly when contracts are used, than it is, for instance, to find the lowest price of a standardized good. I will not deal with these search aspects, but merely note that costly search is likely to lead to a lesser variety of contracts being used, because standardization improves comparability.

Let me next turn to adverse selection issues. Suppose that the only source of asymmetric information is the quality of the lawyer. The lawyer knows his/her quality (the probability of winning) but the client does not. For simplicity, assume a lawyer can be either good or bad. Assume also that in either case optimal risk sharing dictates that the lawyer should be paid a constant fee, because the client is risk neutral. Then it is clear that a bad lawyer would always like to state that he is a good one as long as lawyers share in the rents that the lawyer–client relationship offers (or, alternatively, if the opportunity cost is higher for good lawyers). This would drive good lawyers out of the market. A way to avoid such market deterioration is to design contracts in a way which separates the two groups. For instance, a good lawyer could offer to carry some risk, which the bad lawyer could not tolerate given his lower probability of success. Self-selection would reveal who is who, but at a cost: Optimal risk sharing would have to yield. The only case again, in which lawyers would not have to suffer from excessive risk, is if they were risk neutral. As Grossman (1981) has observed in a somewhat different context, risk neutral lawyers would offer full insurance to a client at the client's reservation utility. A client who receives a fixed return from his/her case does not care who handles it.

In contrast to the moral hazard situation, government intervention could improve the market outcome when adverse selection of the kind described previously is present. The reason is that bad lawyers cause an externality. Although they can operate under efficient risk sharing contracts (because they need not prove that they are bad), they cause good lawyers to carry too much risk. One remedy to this market distortion is to exclude bad lawyers from the market or force them to improve their quality. This may be accomplished by quality certification. Of course, judgment on intervention must be based on an explicit welfare function for the reasons I gave earlier (bad lawyers cannot be reimbursed, since they cannot be identified). Presumably this is of lesser concern if the number of bad lawyers is not large and particularly if their opportunity costs are small. The benefits of such intervention would come from better risk sharing, increased supply of good lawyers and improved matches between lawyers and clients.

I shall hasten to add here that even if certification may be a valuable source of information, it should not necessarily be administered and imposed by the government. I will discuss this further in section 5.

Previously I have presented two explanations for why lawyers use contingent fee schedules. Can we infer from empirically observed contracts which theory is more relevant? This question is of some importance in view of the fact that adverse selection may call for market intervention while moral hazard does not.

Looking at individual contracts, the two theories do not seem observationally distinguishable. Any single contract can be explained either way. However, the aggregate data seems to offer some opportunities to discriminate. Since competence is revealed over time through case histories, there will be a decreased need for senior lawyers to signal quality. This would manifest itself as a difference in aggregate contract composition between junior and senior lawyers; in particular, senior lawyers would share less risk. I do not have the information, but I doubt that such a difference shows up in the data. If so, one would be inclined to conclude that principally, moral hazard (together with risk sharing, of course) is responsible for the fee schedules we observe.

This is not quite correct, though, because the aggregate data reveals that a third explanation is needed to accommodate all the evidence. Both moral hazard and adverse selection considerations predict that a risk-neutral lawyer would fully insure his client. There are strong reasons to believe that in some cases the lawyer (including his/her firm) is indeed risk-neutral relative to his client, partly because he can diversify risk by handling a large clientele. Yet, we do not seem to observe contracts where the client sells all his/her risk to the lawyer for a fixed amount.

One explanation of this would be based on the argument that the client also has an input in the legal process and thereby is subject to moral hazard. But a more important reason, I think, is that information about the chances of a successful case is asymmetric. If so it would be difficult to agree on the size of the fixed payment to the client. The lawyer would be inclined to understate the value of the case if he were better informed and the converse would be true if the client were better informed. This problem can (again partly) be overcome by having the client and the lawyer jointly share in the outcome even if that is suboptimal from a risk sharing point of view.

### 3.2    *Summary*

The lawyer–client relationship fits nicely into the agency paradigm that has recently been extensively studied in the literature. This paradigm offers several potential explanations for contingent lawyer fees. I made an effort to indicate how one might be able to discriminate between competing theories and concluded that moral hazard together with asymmetric information about the client's case would probably best accommodate the evidence. The two alternative explanations, pure risk sharing and (more tentatively) signaling of competence, were dismissed.

Since I used little more than casual observations as supporting evidence, it is clear that my conclusions should be subjected to closer scrutiny in future research. In this regard I think that lawyer contracts provide an accessible and interesting empirical laboratory within which various agency theories can be tested. More research is also needed theoretically. The impact of asymmetric case information is very poorly understood and certainly deserves more attention. The same applies to questions about equilibrium processes in contract markets, where price signals are confounded by insurance and other aspects of contracting. Developing search theory in this direction would seem both feasible and useful.[3]

One of the important insights from the preceding analysis is that market performance is quite dependent on whether adverse selection or moral hazard is the source of problems. Adverse selection results in externalities, which may require intervention, while moral hazard does not.[4] This dividing line reappears in the analysis of medical malpractice. Liability laws influence both care and competence (through self-selection), but the optimal legal design differs depending on which problem is the most serious one. Since Shavell (1978) has recently written an excellent essay on the subject, I refer the reader to his comprehensive analysis for more details. The main point, as I see it, is that competence could be assured by other methods (stricter certification) than liability laws, whereas provision of care could not. In this regard it seems important to ask how detailed medical certification procedures should be and what kinds of alternative signals of competence one could use to aid patients in selecting physicians. By imposing liability laws uniformly on physicians, one signaling option is removed. Would it be unreasonable to consider a system where physicians at least partly self-select liability limits? In theory this could improve information flow and reduce costs due to defensive medicine.

## 4    Reputation

Reputation may serve as a substitute for contingent contracts in situations where there are enforcement problems because contingencies cannot be measured or verified sufficiently well. In the service sector quality may be the most important characteristic of the product being exchanged. This together with the fact that clear measures of quality rarely exist, makes reputation particularly significant for studying market performance in the service sector.

Theoretical work on reputation is only beginning. But it is already apparent that one general model will be insufficient to cover the variety of circumstances in which reputation phenomena are at work.[5] Models and techniques will have to be tailored to specific needs. An essential role will be played by the process by which quality information is communicated between customers. Explicit recognition of the details of communication may ultimately be necessary for a fruitful analysis.

These observations will be illustrated in the ensuing discussion of reputation. I will look at three different situations using three different models. The first one is a model of professional services, the second one a model of price-signalling and the third one a detailed example of how communication determines the effects of increased competition.

### 4.1    Professional reputation formation

Customers use reputation as a way of forecasting future behavior of a seller. Logically, this means that there must be some characteristic of the seller that is not fully known and is being signalled by the seller's past behavior.

In the context of professional services, competence is often imperfectly known. I want to show how this uncertainty can influence care taking and in some instances completely resolve the problem of moral hazard. The argument is originally due to Fama (1980). My discussion is based on a formal model developed in Holmstrom (1982).

Consider again a lawyer who operates in a competitive market for legal services. Assume this time that his/her fee cannot be made contingent on any observable event. Therefore he/she is paid irrespective of the eventual value of the service. Obviously, if the world lasted only for one period, he or she would have no incentive to supply costly care. But if he/she wishes to stay in the profession for a longer time, matters are different. He or she realizes that clients will view his/her performance as a signal about competence. By supplying care, which improves performance, the lawyer can influence future clients' perceptions about competence. Thus, the fact that competence is unknown, leads to incentives for care taking.

The simplest structure would have performance in period $t$, $x_t$, depend on competence ($\eta$) and care ($a_t$) in a linear fashion, that is,

$$x_t = \eta + a_t + \theta_t. \tag{4.1}$$

Here $\theta_t$ is a random noise term – a measurement error or some other exogenous factor influencing performance observations.

Suppose clients pay the lawyer in proportion to their expectations about the lawyer's performance. These expectations are based on past history, because previous performance will give an indication of what the lawyer's competence is. It turns out that under some simplifying assumptions about the probabilistic structure, rational clients will update their estimate about competence by taking an average of what they believed previously ($m_t$) and what their most recent observation of performance ($x_t$) was. More specifically, beliefs about competence will progress according to the rule:

$$m_{t+1} = \alpha_t m_t + (1 - \alpha_t)(x_t - a_t). \tag{4.2}$$

The weights $\alpha_t$ play a significant role in determining the strength of the incentive effects and I will return to them shortly. The presence of $a_t$ in (4.2) needs brief clarification. Clients will in equilibrium know how the lawyer chooses care (because it turns out that this choice is independent of $\eta$). Thus, they know $a_t$. By forming the difference $x_t - a_t$, they get to know what $\eta + \theta_t$ was and this is the only relevant information for updating beliefs about competence. Viewed in a different way, care levels should be filtered away from performance observations because they represent time-varying transient effects.

Given that clients react to new information according to (4.2) and pay the lawyer in proportion to their present beliefs (i.e., pay $m_t + a_t$), how will the lawyer supply care? From (4.1) and (4.2) we see that each unit of extra care in period $t$ will raise the lawyer's fee in period $t+1$ by $(1 - \alpha_t)$, in period $t+2$ by $\alpha_{t+1}(1 - \alpha_t)$, and so on. The discounted sum of these increases represents the lawyer's marginal return from care. Equating this with the marginal cost of care determines the lawyer's optimal choice. Clearly, unless $\alpha_t = 1$, future returns to today's investment in care will be positive and so, due to reputation effects, more care will be supplied than if the world would last only one period.

Now, let me get back to the $\alpha_t$ weights, which are central to determining equilibrium care. These weights depend on how precisely the clients know competence and also how noisy the exogenous disturbance term $\theta_t$ is. If competence is already very well known, then an additional observation of performance will imply little adjustment in beliefs. Clients will credit most of the discrepancy between the observation and their expectation to the exogenous disturbance $(\theta_t)$. The same is true if the disturbance is very noisy. What will happen over time in this model is that clients get better and better informed about the lawyer's competence and eventually know it almost certainly. The lawyer, realizing that clients attach less and less significance to his or her most recent performance, will have a smaller and smaller incentive to supply care. In the limit the last observations on performance will be entirely ignored by clients, because they do not tell anything new about competence. Additional care will have no returns and the lawyer ceases to supply it.

In the previously described scenario reputation works only temporarily. To get a permanent effect one has to assume that competence can change over time. In the simplest case, competence progresses linearly, that is,

$$\eta_{t+1} = \eta_t + \delta_t, \tag{4.3}$$

where $\delta_t$ measures the change in competence. With this alteration, clients will never become fully informed about competence and hence always put some weight on their most recent observations. Starting with some arbitrary precision of information, the system will eventually converge to a state where new observations are just sufficient to keep information about competence from eroding due to the disturbance term $\delta_t$. In such a stationary state, the weights $\alpha_t$ will all be equal and it is easy to calculate precisely the marginal return from increased care, which I will denote as $k$. It will be given by[6]

$$k = \frac{\beta(1 - \alpha)}{1 - \alpha\beta}, \tag{4.4}$$

where $\beta$ is the lawyer's discount factor and $\alpha$ is the stationary value of the weights $\alpha_t$ in the formula (4.2). The precise formula for $\alpha$ is[7]

$$\alpha = 1 + \tfrac{1}{2}r - \sqrt{\tfrac{1}{4}r^2 + r}\,;\, r = \mathrm{Var}(\delta)/\mathrm{Var}(\theta). \tag{4.5}$$

These formulas tell us the following. If $\beta = 1$, so that the lawyer does not discount the future, then $k = 1$ (in 4.4) and the lawyer will get exactly the same returns from reputation as is the marginal value of care to his or her present customer [see (4.1)]. In other words, the lawyer will supply the efficient level of care and moral hazard will not be a problem. On the other hand, if $\beta < 1$, then the equilibrium level of care will be suboptimal (since $k < 1$). How much below the optimum it will be depends, besides $\beta$, on $\alpha$. The higher $\alpha$ is, the farther we are from the ideal solution; and $\alpha$ is higher the less accurately clients can observe performance (i.e., if the variance of $\theta_t$ is big) and the less competence varies over time (i.e., if the variance of $\delta_t$ is small). In other words, accurate observations of performance and competence that changes over time are beneficial to reputation formation and the resolution of moral hazard.

This stylized model of professional service supply shows how reputation acts as an implicit contract in inducing care. It performs exactly as an explicit contract would, if the explicit contract were of the form $s(x) = kx + b$, where $k$ is given by (4.4). The point is that legally such a contract may not be possible to enforce, but it can be enforced by the supplier's concern for future customers. Present customers can rely on it, because of reputation. Notice, however, that implicit contracts are determined by the market and that there is not the same design flexibility that one has when explicit contracting is possible. In the preceding example only linear contracts can be supported by the market.

Implicit contracts, and thereby market performance, can be influenced by changing the information flow, because, as we saw previously, the variance of the two disturbance terms $\theta_t$ and $\delta_t$ affect the contractual parameter $k$. Supplying more accurate information about service performance, for instance, makes $k$ bigger and brings it closer to the right marginal return from care. Publicizing service records (individually or through government action) is one option which I will discuss in the next section. Here I want to emphasize the role of competition. When there are many service suppliers who are subject to similar exogenous disturbances, customers can make sharper inferences about competence by looking at relative performance. The reason is that observing performance of many suppliers reveals information about the exogenous factors that are common to all suppliers and thereby an individual supplier's behavior can be better assessed. Consequently, an increased number of suppliers will improve incentives at least if customers can observe or receive information about how all suppliers perform. On the other hand, if the process by which information about the service is transmitted gets noisier, returns from care taking are reduced.

Another factor that will influence care is the speed by which human capital depreciates. If it happens fast, which it frequently does in professions such as law and medicine, clients will tend to interpret poor performance as a sign of reduced competence. To prevent this from happening, care levels will be increased in equilibrium (in addition to replacement of human capital). This is an example where $\delta_t$ becomes noisier and, as we saw above, that will raise the value of $k$ and improve care taking.

Let me point out one other feature of this model, which is of interest. Before the learning process reaches the stationary state where the precision of knowledge about competence no longer improves because information about performance and movements in competence just offset each other, the seller's returns from care may far exceed their value to the present customer. This can be seen by evaluating the infinite sum of $\alpha_t$'s as described earlier. Such a calculation shows that young professionals have the highest returns from performing well, because when information about their competence is poor, performance will have a big influence on customer's perceptions (i.e., $\alpha_t$ is decreasing in $t$). Consequently, one may expect young professionals to work harder than older ones. This prediction seems to have some empirical support (see also Medoff and Abraham, 1978). Such oversupply of effort will be socially inefficient. If it also becomes individually very costly it may lead young professionals to join firms or professional groups which can help reduce the uncertainty in establishing competence as well as smooth their income stream. This comment applies equally to situations where decisions other than care are involved. For instance, a young physician may be reluctant to take large risks on his/her own, because the market would react much more strongly to adverse outcomes in his/her case than in the case of a better established physician. A young physician would rather seek protection from a professional group like a health care center, which could keep the supply of clients and his or her income less dependent on performance.

### 4.2    Price-signaling and reputation rents

In the previous model the buyer could pay for a service before receiving it and still be assured of proper delivery because he/she knew that it is in the seller's own interest to perform well because of future opportunity costs from cheating. These opportunity costs were induced by the learning process. Next I will describe a model, due to Klein and Leffler (1982) and treated more formally by Shapiro (1981), in which the seller imposes on himself or herself an opportunity cost sufficiently high to make nonperformance suboptimal. Realizing this, the customer can again trust that while he/she pays up front he or she will not be deceived.

The model is quite simple. My description is based on Shapiro's work. Consider a service like a hotel or a restaurant. New customers forecast what service they will get, based on what earlier customers tell about their experience. This may be a complicated rumor process, but for simplicity assume that information about past quality is accurate and publicly available all the time. In this situation it is not unreasonable for a customer to assess that the quality of the service that he will receive will be the same as it was in the previous period. It will turn out that this estimate will be correct in equilibrium. We may call this quality forecast the seller's present reputation.

The seller can demand a price for the service, which is compatible with its expected quality. The precise price schedule as a function of quality will be determined momentarily.

Let the cost of quality supply be given by $c(q)$. There is a lowest level of quality, $q_0$, that can be supplied. Adjusting this level will be an important instrument in government intervention.

A firm with reputation $q$ must be provided with an incentive to maintain that quality level in order that consumer expectations will be fulfilled. This is one equilibrium condition. The other is that the price schedule does not lead to supernormal rents because free entry is assumed. Considering the possibility that the seller cheats by supplying the lowest level of quality, $q_0$, instead of the expected level, $q$, leads to the following restriction on price:

$$p(q) \geq c(q) + \frac{1-\beta}{\beta}(c(q) - c(q_0));$$ (4.6)

where $\beta$ is the seller's discount factor. This inequality has to hold if the seller is to prefer $q$ over $q_0$.[8] On the other hand, free entry implies that[9]

$$p(q_0) - c(q) + \frac{\beta}{1-\beta}(p(q) - c(q)) \leq 0.$$ (4.7)

Together with the boundary condition $p(q_0) = c(q_0)$, (4.7) is the reverse inequality of (4.6) and hence the equilibrium price schedule is uniquely determined with (4.6) holding as an equality.

Looking at equation (4.6) we see that price exceeds cost in equilibrium. This is essential as it provides the rent required to sustain reputation. Given this rent the opportunity cost from cheating is higher than the cost savings from supplying low quality in one period. The size of the price premium depends on the discount factor. As in the previous model, a discount factor close to one will lead to an almost efficient solution, because then the price will essentially equal cost. Notice that the inefficiency of the present model does not appear as inferior quality supply, but as excessively costly quality. Customers will be forced to buy lower quality than they could in a world where quality would be purchased with an enforceable contract.

In the present context, the size of the discount factor could be interpreted in alternative ways, including the speed with which information is transmitted or the frequency with which customers patronize the service. If the latter interpretation is used, the model suggests that increased demand will improve quality.

Since free entry is assumed there must be something to offset subsequent rents. Equation (4.7) reveals that it is the initial investment in establishing reputation. This looks convincing, but is in fact inconsistent with customer rationality. First-time customers will receive a quality in excess of equilibrium price. Therefore customers that patronize established firms which supply quality $q_0$ behave irrationally. They would be better off going to a firm which has just opened its service.

There is another problem as well with rents in subsequent periods. What prevents an established firm from undercutting its competitors (in the same quality class) and getting all the demand? Since price is above cost, this will at least in the short run be a profitable move.

These problems can be resolved by interpreting the model in a slightly different way, namely, so that customers forecast quality based on the price of the services. In this interpretation price acts as a signal of quality. The presumption is that if received quality does not match expected quality, the seller loses his reputation forever. The only quality level at which the seller can attract customers after cheating once is therefore $q_0$. Since the lost rents from such a maneuver exceed the cost savings, the seller can in fact be trusted not to deviate from the price–quality schedule. The choice of price is simultaneously a commitment to quality.

This interpretation accords better with Klein and Leffler's original idea, but now free entry poses a problem. Sellers will earn a positive profit from the beginning, because they do not need to invest $c(q) - p(q_0)$ in forming a reputation. Klein and Leffler conclude that investment in specific capital like advertising and other nonsalvagable assets, is needed to balance off these profits and prevent entry from destroying the rents to reputation that are essential for supporting quality levels above the minimum. If consumers derive any benefits at all from such specific investments, one may envision an equilibrium in which both price and investment signals have to be right before consumers are assured that quality will be what they expect.

Although the idea that price signals quality certainly is appealing and appears to have empirical support, neither Shapiro nor Klein and Leffler provide an explicit analysis of how sellers compete for reputation rents. Indeed, the number of sellers does not have any influence on the price–

quality schedule. This seems to be an issue worth exploring in more depth and requires almost certainly a more detailed study of how consumers actually communicate information. Another part of the model that needs more careful treatment is the question of multiple equilibria. In Shapiro's model, for instance, an alternative is that customers expect low quality irrespective of price. If so, all firms will supply low quality and no price-quality schedule will emerge. Firm-specific investments that have value to the customer are probably important in breaking such a deadlock.

In this context, it is interesting to note that long-term agreements can be used as quality assuring devices if a service relationship is ongoing. Consider for instance a firm that hires janitorial services or food services. To protect the service supplier from losing specific investments in case the customer interrupts the service too early, an agreement of some length is necessary. On the other hand, by bounding the duration of the agreement, the seller's incentives to undersupply quality can be controlled. As in the preceding model, price has to be set above cost in order to induce a rent, which the supplier does not want to forego. Viewed differently, the price will act as a bribe, which makes the customer's only punishment – termination of the relationship at the end of the contract – an effective incentive device. Since the analysis of long-term agreements proceeds much along the lines of price signaling I will not elaborate on it here. What is interesting, though, is that such an analysis can be used to explain contract length in ongoing service relationships. The competition for long-term agreements has also some intriguing features in that rents offered by customers induce externalities onto others. The cost to a seller from termination of a service relationship depends on his or her alternative opportunities. Shapiro and Stiglitz (1982), building on earlier work by Calvo and Wellisz (1978) and Becker and Stigler (1974), have explored externalities of this kind in the context of labor markets. Their insights ought to be adaptable to long-term service relationships as well.

Going back to Shapiro's model for a moment, let me consider market intervention. A government could impose standards on minimum quality, that is, adjust $q_0$. The cost of raising the quality standard stems from lost service of low quality demand. The benefit comes from a cheaper supply of high quality service. As usual, in models of adverse selection, the low quality sellers induce an externality on high quality sellers. In the case at hand this externality can be read off directly from (4.6). The additional cost imposed on high quality supply is proportional to $c(q_0)$. If $q_0$ is raised, $c(q_0)$ goes up and the price premium necessary to support sufficient reputation rents goes down. It is clear that with an explicit welfare function an optimal level of $q_0$ is easily found. Recall though that this is not a Pareto improvement, because customers who prefer low quality (because of price) are cut out by the imposed quality regulation and cannot be compensated for informational reasons.

### 4.3    *Market structure and quality*

The preceding models had little to say about the effects of market structure. In this section I want to look at a very simple example, which I believe will clarify why I think market structure effects must ultimately be addressed with explicit models of consumer communication. It is a variation on a more extensive and carefully developed model of price competition between physicians that Satterthwaite (1979, 1985) has developed.

I will consider a community that is served by $n$ sellers. I have in mind a service like TV repair. I want to study the effect of an increase in the number of sellers. To make matters substantially simpler I will restrict myself to only one service characteristic: quality. The other characteristic is, of course, the price of the service, but I doubt that the point I wish to make will be sensitive to my assumption that price is fixed and the same for all sellers.

There is one unit of demand each period. One may think of the consumers as standing in line and one being served per period. If the consumer has no information about the sellers at the time he/she needs service he will choose one randomly. A service involves some effort by the seller. Let $q$ be the level of care that the seller takes. This determines how long the item, say a TV, will function again. Since exogenous factors also influence how long the TV will last, $q$ induces a probability distribution over the lifetime of the TV. Again, to simplify the analysis, I will assume that once repaired the TV will break down immediately or not at all. Choosing the scale properly the quality of the service, that is, the level of care $q$, can then be taken equal to the probability that the TV remains functioning.

What the customer observes is whether or not his or her TV breaks after the service. If it breaks he/she gets a bad impression of the repair service, if not he or she gets a good impression. With this information he/she returns to the queue of future customers and meets one at random to whom he/she tells his/her experience.

All individuals in this community have a one period memory. Thus, if the most recently served customer does not meet the next to be served, the service information is lost. With $m$ customers this probability is $(m-1)/m$. Finally, if the customer next to be served hears from the previous customer about a particular repair service he or she goes there if it was good and he or she does not go there if it was bad.

Let $p$ be the common price charged and let $c(q)$ be the cost of quality supplied. With the previously described process of communication, the net expected return to the repair service from choosing a care level $q$ is: [10]

$$pq/m + p(m-1)/mn - c(q).$$ (4.8)

Consequently, the optimum choice of $q$ is to set $c'(q) = p/m$.

We see that quality will increase with the rents that are foregone ($=p$) if the customer leaves with a bad impression. Quality will decrease with the size of the community ($m$), because that will reduce the relative efficiency of communication. A notable fact is that the number of sellers $n$ has no influence on quality choice. However, as might be expected, this is a knife-edge case. A slight change of the communication structure will alter the conclusion. The change is the following. Instead of telling that the service experience was either good or bad, the most recent customer may also leave with no particular opinion. That counts as no information and will neither benefit nor hurt the reputation of a repair service. Let the probability of a good, bad, or indifferent service outcome be $\pi_+(q)$, $\pi_-(q)$ and $\pi_0(q)$, respectively. Now the return to service quality is given by: [11]

$$p\pi_+(q)/m + p\pi_0(q)/mn + p(m-1)/mn - c(q),$$ (4.9)

and the optimal choice of quality satisfies:

$$c'(q) = p\pi'_+(q)/m + p\pi'_0(q)/mn.$$ (4.10)

In this case we find that the number of sellers does influence service quality. Specifically, an increase in $n$ will increase quality if $\pi'_0 > 0$ and it will decrease quality if $\pi'_0 < 0$. The earlier described case is the limiting situation where $\pi'_0 = 0$ in which case the number of sellers has no influence on quality.

A way of interpreting these findings is in terms of customer attitudes. If customers expect good quality and therefore only tell their friends when not satisfied, then $\pi'_0 > 0$ (because the good and intermediate outcomes become the same). Such an attitude results in lower quality as $n$ increases. On the other hand, if only good outcomes are communicated, then $\pi'_0 < 0$ and the result is reversed.

My intention is obviously not to claim any generality for these specific conclusions. Rather, I wanted to show that what consumers discuss among themselves may have an influence on how competition affects service characteristics. For this purpose I consider the example sufficient. Clearly, there are a number of dimensions in which the example could be permutated to bring this same point home. Service could be supplied to many customers at the same time, customers could talk to more than one friend about their experience, they could remember their experience for a longer period and they could have a richer scale of opinions about service quality. None of these embellishments influence my general conclusion. Nor is the fact that I have arbitrarily assumed a fixed price important for my purposes. But, of course, if one wants specific predictions about when quality decreases with increased service supply, one ought to model competition (in particular the price dimension) more carefully.

With this disclaimer, let me give another example of how explicit modelling of reputation formation can be applied. Intuition suggests that the value of a good reputation is related to seller size. In my earlier described repair service example one can study that. Without bothering with the trivial details one finds that the effect of merging two or more repair services under one ownership is the same as that of decreasing the number of sellers. Again the outcome depends on customer attitudes and what information is communicated in the market.

In this context it would also be very interesting to explore quality specialization. Implicitly, I assumed previously that customers identify quality with the firm name. In fact, one may expect that the same chain of service stores can maximize its return from reputation by providing homogeneous quality. Varying quality will add uncertainty to the customer's assessment and lower his expected return from purchasing the service. Casual empiricism strongly suggests that this is true and one would like to know what ramifications it has, for instance, on the size distribution of service suppliers.

### 4.4 Summary

Reputation is an important mechanism by which decent service quality can be assured. Presently we do not have a very good grasp of how reputation is best modelled and analyzed. For this reason I presented in some more detail three examples of reputation analysis, which indicate how one might approach this subject and what questions can be addressed. Among the tentative conclusions from these examples are the following: (1) rents are essential for supporting reputation formation; (2) the strength of the reputation effect is positively related to the discount factor, the speed and accuracy of information transmission and the uncertainty concerning the seller; (3) reputation can implicitly enforce contracts that have the same structure as explicit agreement, yet the choice of contracts is more limited.

These conclusions accord well with intuition and suggest that reputation phenomena can be effectively studied by formal models. The big question in my mind, however, is how competition should be included in the picture. The first two models did not and could not address competitive issues at all, while the third example indicated that the effects of competition may be very sensitive to how consumers communicate information. My conclusion is that explicit modeling of communication (as well as search) is essential to analyzing competition for reputation rents and that this is the direction in which future research should go. I see Satterthwaite's (1979, 1985) model as excellent support for this point of view.

## 5     Certification and monitoring

One approach to remedying moral hazard and adverse selection is to go directly to the source of these problems and try to reduce informational asymmetries by monitoring. A central question is whether the government should administer such activities or whether one can trust the market to provide the relevant information endogenously and perhaps more efficiently. This question and related ones have recently been addressed by Grossman (1981), Jovanovic (1982), Shaked and Sutton (1981) and Chan and Leland (1982), among others. I will discuss briefly the main insights of this literature.

We saw earlier that when adverse selection is present, suppliers of bad quality cause an externality by forcing good quality suppliers to engage in costly signaling. For this reason it may well be that the economy would be better off without low quality supply and this could be used as an argument for licensing [see Leland (1979)]. Before jumping to that conclusion, however, one ought to look at what the market could do on its own using certification. If certification were costless, then it is clear that everybody except the lowest quality suppliers would let themselves be certified. It would happen through a sequential process in which the highest quality suppliers first distinguish themselves and thereafter each quality level in turn. Once certified, there would be no further need to distort contracts or use other costly signals. In other words, with costless certification, the market is efficient.

On the other hand, if certification is costly, then all qualities would not be revealed. At some point the marginal value of certification will become smaller than the benefit. The interesting fact is that this critical level is such that there will be excess certification in the market compared to first–best [Jovanovic (1982)]. The reason is that the sellers who certify themselves do not take into account the costs they impose on the uncertified, who will be earning less due to their noncertification. Raising certification costs might in this case be an appropriate policy measure. The same argument applies to other kinds of costly signaling activities such as advertising, information disclosure, use of warranties, et cetera. From a theoretical point of view, all these activities are likely to be conducted in excessive rather than suboptimal amounts. In this light forced disclosure or regulations that impose warranties on sellers need not be welfare improving [Grossman (1981)]. In fact, converse actions like forbidding advertising of price, for instance, may be the appropriate measures to take. Included in these measures to limit signaling are also licensing rules, uniformly imposed warranties or other forms of forced contracts (e.g., physician liability). Needless to say, the tradeoffs are delicate and may be very hard to evaluate empirically. [12]

Thus, one argument against voluntary certification would be that it induces too fierce competition. Another argument for intervention is that consumers may not be as rational and well informed about the content and meaning of various signals as equilibrium models assume. How good is a certified service relative to an uncertified one? Or what does a particular service record indicate? An important point is that the value of a signal – say, informing consumers about service records – is dependent on what other sellers do in terms of disclosure. A kind of network externality appears [see Wilson (1982)] and could lead to situations in which no one signals because going first will not be worthwhile given the signal's poor information content when it cannot be compared to other sellers' signals. One might argue that private firms should be able to capitalize on this joint but unrealized opportunity by engaging in information publication, and indeed we do see such production of consumer information. The problem is that, since information is largely a public good, it may be difficult for firms to appropriate their returns from such investments. These considerations may again rationalize forced disclosure of information and perhaps even public monitoring of service quality.

Wilson (1982) has suggested that network externalities may play an important role in the development of information services such as auditing. In recent years we have seen a proliferation of consulting activities that to some extent at least perform a signaling function. This might be explained partly by the fact that as managers get more specialized (for technological reasons), their relative expertise grows, leading to an increased information gap. As a consequence, incentive problems are aggravated raising the demand for more certification. On the other hand, once signaling of this form gets started, its value multiplies with increased use and may lead to a sudden boom in consulting activity. In other words, what we may be observing is a rapid move between two equilibria: from one of no signaling to one of (perhaps) excessive signaling (compare with the two possible equilibria discussed in section 4.2). It would be interesting to explore a formal model of this process and compare it to the empirical evidence.

A final issue in the context of certification and licensing that I want to mention is the efficiency of letting professional groups administer these processes. Shaked and Sutton (1981) conclude rather convincingly that professionals will accept too few members into their associations or give out too few licenses. The reason is simply that the situation parallels a monopoly. Limiting the supply (by rationing, charging a too high fee, or setting too high standards) inflates the price and provides monopoly rents. This, of course, raises the question of whether professions should be allowed to regulate themselves.

## 6     Conclusions

In this paper I have studied the provision of services within a limited framework. I have emphasized the presence of informational asymmetries and tried to shed some light on what ramifications it has, basing my arguments on recent advances in the theoretical literature on the economics of information and uncertainty. I hope my discussion has shown that this framework is useful for studying the service sector, that information theory is relevant for the issues at hand and that it shows promise for future development.

A central theme of information economics is that incentive problems can usefully be divided into two categories: moral hazard and adverse selection. The value of this categorization rests with the behavioral and policy differences that they imply. The main problem is that observationally the two categories are difficult to distinguish. What we observe can often be explained either as caused by moral hazard or by adverse selection. It seems important therefore to try and develop empirical techniques that can be used to discriminate between the two and this I see as one prime objective of future research.

In assessing the value of the informational paradigm I think it is fair to say that we have been reasonably successful in generating explanations for many of the institutions, formal or informal, which we observe in the service sector (in fact, too many, referring to my previous point), but we are much behind in theories that help us understand how competition within those institutions is enacted. Regarding future theoretical work, my main conclusion is that we ought to study more carefully how customers search and select between service suppliers and that this process requires a more detailed and explicit analysis of information transmission among consumers.[13]

### Notes

1. Some interesting work along these lines has already been conducted; see, for instance, Newhouse et al. (1982) and references therein.
2. Formally, (3.1) is the first-order condition of the optimal program: chose $s_0$ and $s_1$ to maximize $pv(s_1) + (1-p)v(s_0)$ subject to $pu(1-s_1) + (1-p)u(-s_0) \geq K$ [a constant].
3. For a good start on these types of search problems, see Schwartz and Wilde (1982).
4. It should be emphasized that this is not a general conclusion. Moral hazard may sometimes involve externalities as well. An example of this will come up in Section 4.1 in the context of long-term service relationships.

5. For different approaches see Dybvig and Spatt (1982), Holmstrom (1982), Kreps and Wilson (1982), Milgrom and Roberts (1982), Radner (1981), Rubinstein (1979), Rogerson (1982), and Shapiro (1981, 1982).

6. Here $k$ equals $\beta(1 - \alpha) + \beta^2(1 - \alpha)\alpha + \beta^3(1 - \alpha)\alpha^2 + \cdots$, which is the discounted sum of the marginal returns from a unit increase in effort in the stationary state.

7. The derivation of this expression is somewhat more elaborate and given in Holmstrom (1982).

8. To see this, notice that $(p(q) - c(q))(\beta/1 - \beta)$ is the discounted profits from continuing to provide quality $q$, whereas $c(q) - c(q_0)$ is the one period return from cheating and subsequently exiting the market. [Since $p(q_0) = c(q_0)$ in equilibrium, exiting the market is equivalent to staying in and producing $q_0$, which is the quality level expected by assumption after cheating has been observed.]

9. Recall that $p(q_0)$ is the price an entrant gets in the first period irrespective of quality choice. Then (4.7) can be explained in the same way as (4.6) was in Note 8.

10. The components of (4.8) can be explained as follows. The probability that the most recent customer will talk to the next customer in line is $1/m$. If that happens, the probability that he/she will tell that the service was good is $q$, in which case the repair service will receive also the next customer and earn $p$ from him/her. On the other hand, if the service to the recent customer was bad, the repair service will not receive the next customer. The expected value of these outcomes are $pq/m$, the first term in (4.8). If the recent customer does not meet the next in line (the probability being $(m-1)/m$), the new customer chooses at random among repair services, which yields an expected return of $p/n$ to the repair service. This explains the second term of (4.8). The third term is just the cost of providing quality $q$. Note that no discounting is assumed in this calculation, although that is irrelevant for the conclusions I make.

11. The explanation of (4.9) is analogous to that in Note 10.

12. Chan and Leland (1982) provide an interesting model that addresses this tradeoff. Their conclusion is that restrictions on price advertising are not welfare improving. One should bear in mind, though, that their setting has special features and it would be inappropriate to draw the inference that banning price competition would always be undesirable.

13. In addition to earlier references on search I would like to mention the important papers by Wilde (1980, 1981). Although these papers do not study the reputation aspect of firms, they do explore the problem of consumer search when quality cannot be directly observed, which, of course, is a very relevant part of the overall issue.

## References

Akerlof, G. (August 1970), "The Market for 'Lemons': Quality Uncertainty and the Market Mechanism," *Quarterly Journal of Economics* 84, 488–500.

Becker, G., and G. Stigler (January 1974), "Law Enforcement, Malfeasance and Compensation of Enforcers," *Journal of Legal Studies* 3, 1–18.

Begun, J., D. Easley, and M. O'Hara (1982), "Can the Market Provide Optimal Quality in the Presence of Asymmetric Information." Working Paper No. 82-11, Cornell University.

Calvo, G., and S. Wellisz (1978), "Supervision, Loss of Control and the Optimum Size of The Firm," *Journal of Political Economy* 86, No. 5, 943–52.

Chan, Y. S., and H. Leland (October 1982), "Prices and Qualities in Markets with Costly Information," *Review of Economic Studies* 49, 499–516.

Dreze, J., and K. Hagen (May 1978), "Choice of Product Quality: Equilibrium and Efficiency," *Econometrica* 46, No. 3, 493–513.

Dybvig, P., and C. Spatt (1982), "Does It Pay to Maintain a Reputation?" Mimeo, Yale University.

Fama, E. (April 1980), "Agency Problems and the Theory of The Firm," *Journal of Political Economy* 88, No. 2, 288–307.

Grossman, S. (December 1981), "The Informational Role of Warranties and Private Disclosure about Product Quality," *Journal of Law and Economics* 24, No. 3, 461–483.

Holmstrom, B. (1982), "Managerial Incentive Problems – A Dynamic Perspective," in *Essays in Economics and Management in Honor of Lars Wahlbeck*, 209–30.

 (Spring 1979), "Moral Hazard and Observability," *Bell Journal of Economics* 10, No. 1, 74–91.

Holmstrom, B., and R. Myerson (November 1982), "Efficient and Durable Decision Rules with Incomplete Information," *Econometrica* 51, No. 6, 1799–1820.

Jovanovic, B. (Spring 1982), "Truthful Disclosure of Information," *Bell Journal of Economics* 13, 36–44.

Klein, L., and K. Leffler (1982). "The Role of Market Forces in Assuring Contractual Performance," *Journal of Political Economy* 89, No. 4, 615–41.

Kreps, D., and R. Wilson (August 1982), "Reputation and Imperfect Information," *Journal of Economic Theory* 27, 253–79.

Leland, H. (1979), "Quacks, Lemons and Licensing: A Theory of Minimum Quality Standards," *Journal of Political Economy* 87, No. 6, 1328–46.

Medoff, J., and K. Abraham (December 1980), "Experience, Performance and Earnings," *Quarterly Journal of Economics* 95, 703–36.

Milgrom, P., and J. Roberts (August 1982), "Predation, Reputation and Entry Deterrence," *Journal of Economic Theory* 27, 280–312.

Newhouse, J. P., A. P. Williams, B. W. Bennett, and W. B. Schwartz (Autumn 1982), "How Have Location Patterns of Physicians Affected the Availability of Medical Services," *Bell Journal of Economics* 13, 493–505.

Radner, R. (1981), "Monitoring Cooperative Agreements in a Repeated Principal–Agent Relationship," *Econometrica* 49, No. 5, 1127–48.

Rogerson, W. (Autumn 1982), "Reputation and Product Quality," *Bell Journal of Economics* 14, 508–16.

Rosen, S. (1981), "The Division of Labor and the Production of Comparative Advantage," Discussion Paper 81-7, University of Chicago.

Rubinstein, A. (1979), "Offences That May Have Been Committed by Accident – An Optimal Policy of Retribution," in *Applied Game Theory*, S. Brams, A. Shotter, and G. Schrodiauer, eds., 406–13. Wurzburg: Physica Verlag.

Satterthwaite, M. (1985), "Competition and Equilibrium as a Driving Force in the Health Services Sector," Chapter 9 in this book.

 (Autumn 1979), "Consumer Information, Equilibrium Industry Price, and the Number of Sellers," *Bell Journal of Economics* 10, 483–502.

Schwartz, A., and L. Wilde (December 1982), "Consumer Markets Warranties," Social Science Working Paper 445, California Institute of Technology.

Shaked, A., and J. Sutton (April 1981), "The Self-Regulating Profession," *Review of Economic Studies* 48, 217–34.

Shapiro, C. (Spring 1982), "Consumer Information, Product Quality and Seller Reputation," *Bell Journal of Economics* 13, 20–35.

——— (1981), "Premiums for High Quality Products as Rents to Reputation," Discussion Paper No. 6, Princeton University.

Shapiro, C., and J. Stiglitz (April 1982), "Equilibrium Unemployment as a Worker Discipline Device," Discussion Paper No. 28, Princeton University.

Shavell, S. (1978), "Theoretical Issues in Medical Malpractice," in *The Economics of Medical Malpractice*, S. Rottenberg, ed., 35–64. Washington, D.C.: American Enterprise Institute.

Spence, M. (August 1973), "Job Market Signalling," *Quarterly Journal of Economics* 87, 355–74.

Wilde, L. (December 1981), "Information Costs, Duration of Search, and Turnover: Theory and Application," *Journal of Political Economy* 89, No. 6, 1122–41.

——— (July 1980), "On the Formal Theory of Inspection and Evaluation in Product Markets," *Econometrica* 48, No. 5, 1265–80.

Wilson, R. (1982), "Research in Accounting: Perspectives from Multiperson Decision Theory," mimeo, Stanford University.

# Comment: The provision of services in a market economy

## ANDREW POSTLEWAITE

Professor Holmstrom has addressed an issue which is extremely important in a large part of the service sector, the issue of quality certification. In areas such as legal or medical services, the recipient of the services often does not have access to as much information relevant to the problem as does the deliverer of the services. A lawyer generally will know much more about the intrinsic merits of a case than his or her client. A surgeon will clearly know the probabilities of various degrees of success of surgery better than his/her patient. A problem arises in the provision of services that have this "asymmetric information" aspect because there is an uncertain outcome regardless of the abilities and efforts of the deliverer of the services. Lawsuits and patients are lost by the best of the lot. The problem that arises is that in the case of "failure," or unsatisfactory outcomes, the recipient of the services cannot distinguish perfectly between incompetence and bad luck. Furthermore, this inability to perfectly distinguish the two has bad incentive effects on the provider of these services. Why not let up the pace just a bit, even if it increases the chance of failure, if the failure is likely to be ascribed to bad fortune? The less able can enter into the provision of these services if their lessser abilities are partially hidden by the problem of separating low ability from bad fortune. The ability of the more able to make, maintain and spread a reputation is confounded by the "noise effects" of bad luck.

These problems of monitoring and assessing the performance of those who perform services have spawned a literature that goes under the general title "Principal–Agent Problems". The formal analysis of these problems has lent insight into contractual forms we observe, such as lawyers working for fees contingent upon success or the existence of health maintenance organizations.

I would like to reverse the relationship of the service sector and these monitoring problems which Professor Holmstrom has laid out. His thesis has been that parts of the service sector are characterized by these problems. I would like to suggest that these problems have, in fact, spawned large parts of the service sector. Where it is difficult to distinguish chance occurrence from systematic malfeasance, one can make a living by specializing in distinction. Much of the work done by accountants, lawyers and management consultants is of this sort. You may hire a lawyer who will inform you

214

of the various ways in which another's ineptitude or incompetance might hurt you and what your remedies will be if you are hurt. You hire an accountant precisely to investigate and to provide you information as to what is being done in various parts of your company or in some other company. You hire management consultants to design good management compensation schemes for your employees because you will not be able to observe your employees' efforts and actions directly. This year's bottom line is an imperfect indicator at best as to a manager's actions regarding product quality, equipment maintenance and customer relations.

I am suggesting that much of the service sector exists because of principal–agent problems. These service activities exist because monitoring is difficult. If monitoring becomes more difficult, there will be an increase in these service activities to overcome the new problems. Many parts of the service sector have arisen precisely to deal with new kinds of quality assurance problems.

It has become commonplace in recent years to lament the short term outlook of today's managers. Regularly the *New York Times,* the *Wall Street Journal* and other publications report that our productivity problems are due to a failure of modern management to take a longer term view on investment decisions. One could argue this could have been predicted a decade or so ago. Over the last three decades a typical career path of a manager has changed. The length of time a manager is in a particular position has shortened. Managers are rotated among many jobs to expose them to many facets of the corporation. Often the internal structure of the firm causes a manager to switch firms only a few years after joining a company. This in itself is not surprising given the changing nature of corporations.

How is a company to evaluate the performance of a modern peripatetic M.B.A.? In the past, the profitability of the division or unit for which a manager was responsible was the primary factor in judging performance, as it should be. If profits were properly calculated we would have no problem today with such a measure of performance. In fact, profits are necessarily crudely measured. How do we charge off the cost of lost good will when a manager cuts his inventory levels for cost-cutting purposes and cannot fill an order? How do we depreciate machinery more quickly when our manager cuts preventive maintenance by twenty percent? How do we set aside reserves for additional warrantee costs if our manager skimps on quality control? Measured profits only crudely, if at all, take account of these very real costs.

Now if a manager is to manage a division or unit for life, the problem may not be so severe. Today's extra profits are at the expense of tomorrow's. If tomorrow's profits decline dramatically for a modest increase today, the tradeoff will not be worthwhile. But if next year I expect to be in the

Western Division, I'm not going to be as affected by the long term consequences of my decisions today as head of the Eastern Division. And I will
not be affected at all if I am with another firm.

Not surprisingly, we should expect that any increase in the mobility of
managers within or between firms should decrease the concern of these
managers for the longer term. But we can counteract some of these effects.
The problem arose because our measure of profits was not accurate. Had
the profit properly been adjusted to reflect the hidden costs, we could safely
use the adjusted profit for our evaluation.

This then is my theme: A fundamental change in the nature of corporations has given impetus to a need for more accurate accounting. The incentive problems have grown more complex and the usefulness of "service
sector" people – accountants and compensation specialists – has increased.

# Part II: Service productivity, trade, and market structure

Mr. Leveson elaborated on a problem with the conventional statistics for trade in services, specifically foreign direct investment. These statistics measure the initial movement into a market but do not register what may subsequently happen. Consequently, growth in service provision or possible leapfrogging into other countries and markets are not included.

Turning to another area Mr. Leveson summarized the strategy he thought the United States should take in trade negotiations. This critical issue, in his view, has up to now been approached with a "fill in the boxes" plan in mind. The United States has tried to negotiate everything, even areas where the market can function on its own. He proposed that we need to target areas that will be important to the United States and concentrate on issues that we have a shot at winning. The key is to pick our battles carefully. He suggested some specific targets: information, foreign capital flows, and the foreign ownership issue. Some reduction in barriers in these areas could lead to real gains and would appear feasible. Market forces could then create the pressure required to open other markets. In this scenario, later trade negotiations would be a sort of de facto deregulation to ratify changes that had already occurred in the marketplace.

He pointed to the recent Japanese bank holding company act and Japanese telecommunication decisions as evidence that in the longer run certain basic similarities in the way industries and regulations develop will lead to conditions where negotiations will be desirable.

Mr. Gruenstein applauded the discussion so far on measurement of service productivity and output. He offered three additional areas for the conference to consider to broaden its focus: employment issues, regional issues, and cyclical issues. Investigations into these areas should be on the research agenda. He elaborated on each. Colin Clark made clear that the shifts from agriculture to manufacture to services have vast human consequences. Most notably are labor market displacements. Some important questions to work on in this regard are: What service industries will grow in the future? What skills will be needed in these areas? What are the training needs and job policies that will help ensure the requisite skills matchups between jobs and workers? Issues that may not be important on a national level may be crucial regionally. Do we expect any problems from regional specialization in services? Can a regional economy be sustained by services? Or in Felix Rohatyn's words, can we sell each other hamburgers and take in each others laundry. Finally, what does the shift to services hold in store for the cyclical sensitivity of the economy? A decade ago it was thought that this shift would dampen the cyclical sensitivity of the economy, both nationally and regionally. Do we still believe this today?

Ms. Stalson offered some comments on points made earlier. Mr. Kravis had suggested that the bilateral route might be better than a multilateral route in trade negotiations. In Ms. Stalson's view the complications bilateral agreements would pose for multinational corporations are enormous. A more reasonable framework might be an umbrella approach. Some guidelines negotiated in a multilateral sphere could be supplemented with bilateral arrangements. She thought this approach would make things easier all around. She agreed with Mr. Leveson's proposal for a directed approach toward trade issues and seconded his suggested targets: information, capital flows, and foreign ownership and investment. She cautioned that in practice these goals would be difficult to attain, especially the foreign ownership and investment issue. Her understanding was that we are trying to camouflage some of these touchy investment issues in trade clothes. Mr. Leveson added that we are also worried about foreign ownership in the United States.

Mr. Kendrick was impressed with Professor Baumol's analysis of quality-adjusted productivity. He compared the theory to a labor market story with a firm adjusting the labor it hires (marginal product) to fit a competitive wage rate. Responding to Mr. Hulten's remarks on quality change in video games Mr. Kendrick noted that these sort of changes would not show up in his tables (Table 1). Change in quality in the goods and durable goods industries are also probably understated.

Mr. Kendrick thought a more interesting analysis was to break down the changes in these residuals (TFP) into their components. Using a modified Denison growth accounting method, he was able to completely explain the slowdown in productivity growth. Denison was not able to explain all the residual. Mr. Kendrick used a different method to estimate the impact of the cyclical nature of the economy on productivity. In his view the depressing influence of this effect was underestimated by Denison. The cyclical nature of the economy dampens productivity more than might be expected. He thought it would be interesting, but difficult, to apply this sort of analysis to individual sectors or industries. It would be nice to be able to explain why productivity in the services has slowed down less than in manufacturing in the recent past. Mr. Kendrick was optimistic about a reacceleration in productivity growth in this decade. This could be the upside of a Kuznets "long swing," the downside being the recent slowdown in productivity growth.

Mr. Harrison was concerned that the role of services as an intermediate input into goods and other services had been neglected by Mr. Kendrick. As these intermediate services improve there would be an impact on the output and quality of final goods and services. This is particularly true in specialty areas such as accounting, law, and finance where it is extremely difficult to separate out the contribution of services as intermediate inputs in the production of final output. Problems may also exist where the composition of inputs change such as the hardware/software mix in the computer industry. For a large computer, this ratio has shifted from much greater than one to much less than one over the last decade.

Mr. Kendrick responded by noting his numbers do, to a certain extent, capture the effect of changes in the use of intermediate products, including services, on final output. Value added rises more relative to gross output as a result of firms economizing on these intermediate inputs. So the effect shows up indirectly in these measures. Mr. Summers's data, on the other hand, involves only final product and therefore misses these intermediate services.

Mr. Kravis, referring to the issue of services as intermediate inputs, said that these are merely a set of conventions that govern the problem being discussed. He expanded this idea with an example of a shoe factory that initially serves a regional market and then, over time, becomes national. The factory's shipping expenses are larger relative to other production costs in the national market. The same could hold for other inputs into shoes, such as wrapping and packaging. The productivity of these inputs hasn't necessarily changed. There are no pure physical commodities, goods are always combined in some way with services.

Mr. Fuchs found the transportation expense example unconvincing since that item would have shown up in a separate transportation category, not with shoes. Mr. Kravis replied that wrapping and packaging inputs would make his point. Mr. Fuchs said that this sort of productivity identification problem is common to all industries not only services. Much of the gain in productivity in agriculture is attributable to progress in the chemical industry, yet we usually give credit to agriculture. Services are not the only sector affected by this problem.

Mr. Hulten returned to the issue of transmitting productivity change through change in intermediate inputs. He noted there is a small literature on the "transmission of productivity change." He thought that in order for Mr. Baumol's general equilibrium productivity theory to go through with strict index number purity, an assumption on the separability of technologies was required. The specific conditions would preclude the possibility of transmission of productivity change from one sector to another through improved quality or lower priced inputs. On a related point he said the mechanism with prices and consumers adjusting, that Mr. Baumol outlined, would address the problem of quality change in inputs for final output. However, with intermediate goods this change in value might not be captured. For example, video games are now of superior design, although the cost of producing them as well as the twenty five cent price has remained constant.

Mr. Baumol replied that on the margin his relation must still hold. If price is not changing, then consumers surplus must change as more consumers use the better quality video games. Mr. Kravis interjected a question of how to distinguish between income elasticity and technological progress as possible explanations of this consumer shift. Mr. Baumol agreed that Mr. Hulten would be correct if our concern was a separate measure of quality change. He emphasized that a productivity measure to include quality change, devised along the lines of his theory, would work. This convinced Mr. Kravis.

Mr. Inman posed a concluding question for the members of the panel. He noted an argument had been made that services are a key sector in contributing to a positive Balance of Payments. Yet when we look at the details from Mr. Kravis's table, all of the main service components show a growth in imports relative to exports over the decade of the seventies. Given these trends, what is the potential for a continued positive contribution of services to our Balance of Payments?

Ms. Spero thought that this country's policy toward services in trade would be important. The world's economies are becoming increasingly dependent on services. They are seen as the leading edge of growth and policy will be directed toward protection of services. The attitude of developing countries toward U.S. trade proposals for services in the GATT is increasingly protectionist. The initial reaction is, what is good for the U.S. must be bad for the rest of the world. An infant industry argument for services is also being made. The crucial questions are: will protectionism in service industries grow? and what is the potential for growth in service trade within the present regulations?

# Analyses of service industries: the finance, health care, and government sectors

# CHAPTER 8

# The future for financial services

FISCHER BLACK

## Introduction

Financial services include processing payments, loan administration, portfolio management, and selling to individuals or institutions. Currently, these services are provided by banks, thrift institutions, mutual funds, brokers, underwriters, and other firms. (Insurance might be counted as a financial service, but I will ignore it here.)

The boundaries between firms providing financial services are set by historical accident, by regulation, and economic factors. Since I want to look at the future, I will ignore historical accident and current regulation where I see no reason for the regulation to continue.[1] I assume that the spread of knowledge about finance will move the firms supplying financial services, their customers, and regulators in the right directions.

When I speak of banking firms, I mean firms that process transactions by check, credit card, or electronic message; or firms that administer loans. When I speak of investment firms, I mean firms that own shares of other firms. When I speak of securities firms, I mean firms that buy and sell stocks and bonds and other securities. I do not mean to imply that firms in each of these areas should be specialized. A single firm may well do all of these things, even today.

I do not mean to imply that the changes I foresee will come in the near future. They can and should come only when the logic behind them is widely understood and accepted. Even if I am correct about the direction of movement, the process may take decades. Still, most of these changes have already begun. Some, like conversion from individual to institutional ownership of stock, have been underway for decades.

## A world without frictions

Let us imagine a world where information is freely available when it is available at all; where there are no selling costs, at least for financial services; where managing is easy because agents or employees always do exactly what you want them to; and where taxes on capital fall evenly on all kinds of assets.

When there is tax neutrality between debt and equity, and when motivating managers is not a problem, there will be no special reason for firms to have debt. We can imagine that firms are financed entirely with equity. When there is tax neutrality between buying and renting, and when selling costs are not a problem, there will be no special reason for renting or leasing. We can assume that all assets are user owned. Even when the tax advantages of bonds are taken away, the participants in a defined-benefit pension plan will want the plan's assets invested entirely in bonds, so default risk will be minimized.[2] The participants in a defined-contribution pension plan will choose a mix of stocks and bonds to match their preferences for risk and expected return, and will ignore tax factors. When there are no selling or management costs, there will be no obvious reason for investment firms to specialize. All investment firms can own the same share of all assets and individuals will own shares of the investment firms mixed with borrowing or lending.

Banking firms can hold riskless bonds as collateral for their deposits, and can allow borrowers to use collateral to reduce their default risk and borrowing rates. If regulation allows, banks will pay market interest rates on positive balances. A customer with a loan will write checks and make deposits that vary the size of the loan: No account with a positive balance will be needed.[3] Banks will base their charges on the cost of processing transactions and administering loans. Since the cost of maintaining an account with a positive balance is trivial when there are no transactions, they will be able to pay full interest on positive balances. If retail outlets find it less costly to handle currency than to handle checks or credit card transactions, they will offer cash discounts.

In this world, there will be no need for securities firms. Nonfinancial firms will issue their securities directly to investment firms. Individuals will adjust their borrowing and lending to match their spending needs, and will buy or sell shares of investment firms when they want to take more or less risk. Individuals will have no reason to own or trade in the shares of nonfinancial firms.

### Costly information

When information is costly, it is difficult for people to find out about the risk of the assets and liabilities of a banking firm where they have positive balances, so it is especially important for the firm to adopt simple policies to assure people that their balances are safe. For example, the banking firm can decide to hold "reserves" in the form of government securities with a market value equal to 100 percent or more of the value of its deposit liabilities. The banking firm could have a rule that these reserves would be used to pay depositors, in case of financial trouble, before they are used to pay any other creditors.

If debt has an advantage in this world, a banking firm can borrow from investment firms. It will also issue stock to raise some of the money it uses to make loans. I can see no special reason for a banking firm to lend out the money it receives from its deposits. The money a banking firm raises by issuing stocks and bonds will also provide added protection for the depositors, especially if the depositors have a higher priority claim on all the assets of the banking firm than other lenders.

When information is costly, it becomes especially important for individuals to hold shares of investment firms rather than portfolios of shares of the underlying nonfinancial firms. An investment firm will generally be in a better position to evaluate new information affecting some of its holdings, to vote on changes in bylaws or capital structure, or to respond to a tender offer. It will also be in a better position to evaluate new securities, especially initial offerings by small firms, that are brought in by securities dealers or by firms themselves. The problems caused by separation of ownership and control should be eased by this structure. When a firm is largely owned by a small number of investment firms, each of them will have an incentive to seek out the information that will allow it to control the firm in a sensible way. Any problems caused by insider trading should be eased as well. There will be little trading in shares of nonfinancial firms, and most of that will be by investment firms who are aware of the fact that the other side of a trade may have important information that has not yet been discounted.

Securities firms will be wholesalers, rather than retailers, of primary securities. They will advise corporate customers on financing strategy and do some analysis for their investment firm customers. They will sell secondary securities issued by investment firms to individuals. These secondary securities will also be sold directly by investment firms to individuals, perhaps through employers, and the primary securities will also be sold directly by corporations to investment firms.

Accounting firms will help firms disclose the financial results of operations without giving confidential details to competitors. The main device for this is the financial statement, where information is summarized so much that it is helpful to investors but is not very helpful to competitors. Investment firms will promote this kind of disclosure, because it helps them evaluate firms that they are or might be investing in.[4]

### Costly management

Since it is in fact costly to find managers, to put them on the right track, and to measure their progress, it matters how a firm is organized.[5] A merger may make managers work better because it reduces the cost of dealings between the two firms, or because the diversification that results allows the managers to be paid less because they feel more secure. A divestiture may make managers work better because they have more control of and more interest in the success of the firm, or because a high debt ratio makes them work hard to avoid the stigma of bankruptcy.[6] The more diffuse the ownership of a firm, the more costly it is for the stockholders to make decisions on matters like these. Small individual stockholders tend to be poorly informed, slow to act, and easily victimized. The solution to this problem, in my view, is not to have small individual stockholders.

When a firm's stock is held by large investment firms and a few sophisticated individuals, there will be no reason to regulate such things as tender offers. The investment firms will want to make the firms they control vulnerable to tender offers, because that will help motivate managers who risk losing their jobs in a takeover.[7] The premiums needed for a tender offer to succeed will be low. Some tender offers will succeed in a single day.

Mutual institutions tend to have even more small individual owners, at least in theory, than stock institutions. In practice, a mutual institution tends to operate as if the managers were the owners, except that the managers are not free to sell their ownership interests, and takeovers are extremely difficult. The solution to this problem, I believe, is not to have mutual institutions,[8] that is, at least not mutual thrift institutions and insurance companies. Mutual funds are just investment firms of a special kind, and will continue, though possibly with internal managers rather than external management contracts.

In general, of course, investment firms will be the exception to the rule that firms will have no small individual stockholders. Neither takeovers nor close supervision by sophisticated stockholders will work well for investment firms. The investment firms that survive will adopt other ways to motivate managers. The mutual funds form is one such way. A mutual fund stands ready to redeem its shares at net asset value, so if its managers do poorly, their pay and the assets they manage will fall. This works, though, only when it is easy to figure net asset value: When the fund's assets are all shares of stock that trade frequently.

An investment firm that owns shares of small or closely held firms will not be able to redeem its shares continuously at net asset value. Perhaps the way for such firms to survive is to be owned by other investment firms such as mutual funds, rather than being owned directly by individuals.

Why can't the mutual fund device work for a mutual savings bank, where depositors can withdraw their funds if they are not satisfied? Because the depositors in a mutual savings bank are not holders of equity. They do not bear much of the risk in the institution. If the bank holds good collateral against their deposits, and if they receive competitive rates and service, they will have no incentive to withdraw their funds. They have only the power to motivate managers that the customers of all firms have.

## Costly selling

Both wholesale selling and retail selling are costly. I imagine firms selling their own shares to investment firms, and investment firms selling their own shares to individuals. Small firms will sell their shares to venture capital firms, who will sell their shares to investment firms. Securities firms may also take part in the selling, at both the wholesale and retail levels. I think of all selling, but especially retail selling, as being heavily influenced by "reputation." With individuals, both the reputation of the investment firm and the reputation of the securities firm (if any) will count.

I think of the securities firms and the investment firms as large, national firms. Venture capital firms and lending firms might do well with a local emphasis, but their shares will be held by other investment firms such as mutual funds rather than by individuals. If the mutual funds are internally managed, then it seems unlikely that they will offer other financial services such as banking or loan administration. To this extent, firms offering financial services to individuals will specialize. It also seems possible that most selling of mutual fund shares will be done through employers, especially through defined contribution savings and retirement plans; and through banking firms. If this happens, banking and securities firms will be combined, and will offer mutual fund shares that may generally be internally managed.

Loan administration involves reputation too: the reputation of the borrower more than the reputation of the lender.[9] Borrowers will gain by setting up long-term ties with lenders. A borrower who plans to move around will want to deal with a national lender, if possible. Loan administration is simpler if the borrower puts up collateral: mutual fund shares, real estate, or cars. Banking firms will generally set lower interest rates when there is collateral than when there isn't. Both parties may save on costs of renegotiating the terms of the loan or finding a new lender or finding a new borrower if the loan is long term rather than short term.[10] The long-term loan could be at a floating rate, though. If the rate is floating, the payment can still be fixed: If necessary, the amortization rate for the loan can become negative. This need not increase the default risk on the loan, because higher interest rates are generally associated with higher inflation, which means a higher expected future value for both wage income and collateral.

Some financial services are related to the market for self control.[11] People who are budgeting seem to like to keep money in different pockets even when there is a sizable cost in doing so. Thus people and firms who have demand loans may keep positive balances in one or more bank accounts. Others, however, will simply let their negative balances go up and down as payments come in and go out.

If the cost of communications falls dramatically with changes such as the use of glass fibers in cables, then most debits may be handled electronically at the time of payment. In that case, much of the work in processing debits may be done by communications firms. I see no particular gain, though, in mergers between banking firms and communications firms. The banking firms can keep the accounts and buy services from the communications firms.

When selling costs are considered, banking firms may not simply charge for each service at an estimated marginal cost for producing it. For example, explicit charges for the use of teller windows may not cover the cost of making an extra window available. Part of the cost may be covered by general account maintenance charges or even lower-than-market interest payments on positive balances. The banks will search for ways of charging customers that will allow them to charge more when a customer is willing to pay more. Special packages of services, including the use of special teller windows, may be one way to do this.

### Regulation

If the market for financial services takes the forms described, it's not clear what will be left of traditional forms of regulation. Maybe it will take a regulatory push to move people away from trading securities other than mutual fund shares, but once that is done, there will be little need for securities regulation. It may take a regulatory push to move mutual funds toward internal management, but once that is done, there will be little need for investment company regulation. It may take a regulatory push to induce banks to use safe and liquid collateral for their positive balances, but once that is done, there will be little need for banking regulation. It may take a regulatory push to encourage stockholders to adopt bylaws that make takeovers easy, but once that is done, there will be little need for takeover regulation.

Deposit insurance will be mostly unnecessary if deposits are backed with securities, but it won't cost much, so we might decide to continue it. Laws against fraud make sense to me, and it may even pay to use regulatory agencies to help enforce them. Antitrust laws will be applied to banks and investment firms and securities firms, but all these businesses are so fragmented now that mergers do not seem like much of a threat.

## Summary

I see, or want to see, a future where large firms dominate the market for financial services, and where reputation depends on helping individuals reduce costs and avoid unnecessary risks. Banking firms will debit and credit both positive and negative account balances using checks, credit cards, and electronic messages. Depositors may be protected by 100 percent reserves against positive balances, whereas borrowers may reduce their loan administration charges by posting collateral including their homes and cars. Most individuals will own securities through mutual funds, which will play an active role in the firms whose shares they own. Only sophisticated individuals will own or trade stocks and bonds of firms other than mutual funds. Securities firms will buy from and sell to mutual funds and sophisticated individuals. Mutual funds will be sold through employers and banks. Banks and securities firms need not be distinct. If financial firms develop in this way without a regulatory push, there will be no obvious need for banking or securities regulation of any kind.

## Notes

1. For descriptions of the past and present for financial services, see, for example, Friend (1965), Friend (1969), and Campbell (1982a).
2. For discussions of the reasons for having bonds only in a defined benefit pension plan, see Black (1980), Black and Dewhurst (1981), and Tepper (1981).
3. For a more complete analysis of the implications of unregulated banking, see Black (1970).
4. This view of financial accounting is discussed in Black (1976).
5. For a general discussion of choice of organizational form, see Fama and Jensen (1982).
6. Diamond (1982) discusses the incentive effects of a high debt ratio on managers.
7. See Easterbrook and Fischel (1981) for the benefits of deregulating tender offers.
8. For a contrary view, see Fama and Jensen (1982, pp. 43–9).
9. For a model of the role of reputation in corporate borrowing, see Campbell (1982b).
10. Flannery (1982) discusses this reason for having long-term loans.
11. A basic paper on the market for self-control is Thaler and Shefrin (1981). For application of the theory to dividend policy, see Shefrin and Statman (1982).

## References

Black, Fischer (Autumn 1970). "Banking and Interest Rates in a World Without Money: the Effects of Uncontrolled Banking." *Journal of Bank Research* 1: 8–20.
  (September/October 1976). "The Accountant's Job." *Financial Analysts Journal* 32: 18.
  (July/August 1980). "The Tax Consequences of Long-Run Pension Policy." *Financial Analysts Journal* 36: 21–8.

Black, Fischer, and Moray P. Dewhurst (Summer 1981). "A New Investment Strategy for Pension Funds." *Journal of Portfolio Management* 7: 26–34.

Campbell, Tim S. (1982a). *Financial Institutions, Markets, and Economic Activity*. New York: McGraw-Hill.

(October 1982b). "The Role of Implicit Contracts in Resolving Stockholder–Bondholder Conflicts." Unpublished memorandum.

Diamond, Douglas W. (August 1982). "Financial Intermediation and Delegated Monitoring." Center for Research in Security Prices Working Paper No. 82.

Easterbrook, Frank H., and Daniel R. Fischel (April 1981). "The Proper Role of a Target's Management in Responding to a Tender Offer." *Harvard Law Review* 94: 1161–1204.

Fama, Eugene F., and Michael C. Jensen (June 1982). "Agency Problems and the Survival of Organizations." University of Rochester Working Paper No. MERC 82-06.

Flannery, Mark J. (August 1982). "Customer Relationships, Transactor Specific Assets, and Commercial Bank Lending." Unpublished memorandum.

Friend, Irwin (1965). *Investment Banking and the New Issues Market: Summary Volume*. Philadelphia: Wharton School of Finance and Commerce.

(1969). *Study of the Savings and Loan Industry: Summary and Recommendations*. Washington, D.C.: Federal Home Loan Bank Board.

Shefrin, H. M., and Meir Statman (August 1982). "Explaining Investor Preference for Cash Dividends." Unpublished memorandum.

Tepper, Irwin (March 1981). "Taxation and Corporate Pension Policy." *Journal of Finance* 36: 1–13.

Thaler, Richard H., and H. M. Shefrin (April 1981). "An Economic Theory of Self-Control." *Journal of Political Economy* 89: 392–406.

# Comment: The future for financial services

## IRWIN FRIEND

Much of Fischer Black's look into the future of financial services implies a continuation of recent trends toward increased competition, increased computerization, and increased diversification of activities conducted by banks and securities firms. These two types of firms are viewed as integrated, with banks carrying on and even extending the asset management accounts recently introduced by brokerage firms. The more specialized thrift institutions would presumably continue to decline in importance, especially in Fischer's world of tax neutrality among all kinds of assets.

The novelties in Fischer Black's look into the future seem to be (1) a 100% asset reserve in the form of riskless bonds for positive balances held by bank depositors; (2) bank loans apparently based only on borrowing from, and equity securities sold primarily to, investment firms and not on such instruments as cash deposits since Fischer sees "no special reason for a banking firm to lend out the money it receives from its deposits"; and (3) individual ownership of corporate securities largely through internally managed and activist mutual funds, with only sophisticated investors owning stocks and bonds of the nonfinancial firms. (4) In such a world, he says, "there will be no obvious need for banking or securities regulation of any kind." It is not clear to me that these nonregulatory changes he foresees are desirable or feasible or that the need for banking and securities regulation would disappear, though I agree that the need of some forms of regulation would be less pressing.

Fischer does not make explicit exactly why he favors a 100% asset reserve for deposits in the form of riskless bonds or why no bank loans should be financed by money received from depositors. Apart from his statement that he sees no reason for a banking firm to act otherwise, he apparently feels that as a desirable consequence, the need for government deposit insurance would be largely obviated. A possible undesirable consequence would be a rise in the cost of private financing associated with a decline in the cost of public financing, perhaps associated with a drop in the efficiency of the allocation of resources as between these two groups. Are short-term bank loans to disappear in his world or are they to be financed by bank issuance of bonds and stocks or by short-term borrowing from investment firms that raise this money in equity form largely from small investors? Money market funds and brokerage firm cash management accounts would apparently

231

disappear except for institutions that specialize exclusively in the market for U.S. governments. Nor is it clear what Fischer means by riskless bonds as backing for deposits, since there is no obvious way of protecting demand deposits and the bank itself against interest rate fluctuations unless the government will be issuing a sufficient quantity of one-day bills.

As for individual ownership of corporate securities largely through internally managed and activist mutual funds, it might very well be desirable to have indirect ownership largely replacing the remaining direct ownership of such securities especially if one believes in current capital asset pricing and efficient market theory. However, it is not at all clear how such an outcome could be achieved short of the most unacceptable types of government intervention in the market. Stock mutual funds have been stagnant for several decades and have not been substantially rejuvenated even in the relatively strong market of recent months. Moreover, if fund management fees and expenses continue to grow as a proportion of assets, even moderate-size investors might be better off by direct investment in a somewhat less diversified stock portfolio. The implicit assumption that Fischer appears to be making, videlicet that competition would enhance the flow of money into those stock funds with lowest expense and best investment performance, does not seem to be borne out by the historical record. Paying a salesperson to sell fund shares appears to be fully as effective in fund success as superior performance. In the *Study of Mutual Funds* a number of years ago, we found that fund growth was more clearly correlated with fund sales charges and payments to salespersons than with fund performance. Currently, the most serious concern that money market funds have about the new competition by commercial and savings banks and institutions is not in the ability of the latter to achieve higher investment returns or lower costs, or even in their special insurance advantage, but rather in the intention of a number of these institutions to offer substantial selling commissions to brokerage sales representatives now selling money market funds.

Incidentally, Fischer Black may have some misconceptions about other aspects of the historical behavior of mutual stock funds whose accelerated growth he obviously advocates. His assertion that "There will be little trading in shares of nonfinancial firms" as a result of this further institutionalization of the stock market does not seem to have any foundation in the past behavior of mutual funds, which have had substantially larger stock turnover ratios than the rest of the market. I doubt that the tendency of professional managers to trade more actively than other investors generally will be greatly changed by the internalization of mutual funds, which he advocates. Similarly, I have some doubts about the operational significance of Fischer's position that mutual funds will typically be in a better position to evaluate new information than other investors. The overwhelming weight of most academic research on mutual fund performance suggests that the funds have not on the average outperformed individual investors, though Fischer may find very limited support for his position in his own analysis of the performance of a single investment company advisor.

Turning finally to the regulatory implications of Fischer Black's new world, I am skeptical that the need for regulation of the provision of financial services will largely disappear. Let me give some examples in the field of securities regulation. Thus, Fischer seems to believe that the domination of the market by mutual funds and other investment firms will be able to ensure the types of disclosure that would be desirable from the viewpoint of market efficiency and investor equity. However, though I think I am familiar with all the literature in this area, I don't know of any support for this belief. My own evaluation of the empirical evidence, which I recently documented once again,* leads me to conclude that even abstracting from matters of equity, mandated disclosure has contributed to market efficiency without excessive cost and I see no strong case for eliminating mandated disclosure. This does not mean that the disclosure provisions in the securities regulations could not and should not be improved, but I think the burden of proof is on those who advocate either the elimination of or a major reduction in mandated disclosure under the 1933 and 1934 Acts.

Similarly, I question Fischer's statement that once mutual funds move toward internal management, there will be little need for investment company regulation. Since mutual funds will increasingly be investing in inactively as well as actively traded securities, there will be major pricing problems, which judging from past experiences, including that with "letter stock," should probably not be left exclusively to entrepreneurial discretions. Although internalization of management in mutual funds has much to commend it, the statutory requirement for independent directors, which I think has provided some protection for fund shareholders, would presumably disappear.

* Irwin Friend (1984), "Economic and Equity Aspects of Securities Regulation." In *Management Under Government Intervention: A View from Mt. Scopus,* ed. W. Lanzillotti and Y. Peles, 31–58. *Research in Finance, Supplement No. 1.* Greenwich, Conn.: JAI Press.

# Comment: The future for financial services

MARK J. FLANNERY

Professor Black's view of the financial service industry serves to remind us that financial theory must play a central role in analyzing the operations of financial firms. His exposition of the perfectly competitive paradigm challenges the unhealthy tendency of some others to view existing institutional arrangements as immutable, rather than as optimizing responses to economic forces. The view that efficient solutions to economic problems emerge over time – almost regardless of temporary impediments or "institutional details" – is intuitively appealing and provides a useful standard of comparison for any theoretical view of banking firms. In discussing the major themes of Black's paper, I will focus on its implications for financial service firms, collectively referred to as "banks."

## Forces of change in the financial sector

Black relies on "the spread of knowledge about finance" to motivate his view that the financial sector and its constituent firms are heading for substantial changes. He leaves unstated, however, what knowledge is spreading here, and to whom. Although we need not specify the immediate forces for change to discuss long-run equilibrium tendencies, a number of transitional issues that greatly concern practitioners and regulators cannot be evaluated without specifying the sources of pressure to change. What role is played here by reductions in communications and information processing costs? By the recent history of high and variable interest rates? By the postwar rise in real per capita wealth? Is deregulation a cause of change in the financial services industry, or a reluctant response to other exogenous events? I wish we had a more extensive discussion of such questions: Without an assessment of these underlying impetuses, I am unsure why the *existing* structure is not a long-run equilibrium.

Other writers have tried to identify and evaluate the sources of change in this sector. Kane (1981) focuses on a "regulatory dialectic" that emphasizes the central role of regulators and *their* preference functions in shaping the financial services industry. In his view, regulators and their constituents are primarily reacting to exogenous changes in the financial environment. Aspinwall (1982) delineates alternative macrofinancial environments, and discusses the optimal response of banking firms to each possibility. Finally,

234

Silber (1982) goes furthest in applying inductive logic to financial innovations that have emerged over the past twelve years, fitting each one into a general analytical framework. I believe this line of work can yield interesting and instructive insights about the future shape of financial firms, as well as the regulatory process. At a minimum, these papers suggest that some attention must be paid to the forces underlying financial change.

## Financial theory and financial firms

Black's long-run equilibrium view of the banking sector is prominently influenced by the paradigm of perfect competition in financial markets. Yet financial theory is weakest in precisely the dimensions required to motivate and understand financial intermediary firms. Substantially more work must be done to determine how broadly the perfectly competitive paradigm can be applied to the financial services industry. I consider here two, rather broad concerns of banking theory.

### Information, reputation, agents, and efficient markets

It is well known that financial intermediary firms are redundant in sufficiently perfect capital markets. Microbanking models can often be criticized as ad hoc in some regard, and most have been so criticized. Yet banking firms undeniably play a prominent role in real-world financial markets, suggesting that their activities afford efficient solutions to economic problems. I believe the theoretical difficulty with microbank models arises because financial theory cannot rigorously accommodate some of the phenomena that are central to banking: costly and asymmetric information, adverse selection, reputation, incentive compatible contracts, and imperfectly divisible securities, to name several. Individually, each of these issues is difficult to model; simultaneously, the problems quickly become intractable. This situation elicits partial equilibrium, ad hoc efforts to model financial firms – since the alternative is to build no models that correspond to reality.

Several specific examples may clarify my reservations about applying perfectly competitive principles to financial firms. In each case, the indicated difficulty with financial theory seems fundamentally related to the operation of banking firms. The crucial question requiring further research is: How substantially must the competitive paradigm be changed to allow for such phenomena as these?

1. It is well known that perfectly efficient markets cannot support the gathering of costly information required to keep prices fully reflective of available information. Grossman and Stiglitz (1980) conclude that "as soon as the assumptions of the conventional perfect capital markets model are

modified to allow even a slight amount of information imperfection and a slight cost of information, *the traditional theory becomes untenable"* (p. 404, emphasis added). If banks are centrally involved in gathering and processing credit information, it appears the "traditional theory" cannot be employed without modification.

2. Akerlof (1970) first pointed out that information asymmetries can cause market failure. In the context of banking, Stiglitz and Weiss (1981) show that asymmetric information and opportunistic behavior may result in non-price credit rationing, which has no place in perfect capital markets. Can banking firms, which deal largely in nonmarketable, asymmetrically available information, always be expected to behave in the usual neoclassical manner?

3. In the principal–agent context, asymmetric information creates a strong incentive for monitoring. Diamond (1984) has applied these ideas to banking. He views bank equity owners as delegating the responsibility for monitoring bank borrowers to the bank's manager. How can owners give the manager an incentive to monitor? Diamond argues that a broadly diversified portfolio of loans induces the bank manager to monitor appropriately. Unlike the usual capital market prediction, therefore, diversification *within* a firm may be valuable when information is costly to obtain.

4. Finally, current financial theory incorporates reputation effects only minimally, though their importance in selling financial claims is obvious. Does a rating by Moody's or Standard and Poor make a bond more salable? Why do people listen when E. F. Hutton talks? Would depositors prefer large or small banks in the absence of deposit insurance? Without a model of how financial reputations are built and maintained, we cannot hope to address such questions. Black predicts, for example, that banks will attempt to minimize their depositors' information problems by backing deposits 100% with government bonds. (This collateralization is seen as a substitute for FDIC insurance.) It would seem that money market mutual funds have largely the same problem today, yet government bond funds certainly do not dominate the marketplace. How have the funds established their marketable reputations?

Unanswered questions such as these lead me to the conclusion that we don't really know the extent to which perfect competition is consistent with real-world financial markets and institutions. The questions and problems surrounding bank operations in a developed capital market clearly warrant further study. This can take the form of developing innovative bank models, or of applying and adapting existing financial theories to the financial services institutional framework. (Because banks are a particular type of firm, much existing financial theory can be applied directly.) The ultimate motivation for this broad line of research would be to assess the accuracy of Black's long-run characterization of the financial services industry.

*Relationships in banking*

If the relevant object of bank competition is deposit or loan balances (i.e. dollars), the conclusion that marginal cost pricing is efficient follows quite easily under the right circumstances. Deposit balances then earn a rate that fully reflects market interest rates (adjusted for reserves), and all services are priced at marginal cost. Similar predictions occur for bank asset pricing. Once again, however, the correspondence to reality is not entirely convincing. Although money market mutual funds appear to epitomize highly competitive, unregulated banking firms, I am unaware of any fund that employs more than a minimal amount of marginal cost pricing. The usual compensation scheme for fund managers – a percentage of assets – makes the charge per account increase with average balances. Such a schedule contradicts available evidence that bank costs depend more on the *number* of accounts than on the average balance per account. In addition, it seems puzzling that money funds levy no explicit charge per check, even though their contracts with paying banks generally specify explicit item charges.

A second piece of empirical evidence that may contradict the perfectly competitive paradigm concerns the banks' pricing of newly deregulated accounts (e.g., 18-month IRA accounts and the more recent Money Market Deposit Accounts and Super-NOWs). Many banks seem to "front end load" their compensation, offering high rates (relative to the return on open market instruments) for short periods of time in an apparent effort to attract new balances. Why would a bank pay a premium for funds if subsequent competition will enforce the perfectly competitive rate on all balances attracted? It seems that bankers expect to earn back their initial excess payments via subsequent quasirents.

This behavior can be reconciled with the perfectly competitive paradigm (though it needn't necessarily be) by specifying an account *relationship* as the relevant object of bank competition, instead of balances per se. If a new bank–customer relationship entails nontrivial setup costs, both parties acquire an interest in extending the relationship to economize on further transaction costs. Having incurred these initial (nontransferable) costs, bank and customer confront one another in a type of bilateral monopoly. As Williamson (1979) and others have pointed out, even if competition exists before a customer relationship is established, we cannot fully rely on competitive forces to govern the relationship ex post. I have begun to explore the implications of such customer relationships in banking [Flannery (1982a), (1982b)]. The most general conclusion is that, when relationship setup costs are nontrivial, prices often diverge from short-run marginal costs and nonprice rationing can be efficient. At an absolute minimum, our ability to rely on other competitors to police relationships and enforce efficiency is seriously compromised once relationship setup costs have been incurred. Black hints in this direction (without mentioning the bilateral monopoly issue) when he observes that

> When selling costs are considered, banking firms may not simply charge for each service at an estimated marginal cost for producing it. . . . Part of the cost may be covered by general account maintenance charges or even lower-than-market interest payments on positive balances. The banks will search for ways of charging customers that will allow them to charge more when a customer is willing to pay more. Special packages of services . . . may be one way to do this.

## Conclusion

Structural and institutional change in the financial sector is occurring today at a rapid pace. The need for a unifying analytical framework is obvious to those charged with evaluating (and capitalizing on) events as they unfold. Professor Black's paper provides a challenging yardstick against which other views can be measured. We must determine how much banking business can be adequately described by standard competitive theory, and how much must be modeled differently. Identifying the sources and effects of market imperfections in banking offers a challenging and important area for both theoretical and applied research.

## References

Akerlof, George A. (August 1970), "The Market for 'Lemons': Quality Uncertainty and the Market Mechanism," *Quarterly Journal of Economics* 74, 488–500.

Aspinwall, Richard C. (December 9, 1982), "Prospects for Competition in Markets for Consumer Financial Services," presented at the Eighth Annual Conference, Federal Home Loan Bank of San Francisco.

Diamond, Douglas W. (1984), "Financial Intermediation and Delegated Monitoring," *Review of Economic Studies* 51, 393–414.

Flannery, Mark J. (June 1982a), "Retail Bank Deposits as Quasi-Fixed Factors of Production," *American Economic Review* 72, 527–36.

    (1982b), "Customer Relationships, Transactor Specific Assets, and Commercial Bank Lending," mimeograph.

Grossman, Sanford J., and Stiglitz, Joseph E. (June 1980), "On the Impossibility of Informationally Efficient Markets," *American Economic Review* 70, 393–408.

Kane, Edward J. (May 1981), "Accelerating Inflation, Technological Innovation, and the Decreasing Effectiveness of Banking Regulation," *Journal of Finance* 36, 355–67.

Silber, William L. (1982). "The Process of Financial Innovation," mimeograph, presented at the 1982 American Finance Association meetings.

Stiglitz, Joseph E., and Weiss, Andrew (June 1981), "Credit Rationing in Markets with Imperfect Information," *American Economic Review* 71, 393–411.

Williamson, Oliver E. (October 1979), "Transaction Cost Economics: The Governance of Contractual Relations," *Journal of Law and Economics* 22, 233–61.

# CHAPTER 9

# Competition and equilibrium as a driving force in the health services sector*

## MARK A. SATTERTHWAITE

In this paper I set out a particular view of how competition works within the health services sector of the American economy. In order to be as concrete and clear as possible I restrict my specific analysis to one, narrow segment of the health care sector: the market for primary care physicians' services. This segment is small in relative terms. In the year ending June 30, 1979, primary care physicians' services accounted for roughly 7 percent of personal health care expenditures and 0.6 percent of gross national product. In absolute terms, however, it is large. That 7 percent represents approximately $13 billion of the $177 billion that was expended in the U.S. during those twelve months for personal health care.[1]

My immediate goal is to show that conceptualizing the market for primary care physicians' services as monopolistically competitive permits (1) a deeper understanding of issues that affect the efficient and equitable delivery of care and (2) the generation of a substantial number of testable hypotheses. Specifically, why has increasing the supply of physicians, measured in terms of physicians per thousand population, not caused the prices they charge to fall in real terms? This phenomenon, I argue, is best understood to be the long-run equilibrium to which primary care physicians competing under conditions of monopolistic competition naturally tend.

My underlying purpose, however, is not to explain peculiarities of the physicians' services market. I do that as an example to reinforce the general principle that health care, despite its distinctive characteristics, is an economic good that to a surprisingly large extent can be understood by application of microeconomic tools. The particular emphasis I want to add is this: Competition among providers is pervasive and, if their observed patterns of behavior are to be understood, then their competitiveness and the equilibria to which it leads must be explicitly modeled. The analysis here is meant to illustrate the power of this principle by providing new explanations of two well-known empirical phenomena that directly conflict with the economist's usual intuition:

* Robin Allen provided very capable research assistance.

239

1. At any point in time physicians in communities that are well supplied in terms of physicians per thousand population are likely to charge higher fees than physicians in communities that are less well supplied.
2. Increasing the aggregate supply of physicians per thousand population has had no obvious downward effect on physicians' prices.

The fact that these two pricing paradoxes have not been explained satisfactorily in the literature indicates the need for both (1) imaginative theoretical work aimed at understanding the equilibrium behavior of health care providers and (2) careful empirical work that checks the consistency of current theory with the available data.

The specific approach I take in modeling the primary care physicians' services market stems from three observations. First, each physician has monopoly power in the sense that if he or she raises price, then he or she still retains a substantial proportion of his or her original market share. Second, no primary care physician has a monopoly. A consumer may switch from one physician to another because of price, convenience, quality, or a host of other reasons that are quite idiosyncratic to the person. Moreover, entry into a market area is generally easy for physicians. Third, consumers have severe informational problems in making their choices among doctors. The choices they make are based on recommendations from trusted friends, relatives, and associates, not on hard information about the different qualities and costs of care that the community's physicians produce.

To the extent these observations are fundamental to the nature of primary care, they mitigate against using either perfectly competitive theory or pure monopoly theory in its analysis. A unified theory in which the model's logic leads to a balancing of the industry's competitive and monopolistic faces is to be preferred, provided that theory is tractable. My argument for using Chamberlin's monopolistic competition theory is thus pragmatic: It unifies both aspects, is tractable, and gives insights that are otherwise inaccessible. [2]

Health care in general and primary care physicians' services in particular are multidimensional services in the sense that consumers care about the location of services, their technical sophistication, the amenities of their delivery, and so forth, as well as their price. Nevertheless, I make the gross simplification that the nonprice attributes of care are fixed and doctors only consciously control price. The reason for doing this is that the resulting argument is much easier to follow and – quite fortuitously – does not seem to compromise the analysis of the two pricing paradoxes seriously. In principle the analysis can be carried out for more general cases; it is merely more difficult. [3] Many other issues that are important are also excluded from my discussion. For example, health insurance and its effects are completely ignored. This is defensible – barely – because primary care is not heavily insured.

I proceed in stages. First, I develop a theory for describing the demand that primary care physicians face. Next, special attention is given to the role that consumer information plays in determining the price elasticity of demand for physicians. Third and fourth, I analyze the short- and long-run equilibria of the market. Finally, in the fifth section, the two pricing paradoxes are resolved. Throughout the paper a single, parametric example is developed and analyzed.

## 1     Consumer demand for primary care physicians' services

The key step in applying the monopolistic competition model to physicians' services is specification of the demand for each physician's services in a way that captures the propensity of consumers, when all else is equal, to substitute lower priced physicians for higher priced physicians. This propensity places a market discipline on each physician and prevents him or her from raising price with the goal of increasing net income.[4] In particular, the more elastic the demand that the individual physician faces, then the closer to competitive his or her pricing decisions are. Therefore, a critical task in understanding competition among physicians is to derive the determinants of their price elasticity of demand. This can be done by studying the following, simple model that describes the dynamics of how patients enter and leave physicians' practices.[5]

Consider a moderate sized community, labeled $i$, that contains $N_i$ primary care physicians – general practitioners, internists, and pediatricians. $N_i$ might be a number on the order of 100. To a first approximation every consumer in the community has one physician whom he or she considers to be his/her personal physician. The loyalty consumers show to their personal physician ranges continuously from intense all the way down to infinitesimal. The reasons for such consumer loyalty are numerous and include both objective factors such as location and subjective factors such as the trust that the particular physician evokes in the particular consumer. Depending on the degree of loyalty a consumer feels, when circumstances change in a manner that makes the physician less attractive, the patient may or may not seek a different physician. For example, a very loyal consumer tolerates even a large rise in price whereas a minimally loyal consumer takes flight in response to even a small increase in price. Moreover, the reaction a consumer has toward a particular physician is as idiosyncratic as his or her response to a variety of ethnic cooking. People have different tastes and the matching of them to the right doctor, as defined by their own tastes, is important. The implication is that every physician has monopoly power. When a physician raises price, only the less loyal patients are lost to other, competing physicians. Thus, the firm demand curve of the individual doctor is downward sloping as it is for a monopolist and is not horizontal as it is for a perfect competitor.

Suppose the physicians of the community are in short-run equilibrium where (1) none of them has any reason to change his or her price given the prices the others are charging and (2) each one of them has a practice that is neither growing nor shrinking. Even in this steady state, however, numbers of consumers within any given time period may leave the practices of their current physicians and search for new physicians that meet their idiosyncratic needs. This is because individuals are constantly being born, dying, changing their places of residence, and having their tastes evolve. Events such as these guarantee that a physician's practice always is in a state of flux as far as the specific consumers for whom he or she cares. Given this flux, the requirement for a steady-state equilibrium is that, for every physician, the expected number of patients entering his or her practice balance the expected number leaving the practice.

The equilibrium requirement that the number of patients lost equals the number gained can be disaggregated. Consider a particular physician labeled $ij$ (physician $j$ in community $i$) and let the number of consumers in his/her practice be $M_{ij}$. Let $v_{ij}$ be the probability that a randomly chosen consumer with physician $ij$'s practice will within any given week come in for an office visit. Similarly, let $s_{ij}$ be the probability that a randomly chosen member of $ij$'s practice will in any given week decide to leave his or her practice and let $w_{ij}$ be the probability that a randomly chosen consumer who has quit another physician's practice will select physician $ij$ as his or her new physician. The probabilities $v$, $s$, and $w$ are physician $ij$'s visit rate, switching rate, and acquisition rate, respectively. The equilibrium condition that the number of patients leaving must equal the number arriving is then:

$$s_{ij} M_{ij} = w_{ij} \sum_{\substack{k=1 \\ k \neq j}}^{N_i} s_{ik} M_{ik}. \tag{9.1}$$

The expected number of patients doctor $ij$ sees per week is $v_{ij} M_{ij}$. Suppose that the equilibrium in community $i$ being considered is such that every physician has the same size practice and charges the same price, that is, suppose it is a symmetric equilibrium.[6]

This symmetry assumption, equation (9.1), and the assumption that every consumer is a member of exactly one physician's practice implies that $e_q$, the long-run elasticity of demand physician $i$ faces with respect to his or her own price, is:[7]

$$e_q = e_v + e_w - e_s + e_{\times s} \tag{9.2}$$

where $e_v$ is the elasticity of physician $i$'s visit rate with respect to his/her own price, $e_w$ is the elasticity of his/her acquisition rate with respect to his/her own price, $e_s$ is the elasticity of his/her switching rate with respect to his/her own price, and $e_{xs}$ is the cross elasticity of his/her own switching rate with respect to the price of any other physician. In setting up equation (9.2) I follow the convention of letting elasticities be negative numbers; thus the price elasticity of demand, $e_q = (p_{ij}/q_{ij}) \cdot (\partial q_{ij}/\partial p_{ij})$, is less than negative one for the usual case where demand is downward sloping and elastic.[8] The signs of the four elasticities on the right-hand side of equation (9.2) are, respectively, negative, negative, positive, and negative. To consider one case, the reason $e_{xs}$ is negative is that if some physician $ik$, who is distinct from physician $ij$, raises his/her price while all other doctors keep their prices constant, then $ij$'s patients judge physician $ik$ to be less attractive and are consequently less likely to switch to him or her. Thus $s_{ij}$ falls, which implies $e_{xs}$ is negative.

### Relation to Chamberlin's model

Equation (9.2) makes more sense if it is related to Chamberlin's well-known diagram of demand for a monopolistically competitive firm.[9] Figure 9.1 provides the essentials of that diagram. Let $\bar{p}_i$ be the price that all physicians in community $i$ are charging in the symmetric equilibrium. Physician $ij$ takes this as fixed since if he or she should change price, then the other physicians are unlikely to react and also change price. The reason is that $ij$ is just one physician among many physicians in the community and thus has an inconsequential effect on other physicians' demand curves. The $dd$ demand curve represents physician $ij$'s demand as he or she alone changes price. Curve $dd$, called the firm demand curve, is relevant to $ij$ in making maximizing decisions as to what price to charge. The elasticity of this curve

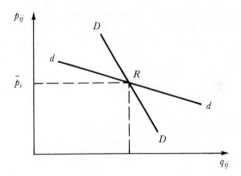

Figure 9.1. Essentials of Chamberlin's diagram of demand for a monopolistically competitive firm

at point $R$ is $e_q$ as defined in equation (9.2) because both it and equation (9.2) take full account of consumers' propensities to substitute less expensive care for more expensive care.

The $DD$ demand curve in Figure 9.1 traces out the quantity demanded from physician $ij$ when all physicians (including $ij$) in the community change their prices together in lock step fashion. For instance, if all physicians in the community increase their prices together, each physician's quantity demanded moves up $DD$ and not up $dd$. The $DD$ curve, which I call the fractional industry demand curve, has elasticity of $e_v$ at point $R$. The reason is that when all physicians change price in unison, then consumers have no reason to switch from one doctor to another on account of price. Therefore, $DD$ includes no intraindustry substitutions and reflects only the fact that as care becomes more expensive, the quantity consumers demand decreases. Consequently, $DD$ is the community's market demand curve for physicians' services divided by $N_i$. Its elasticity, $e_v$, has been extensively studied and estimated because it is the relevant elasticity for evaluating the welfare effects of changes in health insurance coverage.[10]

### Parametric example of demand

This is the appropriate point to introduce the parametric example I carry through the remainder of the paper. Let the quantity demanded from physician $ij$ be

$$q_{ij} = \frac{1}{N_i} \left\{ (A + B\bar{p}_i) + \frac{\beta_i(A + B\bar{p}_i)}{\bar{p}_i} (p_{ij} - \bar{p}_i) \right\}, \qquad (9.3)$$

where $p_{ij}$ is $ij$'s price, $\bar{p}_i$ is the price all other physicians in community $i$ are charging, $A$ is a positive constant, and $B$ and $\beta_i$ are negative constants. My reason for selecting this functional form is that it is the simplest functional form that is consistent with Chamberlin's theory of demand for monopolistically competitive firms. Physician $ij$ takes the price $\bar{p}_i$ that other physicians in the community are charging as given. Therefore, his or her price elasticity of demand evaluated at $p_{ij} = \bar{p}_i$ is

$$e_q = \frac{p_{ij}}{q_{ij}} \cdot \frac{\partial q_{ij}}{\partial p_{ij}} = \beta_i. \qquad (9.4)$$

The graph of equation (9.3) with $\bar{p}_i$ fixed is the firm demand curve, $dd$, in Figure 9.1. The $dd$ curve at point $R$ has price elasticity $\beta_i$. If $\bar{p}_i$ is set equal to $p_{ij}$ and both are varied together, then equation (9.3) becomes

$$q_{ij} = \frac{1}{N_i} (A + Bp_{ij}). \qquad (9.5)$$

This is the fractional industry demand curve, $DD$, in Figure 9.1. Note, in particular, that increasing $N_i$ causes $DD$ to pivot clockwise around its intersection with the price axis. Note also, that if every physician $ij$ in community $i$ symmetrically charges prices $p_{ij} = \bar{p}_i$, then they split the total market for primary care services in the community $N_i$ equal ways.[11] The size of that total market is $A + B\bar{p}_i$ units.[12]

## 2    Consumer information and the elasticity of firm demand

Consumers when they are seeking a new physician who fits their idiosyncratic needs generally rely on the recommendations of trusted relatives, friends, and associates.[13] The gathering of these recommendations takes time and effort; consequently, people search only until they receive a recommendation indicating that some particular physician is likely to be reasonably satisfactory. In other words, individuals search for a new physician in much the way the economic theory of search predicts.[14] That is, the consumer sets a reservation price–needs level and searches until he or she identifies a physician who appears to meet that reservation level. The consumer then tries the physician and, if his or her expectations are met, joins the physician's panel of patients. Otherwise the consumer begins his/her search anew. Presumably in this process the consumer is willing to make tradeoffs between price and the idiosyncratic qualities that are personally important. For example, the consumer is more likely to pick a relatively expensive physician if that physician's office is conveniently located.

If the subjective cost of eliciting detailed and useful recommendations from trusted relatives and friends is low, then the problem of finding a new physician is easier than if the subjective cost is high. When the costs are low consumers are comparatively willing to make the decision to seek a new physician and to set a more demanding price–needs reservation level for their search. The effect such a reduction in the cost of search has on the physician's elasticity of demand is to make it more elastic. This can be understood by examining equation (9.2), which breaks $e_q$ into four components, term by term. A decrease in search costs leaves $e_v$ unchanged since that elasticity relates only to the frequency with which the physicians's current patients request appointments. The second term, $e_w$, is likely to become more negative (more elastic) because consumers who are searching for a new physician become more sensitive about price as they become better informed.[15] For the same reasons $e_s$ and $e_{xs}$, which are the price elasticities of consumers' switching rates, are likely to become more positive (elastic) when search becomes less expensive.[16] Therefore, when the subjective costs of consumers soliciting recommendations from people they trust fall, the elasticity of demand that the individual physician faces is likely to become more elastic.

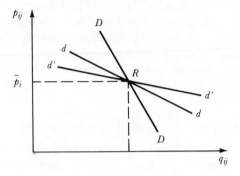

Figure 9.2. Demand curves showing change in elasticity resulting from better consumer information

Figure 9.2 shows in terms of Chamberlin's demand diagram the change in elasticity that likely results from better consumer information: $dd$ is the original firm demand curve and $d'd'$ is the more elastic firm demand curve that results when consumers can search more cheaply. Note that $d'd'$ is just $dd$ pivoted around point $R$ on the fractional industry demand curve $DD$; this is because no reason exists why the cost of search should alter the quantity demanded from each physician when all of them charge the common price $\bar{p}_i$. In terms of equation (9.3), the parametric example of demand, an increase in the price elasticity of firm demand corresponds simply to a decrease in the value of $\beta_i$. Finally, note that it is the use of the monopolistic competition model that allows the effect of improved information to be represented with such simplicity.

### Factors affecting consumers' search costs

The ease with which a consumer searches for a new physician, once he or she has made the decision to do so, depends on two factors: the number of people in the community from whom he or she feels comfortable seeking recommendations and the level of relevant knowledge possessed by those whose recommendations are sought. Both these levels are likely to be low in communities that are experiencing rapid growth, that have a great deal of population flux, and that do not have a high level of social cohesion. For example, if a community is growing very rapidly, relatively few residents have lived in the community long enough to build up a store of knowledge about the characteristics of the local physicians. Moreover, many physicians in the community are too new to have developed a well-defined reputation and, similarly, many residents are too new to have developed more than a few close friends. In such a community consumers are likely to have high costs of search with the result that the community's physicians have more monopoly power (i.e., less elastic firm demand) than they would in a community where consumers have better information.

In addition to these straightforward social and demographic determinants of the cost of search, the number of physicians in the community, $N_i$, may by itself affect the ease or difficulty of consumer search.[17] This effect can be seen by analyzing the polar cases of a small town and a large city. Consider first a small community that has only a few physicians. Each physician in the community, unless he or she is a recent arrival, is certain to have a well-defined reputation as to cost, personality, quality, convenience, and so forth. The reason is that, since physicians are important to people, the town's residents trade stories about their personal physicians. Since the number of physicians is small, no one has any difficulty remembering what story belongs to what doctor. Therefore, each physician has a reputation and each newcomer can easily get a complete rundown on all the physicians because any but the newest resident can report on every physician's reputation.

In a large city the situation is different. Physicians are still important and people still swap stories about them, but the reinforcement necessary for each doctor to acquire a distinct reputation is absent. Because so many physicians practice in a large city and their practices overlap geographically to a great degree, every urbanite hears stories about a large number of different doctors. Except for those blessed with unusual memories the stories become a jumble; people do not remember which story is about which physician. Therefore, when a person is asked for a recommendation, oftentimes they can only report on their own personal physician because they can not remember any specific information about any other physician. This makes search more difficult and means, in conclusion, that ceterus paribus the more physicians serving a community the poorer consumer information is likely to be.

Another factor that may affect search costs is the promotional activities of physicians themselves. If physicians advertise, then their advertisements may contain information that is useful to consumers in making their choices among physicians. Exactly what effect advertising has on consumer demand is ambiguous. In terms of Figure 9.2, advertising may make the market more competitive by twisting each physician's firm demand from $dd$ to $d'd'$. This would be the case if the advertising's primary effect is to make price comparisons easier for consumers. Alternatively, advertising may make exactly the opposite happen with firm demand twisting from $d'd'$ to $dd$. This would be the case if the advertising is successful in more sharply differentiating each physician's services from every other physician's services. Finally, advertising may shift the fractional industry demand curve in or out or cause it to rotate.

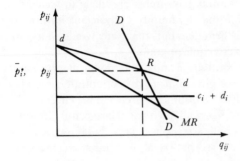

Figure 9.3. Demand curve showing short-run, monopolistically competitive equilibrium


## 3     Short-run equilibrium in a single community

In the short run the number of physicians in a community is fixed. Point $R$ on Figure 9.3 is the short-run, monopolistically competitive equilibrium to which the physicians in a single community tend. Each physician in the community maximizes his or her welfare by setting price so as to equate marginal revenue with marginal cost. Marginal revenue ($MR$) is defined with respect to the physician's firm demand curve $dd$, not the fractional industry demand curve $DD$. Marginal cost has two components: the addition to his or her out-of-pocket practice costs that results from seeing an extra patient and the implicit, personal cost of the time required. Let $c_i$ be the first component and let $d_i$ be the second component. In terms of $\beta_i$, the price elasticity of demand that an individual physician in community $i$ faces, the "set marginal cost equal to marginal revenue" profit maximization rule is:

$$(c_i + d_i) = p_{ij}^* \left(1 + \frac{1}{\beta_i}\right) \tag{9.6}$$

where $(c_i + d_i)$ is marginal cost and the right-hand side is marginal revenue. This expression can be solved for price:

$$\bar{p}_i^* = p_{ij}^* = \frac{\beta_i(c_i + d_i)}{1 + \beta_i}. \tag{9.7}$$

The reason $N_i$ and the constants $A$ and $B$ do not enter into this expression for price is that marginal cost is constant and does not vary with $q_{ij}$. The quantity demanded from each physician in equilibrium is $q_{ij}^* = (A + B\bar{p}_i^*)/N_i$.

Two comparative statics results are interesting for the short-run equilibrium. First, if for some reason consumer information increases and causes the cost of searching for a new physician to fall, then each physician faces

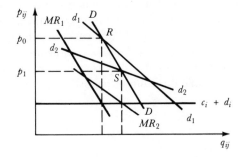

Figure 9.4. Demand curves showing effect on short-run equilibrium if consumer information increases

more elastic demand and, as Figure 9.4 and equation (9.7) show, the short-run equilibrium price falls from point $R$ at price $p_0$ to point $S$ at price $p_1$. Note that both equilibria are on $DD$, the fractional industry demand curve. Because $DD$ is inelastic,[18] each physician's total revenue and, to an even greater degree, income decreases. Second, if the number of physicians in the community increases, then equilibrium price may increase rather than decrease. Figure 9.5 shows this for the case of the number of physicians doubling. The $DD'$ demand curve is half the $DD$ demand curve, as a result of the market being split twice as many ways. The $d'd'$ demand curve has

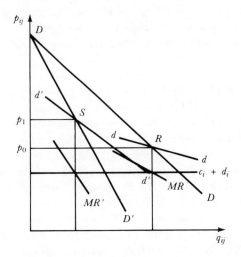

Figure 9.5. Demand curves showing effect on short-run equilibrium if the number of physicians increases

been drawn to be somewhat less elastic than the *dd* curve to capture the harmful effect more physicians may have on consumers' search capabilities. Given a constant marginal cost curve, this less elastic firm demand implies a higher equilibrium price level. If marginal cost had been drawn so that it increases with quantity, as is plausible since marginal cost includes the physician's implicit cost of time, then the direction of price change would be indeterminant.

*Empirical evidence*

The central theme of the theory presented to this point is that consumers play a central role in constraining the pricing decisions of primary care physicians. This theme may seriously conflict with one's own evaluation of how successfully one can shop for a physician. Therefore, a crucial question is: Is this theory consistent with the pattern of prices that physicians are observed to be charging? In particular, does consumer information play the central role that this theory predicts? Definitive answers to these questions do not exist, partly because this theory is relatively new and partly because fully appropriate data has not been collected. To my knowledge, the one study of the physicians' services market that addresses these questions directly is Pauly and Satterthwaite (1981).

We estimated a reduced form, linear version of equation (9.7) using cross-section data from the one hundred largest standard metropolitan statistical areas (SMSA) of the United States. The dependent variable was a sample estimate of the mean price primary care physicians charged in 1973 for a routine office visit. The explanatory variables on the equation's right-hand side were variables that directly or indirectly determine marginal cost ($MC$) or the price elasticity of firm demand. Standard economic variables, such as the average industrial wage rate for production workers, were employed as the determinants of $MC$. The determinants of $e_q$ posed a greater problem. According to the theory that has been described here and in Satterthwaite (1979), consumers' search costs and information levels determine the price elasticity each individual physician faces. No measures, however, exist of search costs or information levels across SMSA's.

Pauly and I were therefore forced to use proxy variables as indicators of consumer information in each SMSA. The five proxies employed were picked strictly on a priori grounds and not on the basis of which candidate proxies had explanatory power in the regression. Two examples of our proxy choices are: proportion of housing units occupied by residents who moved into them between 1965 and 1970 (*MOVED*) and primary care physicians per square mile of urbanized area in 1980 (*MDPCM2*). The reason for including *MOVED* in our set of informational proxies was that people who have recently moved tend to have poorer information about their community's doctors than long-term residents. If a high proportion of the residents of an SMSA fall into this poorly informed class, then two effects follow. First, the new residents are handicapped in their search because of their comparative ignorance. Second, the new residents reduce the search efficiency of all other residents because they are less able to give useful recommendations when asked, that is, their ignorance has external effects. We included *MDPCM2* because it is a measure of the number of primary care physicians who are geographically close enough to a representative SMSA resident to be considered as a potential personal physician. The preceding theory suggests that as that variable's value increases consumers have an increasingly difficult time keeping track of the reputations of the physicians whom they might potentially select. Therefore, high values of these variables should, ceteris paribus, be associated with relatively poor consumer information, relatively price inelastic demand, and relatively high prices.

The results were striking. The variables serving as proxies for consumer information had the effect on price that the theory predicted and were highly significant. This information-based theory explained the 1973 cross-sectional pattern of primary care physicians' prices better than competing theories to a degree that was highly significant statistically. Nevertheless, these results must be interpreted with real care. Proxies for consumer information were used, not actual measures. As is well known, the proxy variables may – and sometimes do – give spurious results. Therefore, a balanced assessment might be that this study lends credence to the importance of consumer information within the market for primary care physicians' services, particularly because the proxies were picked on a priori grounds. Acceptance, however, of the theory as fact must await a study that constructs direct measures of consumer information levels through survey techniques.

The very interesting studies of Benham (1972), Benham and Benham (1975), and Feldman and Begun (1978) provide less direct, but nevertheless important support for the importance of consumer information as a constraint on health care providers. Benham's study showed that restrictions on the advertising of eyeglass prices led to higher eyeglass prices. Benham and Benham's paper extended that result by showing that the advertising restriction also led to a lower quantity of eyeglasses purchased. Feldman and Begun's empirical work compared the constant quality price of optometric examinations in states where both price advertising by optometrists and opticians is forbidden with the price in states where such advertising is permissible. They found that price is on the average 16 percent higher in states where advertising is proscribed.

## 4     Long-run equilibrium across many communities

Historically, the limited number of students that medical schools accommo-
dated in their freshman classes coupled with states' licensure requirements
served as effective barriers to entering the profession of medicine within the
United States. Physicians thus expected to earn long-run financial returns
in excess of what they could have earned if they had not become a doctor.
Once, however, a person surmounted this initial barrier and graduated successfully from an American medical school, then the barriers to entering
the market for primary care physicians' services in any given community
are essentially nonexistent.[19] The physician who wants to practice in a particular community need only obtain his state license,[20] rent and equip an
office, hire a minimal staff, and hang out his or her shingle. If he or she
hustles and is of more or less median attractiveness to patients, then in a
few years the practice will grow to be comparable with the practices of most
other primary care physicians in the community.

Given this easy entry, physicians, particularly physicians just beginning
their private practices, have an incentive to locate in those communities
where their real net income is likely to be maximized. Substantial evidence
exists that physicians do in fact act in this way. For example, Newhouse
et al. (1982) studied physicians' location decisions over the period between
1970 and 1979 and concluded that their choices are consistent with real net
income maximization.

The tendency for physicians to locate in those communities where their
expected real net incomes are highest results in equalization of physician incomes across communities. This is because if physicians did earn significantly higher incomes in some particular community, then that higher income would keep attracting additional physicians – new medical school
graduates especially – to enter that community until the additional supply
of physicians reduced net incomes to the level of other communities. Define
the locational economic profits of a physician to be his or her real net income in excess of what could be earned as a physician in the best alternative
community. Therefore, given the tendency for free entry to equalize real
net income across communities, physicians earn no locational economic
profits over the long run.

This no profit condition is the usual condition for long-run equilibrium
in an industry with no barriers to entry. Therefore Chamberlin's analysis
of long-run equilibrium in a monopolistically competitive industry applies.
The key relationship in that analysis is the shape of the firm's long-run average total cost curve. For a primary care physician $ij$ who lives and works in
community $i$ the long-run average total cost curve ($LRATC$) is the locus of
price–quantity pairs such that he or she is (1) indifferent between every pair

of points on the curve and (2), at any point on the curve, is indifferent between practicing in community $i$ and relocating in the best alternative community that he or she can identify.

Working at the simplest conceptual level, a parametric example of a physician's long-run cost curve in a given community can be constructed as follows. Total costs may be thought of as having two components:

| | |
|---|---|
| $F_i$ | The fixed net income per month that he or she would have to receive as a lump sum compensation in order to make locating in the community $i$ just worthwhile relative to the best alternative community. $F_i$ is the opportunity cost to the physician of living in community $i$. |
| $(c_i + d_i)q_{ij}$ | The variable cost, both in terms of out-of-pocket costs and the costs of time, of caring for $q_{ij}$ patients per month. |

Physician $ij$'s total costs are therefore:

$$C_i(q_{ij}) = F_i + (c_i + d_i)q_{ij} \tag{9.8}$$

and his average total costs are

$$\bar{C}_i(q_{ij}) = (c_i + d_i) + \frac{F_i}{q_{ij}}. \tag{9.9}$$

Figure 9.6 illustrates this *LRATC*. [21]

Long-run equilibrium in monopolistic competition is characterized by tangency between the *LRATC* curve and the firm demand curve, *dd*, because it is the only point at which the firm, when it maximizes, makes precisely zero economic profits. Point $R$ in Figure 9.6 is physician $ij$'s long-run equilibrium point. There the elasticity of the *LRATC* curve equals the

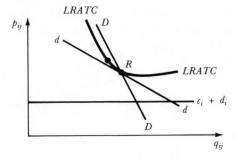

Figure 9.6. Demand curve and average total cost curve showing long-run, monopolistically competitive equilibrium

elasticity of $ij$'s firm demand curve; this follows from the curves being tangent at $A$. In other words, since tangency is necessary for long-run equilibrium, equality of the $LRATC$ curve's elasticity and the firm demand curve's elasticity is also necessary.

The elasticity of the $LRATC$ curve that (9.9) defines is

$$
\begin{aligned}
e_{\bar{C}} &= \left\{ \frac{q_{ij}}{\bar{C}_i(q_{ij})} \cdot \frac{\partial \bar{C}_i(q_{ij})}{\partial q_{ij}} \right\}^{-1} \\
&= \left\{ \frac{q_{ij}}{(c_i + d_i) + F_i/q_{ij}} \cdot \left( \frac{F_i}{q_{ij}^2} \right) \right\}^{-1} \\
&= -\frac{C_i(q_{ij})}{F_i}.
\end{aligned} \tag{9.10}
$$

Movement down it and to the right results in its elasticity decreasing from negative one towards negative infinity, that is, it monotonically becomes more elastic. [22]

For the moment, assume that the firm elasticity of demand in each community $i$ is fixed by demographic and social factors; this ignores the direct effect that the number of physicians in community $i$ may have on the firm elasticity of demand. Therefore, given $e_q = \beta_i$, the only point on the $LRATC$ curve that is consistent with physicians being in long-run equilibrium where $q_{ij}$ is such that $e_{\bar{C}} = \beta_i$, that is,

$$
-\frac{(c_i + d_i)q_{ij} + F_i}{F_i} = -\frac{C_i(q_{ij})}{F_i} = \beta_i. \tag{9.11}
$$

Solving for $q_{ij}$ gives:

$$
q_{ij} = -\frac{(1 + \beta_i)F_i}{(c_i + d_i)}. \tag{9.12}
$$

Only at this quantity does the $LRATC$ curve's elasticity equal the firm elasticity of demand as is required in long-run equilibrium.

As was shown in the discussion of short-run equilibrium, marginal costs of $(c_i + d_i)$ and a firm demand elasticity of $\beta_i$ implies that the optimal price for physicians in community $i$ to charge is

$$
p_{ij}^*(\beta_i) = \frac{\beta_i(c_i + d_i)}{1 + \beta_i}. \tag{9.13}
$$

At this price the quantity demanded from each physician in community $i$ is

$$
q_{ij}^* = \frac{1}{N_i}(A + Bp_{ij}^*(\beta_i)). \tag{9.14}
$$

For long-run equilibrium the quantity in equation (9.14) must equal the quantity in equation (9.12).

The equilibrating variable is the number of physicians, $N_i$, in the community. Equating the right-hand sides of (9.12) and (9.14) and solving for $N_i$ results in:

$$N_i(F_i, \beta_i) = \frac{1}{F_i}\left( -\frac{(c_i + d_i)}{(1 + \beta_i)} \right)(A + Bp_{ij}^*(\beta_i)). \qquad (9.15)$$

This is the number of physicians that can practice in community $i$, earn just enough after their variable costs of $(c_i + d_i)q_{ij}$ to cover their fixed opportunity cost of $F_i$, and be left with zero economic profit. That this is so can be seen by noting that

$$p_{ij}^*(\beta_i) - (c_i + d_i) = \frac{\beta_i(c_i + d_i)}{1 + \beta_i} - (c_i + d_i)$$

$$= -\frac{(c_i + d_i)}{(1 + \beta_i)}. \qquad (9.16)$$

The left-hand side is seen to be the gross profit that community $i$'s physicians earn on each unit of demand. Substituting it for the second factor in the right-hand side of equation (9.15) gives:

$$N_i(F_i, \beta_i) = \frac{1}{F_i}((p_{ij}^*(\beta_i) - (c_i + d_i))(A + Bp_{ij}^*(\beta_{ij})). \qquad (9.17)$$

Its right-hand side is the total gross profits earned by all community $i$'s physicians divided by the fixed costs each must cover; therefore, the result is the number of physicians whose fixed costs can just be covered. If more physicians were to locate in community $i$, then the market would be split more ways, the physicians would not cover their fixed opportunity costs $F_i$, and each one would have an incentive to relocate. Thus, given $F_i$, $N_i(F_i, \beta_i)$ is the long-run equilibrium number of physicians for community $i$.

Assume, for the moment, communities differ only in their levels of consumer information. Thus $\beta_i$ does vary with $i$, but $c_i$, $d_i$, and the intrinsic attractiveness to doctors of the different communities as places to live do not. This means that in long-run equilibrium physicians' net incomes must be equal across all communities, that is, in long-run equilibrium $F_i$ cannot vary across communities. Therefore, the conditions for full long-run equilibrium can be stated as follows. Let $N$ be the total number of physicians and let $I$ be the number of communities. Equilibrium requires

$$\sum_{i=1}^{I} N_i(\bar{F}, \beta_i) = N, \qquad (9.18)$$

where $\bar{F}$ is the common value that $F_i$ assumes in each community in equilibrium.

5     The two pricing paradoxes

*Physician supply, price, and location across communities at a point in time*

The theory of price determination by the intersection of supply and demand curves teaches us that increased supply should lead to a lower equilibrium price. The data, however, is at variance with this simple prediction. For example, as discussed previously, Pauly and I (1981) examined 1973 data on the price that primary care physicians charged for a routine office visit in each of the hundred largest SMSA's. We found that if the local cost of living, cost of inputs, and demographic determinants of demand were controlled for within a regression equation, then the number of primary care physicians per thousand population had a positive and statisically significant influence on the price variable. [23] The theory of long-run equilibrium I develop in this paper implies exactly this observed pattern and the opposite of the pattern that naive application of competitive theory predicts: At any point in time those communities in which physician supply (as measured by physician per thousand population) is low should have lower, not higher prices, than communities in which physician supply is high. That this is so can be seen as follows.

Retain, for the moment, the assumption that communities are identical except for their levels of consumer information. Therefore $c_i$, $d_i$, and, in equilibrium, $F_i$ are identical across all communities. This means the $LRATC$ curve is itself invariant across communities and a single diagram can be used to plot the equilibrium points of several different communities. Figure 9.7

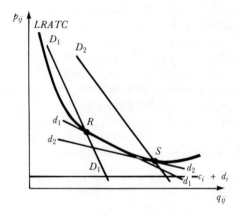

Figure 9.7.  Demand and cost curves showing long-run equilibrium points of two different communities

shows the case of two communities where $\bar{F}$ has been determined by equation (9.18). Let community 1 have poorer consumer information than community 2. This information difference makes the firm demand curves for community 1's physicians $(d_1 d_1)$ less elastic than the firm demand curves for community 2's physicians $(d_2 d_2)$. Thus $\beta_1 > \beta_2$. Point $R$ on the figure is the equilibrium point for each of community 1's physicians and point $S$ is the equilibrium point for each of community 2's physicians. Note that, as is required in long-run equilibrium, $d_1 d_1$ and $d_2 d_2$ are tangent to the $LRATC$ curve at points $R$ and $S$. Also note that the $LRATC$ curve monotonically becomes more elastic as quantity increases.

The fractional industry demand curves, $DD_1$ and $DD_2$ for the two communities necessarily have a common intercept on the price axis because the parameter $A$ is constant across communities. They respectively go through points $R$ and $S$ because, in both short- and long-run equilibrium, the between firm symmetry of the Chamberlin model entails the industry and firm curves intersecting at the equilibrium price–quantity point. Given that both communities are identical except for consumer information, the only way in which $D_1 D_1$ can be below $D_2 D_2$, as the geometry of Figure 9.7 requires, is for the number of physicians in community 1 to be greater than the number in community 2, that is, $N_1 > N_2$.

This, for the case of identical communities, establishes the original assertion: The prices primary care physicians charge tend to be higher in communities that have large supplies of primary care physicians per thousand population than in communities that have small supplies. This conclusion in a certain sense is an upside-down version of the target income theory: [24] physicians in all communities earn the same real income (the target income) due to physicians' rational locational decisions. Therefore, in communities where prices are higher (as a consequence of consumer information differentials) the relative number of physicians must be greater than in communities with lower prices. Otherwise, physicians in the community with higher prices would earn more real net income than do the physicians in the communities with lower prices. The causation here runs in the opposite direction than it did in the original theories' statements: High prices cause high relative supplies rather than high relative supplies causing high prices and high demand.

A reasonable question concerns the robustness of the result just derived. For example, suppose communities differ in how attractive they are to physicians. Does this relaxation of the original assumptions lead plausibly to a different cross-sectional relation between price and supply? Figure 9.8 illustrates that this is a possibility. Let community 2 be more attractive to physicians than community 1; therefore $F_2 < F_1$ as a result of the compensating differential physicians demand as the price for living in community 1 rather

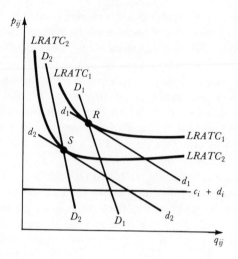

Figure 9.8. Demand and cost curves showing a possible effect of community attractiveness on the long-run equilibrium points of two communities

than community 2. Consequently $LRATC_1$ is above $LRATC_2$.[25] As before consumer information is poorer in community 1 than in community 2; therefore, price is higher in 1 than 2 and $d_1 d_1$ is less elastic than $d_2 d_2$. More physicians, however, practice in community 2 than 1 causing $D_2 D_2$ to be below $D_1 D_1$. Points $R$ and $S$ are the respective long-run equilibrium points for the communities. Therefore, the long-run equilibrium that is illustrated by Figure 9.8 demonstrates the possibility of an inverse relationship between relative supply and price.

But how plausible is Figure 9.8's configuration? The key element in creating it was to make community 1, the informationally poorer community, less attractive to physicians than community 2 and thus force it to have a positive compensating income differential. Thus a sufficient condition for an inverse relation to be observed between price and supply is that the level of consumer information be correlated negatively enough with the size of the compensating income differential physicians need to attract them to the community. An analogous sufficient condition can be derived for marginal costs: The level of consumer information needs to be correlated negatively enough with the level of marginal costs.

My sense is that neither of these conditions is likely to hold strongly enough to cause the predicted cross-sectional correlation between price and supply to switch from positive to negative. I have two reasons for this assertion. First, with respect to the first condition, those communities that are least attractive are likely to have slow rates of growth and therefore, according to the logic of Pauly and Satterthwaite (1981), relatively good consumer information rather than the poorer information the condition requires. Second, as is argued previously, increased numbers of physicians in a community may by itself cause a decrease in the level of consumer information and consequent price increase.[26] Newhouse et al. (1982 pp. 502–3) provide some support for these assertions. They report that physicians in cities over one million population earn about 15 percent less real income on average than other physicians, that is, the compensating differential for very large cities appears to be negative because physicians like to live in them. But large cities are where consumer information is most likely to be poor. Therefore, the correlation between compensating differentials and consumer information is likely to be positive, not negative as a reversal of the price–physician supply correlation would require. Therefore, the observed positive correlation between price and supply is consistent with the theory developed here; little if any reason exists to think that actual conditions are such that in cross section the primary care physician services market should exhibit anything different than a positive correlation between price and supply.

Physicians are unevenly geographically distributed. The analysis of the cross-sectional relation between price and physician supply gives insight to the root causes of this phenomenon. The informational resources of consumers determine the firm elasticity of demand that physicians in a given community face. That elasticity determines the point on physicians' *LRATC* curve where long-run equilibrium occurs for that community. Finally, given the equilibrium point, the equilibrium number of physicians for the community is the number that divides the community's demand for care sufficiently finely to cause the fractional industry demand curve, *DD*, to pass through that point. Thus, if the firm demand curve becomes more elastic, then the equilibrium point moves down and to the right along the *LRATC* curve and the equilibrium number of physicians in the community decreases.

Therefore, according to this analysis, a prime cause of the maldistribution of physicians is the variation in the elasticity of physicians' firm demand curves that exists across communities. If the physicians' firm elasticities of demand are not much less than $-1$, as seems plausible, then small percentage changes in the firm elasticity of demand can cause large changes in the position of the equilibrium point and, consequently, large percentage changes in equilibrium number of physicians. Although this can be seen from careful inspection of Figure 9.7, a more precise understanding can be obtained from equation (9.12), which is repeated here:

$$q_{ij}^*(\beta_i) = \frac{(1 + \beta_i)F_i}{c_i + d_i}. \tag{9.19}$$

This quantity is the number of units of care an individual physician must produce for him or her to be at the point on the *LRATC* curve where its elasticity, $e_{\bar{C}}$, equals the firm elasticity of demand, $\beta_i$. Its elasticity with respect to $\beta_i$ is

$$\frac{\beta_i}{q_{ij}^*(\beta_i)} \cdot \frac{dq_{ij}^*(\beta_i)}{d\beta_i} = \frac{\beta_i}{1 + \beta_i}. \tag{9.20}$$

The number of physicians locating in community $i$ is approximately inversely proportional to $q_{ij}^*(\beta_i)$; therefore, the elasticity of the number of physicians locating in community $i$ with respect to $\beta_i$ is the negative of the elasticity of $q_{ij}^*(\beta_i)$ with respect to $\beta_i$. This elasticity is

$$\frac{\beta_i}{N_i} \cdot \frac{dN_i(\beta_i)}{d\beta_i} \approx -\frac{\beta_i}{1 + \beta_i}. \tag{9.21}$$

A realistic value for $\beta_i$ might be $-2$. When $\beta_i$ takes on this value, this elasticity is $-2$, that is, a 10 percent increase in the magnitude of $\beta_i$ causes approximately a 20 percent decrease in the number of physicians locating in the community. Thus, the number of physicians locating in a community appears to be unfortunately close to being a knife edge phenomenon: Small variations in the community's consumer information levels can cause dramatic variation in the number of physicians locating in it.

### Aggregate supply's effect on price and location

The aggregate supply of physicians relative to population has been rapidly growing in recent years. The number of physicians per thousand population has increased from 1.42 in 1963 to 1.71 in 1978 and is predicted to increase to 2.20 in 1990.[27] What is the likely effect of this increase in the aggregate supply of physicians? The theory I develop in this paper suggests that the increased supply is unlikely to force price down and may even cause it to rise. Physician net incomes are likely to be reduced, but to what degree is open to question. Finally, the increased aggregate supply is not likely to correct the relative maldistribution of physicians, though it certainly increases in every community the absolute supply of physicians.

These predictions may be derived as follows. Equation (9.7) gives, within the context of my parametric example, an expression for the optimal price for a physician in community $i$ to charge. It is:

$$p_{ij}^* = \frac{\beta_i(c_i + d_i)}{1 + \beta_i}. \tag{9.22}$$

Aggregate physician supply does not directly enter into this formula. Nevertheless two variables – $d_i$ and $\beta_i$ – that do enter it may be affected indirectly. First, as more physicians enter community $i$, which is certain to occur as the aggregate supply increases, each physician's patient load tends to fall, with the result that each may work less. Presumably this causes his or her time cost, $d_i$, to decrease.[28] Second, increasing the number of physicians may by itself diminish consumers' capabilities for searching among physicians and, as a consequence, cause physicians' firm demand curves to become less elastic. To the extent this happens the equilibrium prices that physicians charge increase and offsets any tendency toward price decreases that result from reductions in the implicit cost of time.

If these effects are both small or cancel each other out, then physician prices may remain essentially constant with respect to aggregate physician supply. The market, however, is split up among more physicians. Therefore in this, the standard case, the quantity demanded from each declines and each doctor's individual net income suffers, that is, $\bar{F}$ is inversely related to $N$, which is the same prediction the competitive model gives. If this process continues long enough, then $\bar{F}$ is reduced to the income level that physicians are able to earn in professions other than medicine. This process leads to a market limit on the number of individuals who choose medicine as a profession.

A beneficial consequence flows from this: Communities that were too small to support a physician at the fee levels competitive to the fees being charged in neighboring, larger communities are big enough to support a physician when $F_i$ becomes sufficiently small. This prediction has been tested. Newhouse et al. (1982) examined the data from 1970 to 1979 on community size and the presence of physicians from the major specialties. They found that smaller communities that lacked a physician in a particular specialty in 1970 were considerably more likely to have a physician from that specialty in 1979 as a result of the growth in aggregate physician supply that took place over the decade.[29]

Another, more perverse possibility exists than the standard case just outlined. If additional physicians entering a community do cause each of their firm demand curves to become less elastic, then prices do tend to rise even as each community's market for physicians' services is divided among more physicians. This rise in price tends to offset the decrease in net income that occurs if the standard case obtains. At its greatest extreme, price would rise sufficiently such that physicians' net incomes remain constant as aggregate physician supply increases. If this should occur, or come close to occurring, then the market would largely lose the self-limiting property of discouraging individuals from entering medicine as a career.

This scenario where $F_i$ remains invariant as aggregate supply increases implies minimal spreading of physicians to rural communities that are underserved because of their small size. The feedback between the number of physicians in the community and the elasticity of physicians' firm demand curves would not be present in the communities that have no physicians precisely because they have no physicians. Therefore, an increase in aggregate physician supply leaves unaffected the elasticity of firm demand that physicians would face if they should decide to locate in such a community. This implies that the price physicians would charge in those towns also remains constant. As a consequence, because neither $F_i$ nor price necessarily change as aggregate supply increases, the conditions that originally made the community uneconomically small for a physician remain unchanged. The evidence of Newhouse et al. (1982) indicates that this latter scenario has not been occurring to any extreme degree. Whether it has occurred to a significant degree, however, can not be deduced from their analysis.

This paper's analysis suggests that the welfare effects of increasing the aggregate supply of physicians are quite grim. On the plus side are the decisions physicians make to locate in communities that were previously without physicians' services. Presumably the residents of those towns benefit substantially in the form of greater convenience and reduced transportation and time costs. The cost of achieving this benefit through increased aggregate supply is high, in as much as prices are unlikely to fall significantly and may even rise in the vast majority of communities that already are adequately served. Consumers in larger towns and cities already have a wide choice of physicians; more to choose among is not likely to lead to consumers matching themselves more successfully with a physician that meets their idiosyncratic needs and taste. Thus the only gain to consumers in cities is if physicians, in response to sharing the market with more competitors, change the qualitative nature of their services in a way that consumers value highly. The cost to society in increasing the aggregate supply of doctors is (1) the large investment, both public and private, that is involved in training each one and (2) the opportunity cost of engaging in medicine a higher than necessary proportion of the most talented members of our society.[30] Given these costs, increasing aggregate supply appears almost certainly to be an inefficient way to induce physicians to locate in underserved areas. Straight subsidies on a continuing basis would, it appears, be much less expensive.

# 6    Concluding remarks

This paper's body contains an extended analysis of the effects that consumer information levels and the aggregate supply of physicians have on primary care physicians' pricing and location decisions. By explicitly examining these decisions within the context of a monopolistically competitive market structure I have resolved two of the more paradoxical facts of that market:

1. At any point in time physicians in communities that are well supplied with physicians are likely to charge more than physicians in communities that are less well supplied.

2. Increasing the aggregate supply of physicians has had no obvious downward effect on physicians' prices.

If these facts are not placed in the context of monopolistic competition theory, then they might be interpreted as evidence that physicians can manipulate consumers to consume more care than they would freely choose. Physicians may in fact be able to induce consumer demand, but these two facts are not evidence for or against that proposition. Instead, both facts appear to be natural implications of the monopolistically competitive structure of the primary care physician market.

My underlying thesis in this paper, however, does not concern monopolistic competition. It is that health care researchers should let those facts that are most essential about providers, their environments, and the problem under study guide their choice of model. As the study of health services progresses and becomes increasingly sophisticated new models and tools will undoubtedly become important. The many commonalities that exist between the delivery of health care services and the rest of the economy will continue to make it possible for the researcher into health services to adopt many generic ideas from microeconomics. Nevertheless, health care does have a degree of uniqueness that, when it becomes the essence of the problem under study, should be recognized through the creation and analysis of new models. Finally, the models that are constructed in this spirit should be confronted with data in order to check that their testable implications are consistent with the reality of health care delivery. In time this will lead to substantially improved knowledge concerning the structure, competitiveness, and performance of the approximately 10 percent of our economy that is the health care sector.

### Notes

1. Amounts for total personal health care expenditures and expenditures on physicians' services are from Table A-2 of *Health Care Financing Trends* (Fall 1980). The amount for primary care physicians' services was obtained by multiplying the expenditure on physicians' services amount by the proportion of physicians engaged in primary care and then correcting roughly for the lower earnings realized by primary care physicians relative to other physicians. The proportion of physicians in primary care in 1978 is calculated from Chart E-5 in Donabedian, Axelrod, and Wyszewianski (1980). The correction factor for primary care physicians' earnings relative to other physicians in 1978 is estimated from Chart E-39 in Donabedian, Axelrod, and Wyszewianski (1980).

2. Chamberlin's theory (1962) has been criticized on numerous grounds, perhaps most unerringly by Stigler (1950). The criticisms have validity in precisely the same way that my three observations concerning the nature of the primary care market vitiate the usefulness of both perfect competition and monopoly theory in this context. Therefore, the analyst has to make a decision as to which of the available and tractable models comes closest to capturing the essence of the market under study. In this case, since my focus is on the industry's market structure and the role of information within that structure, my conclusion is that the monopolistic competition model is the only one that allows me to treat the important questions in a reasonably unified, albeit imperfect, manner. For some further observations on monopolistic competition, see Demsetz (1968, 1972), Telser (1968), Schmalensee (1972), and Kumar and Satterthwaite (1982).

3. Some progress has been made on the general case. See Satterthwaite et al. (1982).

4. If one accepts the premise that physicians are like other members of the upper middle class and, with few exceptions, would be quite glad to increase their income without increasing their work effort, then one is inexorably lead to the conclusion that the market does constrain physicians in their pricing decisions.

5. This model is developed more formally and in more detail in Satterthwaite (1979).

6. From a methodological standpoint, as Kumar and Satterthwaite (1982) have pointed out, this symmetry assumption is necessary for analyses of this sort to be tractable. Moreover, from a substantive standpoint, the symmetry assumption does not seem too offensive as a good deal of uniformity apparently exists within communities as to how primary care physicians of each specialty structure their practices.

7. This is equation (20) in Satterthwaite (1979). That this is a long-run elasticity should be emphasized. Consumers clearly do not react quickly to physician price changes if for no other reason than that the infrequency of visits means months and months may pass before a given consumer is exposed to the new price.

8. If a physician is maximizing either income or utility (where the utility function's arguments are income and leisure), then his or her equilibrium price is necessarily at a point where the demand he or she faces is elastic.

9. Chamberlin (1962, p. 91).

10. Pauly (1968), Feldstein (1977), and Newhouse et al. (1981) are examples of these studies.

11. Equation (9.3) is set up so that the number of physicians does not affect total consumer demand in a community, i.e., physicians are unable to induce demand.

12. In equation (9.3) the constants $A$ and $B$ do not vary across communities. Thus implicitly all communities are the same size. This restriction, however, is immaterial to the analysis.

13. Booth and Babchuk (1972).

14. See, for example, Lippman and McCall (1976).

15. A detailed, formal analysis of the direction in which $e_w$ changes when search costs decrease is contained in Satterthwaite (1979, Section 5). Inspection of that analysis indicates that a negative change is most plausible for the case of physician services.

16. An outline of this argument, which parallels the argument about $e_w$ in Satterthwaite (1979, Section 5), is as follows. When a physician increases his/her price some consumers currently in his or her patient panel fall below their reservation price–needs reservation level and decide to search for a new physician. Whether the switching rates become more elastic as search costs decrease depends critically on the shape the subjective probability distribution that consumers have regarding the likelihood of finding a physician who meets their needs better than their current physician. Exactly as in the case of $e_w$, plausible shapes for that distribution leads to the switching rate becoming more price elastic as consumers' search costs decrease.

17. Satterthwaite (1979, Section 5).

18. Newhouse et al. (1981) contains estimates of $DD$'s elasticity.

19. In recent years the ability of hospitals to arbitrarily reject a well qualified physician who applies for membership on its voluntary medical staff has been restricted by court decisions. This trend, however, may reverse as the number of practicing physicians increases if hospitals can convince the courts that the medical staff of a hospital has a maximum size that is consistent with the hospital's well-functioning.

20. This is generally easy for a new medical school graduate.

21. A less ad hoc manner of generating the physician's long-run total cost curve would be to endow him or her with a Cobb–Douglas utility function for income and leisure. The $LRATC$ curve is then an indifference curve drawn in $p$–$q$ space. The resulting indifference curve decreases for all $q_{ij}$ less than some critical quantity $q_{min}$ and then increases. To the left of $q_{min}$, which is the relevant segment, the shape is not too different than the shape of the $LRATC$ curve defined by equation (9.9). For the purposes of this paper, therefore, using the simpler functional form of (9.9) is both convenient and sufficient. Woodward and Warren–Boulton (1981) is an example where the Cobb–Douglas form has been used to study physicians' work–leisure–income choices.

22. The $LRATC$ generated by Cobb–Douglas utility has the property that to the left of $q_{min}$ its elasticity is monotonically decreasing. See Note 21.

23. See the coefficient and $t$-statistic of $MDPCPC$ (physicians per thousand population) for the "target income" equation within Table 3 of Pauly and Satterthwaite (1981). The careful reader may raise a question at this point. Table 3 of Pauly and Satterthwaite also contains estimates for the "increasing monopoly" equation and in that equation $MDPCPC$'s sign reverses from positive to negative. The increasing monopoly model, however, includes the information proxies that were discussed in the third section of this paper. They, according to the argument of this paper, are the real driving force behind the variance in prices and physician supply across communities. Therefore, the appropriate interpretation of $MDPCPC$'s positive coefficient in the target income equation is that it serves as a proxy for the missing informational variables.

24. See Evans (1974) for a description of the original target income theory and its more sophisticated successors, theories of physician induced demand.
25. I assume that $c_i$ and $d_i$ are constant across the two communities.
26. In Satterthwaite (1979) and Pauly and Satterthwaite (1981) the argument we made to explain the positive correlation between price and physician supply was solely in terms of the effect that the number of physicians may have on consumer information. No use was made of the long-run equilibrium's properties. That argument and this paper's argument are distinct and complementary, though probably the argument of this paper is more robust. Fortuitously, however, the econometrics in Pauly and Satterthwaite (1981) do not appear to be affected by this new theory because the econometrics employed there explicitly recognized that price in a market does influence the number of physicians who locate there.
27. The first figure is from Rayack (1967, Table 22, p. 73) and the second and third are from the Summary Report of the Graduate Medical Education National Advisory Committee (1980, Table 2, p. 10).
28. Physicians may offset this tendency toward reduced workload by increasing the amount of time they spend with each patient.
29. The information based theory of this paper suggests that the good consumer information small towns are hypothesized to have about their physicians actually makes it harder for such towns to attract a physician. The reason is that the lower prices the good information induces means the market size needed to support a single physician is larger than in a town or city with poorer consumer information.
30. The issue here is an old one: Does monopolistic competition lead to socially excessive investment into an industry?

## References

Benham, L. (October 1972). "The Effect of Advertising on the Price of Eyeglasses." *J. of Law and Economics* 15: 337–52.

Benham, L., and Benham, A. (October 1975). "Regulating Through the Professions: A Perspective on Information Control." *J. of Law and Economics* 18: 421–47.

Booth, A., and Babchuk, N. (1972). "Seeking Health Care from New Resources." *J. of Health and Social Behavior* 13: 90–9.

Chamberlin, E. H. (1962). *The Theory of Monopolistic Competition,* 8th edition. Cambridge, Mass.: Harvard University Press.

Demsetz, H. (Jan.–Feb. 1968). "Do Competition and Monopolistic Competition Differ?" *J. of Political Economy* 76: 146–8.

(May–June 1972). "The Inconsistencies in Monopolistic Competition: A Reply." *J. of Political Economy* 80: 586–91.

Donabedian, A., Axelrod, S. J., and Wyszewianski, L. (1980). *Medical Care Chartbook,* 7th edition. Ann Arbor, Mich.: Health Administration Press.

Evans, R. (1974). "Supplier-Induced Demand." In *The Economics of Health and Medical Care,* ed. M. Perlman, 162–73. London: MacMillan.

Feldman, R., and Begun, J. W. (1978). "The Effects of Advertising: Lessons from Optometry." *J. of Human Resources* 13 (Supplement): 247–62.

Feldstein, M. S. (1977). "Quality Change and the Demand for Hospital Care." *Econometrica* 45: 1681–702.

Graduate Medical Education National Advisory Committee to the Secretary, Department of Health and Human Services. (September 30, 1980). *Summary Report*. Vol. 1. Washington, D.C.: Department of Health and Human Services, Public Health Service, Health Resources Administration, Office of Graduate Medical Education, DHHS Publication No. (HRA) 81–651, 1981.

Kumar, K. R., and Satterthwaite, M. A. "Monopolistic Competition, Aggregation of Competitive Information, and the Amount of Product Differentiation." *J. of Econ. Theory:* forthcoming.

Lippman, S., and McCall, J. (1976). "The Economics of Job Search: A Survey, Part I." *Economic Inquiry* 14: 155–89.

Newhouse, J. P., Williams, A. P., Bennett, B. W., and Schwartz, W. B. (Autumn 1982). "Does the Geographical Distribution of Physicians Reflect Market Failure?" *Bell J. of Economics* 13: 493–505.

Newhouse, J. P., Manning, W. G., Morris, C. N., et al. (December 1981). "Some Interim Results from a Controlled Trial of Cost Sharing in Health Insurance." *New England J. of Medicine* 305: 1501–7.

Pauly, M. V. (1968). "The Economics of Moral Hazard: Comment." *American Economic Review* 58: 531–7.

Pauly, M. V., and Satterthwaite, M. A. (Autumn 1981). "The Pricing of Primary Care Physicians' Services: A Test of the Role of Consumer Information." *Bell J. of Economics* 12: 488–506.

Rayack, E. (1967). *Professional Power and American Medicine: The Economics of the American Medical Association.* Cleveland: The World Publishing Company.

Satterthwaite, M. A. (Autumn 1979). "Consumer Information, Equilibrium Industry Price, and the Number of Sellers." *Bell J. of Economics* 10: 483–502.

Satterthwaite, M. A., Hughes, E. F. X., Pauly, M. V., et al. (July 1981). "Competitive vs. Regulatory Cost Containment: Fundamental Prospects and Problems." Working Paper #59, Center for Health Services and Policy Research, Northwestern University.

Schmalensee, R. (May–June 1972). "A Note on Monopolistic Competition and Excess Capacity." *J. of Political Economy* 80: 586–91.

Stigler, G. (1950). "Monopolistic Competition in Retrospect." In *Five Lectures on Economic Problems,* New York: MacMillan.

Telser, L. G. (March–April 1968). "Monopolistic Competition: Any Impact Yet?" *J. of Political Economy* 76: 312–15.

U.S. Department of Health and Human Services. (Fall 1980). Health Care Financing Administration. Office of Research, Demonstrations, and Statistics. *Health Care Financing Trends.* Baltimore, MD.: HCFA Pub. No. 03073, December 1980.

Woodward, R. S., and Warren-Boulton, F. (1981). "Physician Productivity and Remuneration Method." *Health Care Financing Conference Proceedings: Issues in Physician Reimbursement.* Washington, D.C.: HHS, Health Care Financing Administration, Office of Research and Demonstration, pp. 115–24.

# Comment: Competition and equilibrium as a driving force in the health services sector

JEFFREY HARRIS

I shall address two questions. First, how credible is the evidence in support of Professor Satterthwaite's model of the market for doctors' services? Second, what guidance does his model offer for public policy toward the supply of physicians?

## Analyzing the evidence on doctors' fees

The main motivation for Satterthwaite's model is the problematic observation that doctors' fees are higher in places with a larger supply of physicians. This finding has led a number of economists to reject the conventional competitive model in favor of theories that endow doctors with substantial market power. Though Satterthwaite follows in this tradition, his real innovation is to explain why an increase in the total number of doctors in a market might give each physician more, rather than less, control over price. This is certainly a refreshing alternative to the prevalent notion that more doctors can maintain higher prices merely by drumming up more business. I am concerned, however, that the available cross-section data may not be sufficiently powerful to distinguish Satterthwaite's model from competing theories.

In the conventional, static market model, the equilibrium price and quantity of doctors' services would be determined by the joint solution to

$$P = f(Q, O_D), \quad \text{with } \partial f/\partial Q \leq 0 \qquad (C.9.1)$$

and

$$P = g(Q, O_S), \quad \text{with } \partial g/\partial Q \geq 0. \qquad (C.9.2)$$

In the inverse-demand relation (C.9.1), price $P$ depends negatively on the quantity of physicians' services $Q$, and is also a function of a vector $O_D$ of other demand factors. In the inverse-supply relation (C.9.2), price depends positively on quantity, and is also a function of a vector $O_S$ other supply factors.

Now suppose we have cross-sectional data on physicians' fees, the quantity of physicians' services, and the factors $O_D$ and $O_S$ for various geographically distinct areas. If the observed price–quantity pairs in fact represent

268

equilibrium solutions to (C.9.1) and (C.9.2), and if both the other supply-influencing ($O_S$) and demand-influencing ($O_D$) factors vary across localities, then the observed crude relation between price and quantity will represent neither a pure demand relation nor a pure supply relation, but a combination of the two. Moreover, we cannot ordinarily tease out the individual relations (C.9.1) and (C.9.2) from the data unless we make certain identifying restrictions on the ways that the variables in $O_D$ and $O_S$ enter the equations. In particular, identification of the demand relation (C.9.1) requires that we designate certain supply-influencing variables (i.e., elements of the set $O_S$), which do not affect demand (i.e., are not in $O_D$). In that way, we can trace out a demand curve from observed intersections of supply and demand.

In practice, finding a plausible set of identifying restrictions boils down to searching the available data bases for the right variables. This has not been an easy task. Local wage rates for medical secretaries, for example, may belong in $O_S$ but not in $O_D$. But wage rates may also reflect the local standard of living in an area, which could in turn influence the demand for physicians' services. Similarly, any datum that purports to measure the attractiveness of a metropolitan area as a place for a doctor to reside (an $O_S$ variable) may also gauge the wealth of the area (an $O_D$ variable).

We are left in a quandary. We want to observe the effect of an increase in supply on price. But any measurable factor that might stimulate increased physician supply is likely also to affect demand. Hence supply effects and demand effects are confounded.

What, then, are we to conclude if physician fees are positively related to physician supply? We could say that the demand relation (C.9.1) indeed prevails, but it just cannot be identified from cross-section data. The alternative pursued by Satterthwaite, however, is to replace equation (C.9.1) with the following system:

$$P = f(Q, E, O_D), \quad \text{with } \partial P/\partial E \leq 0 \tag{C.9.3}$$

and

$$E = h(Q, O_E), \quad \text{with } \partial E/\partial Q \leq 0. \tag{C.9.4}$$

In the modified demand relation (C.9.3), $E$ measures the efficiency of consumer search among alternative physicians. When $E$ is low, each doctor has more power to raise price $P$ without losing patients. Moreover, from (C.9.4), an increase in the number $Q$ of doctors makes it more difficult for consumers to learn about any single doctor, thus lowering $E$.

Does Satterthwaite's alternative ease the empirical problem of teasing out supply and demand effects? Since the variable $E$ is a theoretical construct that cannot be directly measured, the best that we can do in practice is to identify the combined solution to (C.9.3) and (C.9.4). Accordingly, inserting (C.9.4) into (C.9.3) and reiterating the supply equation (C.9.2), we get the new system

$$P = f(Q, h(Q, O_E), O_D) \qquad (C.9.5)$$

and

$$P = g(Q, O_S). \qquad (C.9.6)$$

To identify the equation (C.9.6), we now need to designate supply-influencing factors $O_S$ that are contained in neither $O_E$ nor $O_S$. Moreover, we need some restrictions on the functions $f$ and $h$. For if both $f$ and $h$ were linear, we could not distinguish the partial demand effect of $Q$ on $P$ from the total effect of $Q$ on $P$.

Though Satterthwaite does not address these problems in detail, he does refer to the study by Pauly and Satterthwaite (1981). In that paper, the authors stressed the empirical distinction between $O_E$ and $O_D$ variables. For example, they suggested that the extent of residential turnover (what Satterthwaite terms *MOVED*), the population density, and the proportion of female-headed households affect the efficiency of search ($O_E$) but do not affect supply ($O_S$) or demand ($O_D$). Moreover, they postulated, such variables as proportion of the population under 5 years and fraction of females on welfare influence demand ($O_D$) but not supply ($O_S$) or consumer search ($O_E$). But the real issue is the authors' proposal that such variables as hotel expenditures per capita and the rate of recent population growth belong in $O_S$ but not $O_E$ or $O_D$. Moreover, they assumed that $h$ is a specific nonlinear function of $Q$. That is, while $Q$ enters the conventional demand relation as primary care physicians per capita, $Q$ enters the consumer search relation $h$ as primary care physicians per square mile. The latter term is the product of the physicians per capita and the population density.

Some argument can be made for the identifying restrictions chosen by Pauly and Satterthwaite. But it is hardly obvious what might have resulted if even one of their strong assumptions were relaxed. Although the authors claim support for the Satterthwaite theory in preference to others, such a conclusion appears to hinge on the overly precise interpretation of rather fuzzy data.

My guess is that the purportedly paradoxical relation between physician density and physician fees cannot be satisfactorily explained from cross-sectional geographical data. Perhaps examination of fee patterns over time in selected areas would be more useful.

### Physician supply and public policy

Professor Satterthwaite suggests that an increase in the supply of primary care physicians could make consumers worse off. Even within the narrow context of Satterthwaite's monopolistic competition model, I do not believe that such a conclusion is warranted.

In the Chamberlinian story of monopolistic competition, an expansion in the size of a market is ordinarily accompanied by an increase in the extent of product differentiation. At the start, microcomputers offered a few basic packages. As the market grew, specialized home computers, scientific computers, and computerized games appeared. At the start, Camels, Chesterfields, and Lucky Strikes were the three main brands of cigarette. As the market grew, menthol cigarettes, filter cigarettes, 120mm cigarettes, and low-tar cigarettes emerged.

The same phenomena are taking place in the physicians' services market. Starting in the 1960s, the U.S. government markedly increased its subsidy of both the cost of medical care and the cost of medical education. The resulting growth of physician supply has been accompanied by a proliferation of "physician brands." This product differentiation has not been confined to the emergence of new subspecialties based upon new medical techniques. The emergence of new residency programs in primary care and family medicine were also manifestations. Physicians moved increasingly into fee-for-service groups and prepaid ("HMO") group practices. New practice styles, with enhanced use of paramedical personnel, have evolved. Full-time or part-time salaried positions with hospitals have grown. We are seeing more physician-managed diagnostic centers, emergency care centers and ambulatory surgical centers. In dentistry, a related primary care field, we have new retail dental centers. The same has occurred in optometry.

Just as in the classic Chamberlinian model, we have no unequivocal economic basis for claiming that the proliferation of new styles is beneficial or deleterious. Certainly, the evaluation is a lot more complicated than a judgment that we have too many or too few brands of breakfast cereals or cars. My guess, in any case, is that the welfare consequences of such increased product differentiation overshadow the consumer search effects that Professor Satterthwaite has identified. To me, the issue is whether surgicenters offer better medical care, and not whether the proliferation of such centers makes it more difficult to pick a surgeon.

Let me go one step further. An increase in primary care physician supply is likely to affect the whole health care system, not just the narrowly defined market for primary care services. At the first level, an increase in the number of primary care doctors affects the subspecialty market merely because primary care physicians are a major source of referrals to such specialists. At the second level, an increase in physician supply may affect the hospital care market as more and more doctors vie for staff privileges and use of specialized hospital facilities. These questions have not been addressed carefully by Satterthwaite or, for that matter, by other economists.

Professor Satterthwaite is careful to explain that his model applies solely to the primary care market. This is fair enough. But then what model should apply to the other medical care markets? Here, I suggest, we need to pay attention to two critical factors: the extremely rapid pace of technological change in medical care; and the special decision-making role of the physician throughout the medical care system. Perhaps Satterthwaite's provocative model will stimulate economists to tackle these tough problems.

## References

Pauly, Mark V., and Mark A. Satterthwaite (1981). "The pricing of primary care physicians' services: a test of the role of consumer information." *Bell Journal of Economics* 12: 488–506.

# CHAPTER 10

# Government services

EDWARD M. GRAMLICH

Roughly one-third of all services produced and consumed in the United States are sold to federal, state, and local governments. These services (hereafter referred to as public services) have in common with privately sold services one significant analytical property: There is no separate market for resource inputs and service outputs, so it is impossible to arrive at a market-determined measure of production efficiency (or productivity growth). But there is also another property that makes it more difficult to understand and analyze public services: Unlike privately purchased services, the consumption decision is a collective one. With private services we can presume that consumers buy the amount dictated by their willingness-to-pay, and hence that service production and consumption levels are at least roughly appropriate (given the other circumstances of the economy). With public services, we cannot even make this assumption. The fact of collective, political, consumption implies that many groups in a community may be over- or underconsuming public services.

In this paper I highlight the latter difference. The inability to measure production efficiency is an important fact, but since there is no new analytical issue raised in moving from private to public services, there is no particular point in focusing on these measurement issues for public services. But the latter issue, whether services are consumed roughly at appropriate levels, too much, or too little, is both serious and unique, and I focus my efforts there.

The first section of the paper reviews some basic facts regarding public services: what they are, how important they are, how they are provided, how much they have grown over time. The next section considers the normative rationale for public services: why they are necessary in the first place. The third section considers the more detailed question of whether the overall level of public services provided is appropriate or inappropriate, and how this judgment might be made. This section covers many of the arguments that have formed the intellectual support for the tax limitation movement. The final section proposes and evaluates some new institutional arrangements that may improve the checks on the level of public services produced and consumed, ways in which some of the innate private market discipline might be transferred to the public sector. Among the topics

273

Table 10.1. *Government purchased services in relation to other variables, selected dates (%)*

| Item | 1948 | 1958 | 1968 | 1978 |
|---|---|---|---|---|
| Relation to broader variables | | | | |
|   Share of GNP | 8.0 | 12.3 | 14.9 | 15.3 |
|   Share of total government purchases | 64.4 | 58.0 | 65.1 | 74.7 |
|   Share of total purchases of services | 26.9 | 33.0 | 36.3 | 33.6 |
| Composition | | | | |
|   Share that is direct composition of employees | 84.5 | 76.4 | 73.6 | 70.5 |
|     Federal | 43.2 | 37.2 | 30.4 | 22.0 |
|       National defense | n.a. | 29.6 | 23.2 | 14.2 |
|       Other | n.a. | 7.6 | 7.2 | 7.8 |
|     State and local | 41.3 | 39.2 | 43.2 | 48.5 |
|       Education | n.a. | 19.1 | 23.5 | 25.7 |
|       Other | n.a. | 20.1 | 19.7 | 22.8 |

*Source:* Bureau of Economic Analysis, national income accounts issues of the *Survey of Current Business.*

covered are tax limits, privatization, user charges, and internal reform. For each topic I try to describe the present state of knowledge and bring out what seem to be the key research questions.

### Basic facts regarding public services

As mentioned previously, roughly one-third of all services produced and consumed in the United States are public. This share rose steadily until a decade or so past World War II, but as Table 10.1 shows, it has remained quite stable for the past two decades.[1] As the top panel also shows, the share of all government purchases devoted to public services is rising gradually (to about three-quarters), whereas the share of GNP devoted to public services has apparently topped off at about 15 percent.

Exactly what are these public services? The bottom panel of Table 10.1 shows that the largest share, 70 percent in 1978, consists of the compensation of government employees. Indeed, the only government purchases that are *not* considered public services are those purchases that either involve government construction (missile bases, roads, schools), or purchases of durable goods (vehicles, typewriters) and nondurable goods (office supplies, fuel). And, although information on the 30 percent implied by Table 10.1 that is not compensation of employees is scanty, large components of that would involve expenditures for consulting firms, which can essentially be viewed as substituting for direct employee compensation, and for the travel and other services incurred by direct employees. Hence it is at least roughly accurate to think of public services as composed of direct compensation of employees (70%) or indirect compensation-like services (most of the remaining 30%).

The share of public services purchased by federal and state–local governments is behaving much like that of all government expenditures. Driven by the declining share of direct expenditures for national defense (at least until 1980) and the rising share of federal grants to state–local governments, states and localities are buying a large and rising share of all public services. As of 1978, their direct compensation of employees alone comprised half of all public services, and once their indirect compensation-like expenditures were added in (not shown in the table), they purchased about 70 percent of all public services. In turn, roughly half of state and local direct employee compensation involved elementary, secondary, and higher education whereas far and away the largest share of federal employee compensation was, and remains, devoted to national defense. Hence when we talk about public services, we are referring mainly to military direct and indirect employee compensation, the wage bill of teachers and educational administrators, and a minority of public services devoted to all other types of government purchases.

These remarks also imply that the overwhelming means by which public services are produced in today's world is by direct government hire of employees to do whatever job is in question. The last section of the paper asks about different institutional forms for providing public services: These in turn involve potential improvements in the civil service process under which the 70 percent of direct employees are hired, or potential advantages of altering the shares and purchasing more than the present 30 percent from outside the civil service–direct hire system.

### Rationales for public services

There are two main rationales for collective consumption of public services. The first involves what is known as the public goods problem. Many public services – police protection, public parks, the court system – have the physical property that if they are consumed by one individual or group within a community, they are consumed by all. If so, the willingness-to-pay of individual consumers of public services will greatly understate the total community demand for the public service, because these individual demands will not register the demands of others in the community who also benefit from the service. That, in simple terms, is the rationale for having the community decide jointly on consumption levels.

The second, and entirely separate, rationale for collective consumption of public services involves a form of an equity argument. Government policy attempts to ensure an equitable distribution of economic welfare. There are two ways of doing this. One is through direct tax and transfer actions, taking from high income groups and giving to those with low incomes. These direct redistribution policies can be thought of as reducing the variance of rewards in the economic ratrace. They normally do *not* involve public services. But there is a second sense in which public services are provided for equity reasons. In the long run an equitable distribution of economic rewards might also be attained by assuring equality of opportunity, or at least having government policy attempt to mitigate inequalities of opportunity. Putting this another way, the government can and does take steps to try to make the economic ratrace as fair as possible. Toward this end, many subsidized public services are provided, more or less intended to equalize consumption of these services between income groups. Public elementary, secondary, and higher education, an important component of equal opportunities, is either free or highly subsidized for all income groups. Public health insurance and hospital facilities are made available at very low cost to low income groups, to remedy the fact that otherwise these persons would have to do without adequate health care, the lack of which is a hindrance to equal opportunity. Subsidized labor training opportunities are made available to low income groups, again serving the goal of equality of opportunity.

There are other rationales for public sector intervention in private markets. Two prominent examples are the "natural monopoly" problem, which can justify some government physical investment; and information failures or noninsurable risks, which can justify various social insurance programs. For the most part these other rationales do not usually justify public services, and I will treat them only in passing.

Although the basic goals of public service provision – some mixture of the public goods efficiency goal and equality of opportunity – are not often questioned, the particular level of public services consumed, or the aggregate tax cost of public services, often does come under criticism. As a theoretical matter, some of these criticisms could imply that services are underconsumed. However, in practice most are on the side of overconsumption. The next section reviews these criticisms.

## Are the right amounts of public services consumed?

It is difficult to tell whether the right amount of public services is consumed without knowing what that right amount is. The public choice literature gives two standards. The first, really a normative standard, is the Samuelsonian (1954) efficiency condition. At the optimal level of public services, the sum of everybody's marginal valuation of a public service (for either the public goods reason or the equal opportunity reason) should just equal the aggregate marginal cost. If a lower level of services were consumed, aggregate marginal benefits would exceed aggregate marginal costs, and consumption levels should be expanded. Just the reverse would obtain should aggregate marginal benefits fall short of aggregate marginal costs. Used properly, benefit–cost analysis is nothing more than a technique that precisely identifies this Samuelsonian efficiency point.

The other standard for identifying the correct amount is Hotelling's (1929) median voter condition. Whereas the Samuelsonian condition maximizes aggregate satisfaction given the cost of supplying public services, the median voter condition predicts the outcome of what might be termed a perfectly functioning democracy. In this sense it is more a positive than a normative standard. But it is not strictly a positive standard because the median voter result only obtains under a number of strong assumptions. The process works because when voters either vote directly on fiscal choices, or vote for politicians with well-known positions on fiscal issues, there is a tendency for the politician favoring the desires of the median voter in society to win. This in turn would lead politicians to cluster around positions perceived to be taken by the median voter, and to pass these policies. In this sense the median voter model is nothing more than a rigorous prediction of why the tastes of the median voter will dominate in a democracy. When some of these assumptions are not fulfilled – perhaps the information requirement or a requirement that preferences be "single-peaked" [if one's first choice is for an expenditure level of 500, one would not prefer an expenditure level of 300 to one of 400 – see Arrow (1951)] – the median voter result will not be achieved in practice.

This distinction suggests that the budgetary outcomes resulting from Hotelling's median voter outcome and Samuelson's efficient budgetary outcome are generally *not* the same. Whenever tastes are asymmetric and not precisely offset by tax rules for financing public services, the two outcomes will differ [see Bowen (1943) and Bergstrom (1979)]. Many of the imperfections in voting and political behavior represent shortcomings in the way the political system works, but even if it worked perfectly, the outcome would in general not be perfect in the Samuelsonian sense.

What are some of the reasons why even the median voter outcome might not be realized? A long list of possible reasons has been suggested, many of which are quite obvious. A first and fairly obvious reason is the information requirement: Voters must know what political candidates stand for on fiscal choices, indeed the candidates themselves must know. The recent movement toward referenda on tax limitations in many states, whatever one thinks of the outcomes if these limitations are added to the state constitution, is at least a welcome step from this standpoint.

A second type of problem is logrolling, best illustrated by examples in Buchanan–Tullock (1962). There are possible returns to logrolling whenever one group (group A) wants, say, much more spent on particular public service while other groups (groups B and C) want slightly less. In such a case, it will be in the interests of those wanting much more, first to devote more efforts to lobbying, and secondly to try to form coalitions. If they can change the vote of group B or C on this issue, making for a winning coalition, they will vote with B or C on some other issue. From A's standpoint, the gain on this issue exceeds the loss on the issue over which it vote-traded. Presumably the same thing is true in reverse for B or C. Everybody gains, and the logs are rolled.

Although logrolling is a term that evokes the emotional appeal of, say, "rotten boroughs" or "waste, fraud, and abuse," in fact it may sometimes be an efficiency enhancing process. As stated previously, the median voter outcome is not a normative solution, and its main shortcoming is that it does not weight preferences – one who cares deeply about an issue is given the same one vote as one who is practically indifferent. Logrolling is a way in which the median voter process can be combined with a technique for giving greater political weight to more intense preferences. Very often, this will move the political outcome in the direction of the Samuelsonian efficiency point (implicitly computed from a scheme in which intense preferences are given greater weight). Sometimes it will not. Rationalizers of logrolling would be hard-pressed to defend the economic efficiency of the dams and canals that typically are approved as part of Congress's heavily logrolled "public works" appropriation.

The information and logrolling amendments to the median voter theorem show why median voter outcomes may not be realized in practice. But generally they do not point up particular biases in the political process, biases that predict a systematic tendency for over- or underspending on public services (relative to some efficiency standard). But there is a series of models that do point to such a bias. A first class of models of excessive consumption of public services involves both the motives and the strategic positioning of bureaucrats managing public service programs. Because their motives differ, and because they are strategically placed in the political process, these bureaucrats can influence overall demands for public goods and raise public spending above what it otherwise might be. A first model of this type was developed by Niskanen (1971). He argued that since managers of public bureaucracies cannot compete for any profits generated by their agency, they will instead compete to extend their bureaucratic empires, and this will result in excessive spending on public services. Similar motives on the part of legislative oversight committees will also eliminate or weaken some of the normal institutional checks on service expansion. A second model developed by Romer–Rosenthal (1978) and Mackay–Weaver (1978) focuses on bureaucratic control of the political agenda: If bureaucrats can eliminate the median voter choice from the agenda, and force voters to choose between spending levels that are slightly too large or much too small, they can perhaps get slightly excessive spending levels adopted. Note that unlike the logrolling models described previously these bureaucratic aggrandizement models lay little claim to potential economic efficiency: They work not off preference intensities, but off preference differences and the strategic positioning of bureaucrats (unless one were to argue that those who had more intense preferences for public good would actually be employed in these agencies, an argument that ultimately makes it impossible to identify inefficiencies associated with the Niskanen hypothesis).

The Niskanen, Romer–Rosenthal, and Mackay–Weaver hypotheses involve the demand for public goods, but there are potential supply-side imperfections as well. A first is plain old monopolistic market power. As previously noted, public services are essentially wage payments to the suppliers of these services. There is casual evidence that political candidates will sometimes engage in a form of vote-trading by offering higher public wage payments as a means of generating union support. Empirical evidence from Quinn (1979) and Smith (1980) that public sector wages are above those that would be paid for comparable skills in private jobs is also supportive.[2] Not only this, but pension arrangements, disability insurance, tenure restrictions, and the quality of the job all seem to be more favorable for public sector workers [Quinn (1982)]. The analytical case that there are monopolistic wage-rents for public sector workers is strengthened by Inman's (1980) finding that these rents appear to be limited when there are competing suburbs offering an alternative choice of residence for private taxpayers, and by the finding of Ehrenberg–Goldstein (1975) that rents are greater when the suburban employees are also monopolized.

Another type of supply-side imperfection involves the choice of factor inputs. Even if monopolistic rents were absent, public managers are not subject to the discipline of a competitive market, and they have little incentive to conserve on factor inputs or to choose cost-minimizing combinations of factors. This arrangement could lead governments to employ excessive amounts of capital and to have higher production costs than would be the case in the private sector. Empirical support for these propositions is as yet quite limited [see Borcherding–Pommerehne–Schneider (1982)].

All of these arguments for excessive public spending are based on the presumption that public services are supplied by government agencies in a potentially monopolistic position.[3] This is what allows bureaucrats to control the agenda, push up public wages, or inefficiently purchase factor inputs. But there are, in Hirschman's (1970) words, both "voice" and "exit" checks on the monopolistic positions of public agencies, and both of these checks may be responsible for the fact that it is easier to build theoretical models of the overconsumption of public services than to validate the models. Hirschman's voice option is just the median voter democratic check highlighted in Hotelling's theory. If such monopolistic abuses get out of line, it is time for voters to throw the rascals out. Hirschman's exit option is simply that voters can leave the community in response to excessive spending and/or wage levels, high tax rates, or whatever. Tiebout (1956) developed a model that tried to ensure economic efficiency in the provision of public services by allowing voters to shop around among communities.[4] In the strictest version of the Tiebout model, not only would spending levels be those favored by the median voter, but nonmedian voters would gradually be leaving the community to find another where they could be the median, and have their tastes satisfied. These Tiebout checks would also limit public union wage growth by providing jurisdictional competition in the way outlined theoretically by Courant–Gramlich–Rubinfeld (1979) and Epple–Zelenitz (1981), and also in some of the empirical work on public wage differentials. Both the voice and exit checks would seem to prevent the most egregious excess-output biases in the provision of public services.

## New institutional arrangements

Difficulties in measuring the tastes for public goods of various kinds of voters, the motives of bureaucrats, and the skills of public employees will always impede efforts to gauge and evaluate the level of public services consumed. A first important issue on the research agenda is to improve understanding of this issue, perhaps by more surveys of voters or measure of the skills and tastes of public servants. But perhaps a more important issue involves the next question: Suppose we cannot measure exactly whether government services are under- or overconsumed, are there new policies that can help limit the problem? Research and experimentation with these new policies is probably just as important as research on the underlying "problem," and it is to those new policies I now turn.

### An external check – tax limitation

A first important policy designed to deal with the overconsumption of public services is tax limitation. Since 1976 voters in nineteen states have adopted tax limitation measures by popular referenda. These limitation measures vary widely in the items being limited, the nature of the limitation (whether on growth or levels), the ease with which the limitation can be overridden, and whether the limitation is statutory or Constitutional. Given the newness of the movement and the differences in what might be called the experimental treatment, it will be quite difficult to determine the results of this natural experiment. But it is still a very interesting natural experiment, and researchers should not lose a valuable opportunity to assess its implications.

Using a priori theory, one can think of several advantages and disadvantages of tax limitations. The fact that voters are now voting directly on fiscal matters, as opposed to simply electing representatives to make the choices, seems in most cases a step in the right direction. The fact that many limitations are quite difficult to override, hence greatly constraining reversals of the initial decisions, seems quite unnecessary and a step in the wrong direction. The fact that limitations may limit what would otherwise be monopoly rents in public wages is a step in the right direction. But the fact that limitations prevent fiscal choices that voters would otherwise like to make, especially when statewide limitations are enforced on all local governments in a state and effectively constrain local actions with an inflexible central rule, is a step in the wrong direction. Tax limitations can be a very blunt, and perhaps harmful, way to cure whatever problems exist in the supply of public services, and it should be possible for researchers to develop a set of theoretical and empirical working hypotheses to make some sense out of the issue.[5]

The preceding issues are normative – are tax limitations sensible policy measures or not – but with any of the proposals in this area, there is also a positive side. Experiences in the nineteen states with tax limitation amendments could be compared with experiences in the thirty-one without to see whether the limitations, or which limitations, do limit the growth in expenditures and taxes, whether they encourage more use of user charges (typically not limited by the measures), more volunteer efforts, or more movements to provide public services privately. If limitations do limit something, do they limit the growth in the per unit cost of public services (mainly public sector wages), or growth in real levels of services provided? If the latter, is that usually a movement toward or away from the median voter point, toward or away from the Samuelsonian point. Is the behavior of bureaucratic service providers different from before – are aggrandizing bureaucratic managers held in check by the limitations, are efforts to control the political agenda complicated, or what? A new and important phenomenon has been added to an already complex institutional arrangement for providing public services, and it should prove both interesting and challenging to assess its effects.

*Privatization*

The previous arguments for government interference in a market economy were based on consumption considerations. Acting alone, consumers are likely to buy too few public services; acting jointly, they have a chance of buying the right amount. Posing the argument in this manner points up the potential distinction, seldom made in discussions of government spending, between government as a consumer of public services and government as a provider of public services. A second check on excessive public service consumption is to take explicit recognition of this distinction. Is there scope for having public services consumed and financed collectively, but actually provided by private suppliers? This type of check is called the "privatization" of public services.

There are various institutional arrangements by which public services can be privatized. One is simply to allow private firms to supply public services in competition with public agencies. Another is to have governments contract with a private company to supply the services. In the first case there would be private–public sector competition at any point in time; in the second there would not be competition at any given moment, but these contracts or franchises would be renewable, and if the private firm performed poorly, it would lose its franchise.

On the theoretical level, privatization can be thought of as eliminating the vertical integration of a government buying and selling agency. Williamson (1979) has discussed the typical conditions under which such a remedy might be appropriate – the main one being that transactions-specific costs not be incurred in the exchange. This means that there will be many sellers of the public service in question, that the service can be defined in a clear and acceptable way to buyers and sellers alike, and that unplanned and costly contingencies should rarely arise. These conditions certainly are not fulfilled with all public services, but they might be fulfilled with some now vertically integrated into the government.

As an empirical matter, unlike the fairly new phenomenon of tax limitation, various types of privatization experiments have been going on for some time, in a range of different public services and many different countries. Borcherding–Pommerehne–Schneider have summarized a long list of such studies and have found that overall cost levels do seem to be somewhat lower for private than public suppliers of public services, and that there is weak evidence that public suppliers adopt innovations more slowly, give managers longer tenure and price less closely to costs – all the things that might be expected from a lack of market discipline. A more detailed review of the results of trash collection experiments in the United States by Peterson (1981) confirms these conclusions. When private collectors are simply allowed to compete with the public sector, they have *higher* costs, presumably because with this sort of arrangement private collectors cannot capitalize on economies of scale (it is cheaper to pick up all ten cans on one block than to drive around town to pick up ten cans). But when private firms are allowed to contract for the exclusive franchise, they do indeed have lower costs. Both reviews, then, suggest that there are potential supply-side efficiency gains in simply returning some public services to the private sector.

But these gains are not unlimited. It should be noted first that many public services do not satisfy Williamson's conditions as easily as trash collection, and efforts to privatize these services have not worked very well. One area where some pessimism is in order is in education. A decade ago there were initial, somewhat premature, indications that private firms might be able to take preexisting educational technology and translate that into learning gains for educationally disadvantaged students. The results of many costly and complicated social experiments on the topic were, first, that the claim was rejected (firms did no better than normal public schools), and, secondly, that there were many of the sort of costly and unanticipated transactions-specific contingencies that Williamson fears. It became difficult to share the burden of these contingencies between the buyer and the seller. For example, some students attended class all year, used up the suppliers' resources, and then left school just before the exam to determine the firm's incentive payment. The result of a large number of such unforeseen difficulties was that the government sponsor, in this case the Office of Economic Opportunity, never was able to sign final contracts with half of the companies to determine the incentive payments (actually, to recover work-in-progress prepayments later not justified by educational gains). This raised the unpleasant vision of school boards involved in unending contractual hassles with outside firms [insert "fly-by-night" if additional coloring is desired – see Gramlich–Koshel (1975)]. The market test here destroyed the market.

A second problem involves the dual nature of public services. As was pointed out previously, in part they are provided because of consumption interdependencies; but in part they are provided as a way to effect in-kind redistribution of services to disadvantaged groups. Efforts to provide market disciplines are admirable to the extent that they bring down costs: They may be objectionable if they eliminate the internal redistribution. One ominous signpost on this score is that when Peterson evaluated the transfer of city public hospitals to private ownership, he found that costs were reduced, but also that private owners "retreated from the range of redistributive responsibilities that the public sector formerly had accepted." If such is the case more generally, privatizing many public services could be like throwing out the baby with the bath water.

Of course simply to say that there is potential for abuse in a class of policies does not provide grounds for discarding the class. Surely there are potential improvements that could be made in privatizing some public services, and just as surely there are areas that should remain off-limits for private suppliers. Determining just which types of public services can best be provided under which type of arrangements is and will remain an important item on the research agenda.

### User charges

A third type of arrangement for bringing the private market discipline into the supply of public services is through user charges. Whereas privatization substitutes a private for a public supplier with the objective of lowering costs, the user charge approach is to provide a vehicle where the consuming (taxpayer) population can choose to buy as many public services as it wants (normally from a public supplier). There could be some reduction in supply costs, as with privatization, but the main advantage is that consumers would no longer be burdened with the economic inefficiencies resulting from the fact that they get different amounts of public services than they want. Illustrative cases where user charges seem to be ideally suited to pay for public services in a way that minimizes economic inefficiencies are parks and libraries, hunting licenses, and turnpikes and bridges.

But there are problems with user charges, too. One is the natural monopoly problem, previously alluded to briefly. If taxpayer–consumers were given free choice to buy the services of whatever trash company they wanted, competition of this sort would prevent any one company from realizing the advantages of economies of scale. For services of this nature, there might have to be some arrangement for giving consumers free choice within the constraints of an arrangement that lets providers gain the advantages of economies of large scale provision of the public service.

The second potential problem is redistribution. To the extent that redistribution takes place within the public service budget, there may be valid objection to making these services "too voluntary." People, especially those with low incomes, may simply not consume enough public services (education, health, etc.) for their long-run benefit – they may have to be protected from their own decisions. The rationale is similar to that of a mandatory social security system – people may not save enough to sustain themselves in their retirement. But there is at least an imperfect solution to this objection: vouchers. People at whatever income could be given a voucher for consumption of the public service, and they could spend this voucher on the supplier of their choice. The voucher assures that low income people will not underconsume the service, and the fact that vouchers can be spent on various suppliers at least preserves some of the advantages of consumer choice.

Unfortunately, for one reason or another voucher schemes have proven extremely difficult to implement in the United States. Some of the biggest public policy disaster areas around turn out to involve vouchers or voucher-like schemes. Food stamps are vouchers for food consumption, and are widely criticized because there seems little doubt that cash income support payments would be better for recipients. Medicaid is really a voucher plan under which low income people can use their medicaid card to pay for health care. This program is widely criticized because there is no good way to limit the use of the service. Rent supplements are a form of voucher that is widely criticized because of the uneven incidence of benefits. Education voucher experiments were tried on a limited basis in San Jose, California, and were terminated in mid-course. Students in the voucher schools did not perform any better than they would have been expected to on the basis of past performance, and the parents appeared uninformed and distinctly uninterested in exercising their freedom of choice. In each case there are extenuating circumstances: Either vouchers should not have been used in the first place (food stamps), voucher-financed expenditures should have been rationed differently (medicaid, rent supplements), or some other change should have been made. But prospective proposers of new voucher plans should be cautious in proposing a scheme that certainly has not worked very well in other areas.

In any case, although user charges or other schemes of this sort show promise for resolving some of the problems in the provision of public services, the potential seems far from unlimited. Public services in the first place should either be provided because of some supposed consumption interdependency or as a means of making in-kind redistribution. In the former case, a user charge scheme risks not being as economical as other schemes; in the latter case it risks eliminating the redistribution, or causing new problems when it tries to accommodate redistribution. There are undoubtedly some areas – parks, libraries, toll bridges – where user charges seem admirably suited to finance public services in a manner consistent with efficient consumer choice. But it will take more research and experimentation to find other areas, or other user charge-type schemes, where the advantages of this form of financing can outweigh the disadvantages.

### An internal check – improving civil service

Tax limits, privatization, and user charges are all approaches to public service provision that try to improve from without. Either taxes and expenditures are limited, or market-like schemes are set up to promote the normal kind of market efficiencies. But there appear to be limitations with each approach – tax and expenditure limitations cannot abolish the public sector, and market-like schemes cannot be used for all public services. Hence there is, and will remain, scope for improving from within – to arrange schemes that will make the civil service work better. In terms of the Niskanen model, can we arrange incentives for public sector managers to induce them to work hard, not to extend their bureaucratic empires, but to try to maximize satisfaction of the consuming–taxpaying population?

A first point is that internal reform schemes of the sort mentioned are not necessarily substitutes for the external checks mentioned – to a very large extent they are complements. The theoretical and empirical evidence cited previously suggests that monopolistic wage rents are limited when taxpayers have an effective exit possibility, and tax limits and public–private competition of various sorts would only enhance the competitive, cost-cutting behavior of the public sector. There could be undesirable by-products in the process, as mentioned previously, but measures to improve competition should generally improve public agency output efficiency. It, of course, also follows that anticompetitive civil service arrangements, of which job tenure and seniority restrictions are probably the most glaring examples, normally work in the wrong direction.

There have also been purely internal efforts to improve the functioning of the civil service. Probably the most notable is the Civil Service Reform Act (CSRA) of 1978. The goal of this Act was to rely more than before on performance appraisals in determining wage growth for senior level executives, in exchange for which at least the executives choosing to enter the Senior Executive Service would drop their job tenure. In the abstract, this is exactly the type of civil service reform that would seem to be desired: Public bureaucrats could make more and lose more, and both possibilities would give them greater performance incentives. But as so often happens, the actual implementation of this Act seems designed to allow evaluators to learn as little as possible. The performance appraisal systems were slow to get organized, almost no funding was provided for merit pay increases, the pay cap for civil servants was retained, and the whole experiment took place in a time of extraordinary upheaval in the upper level civil service in connection with Reagan's attempt to cut back on government spending [Seashore, et al. (1982)]. Whether CSRA will work now that senior level bureaucrats are being asked to give up a lot for very little, in an environment of fairly intense Executive hostility toward their or their agency's goals, remains to be seen, but the odds are that this will end up being one of life's failed experiments. Perhaps something can be learned from a careful study of it, but at this point it is perhaps more realistic to hope only that efforts to raise the variance of executive pay will not be abandoned.

## Summary

The main lesson here is that the public and private sectors are just plain different. Private services are provided to satisfy privately expressed consumer choices, and consumers acting independently can best express these choices. Public services are provided to deal with cases where privately expressed choices will not lead to ideal outcomes, or cases where there is an intentional attempt to redistribute in favor of disadvantaged groups. Efforts to privatize the provision of public services – whether by tax limits, outright privatization, or user charges – all have gains that are theoretically limited by the fundamentally different nature of the services involved. As an added point, relatively few of these efforts have worked that well, for a variety of reasons – some particular and some that may bespeak of general and common problems. These efforts can and should continue, but there are no panaceas here, and there may not even be that many winning policy proposals. Efforts to reform from within have, if anything, an even worse track record, but that is in part because they have been tried less often.

One does not want to conclude with a counsel of despair either. There are certainly enough inefficiencies in the way public services are now provided that it should be possible to come up with some ways for improving on some of them. The key intellectual question is to try to identify the public goods and redistribution components of various public services, and to try to adapt mechanisms to deal with both. One good thing about this general class of problems is that the tradition of experimentation has been established, and has proven valuable in seeking out at least some nonstarters. There becomes a valuable subsidiary task in devising new experiments and carefully examining some of the old ones.

## Notes

1. The choice of years used for Table 10.1 may appear strange. The published national income accounts data on public services are almost nonexistent before 1947 and, strangely, after 1978. Within those constraints, I chose ten-year intervals.
2. All of these studies are a few years old now, and public wages have generally risen less than private wages in the intervening period. Hence some of the "evidence" on this point may no longer be valid.
3. More arguments are given in Musgrave (1981).
4. In fact, it does not always ensure economic efficiency. See Atkinson–Stiglitz (1980) and Bewley (1981).

288     Edward M. Gramlich

5. There are several recent theoretical discussions of the ins and outs of tax limitation. See Brennan–Buchanan (1980), Courant–Rubinfeld (1981), and Inman (1982).

## References

Arrow, Kenneth J. (1951), *Social Choice and Individual Values,* New York: Wiley.
Atkinson, Anthony B., and Joseph E. Stiglitz (1980), *Lectures on Public Economics,* New York: McGraw-Hill.
Bergstrom, Theodore C. (1979), "When Does Majority Rule Supply Public Goods Efficiently?" *Scandinavian Journal of Economics* 81 (2): 216–26.
Bewley, Truman (May 1981), "A Critique of Tiebout's Theory of Local Public Expenditures," *Econometrica* 49: 713–40.
Borcherding, Thomas E., Werner W. Pommerehne, and Friedrich Schneider (1982), "Comparing the Efficiency of Private and Public Production: The Evidence from Five Countries," mimeo, Institute for Empirical Research in Economics, Zurich.
Bowen, Howard R. (November 1943), "The Interpretation of Voting in the Allocation of Economic Resources," *Quarterly Journal of Economics* 58: 27–48.
Brennan, Geoffrey, and James Buchanan (1980), *The Power to Tax: Analytical Foundations of a Fiscal Constitution,* New York: Cambridge University Press.
Buchanan, James M., and Gordon R. Tullock (1962), *The Calculus of Consent,* Ann Arbor: University of Michigan Press.
Courant, Paul N., Edward M. Gramlich, and Daniel L. Rubinfeld (December 1979), "Public Employee Market Power and the Level of Government Spending," *American Economic Review* 69: 806–17.
Courant, Paul N., and Daniel L. Rubinfeld (1981), "On the Welfare Effects of Tax Limitation," *Journal of Public Economics* 16: 289–316.
Ehrenberg, Ronald G., and Gerald S. Goldstein (July 1975), "A Model of Public Sector Wage Determination," *Journal of Urban Economics* 2: 223–45.
Epple, Dennis, and Allan Zelenitz (1981), "The Implications of Competition among Jurisdictions: Does Tiebout Need Politics?" *Journal of Political Economy* 89: 1197–1217.
Gramlich, Edward M., and Patricia P. Koshel (1975), *Educational Performance Contracting: An Evaluation of an Experiment,* Washington, D.C.: Brookings.
Hicks, John R. (May 1940), "The Valuation of the Social Income," *Economica* 7: 105–24.
Hirschman, Albert O. (1970), *Exit, Voice, and Loyalty: Responses to Decline in Firms, Organizations, and States,* Cambridge, Mass.: Harvard University Press.
Hotelling, Harold (March 1929), "Stability in Competition," *Economic Journal* 39: 41–57.
Inman, Robert P. (1980), "Pensions, Wages, and Employment in the Local Public Sector," *COUPE Papers on Public Economics* 4, 11–57.
(May 1982), "The Economic Case for Limits to Government," *American Economic Review* 72: 176–83.
Kaldor, Nicholas (September 1939), "Welfare Propositions of Economics and Interpersonal Comparisons of Utility," *Economic Journal* 49: 549–52.
Lindahl, Erik (1958), "Just Taxation: A Positive Solution," reprinted in Richard A. Musgrave and Alan Peacock (ed.), *Classics in the Theory of Public Finance,* London: Macmillan.
Mackay, Robert J., and Carolyn L. Weaver (1978), "Monopoly Bureaus and Fiscal Outcomes: Deductive Models and Implications for Reform," in Gordon R. Tullock and Richard Wagner (eds.), *Policy Analysis and Deductive Reasoning,* Lexington: D. C. Heath.

Musgrave, Richard A. (1981), "Leviathan Cometh – Or Does He?" *COUPE Papers on Public Economics* 5, 77–120.

Niskanen, William A. (1971), *Bureaucracy and Representative Government*, Chicago: Aldine-Atherton.

Peterson, George E. (1981), "Pricing and Privatization of Public Services," mimeo, Urban Institute, Washington.

Quinn, Joseph F. (Winter 1979), "Wage Differentials Among Older Workers in the Public and Private Sectors," *Journal of Human Resources* 14: 41–62.

Quinn, Joseph F. (1982), "Compensation in the Public Sector: The Importance of Pensions," in Robert H. Haveman (ed.), *Public Finance and Public Employment*, 227–44, Detroit: Wayne State University Press.

Romer, Thomas, and Howard Rosenthal (1978), "Political Resource Allocation, Controlled Agendas, and the Status Quo," *Public Choice* 33 (4): 27–44.

Samuelson, Paul A. (November 1954), "The Pure Theory of Public Expenditure," *Review of Economics and Statistics* 36: 387–9.

Seashore, Stanley E., et al. (1982), "Organizational Assessments of the Effects of Civil Service Reform," mimeo, The University of Michigan Institute for Social Research, Ann Arbor.

Smith, Sharon (1980), "Public–Private Wage Differentials in Metropolitan Areas," mimeo, Federal Reserve Bank of New York, New York.

Tiebout, Charles M. (October 1956), "A Pure Theory of Local Expenditures," *Journal of Political Economy* 64: 416–24.

Williamson, Oliver E. (October 1979), "Transaction-Cost Economics: The Governance of Contractual Relations," *Journal of Law and Economics* 22: 233–61.

# Comment: Government services

ROBERT P. INMAN

Edward Gramlich has provided us with a concise, clear, and conceptually inclusive view of the provision of government services. He raises all of the right questions – Why government? How does government make choices? What organizational structure might be preferred? – and tells us the best he can within his limited space what we now know about such issues. Since I have no substantive quarrels with anything that Gramlich has said, I propose to use my few pages here to elaborate on the issues Gramlich has outlined. As I see it, the central policy question to be decided for the provision of government services is whether *governments* ought to provide them. What we now call government services are those services that governments provide. But should they? There is nothing magic in the label, and the fact that education, sanitation, health care, and libraries are publicly provided may be as much a result of historic events as sound economic and management decision making. With our renewed interest in the service economy we need to examine carefully the comparative advantages of alternative organizational structures, of which the governmental form is only one alternative. Its competitors, which are markets and voluntary organizations, must be considered as well.

The distinguishing feature of a government organization is its ability to extract resources from its members even though its members may not choose to contribute those resources voluntarily. Governments are coercive; voluntary market exchange and voluntary organizations are not. Why might a society wish to allow a coercive organization to allocate some or all of its resources? The answer must be that we – members of that society – receive benefits in return for having sacrificed partial control over our economic resources. Those benefits are a more efficient and more just economic order, as Gramlich has pointed out. The essential advantage of a coercive organization over a voluntary one is illustrated in Figure 10.1.

Imagine a case of two economic agents trying to decide to provide a public good that provides each with a benefit of $6 but costs a total of $8 to produce. The two agents can cooperate (strategy C) or not (strategy N) in provision of the good. Once the good is provided the benefits are enjoyed by both parties. If both agents cooperate, they share the costs equally and enjoy a net benefit of $2 per person [ = $6 – ($8/2)]. If one agent produces the good but does not receive a contribution from the other, then the producing agent's net benefit is – $2 ( = $6 – $8). In this case, the noncoop-

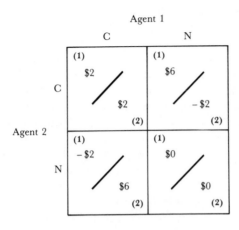

Figure 10.1. Prisoner dilemma and public service provision

erative, free-riding agent enjoys all the benefits at no cost and receives $6 ( = $6 – $0). If the good is not produced by either agent – that is, both act noncooperatively – then each agent receives 0 net benefits. The best outcome for either agent occurs when the other provides the good and he or she free-rides, but if both parties attempt to free-ride the good will not be produced. Unfortunately, the noncooperative, "free-riding" strategy is the dominant (i.e., always best) strategy for both agents. That this is so can be seen from the matrix form of this game in Figure 10.1. Payoffs to each player for each combination of strategies are shown above (for player 1) and below (for player 2) the diagonals in each cell. The joint cooperation strategy (C, C) yields players 1 and 2 $2 each. If player 1 cooperates but player 2 does not, the payoffs are $6 and – $2, respectively. If player 2 cooperates but 1 does not, the payoffs are reversed. If both players adopt the noncooperative strategy, the payoffs are $0 to each. Note that the dominant strategy for both agents is to *not* cooperate. If agent 2 cooperates (C), the best strategy for agent 1 is to not cooperate (N) as $6 > $2. If agent 2 does not cooperate (N), then again the best strategy for agent 1 is to not cooperate (N) as 0 > – $2. Either way, noncooperation is preferred. The same logic applies to agent 2 deciding how to play against agent 1. Since both players find noncooperation the preferred individual strategy, the outcome of this game is in the (N, N) cell where no public good is provided. Yet both agents would prefer the cooperative outcome to this result. Cooperation is preferred, but no agents dare take the chance of suffering large losses if their neighbors cheat. Just as the market has no mechanism to ensure cooperative behavior when there is an incentive to act independently, so too do the players in this (a Prisoner's Dilemma) game lack the means to enforce the cooperative solution. Without such an enforcement mechanism, noncooperation (N, N) is the inevitable result.

Government can be viewed as one rational response to the need for cooperative behavior in economic situations marked by inefficient, noncooperative behavior. In the preceding example, *if* both players could be assured that a coercive government would tax them $4 each and provide the public good, then both would agree that government is a good provider relative to the market alternative (N, N). But the preceding "if" is really the big "If." Once a coercive government with the power to tax has been created, what guarantees do agents have that allocation (C, C) will be provided? The government might well tax each player $4 and not provide the public service at all! Or the government might provide the service, but do it inefficiently and have to tax each agent $7. The payoffs from a coercive government can be negative. The attractiveness of coercive government as an economic organization depends crucially on how responsive it will be to individual preferences for the desired services. Governments have the *potential* to perform more efficiently than markets in the provision of certain services, but there is no guarantee that this potential will be realized. We must examine critically the performance of governments in the same way we examine critically the performance of private firms and markets.

How might we compare the relative performance of alternative organizations in providing services? I have discussed this problem at some length in a recent essay,[1] but it is useful here to summarize the approach. Once we include coercive governments as a possible provider of services to be weighed in the balance with voluntary organizations, we must expand our dimension of comparison from simple economic efficiency to matters of fairness and liberty as well. A government may be economically efficient but it may also be a dictatorship. Do we prefer that organization to inefficient, but voluntary, markets? Maybe, but perhaps not. At a minimum, since we value freedom and since governments are coercive whereas markets are voluntary, governments must be more efficient than markets in the provision of service if they are to be preferred. Increased economic efficiency is the first hurdle that must be cleared in the government provision of services. We can compare the efficiency performance of governments and markets. Each term in the following expressions captures an element of relative organization performance and can, in principle, be measured.

$$\text{\textit{Government Performance}} \qquad\qquad \text{\textit{Market Performance}}$$
$$\{\bar{M} - \theta + (P - m) + (m - \Delta) - (\gamma + \epsilon)\} \quad \text{vs.} \quad \{\bar{M} - \theta + (P - m)\}$$

The two expressions measure the net economic benefits per capita from the allocation of an economic activity (e.g., health care or education) through governments or private markets. The organizational form offering the larger net benefits is to be preferred against the criterion of efficiency. $\bar{M}$ is the fixed level of economic resources per capita that can be consumed if no voluntary trade or governments exist. It measures how well we could do in the "state of nature." The expression $\theta$ is the cost per person of moving from the state of nature to a world with markets and measures the costs of government providing basic property rights and contract enforcement. $P$ is the sum of all consumer and producer surpluses (per capita) that can be earned if the market for goods and services works perfectly – that is, we have no market failures. The economic surplus lost because we do have market failures is measured by $\$m$ per capita. The net gain per capita of going from the "state of nature" to a world with markets is therefore $\{\bar{M} - \theta + (P - m)\} - \bar{M}$, or $(P - m) - \theta$: the net benefit of markets minus the costs of a legal and enforcement system to maintain property rights.

Perhaps we can do better by allowing government to provide services when markets fail? If all the desired transactions the market failed to complete were in fact successfully and costlessly transacted by the government, we would gain a net benefit of $\$m$ per person; just what we had lost through market failures. In fact, however, governments are not likely to negotiate all desired transactions – they may negotiate some undesired ones as well – and the negotiation process of collective choice is itself not costless. The net gains of government will therefore equal $\$m$ per person less the producer-plus-consumer surplus of still uncompleted transactions – denoted $\$\Delta$ per person – less the administrative costs of government. Those administrative costs include: (1) the costs of collecting and processing preference and production cost data – denoted $\$\gamma$ per person – and (2) the costs of enforcing the collective allocation once decided – denoted $\$\epsilon$ per person. Included in $\gamma$ are the costs of actually running a voting or legislative process. Included in $\epsilon$ are the administrative costs of collecting taxes or user fees – that is, the costs of minimizing tax evasion and free-ridership. The net benefits of government itself are therefore $\${m - \Delta - \gamma - \epsilon}$ per person. The overall efficiency performance of an economy with government services, inclusive of endowments $(\bar{M})$ and the value of markets, is $\${\bar{M} - \theta + (P - m) + (m - \Delta) - (\gamma + \epsilon)}$ per person.

Government provision of services will be preferred on the basis of efficiency if:

$$\{\bar{M} - \theta + (P - m) + (m - \Delta) - (\gamma + \epsilon)\} > \{\bar{M} - \theta + (P - m)\},$$

or if:

$$(m - \Delta) > (\gamma + \epsilon).$$

That is, when the net benefits of government provision $(m - \Delta)$ are greater than the administrative and decision-making costs of using governments

$(\gamma + \epsilon)$, then governments are more efficient than markets in providing a service.[2] Against an efficiency criterion government provision is to be preferred.

To be sure, dimensions other than efficiency inform the decision to use private firms or governments to provide services. Fairness (pro-government) and liberty (pro-market) considerations also matter. Balancing the three dimensions – efficiency, equity, liberty – in any particular instance is a delicate problem indeed. That is why I must second Gramlich's concluding plea for experimentation in how we provide services. We have much to learn, not only about the organizational and production technologies of service provision but also about how we value the relevant competing virtues of efficiency, fairness, and freedom in the consumption of those services.

### Notes

1. See R. P. Inman, "Markets, Government, and the 'New' Political Economy," in A. Auerbach and M. S. Feldstein, *Handbook in Public Economics,* North-Holland Publishing Co., 1984.
2. The production costs of providing services are included in $\$m$. Bureaucratic "waste" and the like are included in $(\gamma + \epsilon)$.

# Part III: Analyses of service industries: the finance, health care, and government sectors

Mr. Fuchs asked Mr. Satterthwaite what would happen if he applied his model of the physician market to the extreme limiting case of a market with one physician. Mr. Satterthwaite answered that the one physician would have monopoly power, subject to the constraint that consumers could leave the community. Mr. Fuchs asked Mr. Satterthwaite to identify the point where the physician would operate, in relation to the price–quantity diagrams presented in the paper. Specifically, what sort of demand curve would the community have at this point? Mr. Satterthwaite answered that he would expect a relatively inelastic demand, with a high price. Price would be pushed up until people started to leave the community (assuming we can define what we mean by community). Mr. Fuchs asserted that this conclusion is counterfactual. A monopolist would never operate where demand is inelastic. He added that actual prices in single physician markets tend to be relatively low. Mr. Satterthwaite admitted a failure of the theory of this extreme case. He pointed out that the theory does require at least a reasonable number of suppliers.

Mr. Reiner was interested in the presentation by Mr. Satterthwaite and Mr. Gramlich and the comments of Mr. Harris and Mr. Inman. He pointed out that the discussion has so far considered a binary world composed of government and private for-profit sectors. A major neglected element is the nonprofit sector. The typical situation is more complicated than a simple private-for-profit/government split. Particularly in the health care area, nonprofit institutions play an important role. In many communities, a nonprofit hospital is the dominant establishment. One important question for research is: What is the rationale for nonprofit provision of services? Another might consider a statistical explanation of the varying involvement of nonprofits across services. Lastly, what is the role of the flow of funds from the profit to the nonprofit sector?

Mr. Leveson offered two alternative hypotheses for the apparent tendency of price per visit to fall and quantities to rise as supply falls in physician markets. His first suggestion involved a change in the service mix covered under "price" when supply changes. When the supply of physicians increases we can imagine the lower professional price creating demand for services and we know that this should increase visits substantially. Now it could be that physicians tend to supply diagnostic, as well as treatment services in cases of increasing supply. Since the price of diagnostic services is less, when we consider a "standardized price," adjusted for service mix, this price may actually fall as physician supply increases. Another possibility involves the complementarity of hospital and physician services. With the help of government programs, hospital bed capacity has increased dramatically in the past decades. Since physician services are complementary with hospital services, prices for physicians are easily increased. Mr. Leveson added that both these explanations suggest a further increase in the supply of physicians may lead to a fall in price. This conclusion is obvious in the first story and becomes clear in the second with the supply of hospital beds now fixed by a regulatory constraint.

Mr. Satterthwaite said some of these things may be going on. He emphasized that the real issue here is competition for quality. A troublesome question is why physicians increase the amount of time per patient visit in a situation of increasing supply. To have a complete analysis we need to understand these relations in a competitive setting. We don't yet have this understanding. Monopolistic competition may not even be the appropriate framework within which to carry out this analysis.

Mr. Baumol directed a question to Mr. Gramlich and Mr. Inman. Both of these speakers covered the standard theoretical arguments for government interference in markets, especially government provision of goods and services. These arguments pertain to government financing of goods and services; an additional issue for the government is *financing versus production*. Mr. Baumol wondered if any analysis had been done concerning conditions under which it would be appropriate for government to take the responsibility for actual production of services rather than let the private sector perform that function.

Mr. Gramlich did not know of any existing analysis of this issue, but thought it was an important one. Financing versus production is not a distinction brought out in public finance texts. He added that in practice it may sometimes be difficult to distinguish between public financing and public production. For example, there might be differences between a public hospital and private hospital with public funding, but finding the dissimilarities may be difficult operationally.

Mr. Inman was familiar with some empirical work comparing the relative efficiencies of the two organizational modes. Conceptually, he thought a starting place for this analysis would be a comparison of implicit versus explicit contracting. A Williamsonian framework might provide a normative rationalization for internal organization. Explicit contracting would presumably occur with the most efficient private provider.

Mr. Harris added that some work had been done in this area by Susan Ackerman, using an equity explanation. She argued that government-produced services tend to coexist with privately produced services, resulting in a two-class system, such as we see in education. On the other hand, with a government-financed or subsidized system, private and public consumers tend to coexist. An example of this situation would be a physician who serves both Medicaid and private pay patients.

Mr. Campbell emphasized that a political rationale might well be more important than an economic one in the choice between government financing and production. He reviewed a particular instance involving civil service productivity measures that were developed but never implemented for political reasons. The executive branch of government and some parts of Congress have a real resistance to contracting out. The workings of government itself needs to be considered to understand how these decisions are made. Mr. Cohen added that an important part of the production versus finance issue involves looking at management in profit, nonprofit, and government organizations. We should study the functioning of the various levels in these organizations to help answer this question. Mr. Baumol contrasted the point he was trying to make, concerning how the production versus finance decision ought to be made, with the comments of Mr. Campbell and Mr. Cohen on why these decisions were made in the way they were. Mr. Campbell responded that applying pure economic logic may not be useful here where the public interest demands a more complicated approach than maximizing economic efficiency.

Mr. Aspinwall asked Mr. Black how the changes in financial markets that he predicts will come about. What will be the specific dynamics of the path of change?

Mr. Black's simple answer was if people will be better off with the changes, then the world will evolve toward those better states. The details of this evolution, however, are confusing. He said barriers to change suggest that government intervention may be required to initiate these changes. For instance, it may take an immense amount of education before individuals understand that it is mostly luck and not skill if the price of a stock they picked happens to increase. Government intervention or alternatively some action by firms themselves will be needed to help us along.

Mr. Leveson questioned Mr. Black's position that there are "too many traders of securities." He thought a move in the direction of removing traders from the market would not be in the best interests of either a corporation issuing stock or individual stock owners. The number of traders is a factor in determining the liquidity of the market and that liquidity will influence the value of stock and who is in the market.

Mr. Black answered that individual liquidity was the important factor. Individuals would presumably get liquidity through banks or an investment company. As far as actual trading institutions are concerned, he thought a trade a day or even a trade a week would be adequate for their liquidity needs.

# The future of research and policy for the service economy

# CHAPTER 11

# Productivity policy and the service sector

WILLIAM J. BAUMOL*

Many observers have concluded that the service sector of the economy constitutes a peculiarly pressing and intractable problem for policy to promote productivity growth. It is suggested that, ever since the industrial revolution, productivity in the services has grown far more slowly than that in manufacturing. Moreover, this persistent lag is thought to be a direct manifestation of the technology underlying the service activities and its relation to that of the manufacturing industries. Indeed, though this conclusion has been disputed rather hotly, some analysts have attributed much of the current slowdown of productivity expansion that has plagued the United States for the better part of two decades to the increasing proportion of the nation's labor force that is employed in the service sector.[1]

In this paper I shall argue that matters are rather more complex than some of these assertions suggest. First, the services are too heterogeneous to lend themselves to such simple generalizations. As a result, all services to some degree, and some services to an extraordinary degree, do permit innovation and productivity growth. Moreover, the statistical record indicates that the services have succeeded in both these areas. I will, therefore, try to distinguish several classes of services that typically differ enormously in terms of their susceptibility to productivity growth. I will also show that even those that fall into the category that is most resistant to change offer considerable scope for innovation. This immediately suggests that there is a useful place for policy that encourages productivity in the services and I will, consequently, examine some of the measures that may be appropriate.

## A taxonomy of service activities

The services are generally defined in terms of the intangibility of their outputs. This common feature is, however, no guarantee of similarity in the technology of their supply processes. Indeed, there are enormous differences in the productive techniques employed by the various services: For

* I am extremely grateful to the Fishman–Davidson Center and the National Science Foundation for their support of the research underlying this paper.

example, telecommunications is a very different animal, technically, from teaching or health care, and these, in turn, differ vastly from broadcasting or computation. This observation alone is sufficient to cast doubt on any generalizations about the scope these fields offer for technological progress. Certainly, the preceding list undermines the contention that all services are inherently hostile to productivity growth. Few activities can match the productivity record of telecommunications and computation – their spectacular success has continued even during the long period of productivity malaise that continues to beset the industrialized world. Indeed, the record confirms that services such as these have set a productivity standard even the manufacturing industries so far have not matched and which any sector will doubtless find difficult to meet in the future.

It is, therefore, essential to try to dehomogenize the service sector, breaking it into several narrower groups. For this purpose I will classify the services into three broad categories, which I will call the *stagnant personal services,* the *progressive impersonal services,* and the *asymptotically stagnant impersonal services.* The first of these is illustrated by haircutting, teaching, and live artistic performance. Telecommunications is a clear example of the second type of service, whereas broadcasting, computation and, perhaps, the performance of research and development fall into the third category. It should be emphasized that, even though (for the sake of clarity) the following discussion treats these three groups as separate and distinct, with no overlap, in reality the groups shade off into one another; a particular service may well move from one category to another as circumstances change.

1.  The *stagnant personal services* are defined, roughly, as activities in which quality is highly correlated with labor–time expended, and in which frequently (but not always) there must be direct contact between the consumers and those who provide the labor. These services are also often characterized by the inherent difficulty of standardization of their product. Care of patients by a doctor is a clear illustration. Whereas illnesses and their treatment fall into patterns, there is sufficient variation in the characteristics of medical problems and patients to preclude assembly-line medical treatment (even though it sometimes seems to be upon us). Quality of care is generally taken to be correlated with the amount of time devoted by the doctor. Teaching is similar to the extent that increases in class size impede quality of education. The standard extreme example is a Mozart quartet. The loss of quality that would result from an attempt to speed up the performance is obvious enough.

    The stagnant personal services no doubt constitute the basis for the contention that services in general resist productivity-enhancing change. The string quartet illustration has already indicated the reason. In fact, the available data provided by Fuchs, Kendrick, and Summers (see, for example, their contributions to this volume) and by others show that overall productivity in the supply of these personal services has increased very slowly. That is why elsewhere I have described such outputs as part of the stagnant sector of the economy.[2] As we will soon note, in a number of cases these stagnant services have been replaced in whole or in part by other products whose productivity performance is far superior.

2. The *progressive impersonal services* occupy the opposite end of the spectrum. The case of telephone communications makes clear the nature of these services. Highly dependent upon electronics, they involve virtually no contact between customers and the labor force involved in the production process. Aside from operator-assisted calls, customers need neither know nor care about the activities of the personnel occupied in the process of transmission of messages. As a result, technological developments have yielded an extraordinary record of productivity growth in this industry. Technology has moved from open wire to microwave, coaxial cable, and satellite transmission. Transistors and semiconductors have revolutionized the industry, and real costs have consequently fallen with a persistence and rapidity that few industries can match.

3. The third category of services, to which I have attached the improbable appellation of *asymptotically stagnant impersonal services,* is an amalgam of the progressive and the stagnant services. The history of such a service typically involves periods in which it outperforms, in terms of productivity increases and cost decreases, even the progressive impersonal services. The crucial characteristic of such a service is that its productivity growth is self-extinguishing; the more spectacular its initial productivity growth, the more rapidly it can be expected to come to an end. Computation services constitute a clear-cut example of the outputs in this category and bring out the nature of the underlying technological relationships. For the sake of clarity, assume that the intangible product of computation processes require just two inputs: computer hardware, which is itself a very tangible product of an automated industry, and computer software, which is predominantly produced by human labor. Thus, the hardware input is derived from the progressive sector of the economy whereas the software is produced by the stagnant sector.

The defining attribute of an asymptotically stagnant service, then, is its makeup of these two ingredients. For example, television and radio broadcasting consist of a progressive ingredient (transmission) and a stagnant one (production of the programs that are transmitted). Similarly, research and development has its hardware components and its required inputs of human thought and patient exercise of trial and error, which is, perhaps, fundamentally stagnant.

The most striking behavioral characteristic of an asymptotically stagnant activity is the progression over time of its costs and productivity growth. Computation is again a good example. Technical progress in the computer hardware industry is one of the most spectacular achievements in the recent history of applied science. For decades, the capacity of computer hardware has expanded explosively and, as a result, cost per unit of output (per "computation") has declined just as dramatically. It is, of course, impossible to find any one cost figure that precisely encapsulates the entire recent history of hardware costs for all of the many heterogeneous components involved. Yet the evidence supports the conclusion that a compounded rate of 25 percent per year is a fairly modest estimate of the decline in hardware costs.[3] Taken over two decades the cumulative effect is truly astonishing. At the same time, however, the evidence suggests that the cost of labor, and thus the cost of the software component, has been *rising* at a rate which, according to some estimates, amounts to 6 percent per year [see Burns (1977)].

The consequences for the makeup of computation costs are self-evident. Hardware costs have declined persistently to a smaller and smaller *portion* of total cost of computation. And, obversely, software costs have come to constitute the bulk of the expense of computation. Kubitz (1980), for instance, reports that in 1973 software represented only 5 percent of computer costs, with the remainder devoted to hardware. By 1978 software's share of the costs had risen to 80 percent (p. 143). Schindler (1979) writes that by 1980 software will have exceeded 90 percent of system development costs. Of course, this reversal is the inevitable consequence of the pertinent arithmetic. If 80 percent of a cost figure declines at an annual rate of 25 percent compounded, while the other 20 percent component rises at a rate of 6 percent, a reversal in the proportion of the two cost components requires just about 10 years.

It is this very reversal that causes such services eventually to behave like a service in the stagnant sector. When the preponderant cost element is declining by 25 percent per year, the overall cost of the service will also be falling, given any plausible limits to the cost behavior of the remaining elements. However, when the cost-declining component falls to, say, only 20 percent of the total cost, while the stagnant remainder continues to rise at 6 percent per year, the decline in the total cost of the service will come to an end, and eventually real costs will rise.

That is the typical history of such a service: an initial period of spectacularly decreasing costs, followed by self-extinguishment of the cost component responsible for the decline. Ultimately, as the share of the stagnant input overwhelms the rest, the service as a whole acquires the cost characteristics of that input. Moreover, the more spectacular the cost savings that characterize the initial period in the history of an asymptotically stagnant service, the more rapidly this period will be brought to an end by the continually shrinking share of the very inputs responsible for the plummeting costs: the more successful the productivity growth process from which such a service benefits initially, the more rapidly that service will take on the behavior patterns of a stagnant personal service.

The uses of computers are too diverse to permit any single characterization of their cost trends, but there is no doubt that, despite the continuing fall in the price of computer hardware, in a number of applications computerization has disappointed the hopes of those who expected them to constitute a source of persistently declining costs. One example is the relatively slow adoption by libraries of electronically automated techniques. Although the trend in library expenditures has, in the last decade or so, slowed from its crescendo in the 1950s and 1960s, this diminution in (real) expenditures is not attributable to declining library costs. Rather, libraries have been forced to make painful and much-regretted cutbacks in acquisitions and to undertake other involuntary economies during inflationary times. In other words, the overriding incentive for the adoption of any cost-cutting measures is still very strong. Yet computerized library operations have not brought with them the much-touted cost savings that were expected of them in the 1950s and 60s. Apparently, many libraries have adopted these automated systems *despite* their costs, not because of them. A prime reason for their adoption has been improved service, not reduced cost. For example, Veaner (1979) claims:

With automation we have still failed to realize a significant staff savings (especially in cataloging). . . . as computers and systems become more sophisticated, they require an ever increasing staff of highly sophisticated and expensive software people for maintenance and development. The rise of this personnel component of the computer far offsets any personnel savings in actual library operations. . . . For every decline in [computer] hardware costs, there appears to be a correspondingly greater increase in the cost of staff to support that hardware. . . . (p. 6)

Mick (1979) also reports

. . . computer hardware and software vendors offer the seductive temptations of reduced labor costs and increased production through automation, but although system performance may improve, overall costs rarely go down. (p. 37)

And, according to a recent Mitre study of 193 public libraries, only one third found automated circulation to be less expensive than manual, one-third found it more expensive, and one-third found the cost to be the same [Simpson (1978)]. Thus, despite earlier hopes, electronic library operation has not progressed rapidly toward overwhelming cost superiority [see Baumol and Batey-Blackman (1983)].

### Productivity growth in the three service categories

There is relatively little to add about opportunities for increased productivity in the progressive impersonal services. The record speaks for itself and the sky appears (figuratively and literally) to be the limit. There simply seems to be no reason to expect such a service to suffer from technological lag or to find itself at a disadvantage in productivity expansion in comparison with any or all manufactured products. This observation is important only because it indicates that it is not the intangible nature of a service output that inhibits productivity growth.

It is only when a service is inherently immune to standardization or when a reduction in labor (or other input quantities) automatically triggers a substantial decrease in product quality, as in the stagnant personal services, that resistance to productivity growth affects the services with particular severity. Yet, even in this subsector of the economy, productivity has been stimulated in a variety of ways over the years. First, some of these personal services have priced themselves out of the market and have been replaced by substitutes more readily subject to technical change. Second, in many cases, supporting activities have benefitted from increased productivity and have thereby contributed to that of the related stagnant activities. Third, there have been cases of spectacular "single-shot" innovations. Each of these avenues of productivity increase for the stagnant personal services merits some comment because it suggests some of the possibilities for technological progress that are open to even the least hospitable of the personal services.

There are many examples of the introduction of product substitutes for the personal services. As productivity has grown in the remainder of the economy, real wages have increased everywhere and this has driven up the relative cost of personal servants – butlers, maids, cooks, and so forth. This may not fully explain the virtual disappearance of these occupations, but it surely helps to account for it. However, as we know, their departure has not left a vacuum. Clothes washers and dryers, dishwashers, automatic ovens, blenders, and a host of other household devices have been adopted as substitutes for human household helpers to a degree undreamed of before World War I.[4] Similarly, safety razors and electric razors have served as a partial substitute for barber services,[5] closed circuit TV surveillance systems have cut down on the need for guards and other such personnel, and teaching machines and programmed learning devices threaten to reduce the demand for the services of live instructors.

The second general source of increased productivity in the personal services is to be found in support activities. Restaurants, which are engaged in what is predominantly a handicraft activity, have benefitted from the availability of electric mixers, temperature controls, and freezers. Truck transportation as a substitute for the ancillary services of delivery of raw materials on foot or by horse-drawn vehicles has surely also helped to reduce the labor cost of provision of a restaurant meal. Telephones and electronic devices have decreased the amount of time it takes stockbrokers or even doctors to carry out their work. Even the seemingly irreducible labor content of a half-hour string quartet has proved to be responsive to technological change. When a New York-based quartet is scheduled to perform in Los Angeles, the jet airliner reduces the travel time to a small fraction of what it was only a few decades ago. Thus, even though neither rehearsal time nor actual performing time may have declined one iota, there is no question that the number of musician-hours expended to make the concert possible has gone down considerably.

The last and, perhaps, most noteworthy source of productivity growth in the personal services is the big technological breakthrough. Electronic mail and electronic banking are innovations of this sort that seem to be in the offing. The introduction of frozen foods and supermarkets may be taken as such a breakthrough in retailing services. Perhaps the most spectacular illustration is provided by the mass media and their instantaneous transformation of live sporting events and artistic performances into products in which highly sophisticated electronic elements play a vital role. It is difficult to exaggerate the contribution of this innovation to productivity. The ability to transform an orchestral concert from an activity that serves an audience of 2000 in the concert hall to one that serves 20 million television viewers is an unparalleled leap in productivity. Since the number of labor hours involved in running the concert hall and in transporting the audience to it is probably no smaller than that required to transmit the broadcast, the change represents something like a ten thousand fold increase of productivity at one blow, and it is difficult to think of any spurt in productivity elsewhere in the economy that comes anywhere close to matching it.

We see, then, that even the stagnant personal services are not immune to progress. Indeed, their history provides quite a few examples of spectacular breakthroughs which, although they may be somewhat isolated in their occurrence, are hardly negligible in their effects. There are, however, some reservations that must be expressed about the long-run contribution of these breakthroughs.

First, it must be acknowledged that they typically involve the introduction of imperfect and, perhaps, inferior substitutes for the services previously supplied. The supermarket, whatever its virtues may be, does not offer the personal attention and adaptability to customers that characterize "mom and pop" establishments. And, certainly, many lovers of the arts consider a television or radio broadcast to be a less desirable product than the corresponding live performance. Second, many services that have benefitted from such breakthroughs have often failed to achieve any sustained productivity growth thereafter. Whereas the supply of products such as electronic devices benefits from cumulative productivity gains year after year, live performance, teaching, and retailing go on for substantial periods of time without any noteworthy change in their procedures. In the long run the absence of such persistent and compounding contributions to their productivity growth can constitute a substantial handicap to the personal services.

Finally, it should be noted that even the major technological breakthroughs of the sort I have cited may fail for yet another reason to provide a major long-term contribution to productivity growth: They may involve the substitution for an activity that is preponderantly stagnant of another activity that is asymptotically stagnant. The example of the arts is a clear case in point. The stagnancy attribute of live performance seems obvious enough and the rising relative cost of live performance over substantial periods of time, which we expect to follow from this, has been documented extensively [see, for example, Baumol and Bowen (1966)]. What is less widely recognized is the asymptotic stagnancy of television broadcasting. There, one encounters the same sort of phenomenon that was found to affect computation services. The broadcast of a play, for example, also consists of two main activities. The first is the original live performance that is broadcast directly or recorded on tape or on film. The second is the dissemination of that performance. Now, productivity growth in electronics and telecommunications has certainly helped to hold back the costs of broadcasting, but it has also helped to reduce the progressive components' share in the overall budget of a broadcasting enterprise. Just as in computation, this has served to leave the costs of broadcasting largely and increasingly made up of the live performance component – the input deriving directly from the stagnant sector.

The available figures, such as they are, do not appear inconsistent with the hypothesis. For example, in 1980 technical expenditures amounted to only 10.8 percent of total television broadcast expenses (and, if technical payroll expenses are excluded, this figures drops to 3.7 percent spent on technical activities such as circuit costs). Programming expenses, on the other hand, amounted to about 44 percent of total broadcast costs [*Broadcasting* (1981), p. 54, data for "all tv stations"]. Although the cost of broadcasting per viewer is considerably lower than the cost of live performance per attendee, cost per unit in both these types of artistic activity appears to have risen at rates faster than the economy's overall price level. Moreover, broadcasting cost per viewer does not appear to be rising significantly more slowly than the cost per attendee of live drama, music, or dance. Thus, both broadcasting and live performance seem to be suffering from what has been called the cost disease of the personal services.

Our lengthy discussion has confirmed that, even in the most stagnant of the service activities, anticipatory resignation about the prospects for productivity growth is hardly justified. Productivity growth in the personal services has occurred in the past in a variety of forms, and it will surely occur again. Yet there is no reason to think it will be easy, and certainly little ground for hope that, overall, such services can begin to approach other sectors of the economy in their productivity records.

## Productivity policy

We turn now to the implications of our analysis for productivity policy directed toward the service sector. We will examine first what is implied for the many services supplied by the public sector: education, health care, postal services, police protection, and the like. Then I will turn to the services supplied by the private sector and examine what can be done to encourage productivity growth in this arena. Finally, I will turn away from productivity policy relating primarily to the services and conclude with a few words about policies that can contribute to productivity growth in the economy generally, with the services benefitting only as a particular sector of the economy, along with all the others.

### The public services

Unfortunately, from the viewpoint of its budgetary implications, many if not most government services fall into the category of stagnant personal services. This is true of education and police protection, which are among the largest items in the budgets of municipalities. Similarly, before electronic mail assumes substantial proportions, such necessary components of postal service as sorting and delivery firmly locate this activity in the stagnant category. I have discussed the implications of this phenomenon for public policy rather extensively elsewhere [see Baumol (1967) and Baumol and Oates (1979)]. Consequently, I will offer only a few words on the subject here.

The stagnancy of a service such as education means that it must be subject to the cost disease: Its unit cost, that is, cost per student, can be expected to rise persistently and cumulatively faster than the general price level. Since the mobility of labor dictates that wages throughout the economy must rise more or less in step, when hourly productivity in manufacturing and the progressive services rises, say, 3 percent per year, while the number of students per teacher stays the same, the *relative* cost of teaching must then go up at about 3 percent per year, that is, 3 percent faster than the rate of inflation. If education budgets are increased only, say, 2 percent per year faster than the inflation rate, the public will inevitably perceive that even though expenditures on education are going up at a substantial pace the service is nevertheless deteriorating. People can hardly be blamed for concluding that they are constantly asked to pay more and, in return, are constantly receiving less. Inevitably, bureaucratic inefficiency and corruption are suggested as the obvious explanation. Yet we know from our analysis that there is no need to seek villains to explain the behavior of these costs. The fundamental problem is resistance of the stagnant personal services to technological change.

Wallace Oates has described the problem as "fiscal illusion." It may lead to at least two serious types of misguided policy. First, it may give rise to underfinancing of the services in question: If legislatures join the general public in the belief that inefficiency and skullduggery are the sources of the rising relative costs of the services, they may conclude that additional money spent on them represents good money thrown after bad. The net result may be that the public is deprived of services or condemned to services of poorer quality than they might really want if they understood the nature and necessity of their price. Perhaps even more serious are misguided attempts to deal with the problem, in effect, by declaring it illegal. An example of this is provided by recent attempts to contain the growth of health care costs through a series of restrictions upon hospital decision making. This is not the place to go into a discussion of these health care regulations, but it is clear that some of them, such as certificate-of-need regulations that restrict certain equipment purchases, threaten to impose inefficiencies by unnecessarily circumscribing decision making in hospitals and that other proposed approaches would extend to health care a program of price controls with all of its potentially disastrous consequences [see Joskow (1981)].

### Private policy for the private services

Many services, in all of our three categories, are supplied by the private sector. This is clearly true of communications in the progressive category and broadcasting in the asymptotically stagnant category. Automobile repair, insurance, private health care, commercial theater and, perhaps, retailing can be classed in the stagnant group.[6] Because prices affect volume of business, a firm that supplies services is under constant pressure to contain the growth of its costs and to do what it can to increase its productivity. There is a great deal that private enterprise can do for itself in this regard, though it is not clear that the general approaches to be taken by service industries are materially different from those available to manufacturing. But, although the options and opportunities for self-help are many, there is little that can be said about them that is both substantive and general. Much has been said recently about "quasi-Japanese" business practices such as workers' quality circles and guaranteed job tenure, though opinions on their effectiveness and adaptability to the American scene differ widely. A general call for inclusion of productivity considerations in the strategic planning of business is also very much to the point, even if it smacks uncomfortably of a declaration of loyalty to apple pie and motherhood. All one can say at the level of generalization to which we must be confined here is that there is apparently a good deal of unused opportunity for productivity growth available to business management. Competitive pressures from abroad may well serve to stimulate U.S. manufacturers to devote more effort to the task of taking more effective advantage of these opportunities. The danger here is that because it is relatively difficult to import services, the service industry will be more immune to the pressures of foreign competition and will therefore lag in its productivity enhancement efforts. The relative price effects of the productivity lags that have characterized the stagnant personal services may then have to substitute for foreign competition in forcing these services to improve their productivity records.

## Public policy toward productivity in the private services

Aside from government policy to encourage productivity growth in the economy generally, a number of special issues arise vis-a-vis public policy toward the private services. Although they are not closely related and therefore constitute no coherent story, each by itself is a matter of considerable significance. Here, I will deal with only two such subjects: encouragement of productivity in regulated service enterprises, and the role of research and development, a service activity that is crucial for growth of productivity throughout the economy.

Historically, economic regulation has concentrated upon a variety of services including transportation, telecommunications, banking, and insurance. Many observers have concluded that the very presence of regulation seriously impedes (and may largely preclude) productivity growth in these services. The good productivity record of a number of the regulated enterprises casts doubt on so general a conclusion, but there is one central feature of most economic regulation, which undoubtedly does constitute an impediment to improved productivity. This is the fact that such regulation usually seeks to base itself on the rate of return of the regulated firm. The regulated enterprise is constrained to earning a rate of return no greater than the cost of capital. Although at first glance this seems an arrangement that is both equitable and reasonable, closer examination indicates some of its serious imperfections. Such a regime is equally a source of peril to productivity if its terms are lived up to, and if they are not. In the recent years of rapid inflation, failure to carry out these programs took the form of long delays in the granting or requisite price increases to public utilities and inadequacy of the price adjustments that were permitted. The result was inadequacy of the rates of return permitted to the regulated enterprises, which made it difficult for them to raise capital to modernize or even to maintain their plant and equipment; the detrimental consequences for productivity growth are all too clear.

On the other hand, consider what would have happened had regulators adhered flawlessly and without delay to the rate of return standard. Most public utilities, unlike the railroads, are in a position to adopt prices that will yield overall returns equal to their cost of capital, if only they are permitted to do so by regulation. Under a regime of perfect rate of return regulation this implies that at all times a utility will earn exactly its cost of capital, no more and no less. In other words, its total revenues will always exactly cover its total costs, including the cost of its capital. A moment's consideration confirms that such an arrangement removes all incentive for cost saving, efficiency increases, and productivity growth. If the firm can gain no additional earnings from any of these and loses nothing by slovenly operation and inefficiency, all motivation for productivity improvement is eliminated. The process degenerates into a cost-plus arrangement whose disincentives for efficiency are notorious.

To deal with this problem, the late Arthur Okun and I proposed a regulatory arrangement designed to cope simultaneously with the two threats to productivity that have just been described: The inadequacy of revenues that regulatory lag can impose upon utilities in an inflationary period, and the disincentives for productivity growth caused by the cost-plus characteristic of efficient rate of return regulation [see Baumol (1982)]. I describe this proposal not because I believe it is the only approach or even clearly the best approach possible. Rather, it is offered here as an illustration of the sort of somewhat heterodox devices that may have to be designed to overcome some of the obstacles besetting productivity growth in our economy.

Oversimplifying greatly for the sake of brevity, what we proposed is that once a regulated firm achieves a set of prices yielding revenues adequate to cover its cost of capital, that enterprise henceforth be permitted to adjust those prices automatically, without regulatory hearings, at a rate equal to the rate of inflation *minus its own past productivity growth rate*. Thus, if inflation were proceeding at 9 percent per year and the firm's productivity growth in the past had been 3 percent per year it would be permitted to raise its prices 6 percent, that is, 3 percent less than the rate of inflation. The logic of such a rule is simple. Under its provisions a firm that fell behind its past productivity performance would be penalized by inadequacy of earnings. On the other hand, to the extent that it exceeds its past performance it is rewarded by commensurate profits. There are various subtle issues that must be dealt with to assure the equitability and effectiveness of the proposal. But this is not the place to examine these or other related issues, such as the degree of correspondence between the proposed arrangement and the workings of a free unregulated market.[7] The discussion is sufficient to make my point that productivity policy in general (and that relating to the services in particular) can overcome the various impediments that beset it. But it can do so only through the exercise of a little ingenuity and willingness to deviate at least to some degree from the standard policies that are hallowed only by their longevity and familiarity.

Let me turn now to the second issue to be considered briefly in this section: the role of research and development. As has already been noted, R and D is clearly a service activity whose immediate products are knowledge and ideas, rather than tangible physical entities. There is also considerable evidence that it is one of the economy's prime engines of productivity growth. But Wolff, Blackman, and I have also suggested the (so-far untested) hypothesis that R and D activity falls within the asymptotically stagnant sector of impersonal services [see Baumol and Wolff (1982a, 1982b, 1982c and 1983)]. Here, I do not want to discuss the evidence for or against this hypothesis, but simply proceed on the assumption that it is true and note a few of its implications for policy.

If the hypothesis is valid and at least some R and D activities have now reached the stagnant phase of their histories, it follows that the costs of these activities must be rising relative to those of other economic processes. In private industry this rise in relative cost must constitute a disincentive to make use of R and D and a reallocation of budgets toward an increased share of outlays on other inputs. The consequence may not actually be a decrease in *real* outlays on R and D, that is, in outlays corrected for changes in the economy's overall rate of inflation. But it may nevertheless reduce the amount of R and D activity actually carried out, since the cost of R and D is increasing even faster than the inflation rate. As in our previous discussion of outlays on stagnant services such as education, industry may end up paying more for its R and D and yet getting less of it.

The associated threat to productivity growth is serious, but it is perhaps even more serious where it relates to the funding of *basic* research carried out in the private nonprofit sector. For here the problem of fiscal illusion enters directly. Government and other sources of funds for such research may well be tempted to think that their funding need only keep more or less abreast of the economy's overall rate of inflation. But if basic research has taken on the attributes of the stagnant services, this may mean that fewer and fewer projects can actually be financed, or that they must be funded ever less adequately. According to *Science and Technology*, a National Science Foundation–National Academy of Sciences collaborative publication, "As research becomes more sophisticated, the required instrumentation, facilities, and supporting services become more expensive, adding further costs beyond those due to inflation. Federal agencies can now fund a smaller fraction of worthy research proposals" (p. 470). Although trends seem to vary by field and are not absolutely clearcut, in a preliminary review of three decades of National Science Foundation funding in one research field, physics, we found that the number of research grants per constant dollar awarded fell from a high of .000067 in 1952 to a low of .000008 in 1968, and by 1981 had not risen above .000011.

## Concluding remarks on overall productivity policy

Most of the policy measures that have been proposed to stimulate productivity growth have been discussed widely and need not be reconsidered here. They include reorientation of our tax structure toward the taxation of expenditure rather than income, the taxation of real (deflated) rather than nominal capital gains, and other changes intended as means to encourage saving and investment, increased support for R and D (for basic research in particular), and removal of any regulatory impediments to productivity growth that cannot clearly be justified by comparison of their benefits and costs. The list of standard proposals is, of course, much longer than this, but the preceding sample suggests its general character.

Yet at least one vital ingredient seems to be missing from such programs. If it is true, as is widely contended, that much of the deceleration in productivity growth is attributable to a deterioration in the quality of business management and a decline in entrepreneurial activities, a program to encourage productivity should surely address these issues. Yet, usually little is said on the subject, aside from rousing exhortations about the need for greater efforts and sacrifices and calls for the revival of America's pioneering spirit. Surely, an effective policy must do better than that.

Here, it is inappropriate to offer any long disquisition on the available options, but a few general observations may be suggestive. My conjecture is that the heart of the productivity problem lies in the fact that we have forgotten the basic nature and workings of the competitive mechanism. Compassion for those who fail (which may be judged appropriate so far as it relates to individuals – human beings) is surely entirely misapplied when it is extended to business firms. The genius of the competitive mechanism is its unstinting reward to enterprises that succeed and its unpitying punishment of those that fail. The unparalleled productivity achievements of the free enterprise system (which even Marx was moved to praise extravagantly) may well be attributable to this law of the jungle for business firms. Yet we seem to have forgotten this lesson and have over the years moved toward extension of protection to unsuccessful business firms and even toward punishment of business success whose magnitude is considered excessive. This has manifested itself in a variety of ways. The most obvious of course has been the recent, much publicized bailout of several large firms that were threatened by bankruptcy. It also is illustrated by the fact that virtually every large American firm with an outstanding productivity record has been subject to antitrust prosecution, undertaken either by the government or (even more tellingly) by less successful rivals.

Perhaps the most serious manifestation is the orientation of supply-side economics toward overall reductions in business taxes whose benefits are to be distributed uniformly throughout the business community, regardless of economic performance. Nothing is heard about offering benefits only to those enterprises whose growth or performance in other respects indicates that they have made outstanding contributions toward the national objectives, or denial or reduction of benefits to those who fail to do so. No self-respecting business firm would ever try to stimulate a flagging sales force with a general increase in salaries, totally unrelated to performance. Yet precisely such an approach is advocated for the encouragement of business productivity and growth. Surely, effective policies must do better than that.

### Notes

1. See, for example, Nordhaus (1972), Thurow (1979), and Wolff (1981). It is not part of my objective here to discuss the controversy about the degree of responsibility of the shift toward the services for the slowdown in the economy's productivity growth. However, it may be of some interest to examine one of the arguments that has been used to support the contention that the productivity consequences of the shift have not been substantial. This argument maintains that although productivity *growth* in the services has, indeed, been slow, its absolute level nevertheless remains considerably higher than that in manufacturing, so that the labor force, according to this view, has been moving from an economic sector in which productivity is low to another in which it is high. The consequence, it is held, cannot have been a slowdown in productivity growth in the economy as a whole.

Whatever the validity of the conclusion, a little analysis shows that the argument itself cannot be valid. The productivity of a sector must take account of the multiplicity of its outputs produced by the multiplicity of its inputs, and the appropriate weights that are normally used in constructing the requisite indices of outputs and inputs are the market values of the items in question. In other words, the absolute measure of total factor productivity of a sector must be the total value of its outputs divided by the total value of its inputs. This means that the absolute productivity of the services can be extraordinarily high if the value of their outputs is unusually large relative to the value of their inputs, i.e., if the services are extraordinarily profitable. If this is untrue, *total factor* productivity in the services *cannot* be especially great. *A fortiori,* the services, which are presumably more labor intensive than most economic activities, then cannot be characterized by a relatively high value of their absolute *labor* productivity. For further discussion of these points, see Baumol and Wolff (1982b).

2. See, for example, Baumol (1967), pp. 415–26 and Baumol and Oates (1979), Chapters 10 and 11.
3. The following quotations illustrate the available estimates of the rate of decline of hardware costs:

> The increase in computational power and memory for a fixed price has been approximately exponential over time. Cost-effectiveness doubles every two years – this means, for example, that the cost effectiveness of computing has increased by a factor of more than a million since World War II. It seems likely that this doubling will continue through the 1980s. One crucial factor has been the astonishing increase in the number of active elements on a single silicon chip. [Lipson (1980), p. 23]

> The cost/performance of electronics is improving at a rate variously estimated at from 20–25 percent per year. [Triebwasser (1978), pp. 176–77]

> The most significant...future development involving [data] communications modes will be the drop in the dollar cost of transferring a bit of information from here to there. The carrier component of this cost has been calculated as declining by about 15 percent per year since about 1960, and is forecast to continue at that rate into the 80s. [Ferreira and Nilles (1976), p. 51]

> Kubitz (1980) estimates that computer performance per unit of expenditure has been increasing at 25–30% per year (p. 135).

4. For a charming illustrative essay, see Mitchell (1912).
5. See Bell (1968).
6. Many stagnant personal services are, of course, supplied by the private nonprofit sectors. This is true of college and university education, hospital care, and the performing arts. The problems of this group of suppliers are, by and large, an amalgam of those of the public and the private profit-making sectors, with a dose of fund-raising difficulties thrown in for good measure. Here, it is not irrelevant that fund-raising activity itself should probably be classified as a stagnant service.
7. For a fuller discussion, see Baumol (1982).

## References

William J. Baumol (June 1967), "Macroeconomics of Unbalanced Growth: The Anatomy of Urban Crisis," *American Economic Review* 57, 415–26.

(July 22, 1982), "Productivity Incentive Clauses and Rate Adjustment for Inflation," *Public Utilities Fortnightly (PUF)* 110, No. 2, 11–18.

William J. Baumol and Sue Anne Batey-Blackman (May 1983), "Electronics, the Cost Disease, and the Operation of Libraries," *Journal of the American Society for Information Science* 34, 181–91.

William J. Baumol and William G. Bowen (1966), *Performing Arts: The Economic Dilemma* (New York: Twentieth Century Fund).

William J. Baumol and Wallace E. Oates (with Sue Anne Batey-Blackman) (1979), *Economics, Environmental Policy and the Quality of Life* (Englewood Cliffs, NJ: Prentice-Hall), Chapters 10 and 11.

William J. Baumol and Edward N. Wolff (January 1982a), "Paradox Lost, or How R&D Can Impede Productivity Growth," mimeo.

(December 1982b), "A Paradox in the Measurement of Interdustry Differences in Productivity," mimeo.

(February 1982c), "Productivity and the Shift to the Services," mimeo.

(1983), "Feedback from Productivity Growth to R&D," *Scandanavian Journal of Economics* 85, 147–57.

Carolyn S. Bell (September 1968), "Macroeconomics of Unbalanced Growth: Comment," *American Economic Review* 58, 877–84.

Christopher Burns (April 1977), "The Evolution of Office Information Systems," *Datamation* 23, No. 4, 60–64.

Joseph Ferreira and Jack M. Nilles (October 1976), "Five Year Planning for Data Communications," *Datamation* 22, No. 10, 51–57.

Paul L. Joskow (1981), *Controlling Hospital Costs: The Role of Government Regulation* (Cambridge, Mass.: MIT Press, 162–68.

William J. Kubitz (1980), "Computer Technology: A Forecast for the Future," in F. Wilfrid Lancaster, ed., *Proceedings of the 1979 Clinic on Library Applications of Data Processing, The Role of the Library in an Electronic Society,* 135–61, (Urbana-Champaign, Ill.: University of Illinois Graduate School of Library Science).

Joseph I. Lipson (July 1980), "Technology and Science Education: The Next 10 Years," *Computer* 13, No. 7, 23–28.

Colin K. Mick (1979), "Cost Analysis of Information Systems and Services," *Annual Review of Information Science and Technology* 14, 37–64.

Wesley C. Mitchell (June 1912), "The Backward Art of Spending Money," *American Economic Review* 2, 269–81.

National Science Foundation (1979), *Science and Technology, A Five-Year Outlook* (San Francisco: W. H. Freeman and Co. in collaboration with the National Academy of Sciences).

William Nordhaus (1972), "The Recent Productivity Slowdown," *Brookings Papers on Economic Activity* No. 3, 493–536.

Max Schindler (January 4, 1979), "Computers, Big and Small, Still Spreading as Software Grows," *Electronic Design* 27, No. 1, 88.

George Simpson et al. (1978), *Automated Circulation Systems in Public Libraries* (McLean, Va.: The Mitre Corporation).

"Television Financial Data 1980, FCC Financial Figures" (August 10, 1981), *Broadcasting* 101, No. 6, 54.

Lester Thurow (August 1979), "The U.S. Productivity Problem," *Data Resources Review.*

Sol Triebwasser (1978), "Impact of Semiconductor Microelectronics," *Computer Technology: Status, Limits, Alternatives* (New York: Institute of Electrical and Electronics Engineers, Inc.), 176–77.

Allen B. Veaner (1979), "What Hath Technology Wrought?," in F. Wilfrid Lancaster, ed., *Problems and Failures in Library Automation: Proceedings of the 1978 Clinic on Library Applications of Data Processing* (Urbana-Champaign, Ill.: University of Illinois Graduate School of Library Science).

Edward N. Wolff (1981), "The Composition of Output and the Productivity Growth Slowdown of 1967–76," mimeo.

# CHAPTER 12

# An agenda for research on the
# service sector

VICTOR R. FUCHS

There is a longstanding need for more systematic, scholarly attention to the service sector. There are huge gaps in the data base, major needs for new theoretical models appropriate for the study of service firms and industries, and a large potential demand for analytical studies that use the new models and new data. In this paper I provide a number of suggestions for the direction and focus of research effort. The papers in this collection provide a small but tasty sample of the work that can be done.

The gaps in data result primarily from the heavy hand that history plays in the shaping and funding of the government's statistical programs. Because we were originally an agricultural nation, it is relatively easy to find out how many plums were grown in South Carolina last year, or to obtain other detailed information about minor crops. Because we have been industrialized for a century, the manufacturing sector is also covered thoroughly. The service sector, however, which accounts for more employment and more gross national product than agriculture and industry combined, receives much less attention.

Academic economists have also lagged in their incorporation of services into the mainstream of economics. The typical economics textbook describes farmers who worry about diminishing returns on their land or widget makers who have all the familiar problems of a manufacturing firm. The uninformed reader would never imagine that most of the economy is not involved in farming or manufacturing. Theoretical models require compromises with reality. The compromises that may be appropriate, or the second-order effects that may be neglected in an economy dominated by agriculture and manufacturing, may turn out to be inappropriate or too important to be neglected in an economy dominated by the service industries. For instance, in studying services it may be important to include the consumer as a factor in the production function, to take account of labor-embodied technological change, or to pay more attention to how the timing of demand affects productivity.

How could research on the service industries be organized? One framework that should be congenial to economists is to focus some studies on the

319

demand for services and others on supply. Using conventional techniques economists should be able to develop estimates of the income elasticity and price elasticity of demand for different services. In addition, it is important to study how demographic and social factors affect demand. What role does age play? Marital status? How does the size and structure of families affect the demand for services? One potentially important factor is the role of women in paid employment. We need to know how the growing labor force participation of women interacts with the demand for services. Sometimes there is a clear substitution between production in the market and production in the home (e.g., nursery schools). Sometimes the relationship may be complementary. For example, the demand for vaccinations and medical checkups for children may be complementary with home production and may actually decline when women go into the labor market.

The "feedback loop" between women participating in the labor market and the demand for services needs to be studied. *The growth of a service economy has been, in my opinion, an important factor in the increase in female labor force participation.* Women have always been disproportionately employed in services, and nearly all of the employment growth of recent decades has been in the service sector. The increase in female labor force participation has in turn increased demand for services.

Consider, for instance, the rapid growth of nursery schools. Between the mid-1960s and 1980, enrollment in nursery schools in the United States of children ages 3 and 4 increased from under 10 percent of the relevant population to about 40 percent. If we look at different states at a given point in time, say in 1970, we observe large differences in the percentage enrolled in nursery schools. With regression analysis it is possible to show that the differences across states in 1970 are nicely explained by variations in four variables: the percentage of families headed by women; the labor force participation rates of married mothers of small children; the educational level of women; and, least important, the percentage of the population living in Standard Metropolitan Statistical Areas. These four variables explain 87 percent of the cross-state variation. If the coefficients from that regression are multiplied by the changes in each of the variables between 1965 and 1978, about 85 percent of the increase over time in nursery school enrollments can be explained. The percentage of families headed by females is by far the most important variable; it accounts for about half the total explanatory power. This means that the feedback loop is more complicated than suggested previously. Not only are the growth of service employment and of female employment mutually reinforcing, but both are related to the increase in female-headed families. This increase raises the demand for nursery schools, nursing homes, and similar services, thus feeding back into service employment. These interrelationships need careful study at both the theoretical and the empirical levels.

So much for pure private consumer demand for services; what about collective demand? Many services are subsidized by government. Why? Do these services create externalities? Are they "merit goods"? How much has subsidization contributed to the growth of the service economy? Will resistance to further increases in taxes slow the growth of the service sector?

Another subject in need of research is the demand for producer services. In particular, we need to know how much of the growth of producer services represents a displacement, that is, a movement of services that were being produced within a goods-producing firm to a separate service-producing firm. How much of it is of that character, and how much of it represents a really new service, a change in function that is substituting for some other kind of activity entirely?

With regard to the supply and the production of services, a major subject that has been at the forefront of interest (and deservedly so) is productivity. Professor Baumol's paper treats this subject at length in a highly imaginative way. Following his taxonomy, it may be possible to obtain new insights regarding changes in productivity over time. We also need studies of how service productivity varies across countries and within the United States.

Almost every paper in this volume mentions the difficulty of measuring service output. One special problem arises because in many services the consumer plays an important role in the production process. Consider the function of the consumer in retailing, in banking, and so on. How well the consumer does his/her job will affect the productivity of that activity. This aspect is particularly important in medical care, where the consumer often plays a critical role in the production process with respect to giving a history, compliance with physician advice, and in other ways. Most economic models of the medical care market ignore the production process. They focus primarily on the buyer–seller exchange relationship. It's as if doctors have something to sell and patients have something they want to buy, and that it is possible to understand the process by focusing on this exchange. I submit that this is not possible. The buyer–seller relationship is certainly important, but it is necessary to realize that there is also a production process going on. This involves the patient and the physician working together, not against each other: not competitively, not in an adversarial relationship, but in a cooperative relationship. Economic models of medical care need to incorporate this aspect as well. The point is even relevant in assessing the productivity of Professor Baumol's famous string quartets. I suggest that the productivity of the quartets as reflected in the quality of their performance is affected by what the audience brings to the performance. Their knowledge, their sophistication, their responses will actually affect productivity in a quality-adjusted sense.

Measuring service industry output and productivity is certainly difficult. John Kendrick's paper offers some good advice, particularly his observation that we should concentrate on getting good price indexes to deflate dollar volume rather than trying to calculate quantity indexes directly. He gives several reasons in support of this position and I would like to underscore one in particular. It is usually possible to obtain a useful price index on a *sample* basis because price changes are more uniform across firms within an industry than are quantity changes. By concentrating on the accuracy of a restricted sample of prices and a measure of industry dollar volume, it should be possible to produce a better quantity index than could be obtained by measuring quantity directly.

Another possible way of improving measures of output is to look at what the private sector does about the problem of adjusting for differences in quality. There are many contracts being made all the time in the private sector between firms who sell services and firms who buy services. The firms that sell the services have an internal problem of monitoring quality in order to control what they are doing and to know what they are delivering. The firms that buy the services need to monitor quality in order to know whether they are getting what they are paying for. It should be possible to discover how private firms do this, and thus gain additional insight as to how to measure output in service industries.

Another important aspect of productivity in service industries is the relationship between demand and productivity. We know that the length of run and the size of transactions can affect measures of productivity. This can be critical in a service such as retailing, where the average value of sale per customer can have a large impact on how many goods a checkout person can process per hour. Variability of demand can also affect productivity. It makes a big difference to a service firm whether demand comes smoothly over the day and over the month, or whether it is bunched up in particular hours or particular days. Still another question for study is the effect on productivity of labor-embodied technological change. Economists have written a great deal about capital-embodied technological change, but some improvements in production are achieved only through people's heads and hands and skills. The rate of introduction of the new technology will depend in part on the rate at which new workers with the new skills are added to the labor force. This rate may be affected by institutional arrangements such as tenure, or by the uneven size of cohorts.

The institutional arrangements under which service production takes place is another subject of potential interest. Many services are in the private nonprofit sphere, or in the government sphere. Why is this so? What is the relationship between the type of organization and the subsidization mentioned previously? It is worth noting that some services are produced by government whereas others are subsidized by government but produced elsewhere. Consider, for instance, the change or lack of change in the production of higher education and the production of hospital care. Both these services have experienced an enormous increase in public funding during the last thirty years. In the one case, higher education, the increase in government financing has been accompanied by an increase in government production of higher education through state colleges and universities. By contrast, there has been no increase in the share of hospital care produced in publicly owned and operated hospitals. As a matter of fact, that share has actually diminished slightly.

What explains the differential pattern of change? I have not studied this question, but I will suggest one possible explanation. The pattern may reflect the difference between professors and physicians. Physicians believed, and probably rightly so, that it was in their interest that the expansion of hospital care (albeit government financed) take place in the private sector where they could continue their customary mode of practice. If the expansion took place in government hospitals, they might be forced to become employees of the government. Professors didn't seem to care. It probably didn't matter very much to them whether they were salaried employees of a private institution, or whether they were salaried employees of the University of Michigan or the University of California.

In studies of the for-profit sector, some research should be aimed at the question of vertical integration. We need to know the extent to which the services get produced within goods-producing firms, or are spun off to the service sector. What determines which way they go, and what are the consequences of going one way rather than the other? Another important research topic, suggested by Robert Summers, is the development of an aggregate output index for the service sector, or for some subset of service industries. This index would be analogous to the Federal Reserve Board index of industrial production.

In addition to organizing research under the demand–supply rubric, another useful approach would be in terms of labor and capital, the two main inputs into any production process. On the labor side, there is the question of unions. Until now, unions have been much less present in the service sector than in goods production. We have a few ideas why, but the question deserves systematic study. There has been some growth of unions in the service sector, and we need to understand why that growth has taken place in some industries and not in others, as well as discovering what the consequences of that growth have been. It would also be useful to look at the leadership of service industry unions, at the kinds of activities they engage in, and the kinds of things they press for. There may be significant differences between unions in services and those in goods-producing industries. It is also important to look at the role of self-employment in the service sector and the role of part-time employment. The service sector has always been characterized by greater openness to part-time employees and to self-employment. Is this a function of size of firm, or are there other explanations?

Where is future service employment going to come from? The vast expansion in recent decades has been made possible primarily by the entry of women into the labor force, and more recently by the growth of the teenage population. Both of these sources are going to be played out in the next decade or two. They will not be great sources of labor force growth. If service employment is going to continue to grow rapidly, where will it come from? The elderly are one possibility. Immigration might be another possibility.

Turning to capital, it seems to me that we know very little about the financing of services. Where does the capital come from? What is the role of large firms compared to small firms in the service industries? What role do services play in the demand for investment goods? Is there much investment in physical capital in the service industries? What other kinds of investment occur?

A well-balanced research program on services should include consideration of some economy-wide issues. One subject that surfaces periodically is the effect of the growth of services on the overall productivity of the economy. Some years ago Michael Grossman and I showed that the growth of the service sector is not a major factor in explaining recent slowdowns in productivity. The sector differential in total factor productivity growth is about 1 percent per annum. A shift of ten percentage points in sector shares of employment results in a slowdown of approximately one-tenth of a percent per annum on overall aggregate productivity growth. The slowdown in the 1970s was ten to fifteen times that order of magnitude. The growth of services can't possibly be the cause of this recent slowdown. Nevertheless, the relationship between sector rates of growth of productivity and the overall rate of growth of productivity is something that needs reexamination from time to time.

The cyclical implications of the growth of services also needs study. In our research in the 1960s we found that output and employment were more stable (over the business cycle) in the service sector than in the goods sector. Productivity, however, was more stable in the goods sector than in the service sector. Cyclical fluctuations in productivity tend to be very large in the service industry because of the great stability in employment. As the service sector gets to be a larger and larger share of the total economy, we need to consider the implications for cyclical performance of the economy.

Another topic of economy-wide concern is the use of gross national product as *the* measure of well-being in our society. There's no question that we need to improve our measure of real GNP. There's not much question that it can be improved. Even with improvement, however, we should become increasingly wary of using a single index number, a single summary measure to say how well we're doing as a nation. We need more direct measures of health, education, and other indicators of well-being.

Finally, I suggest that we need to think deeply about what it means to live in a postindustrial society. It should be intuitively obvious that a society in which most of the people are farmers is going to be different from a society in which most of the people are working in factories that produce pinball machines. And *that* society is going to be different from one in which most of the people are playing, or are expected to play, string quartets. The implications for the role of women, the role of government, the role of nonprofit institutions, capital markets, educational programs, unions, and so on, are enormous once the matter is put in those terms. Thus, the challenge facing researchers is also enormous. This volume provides a good start towards meeting that challenge.

# Part IV: The future of research and policy for the service economy

Building on Mr. Baumol's ideas of nonperforming arts and continuing the induced innovation theme, Mr. Leveson argued that induced innovation effects are important in understanding the wheres and whys in the development of new industries. He mentioned a couple of examples. Broadcasting was one area. A movie company in California has bought a Cray super-computer just for special effects in films. In another area, the problems associated with programming computers can be seen as a capital investment bottleneck. One solution on the drawing board is so called expert systems or feedback systems. These will presumably have a positive impact on service sector productivity in the future. In this way, Mr. Baumol's model can be seen as not only a model of dilemmas, but a framework for opportunity and the creation of new industries.

Mr. Black directed a question to Mr. Fuchs and Mr. Baumol. If productivity is defined as output per capita, do you expect the rate of growth in productivity in the future to be lower than it has been in the past?

Mr. Baumol hedged his bet with a yes and no answer. Although he had no special information on the subject, his gut guess was no. He also agreed with Mr. Kendrick's view on productivity growth. There should be some improvement from the especially low rates of growth of the past few years but no large increases.

In his response, Mr. Fuchs noted that the labor force will not be expanding in the future as it has in the past. This changing demographic factor will influence the capital–labor ratio and have a favorable impact on output per worker (and possibly on total factor production). Mr. Fuchs also agreed with Mr. Kendrick's view concerning the underestimate of the importance of cyclicity as a contributor to the low productivity of the past few years. Another consideration here is that productivity fluctuates more in a service-dominated economy than in a goods-dominated economy. In summary, Mr. Fuchs thought growth in productivity in the 1980s would be better than in the 1970s but would probably not return to the historically high rates of the 1950s and 1960s.

Ms. Stalson was concerned that the two speakers had neglected any mention of services in the context of an international economy or in U.S. trade.

327

She thought services are a good prospect for replacing much of the decline that we are and will likely continue to experience in goods export. She hoped future research would include issues relating to services in trade and in an international economy. Mr. Fuchs underscored Ms. Stalson's point. As the United States moves from its dominant role as a producer of goods, we will have to look to other types of activities for trade. "Perhaps the whole world will come here to hear our string quartets."

# Author Index

# Subject Index

331